Sustainable Growth Strategies for Entrepreneurial Venture Tourism and Regional Development

Andreas Masouras
Neapolis University, Cyprus

Christos Papademetriou
Neapolis University, Cyprus

Dimitrios Belias
University of Thessaly, Greece

Sofia Anastasiadou
University of Western Macedonia, Greece

A volume in the Advances in Hospitality, Tourism, and the Services Industry (AHTSI) Book Series

Published in the United States of America by
IGI Global
Business Science Reference (an imprint of IGI Global)
701 E. Chocolate Avenue
Hershey PA, USA 17033
Tel: 717-533-8845
Fax: 717-533-8661
E-mail: cust@igi-global.com
Web site: http://www.igi-global.com

Copyright © 2023 by IGI Global. All rights reserved. No part of this publication may be reproduced, stored or distributed in any form or by any means, electronic or mechanical, including photocopying, without written permission from the publisher. Product or company names used in this set are for identification purposes only. Inclusion of the names of the products or companies does not indicate a claim of ownership by IGI Global of the trademark or registered trademark.

Library of Congress Cataloging-in-Publication Data

Names: Masouras, Andreas, 1980- editor.
Title: Sustainable growth strategies for entrepreneurial venture tourism
   and regional development / Andreas Masouras, Christos Papademetriou,
   Dimitrios Belias, and Sofia Anastasiadou, editors.
Description: Hershey, PA : Business Science Reference, [2023] | Includes
   bibliographical references and index. | Summary: "This book deals with
   tourism entrepreneurship as a social and economic process that is
   encouraged by national systems, identifying ways to develop cultural
   tour marketing and values in entrepreneur venture tourism while
   explaining the scope, definitions, meaning, idea, and structure of
   tourist entrepreneurship venture formation"-- Provided by publisher.
Identifiers: LCCN 2022023483 (print) | LCCN 2022023484 (ebook) | ISBN
   9781668460559 (hardcover) | ISBN 9781668460566 (paperback) | ISBN
   9781668460573 (ebook)
Subjects: LCSH: Tourism. | Entrepreneurship.
Classification: LCC G155.A1 S798 2022 (print) | LCC G155.A1 (ebook) | DDC
   910.68/4--dc23/eng20220723
LC record available at https://lccn.loc.gov/2022023483
LC ebook record available at https://lccn.loc.gov/2022023484

This book is published in the IGI Global book series Advances in Hospitality, Tourism, and the Services Industry (AHTSI) (ISSN: 2475-6547; eISSN: 2475-6555)

British Cataloguing in Publication Data
A Cataloguing in Publication record for this book is available from the British Library.

All work contributed to this book is new, previously-unpublished material. The views expressed in this book are those of the authors, but not necessarily of the publisher.

For electronic access to this publication, please contact: eresources@igi-global.com.

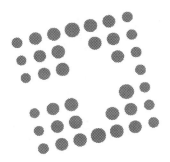

Advances in Hospitality, Tourism, and the Services Industry (AHTSI) Book Series

Maximiliano Korstanje
University of Palermo, Argentina

ISSN:2475-6547
EISSN:2475-6555

Mission

Globally, the hospitality, travel, tourism, and services industries generate a significant percentage of revenue and represent a large portion of the business world. Even in tough economic times, these industries thrive as individuals continue to spend on leisure and recreation activities as well as services.

The Advances in Hospitality, Tourism, and the Services Industry (AHTSI) book series offers diverse publications relating to the management, promotion, and profitability of the leisure, recreation, and services industries. Highlighting current research pertaining to various topics within the realm of hospitality, travel, tourism, and services management, the titles found within the AHTSI book series are pertinent to the research and professional needs of managers, business practitioners, researchers, and upper-level students studying in the field.

Coverage

- Sustainable Tourism
- Tourism and the Environment
- Service Management
- Leisure & Business Travel
- Travel Agency Management
- Destination Marketing and Management
- Service Design
- Customer Service Issues
- Service Training
- Cruise Marketing and Sales

IGI Global is currently accepting manuscripts for publication within this series. To submit a proposal for a volume in this series, please contact our Acquisition Editors at Acquisitions@igi-global.com or visit: http://www.igi-global.com/publish/.

The Advances in Hospitality, Tourism, and the Services Industry (AHTSI) Book Series (ISSN 2475-6547) is published by IGI Global, 701 E. Chocolate Avenue, Hershey, PA 17033-1240, USA, www.igi-global.com. This series is composed of titles available for purchase individually; each title is edited to be contextually exclusive from any other title within the series. For pricing and ordering information please visit http://www.igi-global.com/book-series/advances-hospitality-tourism-services-industry/121014. Postmaster: Send all address changes to above address. Copyright © 2023 IGI Global. All rights, including translation in other languages reserved by the publisher. No part of this series may be reproduced or used in any form or by any means – graphics, electronic, or mechanical, including photocopying, recording, taping, or information and retrieval systems – without written permission from the publisher, except for non commercial, educational use, including classroom teaching purposes. The views expressed in this series are those of the authors, but not necessarily of IGI Global.

Titles in this Series

For a list of additional titles in this series, please visit: www.igi-global.com/book-series

Measuring Consumer Behavior in Hospitality for Enhanced Decision Making
Célia M.Q. Ramos (CinTurs, ESGHT, University of the Algarve, Portugal) Carlos M.R. Sousa (ESGHT, CiTUR, University of the Algarve, Portugal) Nelson M.S. Matos (CinTurs, ESGHT, University of the Algarve, Portugal) and Rashed Isam Ashqar (CinTurs, ESGHT, University of the Algarve, Porugal)
Business Science Reference • © 2023 • 310pp • H/C (ISBN: 9781668466070) • US $225.00

Global Perspectives on the Opportunities and Future Directions of Health Tourism
Oğuz Doğan (Antalya Bilim University, Trkey)
Business Science Reference • © 2023 • 319pp • H/C (ISBN: 9781668466926) • US $270.00

Leadership Approaches in Global Hospitality and Tourism
Ahmet Baytok (Afyon Kocatepe University, Turkey) Özcan Zorlu (Afyon Kocatepe University, Turkey) Ali Avan (Afyon Kocatepe University, Turkey) and Engin Bayraktaroğlu (Anadolu University, Turkey)
Business Science Reference • © 2023 • 341pp • H/C (ISBN: 9781668467138) • US $250.00

Handbook of Research on Sustainable Tourism and Hotel Operations in Global Hypercompetition
Hakan Sezerel (Anadolu University, Turkey) and Bryan Christiansen (Global Research Society, LLC, USA)
Business Science Reference • © 2023 • 677pp • H/C (ISBN: 9781668446454) • US $315.00

Handbook of Research on Urban Tourism, Viral Society, and the Impact of the COVID-19 Pandemic
Pedro Andrade (University of Minho, Portugal) and Moisés de Lemos Martins (University of Minho, Portugal)
Business Science Reference • © 2022 • 722pp • H/C (ISBN: 9781668433690) • US $315.00

Employability and Skills Development in the Sports, Events, and Hospitality Industry
Vipin Nadda (University of Sunderland in London, UK) Ian Arnott (Westminster University, UK) Wendy Sealy (University of Chichester, UK) and Emma Delaney (University of Surrey, UK)
Business Science Reference • © 2022 • 260pp • H/C (ISBN: 9781799877813) • US $215.00

Entrepreneurship Education in Tourism and Hospitality Management
Satish Chandra Bagri (Hemvati Nandan Bahuguna Garhwal University, India) R.K. Dhodi (Hemvati Nandan Bahuguna Garhwal University, India) and K.C. Junaid (Hemvati Nandan Bahuguna Garhwal University, India)
Business Science Reference • © 2022 • 313pp • H/C (ISBN: 9781799895107) • US $230.00

701 East Chocolate Avenue, Hershey, PA 17033, USA
Tel: 717-533-8845 x100 • Fax: 717-533-8661
E-Mail: cust@igi-global.com • www.igi-global.com

Table of Contents

Preface xii

Chapter 1
The Adoption of Corporate Social Responsibility (CSR) Policy in the Tourism Sector: How CSR
Affects Consumer Loyalty in the Greek Hotel Industry 1
    Panagiota Xanthopoulou, University of West Attica, Greece
    Sifis Plimakis, University of Peloponnese, Greece

Chapter 2
Self-Directedness in the Service of Human Resources Management in Tourism and Hospitality:
Perspectives Under the Scope of Adult Education and Lifelong Learning 20
    Mary Viterouli, University of Thessaly, Greece
    Dimitrios Belias, University of Thessaly, Greece
    Athanasios Koustelios, University of Thessaly, Greece
    Nikolaos Tsigilis, Aristotle University of Thessaloniki, Greece

Chapter 3
Capability Building and Development in Socio-Intercultural Entrepreneurship 42
    José G. Vargas-Hernández, Posgraduate and Research Department, Tecnológico Mario
        Molina Unidad Zapopan, Mexico
    Omar C. Vargas-González, Instituto Tecnológico de México, Ciudad Guzmán, Mexico

Chapter 4
The Role of SHRM in Navigating the Hospitality Sector During a Crisis 60
    Dimitrios Belias, Hellenic Mediterranean University, Greece
    Nikolaos Trihas, Hellenic Mediterranean University, Greece

Chapter 5
Future of Sustainable Tourism: Opportunities in Health, Sports, Alternative Tourism, and
Analysis of How Sustainable Tourism Will Be Shaped Post COVID-19 77
    Dimitrios Belias, University of Thessaly, Greece
    Ioannis Rossidis, Hellenic Open University, Greece
    Angelos Ntalakos, University of Thessaly, Greece
    Nikolaos Trihas, Department of Business Administration and Tourism, Hellenic
        Mediterranean University, Greece

Chapter 6
Lego® Serious Play®: Design Thinking as a Tool to Teach the Value Proposition Concept to
Promote the Regional Development of Creative Industries 93
    Miguel Angel Ponce-Camacho, CETYS Universidad, Mexico
    Josue Aaron Lopez-Leyva, CETYS Universidad, Mexico

Chapter 7
Sustainable Growth Strategies for Entrepreneurial Tourism: A Link Between Entrepreneurial
Growth and Regional Development 107
    Eliza Sharma, Symbiosis International University, India

Chapter 8
Traditional Music and Tourism Identity in Cyprus: A Strong Means Strategy to Strengthen
Cultural Tourism 119
    Stalo Georgiou, Neapolis University, Cyprus

Chapter 9
Digital Protection of Traditional Villages for Sustainable Heritage Tourism: A Case Study on
Qiqiao Ancient Village, China 129
    Yixin Zuo, The University of Hong Kong, Hong Kong
    Apple Hiu Ching Lam, The University of Hong Kong, Hong Kong
    Dickson K. W. Chiu, The University of Hong Kong, Hong Kong

Chapter 10
Saving Heritage in War Zones: The Case Study of Ukraine 152
    Stavros Christodoulou, Neapolis Univeristy, Pafos, Cyprus

Chapter 11
Aspects of Total Quality Management: An "Excellence in Quality" Path to a Long-Term Impact
of Effective Teaching in Tourism Education 163
    Despina Konstantinides, Neapolis University, Pafos, Cyprus

Chapter 12
Boutique Hotel by HCH: A New Tourism Trademark as a Tool for the Development of Small
Hotels 181
    Aimilia Vlami, Agricultural University of Athens, Greece

Compilation of References 200

About the Contributors 241

Index 246

Detailed Table of Contents

Preface xii

Chapter 1
The Adoption of Corporate Social Responsibility (CSR) Policy in the Tourism Sector: How CSR Affects Consumer Loyalty in the Greek Hotel Industry 1
    Panagiota Xanthopoulou, University of West Attica, Greece
    Sifis Plimakis, University of Peloponnese, Greece

Corporate social responsibility (CSR) is referred and analyzed as a phenomenon with an economic, cultural, and entrepreneurial dimension. Therefore, it is also considered as a social phenomenon which affects society in many different ways, as it attracts both organizations and governments around the world. The present study analyses the impact of CSR on customers' preference and loyalty in the hotel sector. The authors investigated the main concepts associated with CSR as well as the CSR's policies implemented in the tourism sector. At the same time, specific factors were studied such as customer's satisfaction and how CSR influences consumer's loyalty in a hotel. A semi-structured interview was conducted in 204 visitors in 30 Greek hotels. Findings showed that the average Greek citizen is not particularly familiar with the term of CSR and its activities, and that CSR does not impact on their intention to visit a hotel and then be loyal.

Chapter 2
Self-Directedness in the Service of Human Resources Management in Tourism and Hospitality: Perspectives Under the Scope of Adult Education and Lifelong Learning 20
    Mary Viterouli, University of Thessaly, Greece
    Dimitrios Belias, University of Thessaly, Greece
    Athanasios Koustelios, University of Thessaly, Greece
    Nikolaos Tsigilis, Aristotle University of Thessaloniki, Greece

The tourism and hospitality sector has been greatly impacted by the Covid-19 pandemic with inflows and outflows of tourists abruptly decreasing. In an effort to rebound, nations have embarked on forming policies to aid organizations regain their grounds. Emphasis on the regional development of the businesses, accordingly, can mediate growth. All things considered, organizations of the sector have had to turn to their personnel to seek ways to combat bottlenecks and crises and to upgrade the experience of their customers. The current chapter focuses on the notion of self-directedness and examines its vitality in the survival and recovery of the sector, and its inherent ability led to empowerment, adaptation, and flexibility. This is a literature review which consists of two main influential pillars: the degradation caused by the pandemic and the capability of self-directedness. Thus, the existing literature review, along with up-to-date articles and scientific journals have been processed and scrutinized.

Chapter 3
Capability Building and Development in Socio-Intercultural Entrepreneurship................................ 42
 José G. Vargas-Hernández, Posgraduate and Research Department, Tecnológico Mario
  Molina Unidad Zapopan, Mexico
 Omar C. Vargas-González, Instituto Tecnológico de México, Ciudad Guzmán, Mexico

This study aims to analyze the socio-intercultural entrepreneurship as a capability building and development. The analysis departs from the assumption that entrepreneurship is a cultural embedded concept, although the intercultural category used in entrepreneurial studies has not been founded full conceptual, theoretical, and empirical support. Based on this existing research gap that this analysis reviews, the literature to address the main issues of the socio-intercultural entrepreneurship focusing in the capability building and development to conclude that it is more situational context and environment oriented. The methodology used are the exploratory and analytical tools. Socio-intercultural entrepreneurship competence is highly related to be situational context and environment-dependent on awareness and understanding of cultural differences.

Chapter 4
The Role of SHRM in Navigating the Hospitality Sector During a Crisis.. 60
 Dimitrios Belias, Hellenic Mediterranean University, Greece
 Nikolaos Trihas, Hellenic Mediterranean University, Greece

The hospitality sector is a fragile sector. This means that it is very fragile when a crises hits, such as political, environmental, and financial crises. The operation of hotels relies a lot on the ability of the personnel to offer high quality services. Therefore, HRM plays a strategic role in the sustainability of the hospitality sector, especially during a crisis. For this purpose, the chapter has made not only a literature review into the overall use of SHRM for navigating the hospitality sector during a crisis, but also more precisely for the case of the COVID-19 crisis. Indeed, the related findings – deriving from the existing literature – indicate that there is limited research on this field.

Chapter 5
Future of Sustainable Tourism: Opportunities in Health, Sports, Alternative Tourism, and
Analysis of How Sustainable Tourism Will Be Shaped Post COVID-19.. 77
 Dimitrios Belias, University of Thessaly, Greece
 Ioannis Rossidis, Hellenic Open University, Greece
 Angelos Ntalakos, University of Thessaly, Greece
 Nikolaos Trihas, Department of Business Administration and Tourism, Hellenic
  Mediterranean University, Greece

Tourism today is in a critical crossroad, not only due of the changes on the structure of the tourist industry where the focus has shifted from mass tourism to alternative tourism, but also the question on how the tourist industry will cope with the case of the Covid-19 crisis. Still, the tourist industry does not know what the future of the sector can be. Therefore, the purpose of this paper is to investigate and make suggestions on how the future will shape sustainable tourism. This is a literature review in an ongoing phenomenon which is the Covid-19 pandemic. Hence, this chapter will rely on both the existing literature review and on published scientific papers. Nonetheless, it is crucial to refer to the fact that there is a lack of research on this issue. For this reason, the authors will expand their research on articles and reports published on the internet so to have the latest updates on this issue.

Chapter 6

Lego® Serious Play®: Design Thinking as a Tool to Teach the Value Proposition Concept to
Promote the Regional Development of Creative Industries 93

> Miguel Angel Ponce-Camacho, CETYS Universidad, Mexico
> Josue Aaron Lopez-Leyva, CETYS Universidad, Mexico

This chapter describes the experience of a group of graduate students using Lego® Serious Play® (LSP) and design thinking as tools to learn the value proposition concept to promote the regional development of creative industries. The use of LSP encourages teamwork, co-creation, and motor skills, transporting individuals to a play space, where each opinion has equivalent importance through the use of their hands, learning and reinforcing what they have learned through the techniques of teaching others, practicing doing it and group discussion. LSP facilitates in a short time the experience of creative freedom and the exercise of empathy with the client which refers to one of the phases of the design thinking method, as well as the creation of a conceptual prototype as a metaphor for the value proposition for the client. As a result, a business model canvas, and a value proposal canvas were generated, which help the innovation of the real service analyzed, as well as serve as an innovative tool in the process of teaching-learning for graduate students in the area of innovation.

Chapter 7

Sustainable Growth Strategies for Entrepreneurial Tourism: A Link Between Entrepreneurial
Growth and Regional Development 107

> Eliza Sharma, Symbiosis International University, India

The present study seeks to develop a model that can establish a structural association between development of entrepreneurial tourism, and development of socially-backward communities as well. Keeping in view the promising growth of the tourism sector, and huge opportunities for the entrepreneurs in this sector, this current study will aim to answer the followings research questions: RQ1: What can be the different sustainable growth strategies for the entrepreneurial tourism? RQ2: How different stakeholders can be involved for the sustainable growth of tourism sector? RQ3: How growth of entrepreneurial tourism can be linked to regional development?

Chapter 8

Traditional Music and Tourism Identity in Cyprus: A Strong Means Strategy to Strengthen
Cultural Tourism 119

> Stalo Georgiou, Neapolis University, Cyprus

Music provides an important and emotional narrative for tourists as an expression of culture, a form of heritage, and a significant place. Indeed, it is becoming increasingly difficult to imagine tourism in silence. Music defines and transcends the boundaries of destinations, while emphasizing and even challenging the concepts of tradition and helping to define the identity of visitors. Traditional music is part of the identity of each region and a global artistic language, while its wide appeal enables it to nurture the richest dialogues between different cultures. As a symbol of cultural identity in relation to the past, traditional music is used by many cultural groups and individuals, including nation states, for political empowerment and cultural diplomacy. The cultural tourist identity of a country includes traditional music, traditional dances, improvised street entertainment, tours in concerts, watching music festivals; these are what accompany the visitor-tourist.

Chapter 9
Digital Protection of Traditional Villages for Sustainable Heritage Tourism: A Case Study on
Qiqiao Ancient Village, China.. 129
    Yixin Zuo, The University of Hong Kong, Hong Kong
    Apple Hiu Ching Lam, The University of Hong Kong, Hong Kong
    Dickson K. W. Chiu, The University of Hong Kong, Hong Kong

Similar to the plight of other traditional villages, Qiqiao Ancient Village is declining under the impact of urbanization and the devastation of modernization. Qiqiao is chosen as the case study as it is the second-largest settlement of Confucian descendants, with a rich cultural heritage. In recent years, the local government has taken measures such as cultural heritage restoration and tourism development to protect their traditional village, but the result is unsatisfactory. By field observation and interviewing three groups of stakeholders, the protection project manager, villagers, and tourists, this research analyzed the current situation of Qiqiao and digital protection applications for its heritage tourism to reveal some recent problems. Considering the local economic and technological conditions, this research suggested digital solutions for similar traditional villages in protection projects for sustainable heritage tourism.

Chapter 10
Saving Heritage in War Zones: The Case Study of Ukraine.. 152
    Stavros Christodoulou, Neapolis Univeristy, Pafos, Cyprus

The events of the last days after the invasion of Russia by the Russian troops raise concerns not only about the humanitarian crisis that Ukraine and Europe are facing, but also about the preservation and preservation of the Ukrainian cultural heritage. Thousands of museums across Ukraine store important works of art by Ukrainian and Russian artists; Byzantine artefacts; and paintings, among others by Bellini, Goya, and David; according to a report by the Indian Express. In Ukraine there are seven UNESCO World Heritage Sites. As a result, UNESCO asks for implementation of international humanitarian law, notably the 1954 Hague Convention for the Protection of Cultural Property in the Event of Armed Conflict, and its two (1954 and 1999) Protocols, to ensure the prevention of damage to cultural heritage in all its forms.

Chapter 11
Aspects of Total Quality Management: An "Excellence in Quality" Path to a Long-Term Impact
of Effective Teaching in Tourism Education 163
    Despina Konstantinides, Neapolis University, Pafos, Cyprus

The aim of this chapter is to identify dimensions of total quality management (TQM), which are related to excellence in quality. The identified dimensions are expected to lead to a successful implementation of techniques and customer focus approaches and to teacher effectiveness. In favor of this purpose, the authors have chosen a qualitative and quantitative research approach. The research participants were teachers of general secondary education and teachers at vocational technical schools that include fields of hotel management and professions which belong to the field of tourism education. The importance of this study is revealed through research findings which highlight perceptions of quality with respect to the teaching environment. Teacher involvement in quality improvement educational activities will make them more effective in teaching and school practices. Quality can create an environment where all members of the school community work jointly together to provide students with the resources they need to meet up present and prospect academic and societal requirements.

Chapter 12
Boutique Hotel by HCH: A New Tourism Trademark as a Tool for the Development of Small
Hotels 181
Aimilia Vlami, Agricultural University of Athens, Greece

This chapter examines the purpose and effectiveness of a new tourism trademark, the "Boutique hotel" project, which has been designed and implemented by the Hellenic Chamber of Hotels. The scope is to encapsulate the efforts of the last five years to lay the institutional groundwork for a professionally operated accommodation system of boutique hotels, a relatively new form of accommodation in Greece. This chapter will analyse the goals, terms, and conditions for defining this tourism brand and its operating system. Also, it examines in detail the structural characteristics of boutique hotels in Greece, as they resulted from a survey of the 178 hotels that had received this certification. Boutique hotels in Greece are a successful example of the resilience of hospitality businesses during the periods of both the financial crisis and, subsequently, of the COVID-19 pandemic, given that the very nature of their services and products, enables them to immediately respond and adapt to new situations and cater for evolving consumer needs, ultimately striving for survival and for the return to a new reality of sustainable tourism development.

Compilation of References 200

About the Contributors 241

Index 246

Preface

INTRODUCTION

Entrepreneurial venture tourism is a type of tourism that focuses on supporting and promoting small businesses and startups in the tourism industry. It involves providing opportunities for tourists to engage with local entrepreneurs and experience unique, authentic, and sustainable tourism offerings (Lane, 2005).

Entrepreneurial venture tourism can take many forms, such as:

1. **Ecotourism:** This involves visiting natural areas and engaging in activities that promote conservation and sustainability. Entrepreneurs may provide eco-friendly accommodation, tours of protected areas, or activities like hiking, kayaking or bird-watching (Getzner, Brendehaug, & Lane 2014).
2. **Cultural Tourism:** This involves learning about local customs, traditions and history (Sophocleous, Masouras, & Papademetriou 2019). Entrepreneurs may offer tours of museums, historic sites, or cultural events like festivals or dance performances.
3. **Food Tourism:** This involves experiencing local cuisine and beverages. Entrepreneurs may offer food tours, cooking classes, or visits to local farms or vineyards.
4. **Adventure Tourism:** This involves engaging in physically challenging activities like mountain climbing, white-water rafting, or bungee jumping. Entrepreneurs may provide guided tours, equipment rentals or training.
5. **Wellness Tourism:** This involves activities that promote physical, mental, and spiritual health. Entrepreneurs may offer yoga retreats, spa treatments, or meditation sessions.

Entrepreneurial venture tourism can provide benefits for both tourists and local communities. For tourists, it provides opportunities to connect with local entrepreneurs, learn about the culture and history of a place, and experience unique and sustainable tourism offerings. For local communities, it can provide economic opportunities, create jobs, and promote the development of small businesses.

However, it is important to ensure that entrepreneurial venture tourism is sustainable and does not have negative impacts on the environment or local communities. This can be achieved through responsible tourism practices, such as minimizing waste, supporting local conservation efforts, and respecting local customs and traditions.

Preface

CHALLENGES

Entrepreneurial venture tourism involves the development and operation of tourism businesses by entrepreneurs. Like any other entrepreneurial venture, it comes with its own set of challenges. Here are some of the common challenges faced by entrepreneurial venture tourism:

1. **Financial Constraints:** Starting a tourism business requires significant upfront capital investment, which may be difficult for entrepreneurs who do not have access to adequate funds. In addition, tourism businesses often have long gestation periods before they start generating revenue, which means that entrepreneurs need to have a long-term financial plan in place.
2. **Seasonal Nature of Tourism:** Many tourism businesses operate in locations where tourism is seasonal, which means that they may only be able to generate revenue during certain times of the year. This makes it challenging for entrepreneurs to maintain a stable income throughout the year.
3. **Marketing and Promotion:** With so many tourism businesses competing for customers, it can be challenging for entrepreneurs to market and promote their businesses effectively. Effective marketing and promotion require significant resources and expertise, which may be difficult for small businesses to acquire.
4. **Attracting and Retaining Talent:** The tourism industry requires skilled and knowledgeable employees who can provide high-quality service to customers. However, attracting and retaining talented employees can be challenging for small businesses, especially those located in remote or less attractive destinations.
5. **Regulatory Compliance:** Tourism businesses are subject to a wide range of regulations and compliance requirements, including health and safety regulations, environmental regulations, and licensing requirements. Entrepreneurs need to ensure that they comply with all relevant regulations to avoid fines and penalties.
6. **Competition:** The tourism industry is highly competitive, and entrepreneurs need to differentiate themselves from their competitors to attract customers. This may require investing in unique products, services, or experiences that set them apart from other tourism businesses in the area.
7. **Uncertainty:** The tourism industry is subject to a wide range of external factors that can affect demand, such as natural disasters, political instability, and economic downturns. Entrepreneurs need to be prepared to manage uncertainty and adapt quickly to changing market conditions.

Overall, entrepreneurship in tourism requires entrepreneurs to be innovative, adaptable, and persistent in overcoming challenges and creating a sustainable business.

Sustainable growth strategies in tourism focus on promoting tourism that is environmentally responsible, economically viable, and socially equitable (Vickers & Lyon, 2014). These strategies aim to ensure that tourism contributes to the development of the destination, while minimizing negative impacts on the environment and local communities. Here are some sustainable growth strategies in tourism:

Ecotourism: Ecotourism promotes responsible travel to natural areas that conserves the environment and improves the well-being of local communities. Ecotourism activities typically include nature-based activities such as hiking, wildlife watching, and cultural experiences.

Sustainable Accommodation: Sustainable accommodation focuses on reducing the environmental impact of hotels and resorts, while providing guests with a comfortable and enjoyable experience. Sus-

xiii

tainable hotels use renewable energy sources, minimize water and energy consumption, reduce waste, and promote local products.

Community-Based Tourism: Community-based tourism involves local communities in the tourism industry, empowering them to manage and benefit from tourism in their area. This approach creates opportunities for local people to share their culture, traditions, and way of life with visitors.

Responsible Tourism: Responsible tourism promotes the principles of sustainable tourism, encouraging visitors to minimize negative impacts on the environment and local communities. Responsible tourists seek to minimize their carbon footprint, respect local cultures and customs, and support local businesses.

Green Transportation: Green transportation involves promoting environmentally friendly transportation options, such as cycling, walking, and public transportation. This approach reduces the carbon footprint of tourism and promotes healthy, active travel.

Sustainable Food and Beverage: Sustainable food and beverage strategies focus on promoting local, organic, and sustainably sourced food products. This approach supports local agriculture, reduces food waste, and promotes healthy and sustainable eating habits.

Destination Management: Destination management involves the planning and coordination of tourism activities, ensuring that tourism is developed in a sustainable and responsible manner. This approach involves collaboration between government, businesses, and local communities to ensure that tourism contributes to the overall well-being of the destination.

By adopting these sustainable growth strategies in tourism, destinations can attract responsible tourists who are looking for authentic experiences that are both environmentally and socially responsible. This approach promotes long-term growth and development of the tourism industry, while preserving the natural and cultural resources that make a destination unique.

In addition, Sustainable growth tourism refers to a type of tourism that meets the needs of present tourists while also preserving and enhancing opportunities for future generations (Siakalli & Masouras, 2020). This type of tourism takes into account economic, social, and environmental factors to ensure long-term sustainability. Here are some key points to consider in analyzing sustainable growth tourism:

Economic Impact: Sustainable tourism can have a positive economic impact by creating jobs and generating revenue for local communities. It can also promote local businesses and cultural experiences, helping to preserve unique local traditions and ways of life. However, it is important to ensure that the benefits are distributed fairly, and that tourism does not lead to over-reliance on a single industry or economic inequality.

Social Impact: Sustainable tourism can also have positive social impacts, such as promoting cross-cultural understanding and encouraging respect for local customs and traditions. It can also provide opportunities for local communities to participate in and benefit from tourism. However, tourism can also lead to cultural homogenization and exploitation if not managed carefully.

Environmental Impact: Perhaps the most crucial factor in sustainable tourism is its impact on the environment. Sustainable tourism should minimize its impact on the environment by reducing waste and pollution, conserving natural resources, and protecting local wildlife and ecosystems. It should also support conservation efforts and promote sustainable practices among visitors.

Overall, sustainable growth tourism can be an excellent way to promote economic growth while also preserving local culture and protecting the environment. However, it requires careful planning and management to ensure that the benefits are shared fairly and that the impact on the environment is minimized (Mayer, Habersetzer, & Meili 2016).

Preface

OBJECTIVES

The main objectives of this book on sustainable growth strategies for entrepreneurial venture tourism and regional development are to:

1. Provide an overview of the importance of sustainable growth in the context of entrepreneurial venture tourism and regional development, and highlight the benefits of adopting sustainable practices for both the environment and the economy.
2. Analyze the challenges and opportunities of entrepreneurial venture tourism and regional development and identify the key factors that contribute to sustainable growth in these sectors (Masouras et al., 2019).
3. Showcase successful case studies of entrepreneurial venture tourism and regional development, which have implemented sustainable growth strategies to achieve positive economic and environmental outcomes.
4. Discuss the various approaches and tools that can be used to promote sustainable growth in entrepreneurial venture tourism and regional development, including policy and regulatory frameworks, innovation and technology, and community engagement.
5. Provide guidance and practical advice for entrepreneurs, policymakers, and other stakeholders on how to implement sustainable growth strategies in entrepreneurial venture tourism and regional development, and how to measure and evaluate the impact of these strategies (Scheyvens et al., 2021).

Overall, the book would aim to inspire and inform stakeholders in the entrepreneurial venture tourism and regional development sectors on how to achieve sustainable growth through innovative and effective strategies.

ORGANIZATION OF THE BOOK

The book is organized into 12 chapters. A brief description of each of the chapters follows:

Chapter 1: The Adoption of Corporate Social Responsibility (CSR) Policy in Tourism Sector – How CSR Affects Consumer Loyalty in the Greek Hotel Industry of Greece

As is well known, the complexity of tourism activity lies in the fact that it involves direct contact with all tourism resources during the production process. For Garay and Font, the level of satisfaction through CSR actions in tourism companies with altruistic motives, is higher than others whose motives are purely commercial, although in the end their financial returns are similar. This means that the value system and organizational values of each company are very important.

Chapter 2: Self-Directedness in the Service of Human Resources Management in Tourism and Hospitality – Perspectives Under the Scope of Adult Education and Lifelong Learning

The COVID-19 pandemic has caused significant disruptions in the political, social and economic global environment. By the end of the first quarter of 2020, the pandemic hit tourism the hardest and had brought travel, especially the international one, to an abrupt halt, significantly impacting the tourism and hospitality industry; an industry that accounts for and signifies as a major source of employment, government revenue and foreign exchange earnings.

Chapter 3: Capability Building and Development in Socio-Intercultural Entrepreneurship

The world's population and companies are now more connected and mobile than ever in history, expanded worldwide with access to labor and resources pools but requiring more socio-intercultural communication and entrepreneurial skills. Empowerment and entrepreneurship are defining the engagement rules of this rapidly changing global situational context and environment. Nurturing the culture of empowerment and entrepreneurship is a challenge aimed to design some agile organizations in order to keep pace with the changing economic global situational context and environment.

Chapter 4: The Role of SHRM on Navigating the Hospitality Sector During a Crisis

The hospitality sector is a fragile sector. This means that it is very fragile on crises, such as political crises, environmental and financial crises. The operation of hotels relies a lot on the ability of the personnel to offer high quality of services. Therefore, HRM plays a strategic role on the sustainability of the hospitality sector, especially during a crisis.

Chapter 5: Future Sustainable Tourism – Opportunities in Health, Sports, Alternative Tourism, and Analysis of How Sustainable Tourism Will Be Shaped Post COVID-19

Tourism today is in a critical crossroad, not only due of the changes on the structure of the tourist industry where the focus has shifted from mass tourism to alternative tourism, but also the question on how the tourist industry will cope with the case of the Covid-19 crisis. Still, the tourist industry does not know what the future of the sector can be. Therefore, the purpose of this paper is to investigate and make suggestions on how the future will shape on sustainable tourism.

Preface

Chapter 6: Lego® Serious Play® – Design Thinking as a Tool to Teach the Value Proposition Concept to Promote the Regional Development of Creative Industries

This chapter describes the experience of a group of graduate students using Lego® Serious Play® (LSP) and Design Thinking as tools to learn the Value Proposition concept to promote the regional development of Creative Industries.

Chapter 7: Sustainable Growth Strategies for Entrepreneurial Tourism – A Link Between Entrepreneurial Growth and Regional Development

The multi-billion-dollar tourism industry of today exhibits huge direct and indirect sway over a country's economy and overall development. It has the power to transform entire cities and communities, especially in developing countries. The tourism industry has immense growth potential; it not only generates employment but it can also develop social, cultural and educational values among people. Thus, the development of modern tourism industry is no longer limited to merely economic perspectives; its social impact has attracted significant attention from governments, NGOs, and private organizations.

Chapter 8: Traditional Music and Tourism Identity in Cyprus – A Strong Means Strategy to Strengthen Cultural Tourism

Music provides an important and emotional narrative for tourists, as an expression of culture, a form of heritage and a significant place. Indeed, it is becoming increasingly difficult to imagine tourism in silence. The music defines and transcends the boundaries of destinations, while emphasizing and even challenging the concepts of tradition and helping to define the identity of visitors.

Chapter 9: Digital Protection of Traditional Villages for Sustainable Heritage Tourism – A Case Study on Qiqiao Ancient Village, China

Similar to the plight of other traditional villages, Qiqiao Ancient Village is declining under the impact of urbanization and the devastation of modernization. Qiqiao is chosen as the case study as it is the second-largest settlement of Confucian descendants, with a rich cultural heritage. In recent years, the local government has taken measures such as cultural heritage restoration and tourism development to protect their traditional village, but the result is unsatisfactory. By field observation and interviewing three groups of stakeholders, the protection project manager, villagers, and tourists, this research analyzed the current situation of Qiqiao and digital protection applications for its heritage tourism to reveal some recent problems. Considering the local economic and technological conditions, this research suggested digital solutions for similar traditional villages in protection projects for sustainable heritage tourism.

Chapter 10: Saving Heritage in War Zones – The Case Study of Ukraine

The events of the last months after the invasion of Russia by the Russian troops raise concerns not only about the humanitarian crisis that Ukraine and Europe are facing, but also about the preservation and preservation of the Ukrainian cultural heritage.

Preface

Chapter 11: Aspects of Total Quality Management – An "Excellence in Quality" Path to a Long-Term Impact of Effective Teaching in Tourism Education

The aim of this chapter is to identify dimensions of Total Quality Management (TQM) which are related to excellence in quality. The identified dimensions are expected to lead to a successful implementation of techniques and customer focus approaches and to teacher effectiveness. In order to achieve our purpose, we have chosen a qualitative and quantitative research approach that enabled us to obtain more in-depth findings.

Chapter 12: Boutique Hotel by HCH – A New Tourism Trademark as a Tool for Development Small Hotels

This chapter examines the purpose and effectiveness of a new tourism trademark, the "Boutique hotel" project, which has been designed and implemented by the Hellenic Chamber of Hotels (HCH) over the last 5 years. Specifically, the aim of this chapter is, by examining the evolution of the hotel industry which to a great extent determines the form of tourism consumption and employment in a host country, to encapsulate the efforts of the last five years to lay the institutional groundwork for a professionally operated accommodation system of boutique hotels (BHs), a relatively new form of accommodation in Greece.

Andreas Masouras
Neapolis University, Cyprus

Christos Papademetriou
Neapolis University, Cyprus

Dimitrios Belias
University of Thessaly, Greece

Sofia Anastasiadou
University of Western Macedonia, Greece

REFERENCES

Chell, E., Nicolopoulou, K., & Karataş-Özkan, M. (2010). Social entrepreneurship and enterprise: International and innovation perspectives. *Entrepreneurship and Regional Development*, 22(6), 485–493. doi:10.1080/08985626.2010.488396

Crnogaj, K., Rebernik, M., Hojnik, B. B., & Gomezelj, D. O. (2014). Building a model of researching the sustainable entrepreneurship in the tourism sector. *Kybernetes*, 43(3/4), 377–393. doi:10.1108/K-07-2013-0155

Cunha, C., Kastenholz, E., & Carneiro, M. J. (2020). Entrepreneurs in rural tourism: Do lifestyle motivations contribute to management practices that enhance sustainable entrepreneurial ecosystems? *Journal of Hospitality and Tourism Management*, 44, 215–226. doi:10.1016/j.jhtm.2020.06.007

xviii

Preface

Getzner, M., Vik, M. L., Brendehaug, E., & Lane, B. (2014). Governance and management strategies in national parks: Implications for sustainable regional development. *International Journal of Sustainable Society*, *6*(1-2), 82–101. doi:10.1504/IJSSOC.2014.057891

Lane, B. (2005). Sustainable rural tourism strategies: A tool for development and conservation. *Revista Interamericana de Ambiente y Turismo-RIAT*, *1*(1), 12–18.

Masouras, A., Komodromos, I., & Papademetriou, C. (2019). Cyprus's wine market: Influencing factors of consumer behaviour as part of destination marketing. In Strategic Innovative Marketing and Tourism: 7th ICSIMAT, (pp. 637-644). Springer International Publishing.

Mayer, H., Habersetzer, A., & Meili, R. (2016). Rural–urban linkages and sustainable regional development: The role of entrepreneurs in linking peripheries and centers. *Sustainability*, *8*(8), 745. doi:10.3390u8080745

Müller, S., & Korsgaard, S. (2018). Resources and bridging: The role of spatial context in rural entrepreneurship. *Entrepreneurship and Regional Development*, *30*(1-2), 224–255. doi:10.1080/08985626. 2017.1402092

Schaper, M. (Ed.). (2016). *Making ecopreneurs: Developing sustainable entrepreneurship*. CRC Press. doi:10.4324/9781315593302

Scheyvens, R., Carr, A., Movono, A., Hughes, E., Higgins-Desbiolles, F., & Mika, J. P. (2021). Indigenous tourism and the sustainable development goals. *Annals of Tourism Research*, *90*, 103260. doi:10.1016/j. annals.2021.103260

Siakalli, M., & Masouras, A. (2020). Factors that influence tourist satisfaction: An empirical study in Pafos. In Strategic Innovative Marketing and Tourism: 8th ICSIMAT (pp. 459-466). Springer International Publishing.

Siakalli, M., Masouras, A., & Papademetriou, C. (2017). e-Marketing in the hotel industry: marketing mix strategies. In Strategic Innovative Marketing: 4th IC-SI, (pp. 123-129). Springer International Publishing.

Sophocleous, H. P., Masouras, A., & Papademetriou, C. (2019). Brand as a strategic asset for cultural organisations: A proposal for the forthcoming cultural institution of Pafos. In Strategic Innovative Marketing and Tourism: 7th ICSIMAT (pp. 735-743). Springer International Publishing. doi:10.1007/978-3-030-12453-3_85

Vickers, I., & Lyon, F. (2014). Beyond green niches? Growth strategies of environmentally-motivated social enterprises. *International Small Business Journal*, *32*(4), 449–470. doi:10.1177/0266242612457700

Chapter 1
The Adoption of Corporate Social Responsibility (CSR) Policy in the Tourism Sector:
How CSR Affects Consumer Loyalty in the Greek Hotel Industry

Panagiota Xanthopoulou
University of West Attica, Greece

Sifis Plimakis
University of Peloponnese, Greece

ABSTRACT

Corporate social responsibility (CSR) is referred and analyzed as a phenomenon with an economic, cultural, and entrepreneurial dimension. Therefore, it is also considered as a social phenomenon which affects society in many different ways, as it attracts both organizations and governments around the world. The present study analyses the impact of CSR on customers' preference and loyalty in the hotel sector. The authors investigated the main concepts associated with CSR as well as the CSR's policies implemented in the tourism sector. At the same time, specific factors were studied such as customer's satisfaction and how CSR influences consumer's loyalty in a hotel. A semi-structured interview was conducted in 204 visitors in 30 Greek hotels. Findings showed that the average Greek citizen is not particularly familiar with the term of CSR and its activities, and that CSR does not impact on their intention to visit a hotel and then be loyal.

DOI: 10.4018/978-1-6684-6055-9.ch001

Copyright © 2023, IGI Global. Copying or distributing in print or electronic forms without written permission of IGI Global is prohibited.

INTRODUCTION

Due to the frequent changes in the legislation on social, environmental, and economic issues, organizations are now investing in CSR as a means of raising awareness towards society. Today, there is a strong interaction between consumers and organizations and as a result, a business strategy such as CSR can certify long-term financial viability (Ng & Tavitiyaman, 2020; Dodds & Joppe, 2005. Sustainable development is one of the most important means of achieving economic and social development, as well as a way of preventive treatment of environmental protection. In addition, through many studies (for instance Mohammed & Rashid, 2018; Khan, Yasir & Khan, 2021; Aljarah, Emeagwali, Ibrahim & Ababneh, 2018; Liu, Liu, Mo, Zhao & Zhu, 2019; Glaveli,, 2020; Islam, Islam, Pitafi, Xiaobei, Rehmani, Irfan & Mubarak, 2021; Xanthopoulou & Kefis, 2016; Chatzopoulou & Xanthopoulou, 2021; Kavoura & Sahinidis, 2015; Sahinidis & Kavoura, 2014; Emmanuel & Priscilla, 2022) there was found a significant relationship between CSR and customer trust, which shows that CSR can attract more consumers and "tighten" the company-customer relationships (Schreck, 2011). After analyzing the international literature on "CSR and customer satisfaction," it is concluded that CSR acts mostly positively on customer satisfaction resulting in the improvement of the corporate image, in the strengthening of trust, in the consolidation of loyalty, as well as in the tendency to repurchase and recommend the organization to third parties. However, it is significantly influenced by certain factors, such as pre-existing knowledge of CSR activities, the quality of services provided, the innovation of actions, the type of business and the demographic characteristics of customers. The growing importance of CSR for tourism businesses directs us to further investigate the implementation of CSR in the hotel sector and its impact on the potential tourist/customer. Thus, the purpose of this study is to investigate and analyze consumers' views on how corporate social responsibility of hotels affects their loyalty and intention to visit a hotel. Furthermore, an effort was made to better understand which CSR attributes consumers consider valuable in the hotel sector. From these, the research objectives refer to:

- The impact of CSR on consumers' attraction.
- The impact of CSR on enhancing customers' feelings of trust and security.
- The ways that CSR is implemented in the hotel industry and which of them are more close to customers' preferences

Finally the researchers concluded in the following research questions (RQ):

- *RQ1*. What's the meaning of CSR and how it is related with consumers' behavior?
- *RQ2*. Does CSR create loyalty to a hotel?
- *RQ3*. Does CSR be a criterion for choosing a hotel for a first time or a criterion for customers' previous visit to a hotel?

As is well known, the complexity of tourism activity lies in the fact that it involves direct contact with all tourism resources during the production process. For Garay & Font (2012), the level of satisfaction through CSR actions in tourism companies with altruistic motives, is higher than others whose motives are purely commercial, although in the end their financial returns are similar. This means that the value system and organizational values of each company are very important. Studies have also shown that smaller tourism companies tend to undertake ad hoc CSR actions driven by altruistic motives while larger ones organize strategic CSR programs driven mainly by financial incentives (Garay & Font, 2012; Zientara & Zamojska, 2016). An important difference in the operation of large multinational tourism companies in relation to small and medium-sized enterprises is that in the context of internal CSR they have to pay particular attention to their compliance with the values and basic principles of international human rights organizations. This is due to the fact that they operate in many countries with different levels of social practices than in the country from which they come. Tourism has been widely criticized for its impact on the general public at destinations and the environment and this responsibility for social justice and sustainability of the natural environment is shared by tourists at the same time with all companies involved in the tourism process.

BACKGROUND

Defining CSR

Corporate Social Responsibility is referred as a commitment for companies in order to shape their socio-ethical behavior and optimize the quality of work standards resulting in to exert high influence on financial matters (Hahn et al., 2018; Gond & Nyberg, 2017). European Commission Green Paper defines CSR as the concept of involving companies in voluntary acts with social and environmental content. However, Bowen's book (1953) is considered the beginning of the modern literature on Corporate Social Responsibility, as it is also considered the "father" of CSR. Therefore in this there is a first approach refers to the entrepreneurs and the obligation they have towards the society, to follow the actions and the goals that are desired by it. According to Luo and Bhattacharya (2006), CSR first developed in the United Kingdom and the United States and then in Greece and for this reason was embraced to describe corporate actions and initiatives. Another view of CSR theory is that of Becker- Olsen et al. (2006), who argue that CSR is a motivator and one of the most effective and reliable tools for businesses to improve their image of society, while it is also a significant part of an organizational strategy (Dathe et al., 2022). The first global CSR strategy was announced by the Commission of the European Communities in 2001 with the aim of defining this concept in order for companies to implement this strategy in social and environmental issues of society in combination with the contacts they have with their stakeholders (Hoffman, 2018; Kaplan, 2015). It is observed that many of the terms of Corporate Social Responsibility do not have common characteristics and consist of different factors without this specifying that there is a right and wrong definition of CSR (Tauringana & Chithambo, 2015).

CSR Policies in Hotel Industry: Tools and Impact on Customer's Preferences

The way people experience, consume and share information according to the Travel and Tourism Competitiveness Report 2017 of the World Economic Forum, has now changed greatly from previous years. Businesses in the tourism industry are forced to adapt their business and operational models to the new data of trends and technologies to increase their business performance and customer satisfaction. The degree of consumer satisfaction with the overall tourism product and the experience gained from its consumption, as well as with each of the individual products and services, is therefore an element that must be taken seriously by every person responsible for the marketing of a tourism business or entity in making future decisions related to marketing and sales promotion objectives, in order to ensure a competitive advantage over similar companies, mainly locally but also at a wider level. Therefore, it becomes vital for every business to understand how the consumer thinks and what leads him to the decision to choose specific destinations or individual services and products over others (Middleton et al., 2014). There are many companies in the tourism industry and mainly in hospitality, which find it difficult to increase their market share due to modern phenomena such as increasing international competition, oversupply, slower growth rates, the maturation of certain markets, etc. Thus, companies are more interested before retaining their customers and the benefits are obvious. When customers become loyal, they buy more, they are willing to pay more and recommend more. However, building loyalty among customers is a challenge for hosting, as changing hosting provider carries a risk, as it is difficult to assess the quality of a service before it is consumed (Guzzo et al., 2022). Therefore, in their effort to increase their loyal customers, companies try to develop long-term relationships with them, satisfying their various needs and desires (Martínez & Rodríguez del Bosque, 2013). The study conducted by Fatma, Rahman & Khan, (2016) on the impact of CSR on consumer reactions in the hotel sector, showed that corporate capacity has a strong impact on customer buying intention, while CSR activities influence customer buying intention only in cases where the customer was aware of these activities. In their own study, Canela & Navarro (2017) examined the existing literature, concluding in that there is still no clear characterization of responsible consumers and even less in the case of hotel companies. Their subsequent research was based on this finding and showed that age, nationality and to a lesser extent education, are factors that influence the importance of CSR for the selection of a hotel unit, as well as for repurchase. This data is important for hotels when launching a communication campaign on CSR initiatives, so they know which target groups to target. In addition, the data show that the hotel sector needs to integrate its commitment to CSR actions into its business strategy, both for the social and environmental benefits of the actions themselves and for the very positive impact it will have on business, reputation and increase its competitiveness.

In conclusion, the implementation of CSR actions proves to be an important factor in creating competitive advantages in the hotel industry. From the analysis of the conclusions of all the above surveys, it is concluded that CSR acts mostly positively on customer satisfaction with consequent improvement of the corporate image, the strengthening of trust, the consolidation of loyalty, as well as the tendency for repurchase and recommendation to third parties. However, it is significantly influenced by certain factors, such as pre-existing knowledge of CSR activities, quality of services provided, and innovation of actions, type of business and demographic characteristics of customers, such as nationality, age, and education. The growing importance of CSR for business performance in relation to the proven positive role that customer satisfaction plays in their loyalty to the business and therefore in increasing its sales, especially in a human-centered and highly competitive sector such as tourism, directs us to further research the application of CSR in tourism businesses and its impact on the potential tourist, with the help of primary research that will be analyzed in detail in the following sections.

CSR Policies in the Hotel Sector: Current and Future Trends

Corporate Social Responsibility in tourism is a part of sustainable tourism development. The need to integrate sustainability is very high, as tourism is a sector with great economic and social intensity and efficiency and plays an important role in the economic development of a place and employment. Consequently, due to the type and extent of infrastructure needed to create the so called tourism offer, the environmental and social factor plays a very important role in tourism businesses.

The Adoption of Corporate Social Responsibility (CSR) Policy in the Tourism Sector

Tourism plays a very important role in the fight against poverty, through job creation and the general improvement of the standard of living. The general application of Corporate Social Responsibility in tourism has positive effects on the quality of tourism products, the image of individuals in society and its social partners, the environmental and social criticism of tourism activity and the differentiation of products from the competition, creating more "loyal customers". Corporate social responsibility policies are better known in other industries, where large multinational chains in the field of trade and consumer goods have reached the point of competing in terms of practices, actions and social supply. In the tourism industry, even from large companies, there are not many implementations or practices. The same conclusion was confirmed by a study by Palau (2006), who conducted a study of 24 hotel chains representing 60% of all hospitality chains in the region of Catalonia in Spain. Palau (2006) found that most of these hotel companies do not develop corporate social responsibility strategies due to lack of knowledge about existing international standards such as GRI, SA8000 etc. There is also a low level of business relationship between key stakeholders. Tepelus (2010) links lack of development of corporate social responsibility with lack of consensus on the importance and definition of sustainable tourism. However, many tourism companies, mainly hotels, have made their appearance through environmental social and humanitarian CSR actions. Such may be energy saving, the use of environmentally friendly products, recycling, others in charities, the organization of charitable events, the development and training of staff, compliance with health and safety rules, and more. There are now many tools as well as international standards and guidelines, such as ISO 14001, ISO 26000, on environmental management and CSR principles, GRI, GSTC, EMASIII that are global initiatives and provide the criteria for the establishment of sustainability reports, principles for sustainable tourism, ecological management and more. These help tourism businesses implement sustainable practices, create sustainable products and have a positive social and environmental footprint. Establish various certification bodies for tourism companies in Greece, certifying that they comply with international sustainability standards.

CSR and the hospitality industry have only been linked for a short time, and as a result, hotel owners and operators are beginning to recognize not only the positive but also the negative aspects of this type of business, and they are becoming aware that over a longer time horizon, it is necessary not only to reap financial and human resource benefits from the company, but also to protect and improve the environment around them (Dyrtr, 2006; Franco, Caroli, Cappa & Del Chiappa, 2020; Li, Pinto & Diabat, 2020; Liang & Wong, 2020). Hotels nowadays aren't simply looking for economic indicators; they're also looking for social interactions, whether between employees and management or between the hotel and the general public (Mervart, 2010). At European Commission, tourism issues are the subject of the General Directorate of Business and Industry (DG Enterprise and Industry) and in particular of the Department of Tourism (Unit Tourism) of the said General Directorate. After the publication of the Commission Communication "Agenda for a Sustainable and Competitive European Tourism" in October 2007 and the European Parliament Decision "Renewed Tourism Policy of the European Union" in November 2007, a strong activity of the Department of Tourism on the diffusion and application of the provisions of the above texts. Other important milestones for the social and ethical social responsibility policies of tourism companies are the following:

- *The World Tourism Organization* - UNWTO has developed a code of conduct on "Child protection in tourism" since 2000 to reduce child exploitation and abuse
- *The World Committee for Ethics and Ethics in Tourism* - WCTE has been developed.

- *The ISO 26000* standard concerns the satisfactory and effective implementation of corporate social responsibility in tourism.

Different awards have been introduced for the performance of corporate social responsibility in tourism. Over the years, the evolution of quality standards, as well as the development of the basic principles of corporate social responsibility, the way in which stakeholders position themselves in relation to necessity of implementing social responsibility in tourism will evolve dynamically. The ISO 26000 directive on corporate responsibility in tourism already raises positive expectations today. Thus, more and more tourism companies are adopting socially responsible practices and publishing their social action (Tepelus, 2010; Sugianto & Soediantono, 2022). In addition, it is worth noting that even existing corporate social responsibility initiatives are largely focused on tourism compared to previous years, due to globalization, free trade and of sustainable development. The scope of future initiatives will include much more issues such as fair trade in tourism, pricing policies, supply chain management, labor practices, labor migration, trafficking in human beings and stereotypical discrimination. In this way, emphasis will be placed on poverty reduction as defined by the United Nations Global Compact (Hamid, 2010). At the same time, many tourism companies have been committed to promoting their corporate responsibility and have won several awards for their social action in addition to their environmental awareness. For example, the Accor hotels were awarded for their efforts in combating tuberculosis, malaria and HIV / AIDS prevention, Air France - KLM was awarded for its reduction of carbon dioxide emissions and its active participation in society during the operation of human rights. According to a survey conducted by Metaxas and Tsavdaridou (2010) on the social responsibility of Greek tourism companies, the following conclusions were drawn:
There are fair employment contracts for staff but they have limited capabilities

- Staff training is provided but to a lesser extent after 2009 due to the crisis and many times employees is pushed into self-financing to further develop their capabilities so as not to lose their jobs.
- Priority is given mainly to hotels in hygiene and safety in order to avoid diseases, allergies and other health problems.
- Many tourism companies do sea cleaning, tree planting and other actions for the cleanliness of the societies in which they operate and to avoid complaints from residents.
- The majorities of tourism companies applies quality, safety and environmental standards and publish them to show their social responsibility
- Emphasis is placed on customer satisfaction and the management of public relations with society

RESEARCH DESIGN

Qualitative Research and Data Collection Tool

Qualitative research was used in order to investigate the customer's views on CSR actions and how they impact on their loyalty in a hotel. Jackson, Meade & Ellenbogen, (2006) define qualitative research as a process of searching that is based on different methodological traditions. Ideally, the researcher chooses a topic at the beginning, with the fact that pre-defines questions, or in this case, the problem formulation (Hendl, 2016). A main characteristic of the qualitative method is its reference to the species, i.e. to the

The Adoption of Corporate Social Responsibility (CSR) Policy in the Tourism Sector

character of the phenomenon (Byrd, 2021;Crick, 2021). For the current research, information was collected through the review and study of international literature, as well as the collection of primary data through 204 interviews in 30 Greek hotels, where consumer habits and behaviors in the hotel sector were studied from the view of CSR actions. The quality, expectations and trust that a business generates are very important elements related to consumer behaviors (Coltman et al., 2005; Rita, Oliveira & Farisa, 2019). The benefits offered by an organization determine consumer satisfaction and loyalty as is the case in the hotel industry where visitors can be satisfied with the services provided to them automatically creating a competitive advantage and high profitability for the organization (McDonald & Rundle, 2008; Rita, Oliveira & Farisa, 2019; Evans & Lewis, 2018). In the present study, semi-structured interviews were categorized into non-standard interviews. In non-standard interviews, the researcher prepares a series of questions that he / she would like to be asked in order to be included in his / her research. The difference of this type from the traditional semi-structured interviews is that in the present research the interviews were done some by email and some by phone, so there was no direct personal contact with the respondents (Meho, 2006).

Sampling and Research Sample

Convenience sampling was selected. In this case, immediately available and easily accessible cases are selected (Gravetter & Forzano, 2009). The sample consisted of 204 respondents where they were selected based on the criterion of feasibility. The sampling method chosen is the avalanche method. This method is based on random sampling and is not based on the probability method. This research is based on a number of people who are also participants in the research and share the same sample for analysis. In conclusion, they are considered a subset of the population for research (Goodman, 1961).

The Design of the Interviews and the Thematic Codes

The interviews took place during the period of April 2020 to April 2021 and consisted of 3 thematic axes (see Table 1), based on research questions, asking 18 questions in total. The respondents were not of a specific educational level, marital status, profession. What was required was their experience with any hotel and the identification of the effect of CSR on their choice or the intention to choose the same hotel (loyalty) again in the future knowing the CSR actions that follow.

1. *Selection of respondents.* The first step in conducting the email interviews was to select the respondents. The authors refer to a sample of convenience.
2. *Preparation, interview planning.* The interview questions arose after the completion of the literature review where the aim was to answer the main research questions. The interviews were created based on thematic axes that coincided with the purpose of the research findings and research questions. Each topic consisted of specific questions for discovery and data collection (see Table 1)

Table 1. The 3 thematic axes of the interviews

Thematic Axis 1	
Recognition of CSR by the consumer public	7 questions
Thematic Axis 2	
CSR as a hotel selection criterion	6 questions
Thematic Axis 3	
The effect of CSR on creating loyalty in the hotel sector	5 questions

DATA ANALYSIS

Data analysis was based on content analysis. This process is a continuous interpretation of the findings and decodes the discussions that take place in an interview. The first step in data and sample collection is to record and save the data from the resulting interviews, so that the frequent data are listed and can be categorized and later analyzed. According to Downe - Wamboldt (1992) and Morgan (1993) content analysis uses a descriptive approach both in data coding and in the interpretation of code quantitative measurements. Thematic analysis provides a purely qualitative, detailed view of the data (Braun & Clarke, 2006; Assarroudi, Heshmati Nabavi, Armat, Ebadi & Vaismoradi, 2018). Below (Figure 1) are the initial codes that emerged from the answers of the interviews where they will be analyzed.

Figure 1. Initial codes from answers

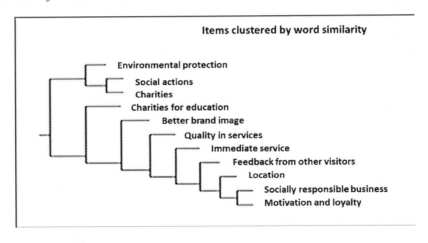

The process of thematic analysis was based on the six stages of Braun & Clarke (2006). In the first stage, the data became familiar. The second stage concerned the coding of the data. Coding through the QSR NVivo 12 program was preferred. Interconnected semantic units were first identified and the data were semantically grouped in relation to the research query. In the third stage, the themes were investigated. In other words, the codes given in the interview data were summarized in themes and sub-themes. The following figure (Figure 2) shows an initial correlation from QSR NVivo 12 based on verbal relevance.

Figure 2. Correlation based on verbal relevance

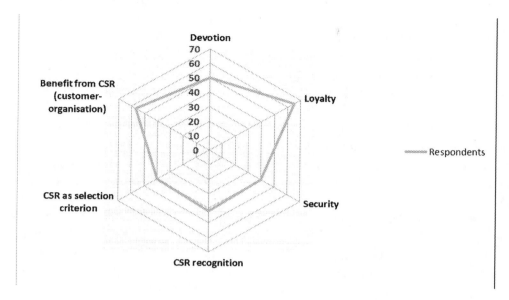

In the fourth stage, the themes were reviewed, so that there are no overlaps and any needs to be merged or separated.

In the fifth stage, the themes were redefined and named. At this stage, the names of the themes of the final analysis were decided, so that they are comprehensive and give the reader a first idea of what each theme includes. The smaller thematic categories were then categorized based on the research questions into three respective thematic axes, which are the following Table (table 2).

Table 2. Codes in three thematic axes

CSR recognition from customers	Customers' criteria for choosing a hotel	The results of CSR in customers
Environmental protection	Quality in services	Motivation and loyalty
Incensement in corporate reputation	Immediate services	Better brand image
Charities	Location	Socially responsible business
Charities in education		

According to Gibs (2007), each code can intersect and record specific passages that explain the theory itself by linking their meaning and the code to a name. As a result, anything that is repeated in the text is categorized so that a set of ideas on the subject can be found and analyzed. In addition, the approach of the present research is the inductive one as the data of the interviews have been codified and grouped in relation to the research questions that have been formed in 3 thematic axes. From the above table 2 emerge the codes which will be analyzed based on the most common answers given by the respondents. As to whether CSR is recognized, the resulting codes are original and very often environmental protection was mentioned. Also it was mentioned the strengthening of corporate reputation, donations, social activities and sponsorships in education. The feelings received from most of the responses, at least through telephone interviews, 3 in 4, referred to definitions and concepts that, however, seemed to have been studied or read and they did not actually know inwardly what they were saying. Specifically, Respondent (R) 4 claimed that "he knows CSR as a voluntary act of companies as well as environmental issues", however it was understood that the respondent was studying, memorizing the definition. Generally, the answers confirm the economic, legal, ethical, philanthropic, environmental and stakeholder dimensions (Pérez-Aranda & Boronat-Navarro, 2022).

The next category highlighted important codes and information on a hotel's actual preference criteria. The words security, reliability, prompt service, but also location was repeated. In conclusion, consumer criteria revolve around service and ease of access. In fact, some of them mentioned another criterion that could make them change the hotel they prefer if they find more affordable financial packages.

The third category refers to the reasons for attracting the respondents and what they feel it really offers. So regardless of whether everyone knew the real importance of CSR, whether such actions were a criterion for the preference of a hotel or whether they believe or not that CSR is a criterion for choosing a hotel, what is ultimately created is a positive profile associated with the organization, motivates them to stay true to it and trust it more and the reason is that in this way they show socially and environmentally responsible organizations. They referred to the importance of preserving and balancing the environment, both through simple recycling and socially, for example by providing employment opportunities to vulnerable groups. Based on the subject codes to be analyzed, a thematic map (Figure 3) was created in order to summarize the important results and data as well as to codify the findings of the present research (Braun & Clarke, 2006).

In the sixth stage, the final analysis was done. The initial goal was to identify phrases that would first lead to the organization of the individual themes and then to the concentration of the content of these interviews.

Results

Following is the analysis of the participants' answers per research question (RQ).

For the RQ1 "what's the meaning of CSR and how it is related with customers", it was initially answered by the various concepts and definitions of its literature where it is expressed and found that Corporate Social Responsibility has evolved over time and more and more companies choose it to be able to compete in the market but also to offer social work. In terms of loyalty, albeit with a small difference, most responded positively to whether CSR actions are a reason to stay loyal to a hotel, yet others did not see it as an important reason to stay or change hotels in the future and opt for a competitive one. The result of the question whether they knew the concept of Corporate Social Responsibility was positive, as well as the 204 who knew it and some even referred to terms such as "sustainable development", which is positive for society. Most of respondents (57) mentioned environmental aid quite often, which means that CSR has been formulated in the minds of the consumer as an action to protect the environment. Another equally important term was "bullying" and helping to combat it with widespread CSR actions, as well as the financial support that companies believe they offer to other financially affected organizations. Finally, 35 participants reported on issues of internal corporate social responsibility and specifically on actions of the company towards employees. Indicatively, R3 referred to "actions of an organization in supporting country's culture and in collaborations for sustainable development", in contrast to R8 who

Figure 3. The thematic map

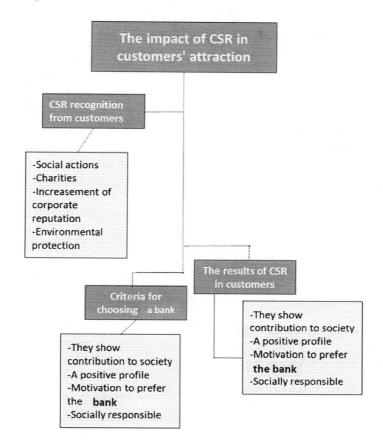

was not aware of CSR actions of the hotels he has visited. These results confirm the economic, legal, ethical, philanthropic, environmental and stakeholder dimensions of CSR.

In the RQ2 whether CSR is a factor that creates loyalty to a hotel, 202 out of 204 answered in the negative, claiming that CSR is not a reason for loyalty to a hotel but for the service, the privacy it offers as well as the accessibility in terms of location. Specifically, regarding "the impact of CSR on consumer attraction and loyalty" some of the answers were:

- R102 stated characteristically that "the reason for his loyalty was the service offered by the hotel as well as its sense of privacy. Similarly, another statement of R35 was that "loyalty is created through good and fast service".
- However, 163 out of 165 respondents stated that although CSR is not a reason to stay loyal to a hotel, it creates a sense of security and trust for them, as such actions create a more socially and environmentally conscious image for customers and this makes them more trustful.
- R11 claimed that "he would be interested in visiting a hotel that implements more CSR programs and this would provide him with greater security in terms of the quality of his services but also in terms of the human resources that the organization employs".

- Respectively, R167 stated that "he feels more secure knowing that the hotel it is visiting is environmentally and socially aware, through CSR actions", in contrast to R3 who stated that "his sense of security does not increase".

Finally, the results of the RQ3 "whether CSR is a criterion for choosing a hotel and whether CSR was a criterion for customers' previous visit to a hotel" were also interesting. All respondents answered no, that it is not a selection criterion and focused on the criteria of service and location. This is probably due to the fact that while they know CSR as a concept and the actions it includes, however, the concept and the substantial result that it can give to an organization have not been fully defined. In addition, weight was given to the question of whether they themselves benefit from the CSR actions carried out by the hotels they have visited where 200 out of 204 believe that these actions are only of interest to the organization, as they enhance its reputation.

FUTURE RESEARCH DIRECTIONS

The topic of Corporate Social Responsibility may be unknown to many but it is an interesting topic to study. For this reason it would be prudent to carry out further research in the future, especially in the hotel industry which is still lagging behind other sectors. Until recently, hotels were more concerned with environmental issues; nevertheless, they must not overlook the importance of other issues, such as labor issues. Problems in the workplace, such as gender equality and fair remuneration, have already been mentioned. These two issues, labor and the environment, are the context in which hotels can successfully and responsibly take individual steps toward completely integrating CSR policies into their operations. Other challenges that should be examined include environmental concerns, which are one of the most common CSR initiatives used by hotels. Also another proposal for the analysis of new aspects and horizons of CSR would be the combination of qualitative and quantitative research data collection. For example, a research could be conducted in this way that compares the application of CSR in wider companies of both the Greek market and the European one. Finally, a survey of executives and employees is proposed in the future, as this would highlight the recognition of CSR by employees themselves and whether their involvement can improve the transmissibility of CSR actions to consumers, which will maintained a competitive advantage and perhaps faster recognition of Corporate Social Responsibility by the public. When gathering this kind of information from customers it is interesting to understand which customer groups, have which preferences and values, therefore, demographic factors and especially the opinions of different age groups or gender concerning the impact of CSR actions in their loyalty is also of interest (Yuen, et al., 2016; Quintana-García, Marchante-Lara & Benavides-Chicón, 2018). Finally, future studies could also ascertain the mediating role of other variables on the linkage between CSR and loyalty that may include positive word-of-mouth, trust or credibility.

CONCLUSION

In the context of tourism and hospitality CSR covers several aspects such as employment, human rights, environmental ethics, or community and the economic, social and environmental areas. In the present research, with the help of the literature review, the role of Corporate Social Responsibility was investigated and studied both conceptually and specifically in the hotel industry.

A significant finding that differs from the literature refers to the weaker relationship that was found between CSR and customers' loyalty. After the completion of the research conducted with the help of interviews and after the contribution of 204 respondents, it seems that the motivation for their stay was not CSR but the services offered the immediate service and the ease of access. In terms of how much CSR actions attract consumers security was the most positive emotion that overwhelmed them. Respondents seem to trust and feel more secure with a socially and environmentally aware hotel, while with a small difference for most was the loyalty, to remain loyal to a hotel as a sign of reward in their social work. Another positive in attracting them is that although CSR has no deeper value in Greece and what it offers is not widespread enough, the consumer public is looking for information about the hotels they are going to visit. However, the variable of their loyalty to the respective hotel showed negative results as most answered that Corporate Social Responsibility is not a reason for their loyalty. This finding confirms the study of Hagelborg (2018) who pointed a weak and negative affect of CSR on customer loyalty. Authors also conclude in that more and more hotel units in Greece implement CSR programs and integrate this strategy in their business. This is an incentive for more people to know its broader meaning but also how much they benefit themselves. From the data obtained in the survey, the majority argued that such programs only help the organization. However customers are affected by CSR practices and this recognition could significantly help hotels focus on improving their service quality (Foote et al., 2010) and lead to improved customer satisfaction (Su & Swanson, 2017).

Regarding the first research question, through the literature study it emerged that there is therefore a discrepancy between bibliography and primary research. More specifically, the data of the results of the primary research show some convergences and discrepancies, compared to the data of the literature review. Regarding the second research question, the data from the primary research which showed that the reasons for consumer loyalty and attraction are not CSR actions, may confirm the perception of Davis (1973), who argued that most companies are not able to support such actions due to lack of specific means, so rightly yet hotels cannot delimit and pass this image on to the consumer public. A discrepancy between primary research and literature review confirms a study conducted in 2009-2010 (Aspridis et al., 2014) which found that companies implementing CSR actions receive greater loyalty from the consumer public. After conducting this research, it was found the opposite and in fact the majority of visitors argue that CSR actions are not a reason for their loyalty, which does not support previous findings (for example Pérez & Rodríguez del Bosque, 2015; Kim & Ham, 2016).

Although the satisfaction and commitment, as well as the negative or positive perception of the consumers, through the second research question, depends on the trust created by the respective company (Sirdeshmukh et al., 2002), the convergence that exists in this research with The corresponding literature is that consumers may believe that the CSR actions implemented by the hotels are superficial and that it only contributes to the increase of their profits and its corporate reputation and recognition. This result do not agree with the findings of other studies such as the study of Latif, Pérez and Sahibzada (2020) who found that customer satisfaction and corporate image were identified as significant mediators of the CSR-loyalty link, but service quality and corporate reputation were found insignificant. This and the fact that organizations are affected by such negative reviews, as reported by Carroll (2015), are consistent with the results of this survey, which showed that the majority of participants believe that CSR actions benefit only organizations. As the role of tourism in global development is very large and its impact on societies and the environment as well, it is necessary to have control and certification as well as development based on the sustainability of the environment and society. After all, sustainable development and CSR are not a fad, but a necessity and a condition for long-term economic growth and prosperity of businesses and residents of a place.

REFERENCES

Aljarah, A., Emeagwali, L., Ibrahim, B., & Ababneh, B. (2018). Does corporate social responsibility really increase customer relationship quality? A meta-analytic review. *Social Responsibility Journal*, *16*(1), 28–49. doi:10.1108/SRJ-08-2018-0205

Assarroudi, A., Heshmati Nabavi, F., Armat, M. R., Ebadi, A., & Vaismoradi, M. (2018). Directed qualitative content analysis: The description and elaboration of its underpinning methods and data analysis process. *Journal of Research in Nursing*, *23*(1), 42–55. doi:10.1177/1744987117741667 PMID:34394406

Becker-Olsen, K. L., Cudmore, B. A., & Hill, R. P. (2006). The impact of perceived corporate social responsibility on consumer behavior. *Journal of Business Research*, *59*(1), 46–53. doi:10.1016/j.jbusres.2005.01.001

Bhattacharya, C. B., & Sen, S. (2003). Consumer–company identification: A framework for understanding consumers' relationships with companies. *Journal of Marketing*, *67*(2), 76–88. doi:10.1509/jmkg.67.2.76.18609

Bhattacharya, C. B., & Sen, S. (2004). Doing better at doing good: When, why, and how consumers respond to corporate social initiatives. *California Management Review*, *47*(1), 9–24. doi:10.2307/41166284

Bowen, H. R. (2013). *Social responsibilities of the businessman*. University of Iowa Press. doi:10.2307/j.ctt20q1w8f

Braun, V., & Clarke, V. (2006). Using thematic analysis in psychology. *Qualitative Research in Psychology*, *3*(2), 77–101. doi:10.1191/1478088706qp063oa

Byrd, R. (2021). Qualitative research methods.

Canela, J., & Navarro, M. (2017). Profile of the consumer who values responsible and smart tourism in the hotel industry. *Management Decision*, *50*(5), 972–988.

Carroll, A. B. (2015). Corporate social responsibility (CSR) is on a sustainable trajectory. *Journal of Defense Management*, *5*(2), 1–2. doi:10.4172/2167-0374.1000132

Chatzopoulou, E., & Xanthopoulou, P. (2021). What drive customers to spread the word and be loyal? Factors influencing e-loyalty and eWOM to OTA's websites. *International Journal of Cultural and Digital Tourism*.

Coltman, T. R., Devinney, T. M., Midgley, D. F., & Venaik, S. (2008). Formative versus reflective measurement models: Two applications of formative measurement. *Journal of Business Research*, *61*(12), 1250–1262. doi:10.1016/j.jbusres.2008.01.013

Crick, J. M. (2021). Qualitative research in marketing: What can academics do better? *Journal of Strategic Marketing*, *29*(5), 390–429. doi:10.1080/0965254X.2020.1743738

Dathe, T., Dathe, R., Dathe, I., & Helmold, M. (2022). CSR as Part of the Corporate Strategy. In *Corporate Social Responsibility (CSR), Sustainability and Environmental Social Governance (ESG)* (pp. 1–22). Springer. doi:10.1007/978-3-030-92357-0_1

Davis, K. (1973). The case for and against business assumption of social responsibilities. *Academy of Management Journal*, *16*(2), 312–322. doi:10.2307/255331

Dodds, R., & Joppe, M. (2005). *CSR in the Tourism Industry?: The Status of and Potential for Certification, Codes of Conduct and Guidelines*. IFC.

Downe-Wamboldt, B. (1992). Content analysis: Method, applications, and issues. *Health Care for Women International*, *13*(3), 313–321. doi:10.1080/07399339209516006 PMID:1399871

Dyrtr, Z. (2006). *Good business name* (1st ed.). Alfa Publishing.

Emmanuel, B., & Priscilla, O. A. (2022). A Review of Corporate Social Responsibility and Its Relationship with Customer Satisfaction and Corporate Image. *Open Journal of Business and Management*, *10*(2), 715–728. doi:10.4236/ojbm.2022.102040

Evans, C., & Lewis, J. (2018). *Analysing semi-structured interviews using thematic analysis: Exploring voluntary civic participation among adults*. SAGE Publications Limited.

Fatma, M., & Rahman, Z. (2015). Consumer perspective on CSR literature review and future research agenda. *Management Research Review*, *38*(2), 195–216. doi:10.1108/MRR-09-2013-0223

Font, X., & Lynes, J. (2018). Corporate social responsibility in tourism and hospitality. *Journal of Sustainable Tourism*, *26*(7), 1027–1042. doi:10.1080/09669582.2018.1488856

Foote, J., Gaffney, N., & Evans, J. R. (2010). Corporate social responsibility: Implications for performance excellence. *Total Quality Management*, *21*(8), 799–812. doi:10.1080/14783363.2010.487660

Franco, S., Caroli, M. G., Cappa, F., & Del Chiappa, G. (2020). Are you good enough? CSR, quality management and corporate financial performance in the hospitality industry. *International Journal of Hospitality Management*, *88*, 102395. doi:10.1016/j.ijhm.2019.102395

Garay, L., & Font, X. (2012). Doing good to do well? Corporate social responsibility reasons, practices and impacts in small and medium accommodation enterprises. *International Journal of Hospitality Management*, *31*(2), 329–337. doi:10.1016/j.ijhm.2011.04.013

Glaveli, N. (2020). Corporate social responsibility toward stakeholders and customer loyalty: Investigating the roles of trust and customer identification with the company. *Social Responsibility Journal*.

Gond, J. P., & Nyberg, D. (2017). Materializing power to recover corporate social responsibility. *Organization Studies*, *38*(8), 1127–1148. doi:10.1177/0170840616677630

Goodman, L. A. (1961). Snowball sampling. *Annals of Mathematical Statistics*, *32*(1), 148–170. doi:10.1214/aoms/1177705148

Gravetter, F. J., & Forzano, L. A. (2009). Research methods for the Behavioral Science. Wadsworth, Cengage Learning.

Guzzo, R. F., Abbott, J., & Lee, M. (2022). How CSR and well-being affect work-related outcomes: A hospitality industry perspective. *International Journal of Contemporary Hospitality Management*, *34*(4), 1470–1490. doi:10.1108/IJCHM-06-2021-0754

Hagelborg, E. (2018). *CSR as a customer loyalty driver: Within the energy industry*. Semantic Scholar.

Hahn, T., Figge, F., Pinkse, J., & Preuss, L. (2018). A paradox perspective on corporate sustainability: Descriptive, instrumental, and normative aspects. *Journal of Business Ethics*, *148*(2), 235–248. doi:10.100710551-017-3587-2

Hendl, J. (2016). *Kvalitativní výzkum* (1st ed.). Portál.

Hoffman, A. J. (2018). The next phase of business sustainability. *Stanford Social Innovation Review*, *16*(2), 34–39.

Islam, T., Islam, R., Pitafi, A. H., Xiaobei, L., Rehmani, M., Irfan, M., & Mubarak, M. S. (2021). The impact of corporate social responsibility on customer loyalty: The mediating role of corporate reputation, customer satisfaction, and trust. *Sustainable Production and Consumption*, *25*, 123–135. doi:10.1016/j.spc.2020.07.019

Jackson, M. N., Meade, M. A., & Ellenbogen, P. B. K. (2006). Perspectives on networking, cultural values, and skills among African American men with spinal cord injuries: A reconsideration of social capital theory. *Journal of Vocational Rehabilitation*, *25*, 21–33.

Kaplan, R. (2015). Who has been regulating whom, business or society? The mid-20th-century institutionalization of 'corporate responsibility' in the USA. *Socio-economic Review*, *13*(1), 125–155. doi:10.1093er/mwu031

Kavoura, A., & Sahinidis, A. G. (2015). Communicating corporate social responsibility activities in Greece in a period of a prolonged economic crisis. *Procedia: Social and Behavioral Sciences*, *175*, 496–502. doi:10.1016/j.sbspro.2015.01.1228

Khan, M. A., Yasir, M., & Khan, M. A. (2021). Factors Affecting Customer Loyalty in the Services Sector. *Journal of Tourism and Services*, *12*(22), 184–197. doi:10.29036/jots.v12i22.257

Kim, M., Yin, X., & Lee, G. (2020). The effect of CSR on corporate image, customer citizenship behaviors, and customers' long-term relationship orientation. *International Journal of Hospitality Management*, *88*, 102520. doi:10.1016/j.ijhm.2020.102520

Latif, K. F., Pérez, A., & Sahibzada, U. F. (2020). Corporate social responsibility (CSR) and customer loyalty in the hotel industry: A cross-country study. *International Journal of Hospitality Management*, *89*, 102565. doi:10.1016/j.ijhm.2020.102565

Li, Y., Pinto, M. C. B., & Diabat, A. (2020). Analyzing the critical success factor of CSR for the Chinese textile industry. *Journal of Cleaner Production*, *260*, 120878. doi:10.1016/j.jclepro.2020.120878

Liang, T. C., & Wong, E. S. F. (2020). Sustainable development: An adaptive re-use solution for the hospitality industry. *Worldwide Hospitality and Tourism Themes*, *12*(5), 623–637. doi:10.1108/WHATT-06-2020-0047

Liu, M. T., Liu, Y., Mo, Z., Zhao, Z., & Zhu, Z. (2019). How CSR influences customer behavioural loyalty in the Chinese hotel industry. *Asia Pacific Journal of Marketing and Logistics*, *32*(1), 1–22. doi:10.1108/APJML-04-2018-0160

Luo, X., & Bhattacharya, C. B. (2006). Corporate social responsibility, customer satisfaction, and market value. *Journal of Marketing*, *70*(4), 1–18. doi:10.1509/jmkg.70.4.001

Martínez, P., & Del Bosque, I. R. (2013). CSR and customer loyalty: The roles of trust, customer identification with the company and satisfaction. *International Journal of Hospitality Management*, *35*, 89–99. doi:10.1016/j.ijhm.2013.05.009

McDonald, L. M., & Rundle-Thiele, S. (2008). Corporate social responsibility and bank customer satisfaction: A research agenda. *International Journal of Bank Marketing*, *26*(3), 170–182. doi:10.1108/02652320810864643

Meho, L. I. (2006). E-mail interviewing in qualitative research: A methodological discussion. *Journal of the American Society for Information Science and Technology*, *57*(10), 1284–1295. doi:10.1002/asi.20416

Metaxas, T., & Tsavdaridou, M. (2010). Corporate social responsibility in europe: Denmark, Hungary and Greece. *Journal of Contemporary European Studies*, *18*(1), 25–46. doi:10.1080/14782801003638679

Middleton, A., Gunn, J., Bassilios, B., & Pirkis, J. (2014). Systematic review of research into frequent callers to crisis helplines. *Journal of Telemedicine and Telecare*, *20*(2), 89–98. doi:10.1177/1357633X14524156 PMID:24518928

Mohammed, A., & Rashid, B. (2018). A conceptual model of corporate social responsibility dimensions, brand image, and customer satisfaction in Malaysian hotel industry. *Kasetsart Journal of Social Sciences*, *39*(2), 358–364. doi:10.1016/j.kjss.2018.04.001

Ng, A. W., & Tavitiyaman, P. (2020). Corporate social responsibility and sustainability initiatives of multinational hotel corporations. In *International business, trade and institutional sustainability* (pp. 3–15). Springer. doi:10.1007/978-3-030-26759-9_1

Pérez, A., & Del Bosque, I. R. (2015). Corporate social responsibility and customer loyalty: Exploring the role of identification, satisfaction and type of company. *Journal of Services Marketing*, *29*(1), 15–25. doi:10.1108/JSM-10-2013-0272

Pérez-Aranda, J. A., & Boronat-Navarro, M. (2022). Which corporate social responsibility issues do consumers perceive as relevant to be evaluated in the hotel sector? *European Journal of International Management*, *17*(1), 60–85. doi:10.1504/EJIM.2022.119746

Quintana-García, C., Marchante-Lara, M., & Benavides-Chicón, C. G. (2018). Social responsibility and total quality in the hospitality industry: Does gender matter? *Journal of Sustainable Tourism*, *26*(5), 722–739. doi:10.1080/09669582.2017.1401631

Rita, P., Oliveira, T., & Farisa, A. (2019). The impact of e-service quality and customer satisfaction on customer behavior in online shopping. *Heliyon*, *5*(10), e02690. doi:10.1016/j.heliyon.2019.e02690 PMID:31720459

Sahinidis, A. G., & Kavoura, A. (2014). Exploring corporate social responsibility practices of Greek companies. *Zeszyty Naukowe Małopolskiej Wyższej Szkoły Ekonomicznej w Tarnowie*, (2 (25)), 185–193.

Schreck, P. (2011). Reviewing the business case for corporate social responsibility: New evidence and analysis. *Journal of Business Ethics*, *103*(2), 167–188. doi:10.100710551-011-0867-0

Sirdeshmukh, D., Singh, J., & Sabol, B. (2002). Consumer trust, value, and loyalty in relational exchanges. *Journal of Marketing*, *66*(1), 15–37. doi:10.1509/jmkg.66.1.15.18449

Su, L., Swanson, S. R., Hsu, M., & Chen, X. (2017). How does perceived corporate social responsibility contribute to green consumer behavior of Chinese tourists: A hotel context. *International Journal of Contemporary Hospitality Management*, *29*(12), 3157–3176. doi:10.1108/IJCHM-10-2015-0580

Sugianto, S., & Soediantono, D. (2022). Literature Review of ISO 26000 Corporate Social Responsibility (CSR) and Implementation Recommendations to the Defense Industries. *Journal of Industrial Engineering & Management Research*, *3*(2), 73–87.

Tauringana, V., & Chithambo, L. (2015). The effect of DEFRA guidance on greenhouse gas disclosure. *The British Accounting Review*, *47*(4), 425-444.

Tepelus, C. (2010). 6 Corporate Social Responsibility. *Understanding the sustainable development of tourism*, 110.

Xanthopoulou, P., & Kefis, V. (2016). Redefining CSR as an innovative tool in crisis times: The Greek approach. *International Journal of Social Research Methodology*, *4*(4), 1–18.

Yuen, K. F., Thai, V. V., & Wong, Y. D. (2016). Are customers willing to pay for corporate social responsibility? A study of individual-specific mediators. *Total Quality Management & Business Excellence*, *27*(7-8), 912–926. doi:10.1080/14783363.2016.1187992

Zientara, P., & Zamojska, A. (2018). Green organizational climates and employee pro-environmental behaviour in the hotel industry. *Journal of Sustainable Tourism*, *26*(7), 1142–1159. doi:10.1080/0966 9582.2016.1206554

KEY TERMS AND DEFINITIONS

Consumer Behavior: Consumer behavior is the study of how individuals and organizations make decisions to purchase, use, and dispose of products and services. It involves analyzing factors that influence consumer decision-making such as cultural, social, psychological, and economic factors.

Corporate Responsibility: Corporate Responsibility refers to the ethical and social obligations that companies have towards society, stakeholders, and the environment. It involves adopting policies and practices that promote sustainability, accountability, transparency, and ethical behavior in all aspects of the company's operations.

Customer Loyalty: Customer loyalty refers to the tendency of customers to repeatedly purchase products or services from a company or brand. It is influenced by factors such as customer satisfaction, trust, and perceived value, and can be fostered through effective marketing, customer service, and relationship-building efforts.

Customer Trust: Customer trust refers to the belief and confidence that customers have in a company or brand to deliver on its promises and commitments. It is a key component of building customer loyalty and can be influenced by factors such as product quality, customer service, and corporate reputation.

Hotel Industry: The hotel industry is a sector of the hospitality industry that provides lodging, accommodation, and related services to travelers and tourists. It includes a variety of establishments such as hotels, motels, resorts, and guesthouses.

Hotel Management: Hotel management refers to the process of overseeing the operations of a hotel or hospitality establishment. It involves managing the staff, financial resources, marketing and sales, customer service, and overall guest experience.

Sustainability: Sustainability refers to the ability to meet the needs of the present without compromising the ability of future generations to meet their own needs. In the context of business and tourism, sustainability involves adopting practices that minimize negative impacts on the environment, society, and economy, while maximizing positive contributions to these areas.

Tourism Policy: Tourism policy refers to the set of guidelines, regulations, and measures adopted by governments and tourism organizations to promote and manage tourism activities. It includes policies related to tourism infrastructure, destination development, environmental protection, cultural preservation, and community involvement.

Chapter 2
Self-Directedness in the Service of Human Resources Management in Tourism and Hospitality:
Perspectives Under the Scope of Adult Education and Lifelong Learning

Mary Viterouli
University of Thessaly, Greece

Athanasios Koustelios
University of Thessaly, Greece

Dimitrios Belias
University of Thessaly, Greece

Nikolaos Tsigilis
Aristotle University of Thessaloniki, Greece

ABSTRACT

The tourism and hospitality sector has been greatly impacted by the Covid-19 pandemic with inflows and outflows of tourists abruptly decreasing. In an effort to rebound, nations have embarked on forming policies to aid organizations regain their grounds. Emphasis on the regional development of the businesses, accordingly, can mediate growth. All things considered, organizations of the sector have had to turn to their personnel to seek ways to combat bottlenecks and crises and to upgrade the experience of their customers. The current chapter focuses on the notion of self-directedness and examines its vitality in the survival and recovery of the sector, and its inherent ability led to empowerment, adaptation, and flexibility. This is a literature review which consists of two main influential pillars: the degradation caused by the pandemic and the capability of self-directedness. Thus, the existing literature review, along with up-to-date articles and scientific journals have been processed and scrutinized.

DOI: 10.4018/978-1-6684-6055-9.ch002

Copyright © 2023, IGI Global. Copying or distributing in print or electronic forms without written permission of IGI Global is prohibited.

INTRODUCTION

The COVID-19 pandemic has caused significant disruptions in the political, social and economic global environment. By the end of the first quarter of 2020, the pandemic hit tourism the hardest and had brought travel, especially the international one, to an abrupt halt, significantly impacting the tourism and hospitality industry; an industry that accounts for and signifies as a major source of employment, government revenue and foreign exchange earnings. The duration of the global lockdown, as well as the remaining limitations and restrictions, have generated implications on the sector, hard to overcome. Many countries – if not all – both developed and developing, have experienced a dramatic contraction in GDP, and a subsequent rise in unemployment and poverty. Domestic tourism has mainly been the only functional subsector (UNWTO, 2022), since tourists have turned to closer to home destinations for a variety of reasons (Belias, Rossidis, & Valeri,2022)

Subsequently, the tourism standstill made quite a number of tourism and hospitality employees turn to other sectors and fields for work and employability (Belias & Trihas, 2022). In turn, this employee drain caused further problems in the industry and the need for qualified and talented personnel became more important than ever. The sector needs to recover and in order to do so, it needs 'its' people; people who are able to cope with problems and find solutions; people who are capable of dealing with and overcoming crises; people who are self-driven and autonomous to lead by example; people who keep pace with changes and innovations (Viterouli & Belias, 2021). What other kind of growth strategy could prove more efficient and sustainable other than the promotion, empowerment, and enrichment of a sector's personnel?

A high staff turnover can lead to negativity in the work culture and is damaging for the general performance, feeling of safety and security, motivation, and productivity altogether; not to mention the fact that the costs of recruiting, training and developing newcomers are substantial. Thus, addressing the problem has become a priority. Staff retention, motivation and performance have to improve, so as the sector's return on investment improves and its performance recovers.

BACKGROUND

The aim of this chapter is to investigate the relationship between the tourism and hospitality employees and lifelong learning and show that the latter can aid the former in becoming more independent, flexible and adaptable in order to help the sector regain its ground and prosperity. Self-directedness, taught via Knowle's Andragogy (1984), is proposed as a sustainable growth strategy that will help in this venture, essentially. Training and lifelong learning is considered crucial for Tourism Rebound and Inclusive Community Development (UNWTO; 2020, 2022). Empower; safeguard; prosper; and collaborate are the four pillars that measure and promote the Sustainability of Tourism. Domestic tourism continues to be the most crucial subsector in the recovery of the overall tourism sector, while international tourism continues to be volatile. Tourists have sought densely populated areas close to home to avoid travel limitations and, naturally, infection. It has felt safer to go on vacation within one's own country since he/she knows what to expect. Tourists and visitors started enjoying open-air experiences and rural tourism more. Therefore, a new trend has been created and this particular segment of tourism has given tourism stability and a chance to survive.

Tourism, as a vital lifeline, for many countries and peoples should overcome its current state and recover, and in order to do so the knowledge and competences of its human resources will be needed; knowledge and competences that can be supported and enhanced via self-directedness.

MAIN FOCUS OF THE CHAPTER

With tourism and hospitality having turned to domestic schemata and being so fast-paced and radically changing, people working in the sector are expected to be multi-taskers more often than not. They are expected to adapt to change almost immediately, to be internally motivated, and self-directed to overcome barriers and cope with demands (Belias et al., 2022). Building these capabilities in the tourism and hospitality can eventually aid in the rebound of the sector, after all, investment in training and educating the staff is investment in the longevity of the sector and every business individually. Offering potential and chances for enhancement, and reinforcing skills and capabilities fortifies retention of quality and talented personnel who are satisfied with their work and look into the future with hope and anticipation (Rossidis & Belias, 2020). Closing the gap between where an employee actually is and where he/she wants to be is imperative.

Lifelong learning and adult education can and should be used as a consistent basis for closing this gap (Merriam & Bierema, 2013) and offering further development, and most importantly, stimulation and a means or an outlet for (re)engineering. As a labour intense industry instilling motivation in every employee is how basically performance should be driven (Viterouli et al., 2022). This luminal transition requires adaptation skills and new kinds of knowledge. For this reason, employees should be managed, motivated, rewarded and enriched so as to reach their full potential and contribute to the business recovery and kick-start for and to a post-crisis 'new normality' and this is where the chapter's originality and value lies; to promote employees advancement for a scarcely researched field, i.e. self-directedness, in the tourism and hospitality sector.

UNDERGOING CONDITIONS

Current Status in Tourism and Hospitality

The Tourism and Hospitality sector has faced unprecedented challenges, hardships and uncertainties during the past few years. Globally and domestically, no company or organization has remained unaffected from the social, political and economic impacts of Covid-19 pandemic (Ntalakos et al., 2022a). Recovery and Resilience plans have been put into action, in Europe and the rest of the globe, to help enterprises cope with the consequences of its disastrous traversal, recover and adjust to the 'new reality', which has been forged by it. Within these turbulent and volatile schemata, leaders, across sectors, are asked to take initiatives, stabilize their businesses' turnover, boost its productivity to compensate for lost time, profit and inputs, and maintain their perseverance to survive.

Reflection of past actions and experiences, and elaboration of future perspectives and changes is troubling every business entity, let alone tourism businesses. Undertaking strategic, financial, and operational planning for the time ahead and cogitating trends and development in the Greek domain, for instance, are some of the steps local Tourism and Hospitality Sector enterprises have taken to mitigate the continuing and unpredictable effects of the pandemic (Belias et al., 2020a). We have borne witness to severe health measures, jeopardized livelihood for many of our fellow citizens, restrictions on mobility and travelling, lockdowns, mass deaths; circumstances that have altered our perceptions and attitude towards things and life itself. Travelling was no more a priority of the lot, but a necessity of the few and that is how hospitality, somehow, survived.

According to World Tourism Organization (UNWTO, 2022) - which is the United Nations specialized agency mandated with the promotion of responsible, sustainable and universally accessible tourism - global tourism experienced merely a 4% upturn in 2021 in comparison to 2020, but still remained a roughly 72% below the levels of pre-pandemic year, 2019. Due to Covid-19, the year 2020 is considered the worst year ever, on record, for tourism. The first quarter of 2021 showed tourist numbers down by 83% in Europe compared to the first quarter of 2020; followed by Africa (-81%), the Middle East (-78%) and America (-71%). Of course, we shouldn't fail to mention that this all follows on from the 73% fall in worldwide international tourist arrivals recorded in 2020 (UNWTO, 2021). The second half of 2021 showed a slight rebound; but still with international arrivals down 62% in both the third and fourth quarters, compared to the same periods in 2019.

Covid-19 in Arrivals and Tourists in Departures.

Europe and the Americas recorded arrivals up 19% and 17% respectively, but, still both remained 63% below 2019 levels. Africa saw a 12% increase in 2021 compared to 2020, though remained 74% below 2019 levels. Contrarily, in the Middle East arrivals declined 24% compared to 2020, and 79% over 2019. In Asia and the Pacific too, arrivals dropped 65% from 2020 levels and 94% when compared to pre-pandemic values (UNWTO, 2022).

Figure 1. International tourist arrivals 2021
(UNWTO, 2022)

The economic contribution of tourism (Tourism Direct Gross Domestic Product) was estimated in 2019 at US$ 3.5 trillion, whereas in 2020 at US$1.6 trillion and accordingly in 2021 at US$1.9 trillion.

Table 1. Unprecedented impact from Covid-19

	2019 (pre-pandemic year)	2020	2021*
International tourist arrivals (overnight visitors)	1.5 billion	400 million	415 million
Export revenues from international tourism (international tourism receipts + passenger transport)	US$ 1.7 trillion	US$ 638 billion	US$ 700-800 billion
Tourism Direct Gross Domestic Product (TDGDP)	US$ 3.5 trillion	US$ 1.6 trillion	US$ 1.9 Trillion

Source: UNWTO, World Tourism Barometer, 2022 (*Preliminary Results)

The latest UNWTO Panel of Experts (UNWTO, 2022) survey indicates that 61% of tourism professionals expect better performance in 2022 in comparison to that of 2021. Nevertheless, a high percentage of them (64%) strongly believes that tourism will return to 2019 levels after, at least, 2024. Unfortunately, Omicron variant of the pandemic has left little room for complete recovery in 2022, along with the continuous increase in Covid-19 cases and the recent surge of infections.

Therefore, while international tourism struggles to rebound, domestic tourism (subsector) continues to be the key factor in the recovery of the overall tourism sector, since demand for destinations which are closer to home and lower in population density is continually increasing, making it the least volatile tourism group. Tourists have turned to open-air activities, nature-based products and rural tourism, mainly due to travel limitations and infection-free likelihood in open-air experiences. Their quest is based primarily on sustainability, authenticity and localhood, trying to enrich their encounter and ventures with a diversity of people and places around, share visual stories, learn about local products and support local communities and businesses. Overall, 2021 has seen a significant increase in spending per trip and longer stays, even if the amount of money spent per day was lower and foreign exchange wasn't brought as intensely as previously to countries by the external inflows. Nevertheless, under the circumstances, the robust segment of domestic tourism has given tourism stability and a chance to survive.

Preparing and Thinking Ahead

The harshness of the pandemic has entrained enormous uncertainty and uncalculated risks. However, it has given us the time and the opportunity (or rather, inflicted them on us as non-negotiable) to rethink, revise and consolidate actions of the past, reinvent the way it does tourism, and consider needs and steps for the future.

The World Tourism Organization in the AL ULA Framework for Inclusive Community Development (ICD) through Tourism (2020) suggested four main pillars of action to Measure the Sustainability of Tourism (MST) in its economic, environmental and social dimension. The pillars were holistic and the proposed programmes and interventions in accordance to the respective pillars of action were flexible, inter-related and mutually dependent on each other to maximize the impact and outcomes of each of the interventions.

Figure 2. Framework for ICD through tourism
(UNWTO, 2020)

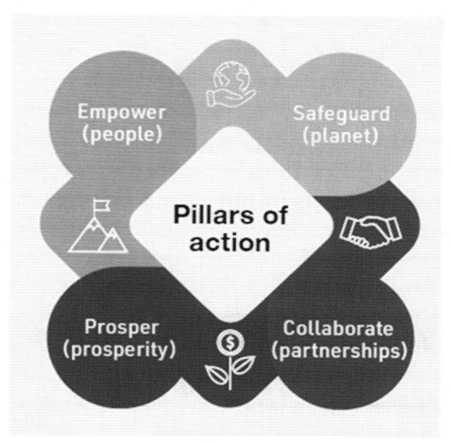

This approach has encouraged cohesion and collaboration between communities and tourism stakeholders, and promoted global cooperation and endurance. The key measurement areas of the Measuring the Sustainability of Tourism (MST) initiative aligned to the pillars of the Framework for ICD through tourism are outlined below:

The impact of COVID-19 on tourism demands collaboration between and among the public and private sector, communities, and stakeholders and requires important actions from all players to support the millions of livelihoods at risk. It has been seen as an opportunity to re-embark on a new basis and new perceptions towards a more sustainable, resilient and inclusive tourism sector. There has been a turn towards domestic, regional and local tourism and a focus on finding recovery schemes and strategies through accelerating digital transformation, innovation and sustainability in the sector.

Crisis management has been brought into force with various methods and resources (Rossidis, Belias and Vasiliadis, 2021). Measures such as the pillars proposed above have offered stakeholders means to reduce tension and relieve unpredictability and fear. Education is one of these means, and indeed an important one, which is referred in three out of the four pillars mentioned above. That alone attaches considerable importance on it. In fact, one of the recommendations in the 'Inclusive Community Development Through Tourism' report is to "promote human capital development through targeted policies and

Table 2. Measuring the sustainability of tourism (MST) pillars

EMPOWER	SAFEGUARD	PROSPER	COLLABORATE
Focus on the economic and social dimensions of MST including:	*The measurement fields in MST include:*	*Fields to be considered in line with MST include:*	*Relevant measurement areas in MST include:*
• Tourism supply and use accounts analysis; • Employment in tourism; • Demographics of tourism establishments; • *Education*; • Community and local perception; • Tourism governance; and • Decent work. Special attention should be paid to gender indicators.	• Water use in tourism industries (including wastewater flows); • Water resources; • Energy use in tourism industries; • GHG emissions by tourism industries; • Solid waste by tourism industries; • Land use and cover (including marine areas), ecosystem condition and services for tourism related areas; • Wildlife in protected areas/parks; • Green jobs; and • Visitor movement and culture/heritage can be used to measure and monitor the impact of the proposed interventions.	• Tourism supply and use accounts analysis (derivation of GDP, GVA, etc.); • Tourism expenditure; • Employment and decent work in tourism; • Investment and infrastructure; • Health outcomes; • *Education*; • Community cohesion; and • Crime	• Demographics of tourism establishments; • Investment and infrastructure; • Ecosystem condition and services for tourism related areas; • Green jobs; • *Education*; • Community; • Accessibility; and • Tourism governance.

Source: UNWTO, 2020, p. 18

programmes for education and capacity building…that enable efficient decision-making and leadership concerning tourism" (UNWTO, 2020, p. 34-35).

RECOMMENDATIONS TOWARDS TOURISM STABILITY

HR's Critical Role for Tourism and Hospitality Businesses

The tourism industry provides indispensable employment to millions of people around the world. These people are determinant to the service and product offering of the sector, setting the role of Human Resource Management (HRM) as an integral part of the strategic management of Tourism and Hospitality enterprises, and perhaps now more than ever (Belias, Rossidis and Papademetriou, 2021). We have seen the challenges employees, in all kinds of businesses, had to face concerning Covid-19, specifically, in sectors involving (in-person) service provision, such as tourism. Naturally one can say that different situations require different approaches and, likewise, different solutions. But, who could have predicted what was to come? Who would have foreseen such disastrous outcomes in every aspect of one's life and well-being?

The combination of a well-prepared crisis management team, leadership and skilled employees is the key answer to any crisis that might occur (Drašković and Džunić, M., 2020). This deduction leads to the assumption that the importance of the human capital is essential for a well-planned and efficiently implemented crisis management strategy. The quality of human resources determines organizational

Self-Directedness in the Service of Human Resources Management in Tourism and Hospitality

adaptation and performance (Masouras, 2019). The role of the HRM, the role of managers, and specifically the role of the managerial staff directly contribute to the realization of the organizational goals of the organization (Belias, Velissariou and Rossidis, 2019). Marsha and Tucker (1992) had claimed that societies that will strive are those based on learning and the application of acquired knowledge. Ashton and Green (1996) had stated that the key to organisational competitiveness is when and where the workforce develops and advances through education and training. Intellectual power and potential is the answer to any challenge or venture (Viterouli and Belias, 2021). We can teach skills, but we cannot instill character and potential. These have to do with one's soft skills and prospective. Thus, looking for potential rather than only skills and capabilities should be the new trend and demand.

In service businesses, the customer's satisfaction depends highly on the interpersonal contact they will have with the personnel (Blštáková et. al, 2020). Many researchers have argued that there is a tight and positive correlation between the satisfaction of internal customers (i.e. employees involved in the production-service chain) and external (final) customers. This view is a basic principle of Total Quality Management (TQM) (Ciampa, 1992). TQM has become, by and large, popular in the tourism and hospitality industry due to its unique nature and to high global competition. Nevertheless, TQM application varies across businesses (Kulenović, Folta and Veselinović, 2021, p. 5-6). Al-Ababneh (2021) claimed that few studies have been conducted to investigate the implementation of TQM in the hotel industry, and proposed a 12 Critical Success Factors key (CSF), leaving his findings as the most up-dated research that determines the successful implementation of TQM principles, as shown below:

Figure 3. Critical success factors (CSFs) of TQM implementation
(Al-Ababneh, 2021)

Hence, retrieving on our previous internal-external customers concept, it would be safe to say, as TQM, Organizational Behavior (internal client) and Marketing (external client) proclaim it, that a way to combat service quality diversity, which may derive from disengagement, displeasure or discomfort of the employees, is primarily to treat them as if they were the customers, cater for their needs and aspirations so that they take care of the business they work for, especially in such a turbulent era. It is, indeed, a chain reaction, where the level of internal quality and mutuality of the business is vividly reflected on the external customer's receipt of service and experience.

Yet, one should also bear in mind, that the nature of this kind of service is as perplexing as the heterogeneity of the sector. There is a wide range of profiles and engagement plots in the tourism and hospitality personnel. One key element integral and critical to all the pieces of information outlined so far (the European Union's Recovery and Resilience plan, the Crisis Management Constituents, the TQM's implementation scheme), is the education and training of the staff. Every plot, policy and strategy is formed and applied based on the current and potential knowledge of the human resources. Education and training alike are the master key to any 'key-lock' based problem or bottleneck. So, the actual question that would prove meaningful in the tourism and hospitality sector is not solely "What" to teach them, but "How" to do so, too; since what is not taken into consideration, usually, is the pace and style of teaching, and whether or not the abilities of employees, vertical and horizontal, can be literally and pragmatically enhanced by certain types of teaching and training.

Different tourism groups, for example, most likely appreciate customized tourism products. To satisfy each and everyone's expectations, specializations (Ntalakos et al., 2022b) in respective fields such as eco-, adventure, health, education and tangible/intangible cultural tourism is imperative. *This is the "what"*. Respective on-the-job training or informal learning along with matching specializations in training institutions/schools, twinning arrangements, apprenticeship strategic partnerships, tailored teaching/training styles, methods and practices, and systematic and sustained self-educating activities will and can help improve and advance skills, capabilities and mentalities (in attitudes and values). *This is the "how"*; and this is, exactly, where the emphasis should be placed.

Issues With the Current Status of HR Development

The multifariousness of the sector and its people, and the consecutive problems it has faced, have left little room for actual learning to take place. According to the World Travel and Tourism Council (2021), the sector has seen incredible staff shortages (not to mention, shortages of qualified human resources), which are, to date, rising. During the crisis, a large number of employees chose to move to other sectors (mainly because of the fear of unemployment), was entirely out of the labour force (laid off - unemployment status) or was furloughed until further notice. Thus, HR development should be reckoned with, since sufficient and skilled labour force is required to fill the available vacancies and enable the sector to recover.

Addressing the lack of the tourism labour force supply (Belias et al., 2020b) and the insufficiencies of the sector, involves prioritization and implementation of various policies and initiatives via multi-stakeholder collaboration. The WTTC's analysis (2021) recommends some key adjustments:

- *Facilitate Labour Mobility*: bridging a skill gap requires enabling and clearing the way of staff mobility and talent mobility within and across borders.

- *Facilitate Remote Work:* Enabling telecommuting, in hybrid and remote work schemes, could prove to be an efficient tool in addressing talent shortages since you increase flexibility.
- *Enable Decent Work and Provide Social Safety Nets:* Decent work (fair, safe, productive and meaningful) on its own, is a stimulus for attracting qualified personnel and, of course, retaining it.
- *Upskill and Reskill Workforce and Retain Talent:* Enhancing both vertical and horizontal skills can strengthen the personnel's potential, respective to current and anticipated needs, and reinforce its capabilities within and across sectors.
- *Create and Promote Education and Apprenticeships:* Bridging skills gaps and molding a workforce that can adapt to changes and combat crises effectively is the aftereffect of tailored education and training that is linked to talent and recruitment needs and retainment.

All in all, the above guidelines can be the means to an end; to balance supply and demand instability and refrain from the lack of talented human capital; to fill in the gaps in skills and in the availability of tourism training infrastructure along with qualified trainers and teachers; to intensify the attention given to the conditions of work in the tourism sector and to improve them; and ensure that shortages, inequality and uncertainty do not remain an issue in the longer term.

The Need for Trained and Skilled Manpower

Mega trends such as the ones we have been experiencing during the last few years, i.e. technological changes and modernization (Papademetriou, Masouras and Ioannou, 2020), globalization, demographic changes and more recently, the Covid-19 pandemic, have necessitated the existence and application of skills development (Rossidis and Belias, 2020) and lifelong learning in the tourism and hospitality sector as well, since we have seen Adult Education thriving in many other sectors. That is why, integrating Adult Education principles into the HR development processes is required. The Organisation for Economic Cooperation and Development (OECD) has released its *Skills Outlook 2021: Learning for Life Report* that assesses the essential nature of skills in the modern world, particularly in light of the Covid-19 pandemic, and the need to adapt to a fast-changing global environment, so that people can be empowered, skilled and trained to keep up with innovations, such as environmental and technological advancements.

Adult education principles and lifelong learning itself are human-centred approaches to one's enhancement. They place the individual at the centre of socio-economic and organisational/business practices. This kind of learning offers potential; potential for improvement, for self-directedness, for transformation; it smooths changes and transitions and reduces inequalities and injustices, by creating a virtuous circle between employment and productivity/quality standards. Overall, it has the leverage to form and transform employees into qualified assets that can offer new possibilities and chances to the business and, likewise, the sector.

Learning Context and Training Methods Under the Scope of Adult Education Models

"Education is not preparation for life; Education is life itself." ~ John Dewey, philosopher & educator

Adult Education, as a practice, involves *Adult Basic Education* where one is taught basic learning and survival skills, (usually refers to the undereducated); and *Continuing or Lifelong Education* where efforts are made for personal and professional growth (usually refers to the highly educated). Lifelong education encompasses much more than adult education; it includes all levels, bands, unit standards, learning areas and qualifications of the National Qualifications Framework (NQF). Thus, Adult Education (AE) could be regarded as a sub-category or a branch of Lifelong Education, and can be seen in any of the following three contexts:

- *Formal – structured learning*: which typically carries credentials and takes place in an education or training institution, usually with a set curriculum;
- *Non – formal learning*: which typically carries no credentials and is usually organized by educational institutions. It may be either provided in the workplace or through activities of civil society organizations;
- *Informal learning*: which mainly results from daily life activities related to work, family, community or leisure, and is on-going. *(Spencer and Lange, 2014).*

Adult education began to emerge as a field of study in the late 1930s. Eduard C. Lindeman (1926) was the first expert who gave a systematic account of adult education as a lifelong process and described it as cooperative, non-authoritarian and informal based on each learner's experience. Since then, a lot of theories were brought to light. Some of the most popular adult learning theories are: *Experiential Learning,* which was developed by David *Kolb* and Ronald *Fry* in the 1970s, and puts the learner at the center of the learning experience, stating that active participation is the key to every outcome, since learning takes place only when the participant reflects upon what one is doing (learner's internal cognitive processes). This type of learning has been broadly used in corporate training in the past years; *Self-Directed Learning (SDL),* where *Garrison's* Model (1997) integrated Self-management (contextual control), Self-Monitoring and Motivation; *Project Based Learning (PBL)* by John *Dewey* in 1897 holds that learners acquire deeper knowledge through active exploration of real-world problems and challenges; *Action Learning* which was developed by Reg *Revans* in 1982 involves taking action and reflecting upon the results; The *learning process* and the meaning of experience which *Jarvis* defined as *"a continuous process which seeks to give a meaning to the daily experience, connecting the human conscience with time, space, society and their multiple relationships"* (1991, p. 11); *Critical Pedagogy* by Paulo Reglus Neves *Freire* who claimed that this problem-solving education should be the means by which the oppressed could aim to regain their sense of humanity and improve their level status and *Transformational Learning (TL),* which was developed by Jack *Mezirow* in 1978 and elaborated on the process of "perspective transformation", by challenging routed (pre)existing beliefs and values through critical thinking; and *Andragogy,* which was developed by Malcolm *Knowles* in 1968 and regards adults, as autonomous beings that need to be involved in the planning and evaluation of their instruction (self-management).

Adult learning theories have the individuals at its nucleus and their main goal is their advancement and fulfillment in a variety of contexts and masteries so as to keep up with change (societal, institutional or whatever sort). Individual, vocational and professional competence in the workplace can be enhanced if at least one of these theories, or combined better yet, is implemented in training, since there is a positive correlation between organizational performance and learning at the workplace (World Bank, 2019).

PROSPECTS OF HUMAN RESOURCES' EMPOWERMENT

Lifelong Learning and Adult Education Tactics in Aid of the Rebound

Tourism and hospitality, unfortunately, has been an industry that offers career perspectives to few and internal recruitment for upscaling has been scarce. Creating a virtuous circle by providing better opportunities for skills upgrading and profiling, and talent attraction and retainment could prove to be determinant in boosting tourism performance (Belias, Vasiliadis, and Mantas, 2020). The pandemic has induced shocks to labour markets, such as this, creating an inherent need for skilled and adaptable workers. The greater the cultivation and the development of skills, the less the feeling of insecurity and dispensability of the individual.

Lifelong learners are not mitigated by changes or crises, since they have been armed and equipped with the tools and means to overcome challenges. This kind of learning can build a concrete foundation with transferable skills learnt across many sectors and environments. This way citizens can become able to keep pace with the innovations and transformations of the market and align with it, take on various current and future roles and move from sector to sector adapting to its needs effortlessly. This is AE's core; to increase the citizens' adaptability and self-directedness power (Viterouli, Belias and Koustelios, 2021), not only for the sake of the individuals themselves, but for the economy as well. In this case, even when an individual loses his current job, being able to adapt to a new job or a new sector altogether is crucial.

Having skills is, therefore, an invaluable trait, as individuals can adapt to different situations or circumstances and pick up new skills or knowledge (e.g. working remotely) more efficiently and quickly compared to peers or other counterparts, who may be less predisposed to skills development and learning. Opportunities for the individuals can be paraphrased as chances for the sector itself (Viterouli et al., 2022). When individuals have learnt to cope with hardships and control variables one way or the other, they will be capable of dealing autonomously with new trends and demands that the sector commands in order to recuperate and revive. The human capital is the foundation on which the sector is built and expanded (Koutiva et al., 2019). If the basis is solid and empowered, then the rest cannot fall apart, they will sustain, readjust and 'scrape the bottom of the barrel' as efficiently as possible.

Approaches to Lifelong Learning

Meeting skills demands requires differentiated approaches. In order to design effective skills policies, learning needs to be perceived and viewed not only from a lifelong perspective, but also 'lifewide' (Tran, 2021). This entails looking at education not only in more formal institutions, such as schools and universities, but also in non-formal learning settings, such as on-the-job training and informal learning, for instance from co-workers. Addressing to skills and employability demands does not necessarily correlate with and upon graduation from formal education. "Institutional commitment to employability and skills demand should be seen as multifaceted – and not limited to curricular and extracurricular activities for students during their first foray into higher education". (European University Association Report, 2021, p. 3)

Learners return to education during different life phases and stages for a variety of reasons, needs and motivations. Models of continuous learning can allow flexible and customized engagement with formal education, and provide credentials that are time-flexible, cost-efficient and work-related. Through a variety of intergenerational environments (online, in-person, or hybrid), that are available nowadays, long-term learning can give access to training and learning to every individual that seeks to integrate it into one's life and career. Intergenerational learning, for instance, can develop transferable communication skills and provide open and free exchange of knowledge and skills, perspectives, values, and ideas between individuals and groups with different life experiences (wisdom exchange across generations) that may not be available through learning materials alone (Meuser, Gugliucci and Weaver 2020).

Lifelong learning is an interactive process that has the capacity to support a variety of individual circumstances and objectives. It can reskill and upskill learners, by considering and overcoming challenges and limitations that they may face, i.e. internal constraints; time, family, work barriers, or whatever sort. By focusing on the way, the length and scope of learning, clarity, openness and willingness to participate will grow, given the variety of approaches to skills development. *Learning – Unlearning - Relearning* is a cycle that leads to one's advancement (ECampusOntario, 2021). That being the case, supporting a lifelong journey requires a dynamic understanding of learning, the formation of personalized and adaptable approaches, and the empowerment of learners to turn to self-directed learning.

Self-Directedness as Means of Resilience, Recovery, and Performance

Self-directedness (self-concept) is one of the three aspects of human character in Cloninger's *Temperament and Character Inventory (TCI), his* biopsycho-socio-spiritual model of personality (Cloninger et al., 1993, Cloninger, 2004), the other two being *Cooperativeness* and *Self-transcendence;* all consisting of sub-categories. In the TCI, self-directedness consists of five subscales:

- Responsibility vs. Blaming (SD1)
- Purposefulness vs. Lack Of Goal Direction (SD2)
- Resourcefulness vs. Inertia (SD3)
- Self-Acceptance vs. Self-Striving (SD4)
- Congruent Second Nature vs. Incongruent Habits (SD5)

The self-concept character trait is regarded as the executive branch of a person's system of mental self-government and self-determination, that is, the ability to regulate and adapt behavior to the demands of a situation in order to achieve personally chosen goals and values. People who are self-directed tend to accept responsibility towards and have control over their actions, beliefs and behaviour. Attitudes they have, situations they are in and problems they face, all reflect their own choices. That is why, they strike others as reliable, mature and trustworthy individuals. Organizations need well-trained and educated staff, who regularly take the initiative in both learning and career processes to assess their learning and workplace needs, to plan and to follow through with enhancing their skills.

The self-directedness notion lies within the principles of all Adult Learning theories, since it is a core concept of lifelong learning. Nevertheless, research has shown that most adults lack in self-directedness in conventional learning environments via instructional methods; have a disposition for non-participatory practices and late submission of work; and tend to be unprepared in their assignments or tasks (Ngozwana, 2020). Naturally, learners may demonstrate different levels of self-direction in different learning environments, work situations or time periods (Candy, 1991). Inclination towards self-directed learning could be boosted by a supportive learning climate and a facilitating instructor. Therefore, self-directedness in learning is the outcome of multiple factors interaction (Hutasuhut et. al., 2020).

Self-Directedness in the Service of Human Resources Management in Tourism and Hospitality

Self-directedness was first referred to and popularized in *Andragogy Theory* (Knowles, 1968). *Andragogy is the art and science of helping adults learn* (Knowles, 1984). The word originates from the Greek ανδρ- (andr-), which means 'man', and αγωγή (agogi), which in turn means 'leader of', from the verb άγομαι (agome). Knowles (1975) defined *self-directed learning* as a process in which individuals take the initiative, with or without others' aid, in identifying their learning needs, formulating learning goals, determining respective needed resources for learning, and, finally, selecting and implementing the appropriate learning strategies and evaluating learning outcomes. Accordingly, he described self-directed learners as those who regard themselves independent and active learners (self-awareness/self-concept). Naturally, other definitions were later formulated too.

Garrison (1997) defined self-directedness in a learning environment as an approach where learners are stimulated to assume personal responsibility and control of the process, as far as cognition and context are concerned, and construct meaningful learning outcomes. He presented a respective three-dimensional model which integrates self-management, self-monitoring and motivation. Self-directed learning is also defined as a form of study where individuals take primary charge of planning, continuing and evaluating their learning experiences (Merriam, Caffarella and Baumgartner, 2007). Initiative, active involvement and control of the learner over the learning process is imperative and an integral part of autonomy and self-directedness (Merriam and Bierema, 2013; Grover, 2015). The learner has the ability to understand and choose what needs to be studied and how; thus, self-directed learning includes the conceptualization, design, implementation and evaluation of learning by learners themselves according to their needs and preferences (Brookfield, 2009) and is viewed as a natural form of learning where adults pursue learning to face their daily problems (Brockett and Hiemstra, 1991). Taylor (1995) defined self-directed learners as demonstrating a greater awareness and motivation to take responsibility in making learning meaningful and confronting problems as challenges. Accordingly, Candy (1991) presented a four-dimensional model of self-directedness in learning, where the following attributes were included: personal autonomy (deciding and taking action); self-management (willingness and ability to manage one's own learning); learner's-control of instruction; and autodidacticism (self-education).

It is evident from the aforementioned that employees who are self-initiated in a learning environment will also be self-initiated in a work environment too. This element is precisely what every business needs; human resources that have the zeal, the cognition and brainpower to deal with incidents and issues come what may.

PROSPECTIVE DIRECTIONS, SOLUTIONS, AND SUGGESTIONS

Andragogy's Importance for Self-Directedness in Tourism and Hospitality Employees

Self-directed learning has evolved throughout the time and has turned into a well-developed and established concept. However, the principles of Knowles theory (1984) still serve their purpose and are considered applicable even to-date. Knowles believed that adults learn effectively when they are internally motivated to acquire a new skill or piece of knowledge, and are free to direct their own learning, by integrating their real–life context into it. They must feel that they need to learn something (content – connection – application) and, that they have chosen so; this will sustain the whole process. They learn best by doing (practice) and actively participating in the learning interaction; that is why they need to be considered as equal partners in the process. Problem solving is the best means for learning and informal situations pose a better chance to grasp content and achieve goals. Maturity and socialization changes one's self-concept, where he/she moves from that of a dependent personality towards one of a self-directing individual.

The application of Andragogy is important to both adult learners and adult educators alike, that is why, the educator needs to be a facilitator of the process and aid the learner in any way possible (Brockett and Hiemstra, 1991). This way, the learner is driven to become a deep learner and an active participant of and in the process. Hence, characteristics of the andragogical learner and the andragogical educator/environment (as listed below) should be taken into serious consideration.

Table 3. Characteristics of the learner and characteristics of the educator/environment

Characteristics of self-directed learners:	Competencies that self-directed learning requires from the educator:
They set clear goals for themselves.	The ability to enter into a close, respectful and learning friendly relationship with learners.
They shape their learning process in line with goals and plans.	The ability to establish an environment which is physically and psychologically comfortable, open to interaction, based on cooperation.
They monitor their own learning process.	The ability to take responsibility for determining one's own learning needs.
They evaluate the outcomes of their own learning.	The ability to set goals.
They are autonomous.	The ability to plan, implement and evaluate learning activities.
They have self-motivation.	The ability to help learners to self-direct their learning.
They are open to learning.	The ability to be a facilitator and a source.
They are curious.	The ability to effectively use small group processes.
They are willing to learn.	The ability to evaluate learning processes and outcomes.
They value learning.	
They have self-control.	Source: Knowles, 1977 cited in Kasworm, 1983
They take initiative to learn.	
Source: Knowles, 1975; Knowles, 1977; Jennett, 1992 cited in Brockett and Hiemstra, 1991	

Addressing learning styles, and in particular self-directed learning, with tourism employees can create a catalyst for self-discovery among personnel and self-recovery for the business as an entity, which could lead to ongoing intentional learning within the tourism and hospitality environment and could evoke notions such as potential, initiative and self-management. The ratiocination behind lifelong learning is that it can stand as a competitive advantage for the tourism and hospitality industry and enhance service delivery, especially within this era of uncertainty that the pandemic has caused.

Ways to Overcome Barriers to Self-Directedness

Andragogy, as well as any other Adult Education Theory, can only be effective in essence when the employee (individual) has a desire to participate and learn. However, in reality, this is not always the case.

Self-Directedness in the Service of Human Resources Management in Tourism and Hospitality

There is many a case where employers are conducting training courses for their personnel, which might be of no interest to them or of no good use or suitability whatsoever. This lack in interest will result in diminished or diminishing motivation (McGrath, V., 2009), since they perceive no relevance to what they are actually doing in the workplace or no actual linkage that will make them perform better.

Moreover, previous negative learning and training experiences, low self-esteem and time constraints or pressures might become barriers to present or future learning. Time constraints and pressure may result from prior or simultaneous work responsibilities or family engagements, preventing individuals to participate in a training course or to engage in it, as they would otherwise have. Likewise, some trainees may not be ready or able to be challenged (themselves or their beliefs), and that can lead to them feeling uncomfortable or even threatened. That, in turn, can affect or alter one's self-esteem and avert or detain any form of new learning from taking place.

It is wise to bear in mind that the ability and will to self-direction is not an inherent quality and is not expressed similarly in all situations and circumstances. Hence, finding ways to reinforce self-initiation and combat barriers that may arise during the process is imperative. Educators have a key role in helping trainees overcome or counteract constraints and limitations.

People enter the learning processes having already formed their own agendas. They have their own predispositions, beliefs, grounded knowledge and biases. Educators can combat different kinds of bias by promoting a climate that provides a safe environment for the individuals and fosters assertiveness and autonomy in them. An environment where they can feel free to simply be themselves, express themselves and drive themselves where they choose to with the aid of others (peers and trainer) so as to fruitfully learn. After all, Knowles stated that it is the adult educator's job to urge them to assume responsibility for their own learning and style; instill new learning tactics and patterns into the learners; and clear them of old practices, methods and mentality (Knowles et al, 1998).

Encouragement of active participation, constructive interaction and equality setting among and between all members of the process can lead to self-liberation, self-awareness and maximization of one's self-esteem. By becoming facilitators and provocateurs of the process, trainers - whether they are the supervisors, the coordinators or the moderators - can cultivate inner qualities of the employees that will lead to learning independency and work skills development that will equip them with the necessary resources and appropriate means and competencies to overcome challenges (Belias, Mantas and Tsiotas, 2019) that have to do with the service delivery and the customer satisfaction of their post (and not only).

Amplifying masteries and capabilities is also relevant to the content and context of what is being taught and its coherence and cohesion with one's needs and wants. If a waiter's need is to learn how to serve and he is being shown how to carry luggage, for instance, naturally he/she will pay no attention whatsoever and will lose interest there and then (Belias et al., 2017b). Servers, for example, would like to improve their skills on convincing customers or up-selling cleverly; they would also like to endorse their customer service skills so as be tipped more. A manager of a hotel, on the other hand, could make use of managerial guidelines, leadership styles and communication skills that can help him/her manage the staff in a more productive and teamlike manner so as to heighten the service of the hotel, and naturally its reputation and impact.

Thus, it all has to do with the environment, the people involved in the process and the situational needs and contents of learning. Learning should add up to somebody's status, not burden or garble it. Learning should be sought, not inflicted upon. That being the case, the individual should be the nucleus of the process and his/her needs, aspirations and wants should be the sphere where everything revolves around. That is the way that self-directedness will be fostered, soft and hard skills will prove out to be

FUTURE RESEARCH DIRECTIONS

Once self-directedness readiness of employees has been developed, the ability of a tourism and hospitality organization to adapt to change and crises is inevitably strengthened, since learning gaps are bridged, the variables that promote the self-directed capabilities are understood and promoted, and the attached barriers are effectively combated.

As human resource departments look for advantages in all segments of and throughout their organizations (Belias et al, 2017a), self-directedness processes should be considered to promote continuous learning opportunities for employees in the tourism and hospitality industry. Self-initiation in learning is significant in the labour market and further pursuit of education and training chances should be intensified, especially in sectors that are mainly or solely service-driven.

Employability should be approached differently, nowadays, since a university degree is not considered sufficient any longer. Different profiles of people in the tourism and hospitality sector demand different approaches from the customary training methods and the obsolete education standards and curricula, which are not, sufficiently, based on occupational and functional analyses and needs. Using the breadth of their experiences and linking them to new, arisen experiences is imperative for enhancing self-initiation in one's personnel. Andragogy can aid in doing exactly that and so much more. Bringing into one's job qualities that are cherished by customers can be taught and applied, as long as the right methods and tactics are put into force. Everybody can be lured into learning and progressing provided that the process is tailored to their individuality.

CONCLUSION

Humanity has undergone and endured a crisis that is still, to date, existent. Crises management has been called upon on several occasions and leaders should not fail to recognize that combating crises also involves, and to a great extent, self-directedness skills, i.e. consolidating, taking control of things and showing initiative to overcome hardships. Proper organisation of activities which is reflected in the engagement of the right person in the right place, means relying on the knowledge of the organization's employees and extracting the maximum ability and potential for the most efficient and productive achievement of business and sector results and goals (Drašković and Džunić, 2020).

The industry has faced problems by both the trade itself and by industry practitioners and organizers. These problems can be handled by qualified, talented people. For instance, skills at the management level are particularly lacking in many countries. That is why, technology and knowledge skills is an important element in tourism and hospitality staff's development. Pinpointing the skills and capacities people in this sector lack is important so as to target them. Once we define the competencies that contribute to the realization of the organizational objectives and what one should and is determinant to foster, business competencies can be achieved. Additionally, to professional knowledge and skills, though, one's personal traits, abilities and attitudes also determine the level of individual competence.

Human resources development departments in the tourism and hospitality sector can cultivate cognition, critical thinking and commitment into their people via lifelong learning schemes. Self-directedness, within lifelong learning, embraces the scope of choices; one identifies and acknowledges the range of choices (and solutions) available. Yet, the propensity and ability to self-direct is influenced by a variety of factors, that is why, individuals tend to focus their attention, reflect, critically judge, prioritize and appreciate parameters and alternatives for decision making differently in different situations. Therefore, by fortifying the people with qualities and skills, one refortifies the whole sector. Focusing on internal training and service quality issues means undoubtedly having the grounds and chance to improve external service quality and inflows.

REFERENCES

Al-Ababneh, M. M. (2021). The implementation of Total Quality Management (TQM) in the hotel industry. *International Journal of Tourism and Hospitality*, *1*(1), 25–34. doi:10.51483/IJTH.1.1.2021.25-34

Ashton, D., & Green, F. (1996). *Education, training, and the global economy*. Edward Elgar.

Belias, D., Mantas, C., & Tsiotas, D. (2019). The impact of corporate culture in the performance of the front desk employees - The case of five-star hotels in Greece. In *Smart tourism as a driver for culture and sustainability* (pp. 563–576). Springer. doi:10.1007/978-3-030-03910-3_38

Belias, D., Papademetriou, C., Rossidis, I. and Vasiliadis L. (2020a). Strategic Management in the Hotel Industry: Proposed Strategic Practices to Recover from COVID- 19 Global Crisis. *Academic Journal of Interdisciplinary Studies, 9*(6).

Belias, D., Rossidis, I., Papademetriou, C., & Lamprinoudis, N. (2020b). The Greek Tourism Sector: An analysis of Job Satisfaction, Role Conflict and Autonomy of Greek Employees. *Journal of Human Resources in Hospitality & Tourism*.

Belias, D., Rossidis, I., Papademetriou, C., & Mantas, C. (2021). Job Satisfaction as Affected by Types of Leadership: A Case Study of Greek Tourism Sector. *Journal of Quality Assurance in Hospitality & Tourism*.

Belias, D., Rossidis, I., Sotiriou, A., & Malik, S.Case Study in Greek Seasonal Hotels. (2022). Workplace Conflict, Turnover, and Quality of Services. Case Study in Greek Seasonal Hotels. *Journal of Quality Assurance in Hospitality & Tourism*, 2022. doi:10.1080/1528008X.2022.2065655

Belias, D., Rossidis, I., & Valeri, M. (2022) Tourism in crisis: the impact of climate change on the tourism industry. Valeri M. (Eds.), Tourism risk. Crisis and Recovery Management? Emerald. doi:10.1108/978-1-80117-708-520221012

Belias, D. and Trihas, N. (2022). Investigating the Readiness for Organizational Change: A Case Study from a Hotel Industry Context/Greece. *Journal of Tourism & Management Research*.

Belias, D., Trivellas, P., Koustelios, A., Serdaris, P., Varsanis, K., & Grigoriou, I. (2017a). Human Resource Management, Strategic Leadership Development and the Greek Tourism Sector. Tourism, Culture and Heritage in a Smart Economy, 189-205. In V. Katsoni, A. Upadhya, & A. Stratigea (Eds.), *Tourism, Culture and Heritage in a Smart Economy. Springer Proceedings in Business and Economics*. Springer.

Belias, D., Vasiliadis, L., & Mantas, C. (2020). *The Human Resource Training and Development of Employees Working on Luxurious Hotels in Greece*. Cultural and Tourism Innovation in the Digital Era. doi:10.1007/978-3-030-36342-0_49

Belias, D., Velissariou, E., Koustelios, A., Varsanis, K., Kyriakou, D., & Sdrolias, L. (2017b). The Role of Organizational Culture in the Greek Higher Tourism Quality. In A. Kavoura, D. Sakas, & P. Tomaras (Eds.), *Strategic Innovative Marketing. Springer Proceedings in Business and Economics*. Springer. doi:10.1007/978-3-319-56288-9_10

Belias, D., Velissariou, E., & Rossidis, I. (2018). The contribution of HRM on the development of effective organizational culture in hotel units - The case of Greek hotels. In Exploring smart tourism: The cultural and sustainability synergies. Springer.

Belias, D., Velissariou, E., & Rossidis I. (2019). The contribution of HRM on the development of effective organizational culture in hotel units - The case of Greek hotels. *Smart Tourism as a Driver for Culture and Sustainability*, 603-618.

Blštáková, J., Joniaková, Z., Jankelová, N., Stachová, K., & Stacho, Z. (2020). Reflection of Digitalization on Business Values: The Results of Examining Values of People. *Management in a Digital Age Sustainability, 2020*(12), 5202.

Brockett, R. G., & Hiemstra, R. (1991). *Self Direction in Adult Learning Perspectives: on Theory, Research and Practice*. Routledge.

Brookfield, S. D. (2009). Self-directed learning, in International Handbook of Education for the Changing World of Work. Springer Science and Business Media.

Candy, P. C. (1991). *Self-Direction for Lifelong Learning: A Comprehensive Guide to Theory and Practice*. Jossey-Bass Publishers.

Ciampa, D. (1992). *Total Quality: A User's Guide for Implementation*. Addison-Wesley.

Cloninger, C. R. (2004). *Feeling good: The science of well-being*. Oxford University Press.

Cloninger, C. R., Svrakic, D. M., & Przybeck, T. R. (1993). A psychobiological model of temperament and character. *Archives of General Psychiatry, 50*(12), 975–990. doi:10.1001/archpsyc.1993.01820240059008 PMID:8250684

Dewey, J. (1897). My Pedagogic Creed. *School Journal, 54*(3), 77–80.

Drašković, B. and Džunić, M., (2020). *The Importance of Human Resources for Effective Implementation of Crisis Management Tools in Tourism and Hospitality Industry*. 5th International Thematic Monograph: Modern Management Tools and Economy of Tourism Sector in Present Era.

ECampusOntario, Virtual Learning Strategy (VLS), (2021) *Foresight Report: Lifelong Learning Empowering lifelong learners and creating opportunities for growth.* VLS Reports Outline.

Eduard, L. (1926). *The meaning of adult education.* New Republic.

Encarta. (2008). Lifelong learning. *Encarta.* http://encarta.msn.com/dictionary_561547417/lifelong_learning.html

European University Association ASBL. (2021). *Meeting skills and employability demands: Thematic Peer Group Report. Learning & Teaching Paper #13. 12 Mar 2021. Report* (P. McSweeney & T. Zhang, Eds.).

Freire, P. (1970). *Pedagogy of the oppressed.* Seabury Press.

Garrison, D. (1997). *Self-directed learning: toward a comprehensive model.* Academic Search Complete.

Garrison, D. R. (1997). Self directed learning: Toward a comprehensive model. *Adult Education Quarterly, 48*(1), 18–29. doi:10.1177/074171369704800103

Grover, K. (2015). Online social networks and the self-directed learning experience during a health crisis. *International Journal of Self-Directed Learning, 12,* 1–15.

Hutasuhut, I., Adruce, S., A., Z. and Jonathan, V. (2020). How a learning organization cultivates self-directed learning. *Journal of Workplace Learning, 33*(5), 334-347

Kasworm, C. E. (1983). An examination of self-directed contract learning as an instructional strategy. *Innovative Higher Education, 8*(1), 45–54. doi:10.1007/BF00889559

Knowles, M. (1980). *The modern practice of adult education: Andragogy versus pedagogy.* Cambridge Adult Education.

Knowles, M. S. (1968). Andragogy, not pedagogy. *Adult Leadership, 16*(10), 350–352, 386.

Knowles, M. S. (1975). *Self-Directed Learning: A Guide for Learners and Teachers.* Cambridge Books.

Knowles, M. S. (1984). *Andragogy in action: Applying modern principles of adult learning.* Jossey-Bass Publishers.

Knowles, M. S. (1984). *The adult learner: A neglected species.* Gulf Publishing.

Knowles, M. S. (1989). *The making of an adult educator.* Jossey-Bass.

Knowles, M. S., Elwood, R., Holton, R. III, & Swanson, A. (1998). *The Adult Learner: The Definitive Classic in Adult Education and Human Resource Development* (5th ed.). Heinemann.

Kolb, D. A., & Fry, R. (1975). Toward an applied theory of experiential learning. In C. Cooper (Ed.), *Studies of group process* (pp. 33–57). Wiley.

Koutiva, M., Belias, D., Flabouras, I., & Koustelios, A. (2019). The Effects of Workplace Well-being on Individuals Knowledge Creation Outcomes. A Study Research among Hotel Employees. *International Conference on Strategic Innovative Marketing and Tourism.* Springer.

Kulenović, M., Folta, M., & Veselinović, L. (2021). The Analysis of Total Quality Management Critical Success Factors. *Quality Innovation Prosperity, 25*(1), 88–102. doi:10.12776/qip.v25i1.1514

Lema, J. (2009). Continuous learning: A competitive advantage for the tourism industry. *International Journal of Tourism and Travel, 2*(2), 16-30.

Marshal, R., & Tucker, M. (1992). *Thinking for a living*. Basic Books.

Masouras, A. (2019). *Entrepreneurship in Small and Medium-Sized Enterprises*. Nova Science Publishers.

Mcgrath, V. (2009). Reviewing the Evidence on How Adult Students Learn: An Examination of Knowles' Model of Andragogy. *Adult Learner: The Irish Journal of Adult and Community Education*, p 99-110.

Merriam, S. B., & Bierema, L. L. (2013). *Adult Learning: Linking Theory and Practice*. Jossey-Bass, John Wiley and Sons.

Merriam, S. B., Caffarella, R., & Baumgartner, L. (2007). *Learning in Adulthood: A Comprehensive Guide*. Jossey-Bass Publishers.

Meuser, T., Gugliucci, M., & Weaver, S. (2020). *Intergenerational Learning in Higher Education*. The Evolllution. https:// evolllution.com/attracting-students/todays_learner/intergenerational-learning-in-higher-education/

Mezirow, J. (1978). Perspective Transformation. *Adult Education Quarterly*, *28*(2), 100–110. doi:10.1177/074171367802800202

Ngozwana, N. (2020). The Application of Adult Learning Theory (andragogy) by Adult Educators and Adult Learners in the Context of Eswatini. UJOE, 3(1).

Ntalakos, A., Belias, D., Koustelios, A., & Tsigilis, A. (2022a). Effect of Covid-19 on the Tourism Industry: Opportunities and Threats in Covid-19 Era. *4th International Conference on Finance, Economics, Management and IT Business*. Scitepress. 10.5220/0011065200003206

Ntalakos, A., Belias, D., Koustelios, A., & Tsigilis, A. (2022b). *Organizational Culture and Group Dynamics in the tourism industry*. 5th International Conference on Tourism Research 2022 (ICTR22) Porto, Vila do Conde, Portugal (ESHT). 10.34190/ictr.15.1.150

Papademetriou, C., Masouras, A., & Ioannou, A. (2020). Social Networking Sites: The New Era of Effective Online Marketing and Advertising. In *Strategic Innovative Marketing and Tourism* (pp. 443–448). Springer., . doi:10.34190/ictr.15.1.150

Pawar, D. V. (2014). Internal and External Customers. International Journal for Research in Management and Pharmacy, 3(5).

Revans Reg, W. (1982). *The Origin and Growth of Action Learning*. Chartwell-Bratt.

Roccas, S., Sagiv, L., Schwartz, S. H., & Knafo, A. (2002). The Big Five Personality Factors and Personal Values. *Personality and Social Psychology Bulletin*, *28*(6), 789–801. doi:10.1177/0146167202289008

Rossidis, I., & Belias, D. (2020). Combining Strategic Management with Knowledge Management: Trends and International Perspectives. *International Review of Management and Marketing*, *10*(3), 39–45. doi:10.32479/irmm.9621

Rossidis, I., Belias, D., & Vasiliadis, L. (2021). Strategic Hotel Management in the "Hostile" International Environment. In V. Katsoni & C. van Zyl (Eds.), *Culture and Tourism in a Smart, Globalized, and Sustainable World. Springer Proceedings in Business and Economics*. Springer. doi:10.1007/978-3-030-72469-6_21

Rossidis, I., Belias, D., & Vasiliadis, L. (2021). Strategic Human Resource Management in the International Hospitality Industry. An Extensive Literature Review. In V. Katsoni & C. van Zyl (Eds.), *Culture and Tourism in a Smart, Globalized, and Sustainable World. Springer Proceedings in Business and Economics*. Springer. doi:10.1007/978-3-030-72469-6_22

Rothmann, S., & Coetzer, E. P. (2003). T*he Big Five Personality Dimensions and Job Performance. SA Journal of Industrial Psychology*, *29*(1), 68–74. doi:10.4102ajip.v29i1.88

Spencer, B., & Lange, E. (2014). *The Purposes of Adult Education: An Introduction* (3rd ed.). Thompson Educational Publishing.

Tari, J. J., Claver-Cortes, E., Pereira-Moliner, J., & Molina-Azorin, J. F. (2010). Levels of quality and environmental management in the hotel industry: Their joint influence on firm performance. *International Journal of Hospitality Management*, *29*(3), 500–510. doi:10.1016/j.ijhm.2009.10.029

Taylor, B. (1995). *Self-directed learning: revisiting an idea most appropriate for middle school students.* Paper presented at the Combined Meeting of the Great Lakes and Southeast International Reading Association, Nashville, TN.

Tran, D. (2021). *OECD Skills Outlook 2021: why lifelong learning is essential for modern society. Digital skills and Jobs Platform.* European Union. https://digital-skills-jobs.europa.eu/en/latest/news/oecd-skills-outlook-2021-why-lifelong-learning-essential-modern-society

Viterouli, M., & Belias, D. (2021). *True Organizational Learning Culture as a key to unlocking Operational Performance: A Critical Review.* International Business Information Management Association, 37th IBIMA Conference, Cordoba, Spain.

Viterouli, M., Belias, D., & Koustelios, A. (2021). *Organizational Performance Enhancement via Adult Education Driven Principles in HR Management.* Leadership and Governance (ECMLG 2021), 17th European Conference on Management, Valletta, Malta.

Viterouli, M., Belias, D., Koustelios, A., & Tsigilis, N. (2022). Refining Employees' Engagement by incorporating Self-Directedness in Training and Work Environments. *Proceedings of the 18th European Conference on Management Leadership and Governance*. ACI.

World Tourism Organization. (2020). *AL ULA Framework for Inclusive Community Development through Tourism Executive Summary* IE University, Spain.

World Tourism Organization (2022). *World Tourism Barometer,* 20(1). WTO.

World Travel and Tourism Council. (2021). Staff Shortages. World Travel and Tourism Council.

Chapter 3
Capability Building and Development in Socio-Intercultural Entrepreneurship

José G. Vargas-Hernández

Posgraduate and Research Department, Tecnológico Mario Molina Unidad Zapopan, Mexico

Omar C. Vargas-González

Instituto Tecnológico de México, Ciudad Guzmán, Mexico

ABSTRACT

This study aims to analyze the socio-intercultural entrepreneurship as a capability building and development. The analysis departs from the assumption that entrepreneurship is a cultural embedded concept, although the intercultural category used in entrepreneurial studies has not been founded full conceptual, theoretical, and empirical support. Based on this existing research gap that this analysis reviews, the literature to address the main issues of the socio-intercultural entrepreneurship focusing in the capability building and development to conclude that it is more situational context and environment oriented. The methodology used are the exploratory and analytical tools. Socio-intercultural entrepreneurship competence is highly related to be situational context and environment-dependent on awareness and understanding of cultural differences.

INTRODUCTION

The world's population and companies are now more connected and mobile than ever in history, expanded worldwide with access to labor and resources pools but requiring more socio-intercultural communication and entrepreneurial skills. Empowerment and entrepreneurship are defining the engagement rules of this rapidly changing global situational context and environment. Nurturing the culture of empowerment and entrepreneurship is a challenge aimed to design some agile organizations in order to keep pace with the changing economic global situational context and environment.

DOI: 10.4018/978-1-6684-6055-9.ch003

Copyright © 2023, IGI Global. Copying or distributing in print or electronic forms without written permission of IGI Global is prohibited.

Capability Building and Development in Socio-Intercultural Entrepreneurship

The analysis of social entrepreneurship from a cultural perspective is limited (Dancin, Dancin, & Tracey, 2011) and more from the point of view of socio-interculturality. The study and analysis of individual cultural differences and its influence on socio-socio-intercultural entrepreneurship have been neglected. However, the studies on socio-intercultural entrepreneurship are on the rise in a globalized world. Since the 1970s, the study of entrepreneurship has intensified and has become one of the most prolific and dynamic academic fields in management, economics, regional sciences, etc. (Aldrich, 2012; Shane & Venkataraman 2000).

Socio-intercultural entrepreneurship in global business is supported by the socio-intercultural framework and foundational concepts based on baseline understanding of socio-intercultural communication which can be applied in diverse cultures beyond the cultural learning of traditions, heritages, behaviors, values, customs, etc. of specific cultures.

This analysis approaches the socio-intercultural entrepreneurship focusing on the knowledge of determining and understanding the socio socio-intercultural situational context and environment facing the global business to establish common concepts to be used in the socio-intercultural communication regardless of specific cultures and situations. A deep knowledge of socio socio-intercultural systems applied in some different situational context and environments is a requisite to develop entrepreneurial skills to be used and implemented in entrepreneurial practices and tasks.

The paper is organized after this brief introduction, to state the relevance of the analysis as the motivation to review the main concepts and theories conducted to establish the basis for the study of the socio-intercultural profile of entrepreneurship. This entrepreneurial profile is complemented with the relevant findings of empirical research aimed to determine the required capability building and development for socio-intercultural entrepreneurship. Finally, some concluding remarks are offered.

RELEVANCE OF THE STUDY

Global and international organizations, companies, firms, and people working across diverse cultures require to overcome cultural bias and preconceptions by promoting socio socio-intercultural entrepreneurial management that is adaptable and open minded to new situational contexts and environments, situations and individuals, to live, work, communicate and learn together. Dissimilar cultures around the shrinking world are influencing each other and leading to sources of synergies but also of conflicts which require the implementation of a socio-intercultural entrepreneurial capabilities, competences, and skills.

Socio-intercultural entrepreneurial competence in a borderless world becomes crucial for the diversity in global business projects and ventures, which requires to develop competencies and skills to interact socio-interculturality and understand the diverse cultural backgrounds of individuals. However, socio socio-intercultural entrepreneurship is beyond sociocultural diversity initiatives.

Socio-intercultural entrepreneurial practices facilitate the understanding and use of cultural backgrounds of individuals to achieve innovation and creativity in decision making as the ultimate competitive advantage in any type of situational context and environment. The socio socio-intercultural entrepreneurial practices at the workplace aims at building its policies and individual identity based on the recognition that socio cultural diversity is the source and resource for economic growth, social development, and environmental sustainability.

The continuous transformation of organizations leads to motivational processes of individuals who have initiative and develop creative attitudes to create and innovate based on technological advances.

The strong achievement motivation of entrepreneurs contributes to explain they commitment for entrepreneurship.

CONCEPTUAL AND THEORETICAL FRAMEWORK

Being an entrepreneur is fundamentally a personal act (Baum, Frese, Baron, & Katz 2007) so that personal factors influence organizational success. Entrepreneurship is a term that has been used since the 1980s, in reference to the entrepreneurial spirit training system that emphasizes the development of skills for self-generation of employment (Del Solar, 2010, p.16). The concept of entrepreneur does not have a single definition. The entrepreneur is defined as the owner and manager of a company (Brockhaus 1980) that involves a new business or a new proposal in the organization (Lachman, 1980). Entrepreneurship is concerned with the discovery and exploitation of profitable opportunities (Shane & Venkataraman, 2000, pp. 217–226).

An entrepreneur is the person who starts a business initiative, creates his own company, alone or in association with its promoters, assuming the financial risks that this entails, contributing his work and taking care of the management of the company (Moriano, Trejo, & Palací, 2001, p. 230). The entrepreneur is an innovative businessman who is willing to take risks, although the one who risks is not always an entrepreneur, just as creating a company is being an entrepreneur. The entrepreneur looks for opportunities and through innovation processes create a company and generate wealth (Stevenson, 2000, cited in Formichella 2004, p.10). It is concluded here that the entrepreneur is an independent, risk-taking individual organizing the people and resources necessary for creating and developing new business ventures.

Entrepreneurship is defined as the project development that has economic, socio-political, and other purposes. Entrepreneurship is the personal attitude to take on new projects, by innovating and adding value to an existing product, and advance in their goals and objectives. Entrepreneurship shares the elements of innovation and uncertainty. In this sense, entrepreneurship is defined as the sharing of uncertainty and innovation to the development of a project that pursues a certain economic, social political, and other purpose (Bittán 2017). Entrepreneurship is an innovative instrument for dealing with complex social needs (Peredo & McLean 2006). Entrepreneurship is the ability to act positively and creatively promptly in the face of setbacks and in difficult or new situations (Goleman 2005, p. 157).

The conceptualization of entrepreneurship is related to the drive for innovation and economic competitiveness in socio-productive contexts and environments. The entrepreneur dedicates time and efforts to the creation and development of business organizations, assuming psychological, financial, social risks, etc., undergoes processes of creating products or services with added value, with benefits and monetary rewards and more personal (Hisrich & Peters 1992; Sadler-Smith, Hampson, Chaston, & Badger 2003).

The conceptualization of the social entrepreneur focuses on individual characteristics, actions, processes, resources, and mission (Light, 2009, Sullivan Mort et al., 2003; Tracey et al., 2011; Dancin, Dancin, & Tracey, 2011; Peredo & McLean, 2006). There is no consolidated definition of social entrepreneurship while the debate focuses on the change in the Welfare State (Dees, 1998, Mair and Martí, 2006). Recently, the analysis of social entrepreneurship has emerged from theoretical and practical perspectives on entrepreneurship and from other approaches to define the specificities of social entrepreneurial activities (Alvord, Brown & Letts, 2004).

Capability Building and Development in Socio-Intercultural Entrepreneurship

The definition of social entrepreneurship gives certainty to measure the results of their activities as something tangible considering that a certain degree of ambiguity is inevitable (Dees, 1998, Martin & Osberg, 2007, Peredo and McLean, 2006, Weerawardena & Mort, 2006). The social entrepreneur emerges in a specific situational context and environment of uncertainty Sarasvanthy (2001, 2004). Social entrepreneurs take advantage of environmental uncertainty in entrepreneurial activities (Wennekers, VanStel, & Noorderhaven, 2010). The entrepreneur seeks to avoid uncertainty through the normalization of activities, a feature that can be contradictory to the high levels of uncertainty that occur in business development. This situation allows entrepreneurs to change their strategies in uncertain environments and depending on the transformations of the scarce resources available to them.

The behavior of the social entrepreneur is explained from an socio-intercultural perspective because it is born in an environment of uncertainty according to the effectuation theory (Sarasvanthy 2001, 2004) which arises from organizational learning under the assumption that entrepreneurs are based on instinct and intuition to determine possible strategic alternatives in decision making (Mitchellet al., 2007).

The effectuation theory enables the study of decision-making strategies in environments characterized by high levels of uncertainty and resource limitations (Smith & Stevens, 2010). The effectuation theory is based on the organizational learning of administrators who make decisions about strategic alternatives based on instinct and intuition (Mitchell et al., 2007), which allows changing strategies under conditions of uncertain environments to transform available resources they are scarce.

The effectuation theory method offers possibilities for the study of social entrepreneurship characterized by a high degree of uncertainty and resource limitations, for the formulation and implementation of strategies in decision-making (Smith & Stevens, 2010). social entrepreneurs take environmental uncertainty as a guide for business activity (Wennekers, Van Stel & Noorderhaven, 2010).

The concept of socio-intercultural sensitivity measures the levels of entrepreneurial skills. Socio-intercultural entrepreneurship is a high-risk activity, due to the factors that influence its social, economic, political, cultural and technological development. Socio-intercultural sensitivity has been defined as those human capacities to emit positive emotions and control those emotions that can harm socio-intercultural communication (Vilá, 2006). Hammer, Bennett, & Wiseman (2003) define socio-intercultural sensitivity as the ability to identify and appreciate the most relevant cultural differences. Socio-intercultural sensitivity is the individual ability to develop positive emotions towards understanding and appreciation of cultural differences capable of promoting effective and appropriate behaviors in socio-intercultural communication (Chen and Starosta, 1997 p. 5).

Socio-intercultural entrepreneurship is a concept that is relevant to any individual regarding if he or she is involved in business as the investor, the negotiator, the global project manager, etc. A conceptual framework of socio-intercultural entrepreneurial practices is based on shared heritage, behaviors, values, beliefs, etc., developed in cultural value creation leading to inter and intracultural creativity and innovation, forming micro cultures as an socio-intercultural assets contributing to the economic growth, social development and environmental sustainability.

A conceptual and theoretical framework for micro- socio-intercultural entrepreneurship are based on a range of contributions from the intra and inter sociocultural creativity and innovation processes creating cultural economy value beyond the cultural economy. Socio-inter culturalism goes beyond rational communication through concepts such as multilingual learning that goes beyond cultural, educational, social, economic positions, etc. (Fornet Betancourt 2009, 2005, 2000). Small groups of people framed as micro socio cultures sharing common heritage, behaviors, cultural values, beliefs, customs, traditions, etc., may be the base to develop a conceptual framework to support the socio socio-intercultural entrepreneurship development.

Socio-intercultural entrepreneurship integrates differentiated socio-cultural groups to undertake something that is possible for subgroups that require working on a common project with the guidance of an entrepreneur who makes use of their skills and abilities to promote socio-intercultural cooperation for the creation of joint ventures between socio-cultural groups.

SOCIO-INTERCULTURAL ENTREPRENEURIAL PROFILE

The individual characteristics of entrepreneurs are explained from the characteristics of the environment (Dancin, Dancin & Tracey, 2011, Martin & Osberg, 2007). One of the entrepreneurship models that is explained in the economic environment of new business creations is that of Rauch and Frese (2007), it involves personal characteristics such as knowledge, skills, autonomy, locus of control, with the environment of the organization in situations such as organizational life cycle, risk factors, etc. with business results. The entrepreneurship model is based on personal and organizational characteristics to explain the phenomenon.

The personal characteristics of the social entrepreneur explain their behaviors and allow their comparison. The characteristics of socio-intercultural entrepreneurship are conceptualized at the interface between thought and action, innovation as a social commitment, and the creation of competitive markets. The characteristics of the entrepreneur according to Viera, Pérez and Paredes (2008, p.49), are the entrepreneurial spirit or entrepreneurial capacity to carry out productive actions and the psychosocial motivation to undertake.

The motivational disposition of the entrepreneurs encourages them to venture out and face the challenges of new cultural, economic, social and organizational contexts and environments. The authors Pablo, Begoña and Bueno, (2004 p. 818) classify the entrepreneurial profile in factors related to the personality of the individual or the psychological traits, the personal profile defined by the aptitudes, the motivations or drives of an individual to embark on a project; the capacities and competences, the abilities and knowledge of the individual resulted from the evolution of the aptitudes developed throughout life, learning and experiences.

The motivation of the entrepreneur is the force that induces to take action and the decision that have an influence on the lives of people (Porras, Oliveras, & Vigier 2013). The psychological factors of the entrepreneur such as the motivational features, capacities and competences gathered through the experience that make to take action. These factors of the entrepreneurial profile show the psychological features of the entrepreneur (Pablo, Begoña and Bueno, 2004 p. 818). Entrepreneurs are more motivated to achieve, take risks and are innovative (Hodgetts & Kuratko, 2001). The motivational component of socio-intercultural competence includes self-efficacy and goal setting (De la Garza & Egri, 2010; Earley & Peterson, 2004).

Entrepreneurship is driven by leadership open to innovation, new ideas, to experiment and learn. Leadership may help to drive the desired entrepreneurial behavior as an outcome through encouragement and role modelling providing the confidence to individuals to behave like entrepreneurs. Leadership development is crucial to create a culture of entrepreneurship and empowerment. Entrepreneurs exercise leadership that involves behaviors, skills, abilities, knowledge, variables and personality traits to solve organizational problems (Connelly et al., 2000; Zaccaro, Mumford, Connelly, Marks, & Gilbert, 2000).

Capability Building and Development in Socio-Intercultural Entrepreneurship

The attributes of the entrepreneur characterize him as a person who assumes responsibilities, is free to make decisions and establishes goals and achieves them with his own effort (McClelland, 1971). People gifted with entrepreneurial aptitude take advantage of opportunities to achieve their goals and motivate others to achieve them even at the cost of forcing the rules in many cases and avoiding bureaucratic limitations.

The theoretical literature associates the entrepreneur with people who have internal control as a relevant personality trait (Shapero, 1975; Gartner, 1985; Shaver & Scott, 1991; Lee & Tsang, 2001). The locus of control is a differentiating and stable personality trait of individuals (Levenson, 1974). Individual internal locus of control is linked to entrepreneurial behavior and can be taken as an analysis construct, assuming that the highest the internal locus of control at work exerts indirect influence showing greater entrepreneurial behavior.

Entrepreneurial behaviors as independent means of achieving personal goals, are supported and attracted by the social norms. Some of the entrepreneurial behaviors are the culture management and vision management. Some of the non-entrepreneurial behavior are process management, stakeholder management, as well as contexts and environments, and development management. Finally, the general behavior: performance management.

Entrepreneurs seek new business opportunities through the creation of business organizations because they develop skills, knowledge, experiences, personality traits and behaviors. Socio-intercultural entrepreneurship interactions are not guarantee by the understanding of the own sense of identity and personality traits which may have different meanings in different cultures (Walker, 2003, p. 203).

Social entrepreneurship initiatives are a distinctive trait associated with taking advantage of benefits (Dancin et al., 2011). Social entrepreneurship is based more on the socio-intercultural traits of a society to create more favorable social and economic environments for the development of initiatives that generate economic growth, equity, inclusiveness and social justice, as well as environmental sustainability and biodiversity of socio-ecosystems. The characteristics of social entrepreneurship are linked to some cultural traits Apetrei, Ribeiro, Roig, & Mas 2013) proposed by Hofstede (2001), that creates a favorable environment for the increase of social economy through the development of social entrepreneurship.

Socio-intercultural competence is defined as the complex behavioral action pattern that implies the management of knowledge, skills, values and motivational dispositions that are expressed in situations of an socio-intercultural relationship. Socio-intercultural entrepreneurship understanding as a competence is a source of competitive advantage in large organizational processes such as negotiating, entering into new markets or products, opening new business units and ventures, merging and acquiring new business etc. These entrepreneurial competencies are managed by the entrepreneur as an entrepreneur or small business owner with a focus on profitability and growth. The entrepreneur's competencies are grouped into three factors (Sadler-Smith, Hampson, Chaston, & Badger, 2003).

Other competences that help the entrepreneur to achieve her objectives are socio-intercultural competence and negotiation skills. Development of socio-intercultural entrepreneurial competence involves the transference of skills that help people to become more self-aware of the needs of others, growth their mindset to be more effective by making more creative and innovative decisions. Socio-socio-intercultural entrepreneurship facilitates to understand and foster individual self-awareness, create, and transform identities of individuals with differing cultural backgrounds (Martin & Nakayama, 2010).

RELEVANT FINDINGS OF EMPIRICAL STUDIES

Entrepreneurship is a cultural embedded concept, although cross-cultural, cross-national and intercultural categories used in entrepreneurial studies have not founded full empirical support (Lee & Tsang, 2001).

Empirical studies on socio-intercultural entrepreneurship define the variables of socio-inter culturality and entrepreneurship to establish their relationships and statistically measured in different situational contexts and environments. There is plenty of room for opportunities to study these relationships associated socio-interculturality and entrepreneurship concepts with a sufficient level of depth and scope. Research has reported a relationship between entrepreneurial orientation, entrepreneurial skills, entrepreneurial intentions, and environmental factors (Ibrahim & Masud 2016).

Besides the national culture, the individual variables internal locus of control and the level of studies are related to greater individualism but the results do not have a direct association with entrepreneurial behavior. These results question the trait approach to the locus of control as an attribute that encourages entrepreneurial behavior (García, García, 2007).

Entrepreneurial behavior of individuals is motivated and influenced by the average demographic variables in a profile which may be estimated, analyzed and explained in terms of association with male sex (Begley & Tan, 2001; Cowling & Taylor, 2001; Ardichvili & Gasparishvili, 2003; Acs et al., 2005), young and mature but not old (Ardichvili & Gasparishvili, 2003; Acs et al., 2005) higher level of education (Harmadyova, 1997; Ardichvili & Gasparishvili, 2003; Acs et al., 2005). The demographic profile variables such as age, gender, level of education of the individuals, etc., are linked to entrepreneurial behavior. Research results find a positive association between education and entrepreneurial behavior (Wang & Wong, 2004).

The educational level is a relevant quality of the entrepreneur (Lee & Tsang, 2001). The variable gender has shown on the studies, a negative effect on entrepreneurial behavior. On the other hand, the gender variable, which turns out to be explanatory of entrepreneurial behavior according to the results obtained from the structural equations model, has a negative effect on entrepreneurial behavior, indicating the greater presence of this behavior. However, a study carried out by Verheul et al. (2006), found that unemployment exerts a more positive influence on the entrepreneurial behavior of females than males.

It has been reported (Diario Gestión 2015 and Revista Andina, 2017) that in the city of Tacna there is historical background for the development of socio-intercultural entrepreneurial activities in formal and informal merchants established in free zone and as the result of the presence of foreign tourists. According to INEI (2018), Tacna has almost 350 thousand inhabitants in the gymnasium area related to socio-intercultural entrepreneurship characterized in emerging services based on body care, cosmetic and global health trends besides the most traditional and conventional business, commercial, trade and mining activities (Diario Correo 2014). All these entrepreneurial activities have risen concerns from the existing relationships between socio-interculturality and entrepreneurship sensitivities.

Different cultural dimensions have different effects on socio-intercultural entrepreneurial activities and opportunities as an important factor for the creation of a firm and economic growth and regeneration (Radziszewska Czestochowa, 2014). The cultural values of the Hofstede dimensions have been related to the socio-intercultural characteristics of social enterprises in such a way that it facilitates the understanding of those cultures that are more involved in the socio-intercultural activities of enterprises with a social orientation. The cultural dimensions of Hofstede's model are based on value continuums ranging from individual to collective values, from male to female, those related to the avoidance of uncertainty and the distance from power.

Capability Building and Development in Socio-Intercultural Entrepreneurship

The cultural dimensions more related to entrepreneurial activities, according to Hofstede (2001) include individualism, collectivism, masculinity, feminine, uncertainty avoidance, power distance. Individualism, low power distance, low uncertainly avoidance, long term orientation, human orientation, performance orientation and future orientation, are the cultural dimensions that influence more positively on entrepreneurship. Conclusions have been advanced that cultural values such as collectivism, femininity, higher level of uncertainty (Apetrei, Ribeiro, Roig, & Mas, 2013).

This individualistic cultural orientation has a direct positive effect on the locus of control that influences entrepreneurial behavior through educational level. In individualistic oriented cultures there are more entrepreneurs than in collectivistic cultures (Hofstede, 2001). Individualistic cultures support the individual initiative and autonomy leading to pursue individual interests and to low level of organizational loyalty. When investigating the locus of control, the cultural level of the individual is determinant of entrepreneurial behavior. Independent and individual entrepreneurial behavior aimed to achieve personal goals is supported by social norms. Low level of individualism leads to fewer entrepreneurial initiatives. On the other side, high level of individualism results in more entrepreneurial activities and ventures.

Collectivism of groups in societies is assumed to be negatively related to entrepreneurial activities and measures the individuals' expressions of pride, loyalty and cohesiveness (House et al., 2002, pp. 3–10) depending heavily on personal relationships and group goals.

The masculinity dimension has not been found to have a significant effect on entrepreneurial behavior not confirming the theoretical relationship based on the assumption that assertiveness, competitiveness and the need of achievement of male societies may have an accentuated entrepreneurial behavior. On the other side, Ardichvili and Gasparishvili (2003) found a negative association between masculinity and entrepreneurial behavior. Entrepreneurship attracts individuals as a means of achieving economic benefits and social status in higher masculine oriented cultures. High masculinity leads to entrepreneurship activities while low masculinity has the tendency towards less interest in entrepreneurial activities. In societies with more predominant masculine values, the entrepreneurs tend to attend success in entrepreneurial ventures and are more esteemed and recognized.

Feminine oriented cultures have less interest in entrepreneurial activities (Hofstede, 2001). The feminine cultural values in balance and combination with other values, promote social entrepreneurship is validated for certain cultures. Feminine values culture has a people orientation and including masculine values may develop socio-intercultural dimensions of entrepreneurship.

Power distance between individuals measures the degree of unequally distributed power relationships in societies. Power distance have a positive effect on entrepreneurial behaviors and activities linked to independence. Higher power distance limits the upward social mobility in society, with little acceptance for innovation and initiatives to create new business. Cultures with low power distance allows more entrepreneurial activities. In this sense, entrepreneurship is a tool used to achieve more independence and increasing the power position of individuals (House et al., 2002, pp. 3–10).

The socio-intercultural dimensions recognize cultural traits that promote innovation closely related to social entrepreneurship, such as the distance from power that measures power and the interpersonal relationship between leader and subordinate (Hofstede, 2001, p.83). According to Hofstede, in long term oriented and low power distance cultures favor entrepreneurship. The general consequence of low power distance is that allows access to entrepreneurial resources and opportunities. High power distance restricts access to entrepreneurial resources and opportunities making difficult entrepreneurship to emerge. Democratic pluralism has a close similarity to socio-interculturalism because it ensures consistency and socio-intercultural peace, apart from promoting discrimination or hostility between cultures (Pizzorno, 1985; Calderón and Gamarra, 2004 p.114).

The uncertainty faced by the entrepreneur when making decisions may explain the existence of patterns and mechanisms in the emergence and development of business. The premise that is based on the fact that cultures with a higher degree of uncertainty create a work environment that stimulates social entrepreneurs is highly questionable, since one of the functions of culture is to provide greater certainty in socio-intercultural management. Low uncertainty increases the willingness to take risks while increasing the individual initiative of entrepreneurial ventures.

The uncertainty of situational context and environment in cultures stimulates social entrepreneurs. In socio-intercultural management, the concept of uncertainty is framed with the uncertainty avoidance dimension of Hofstede (2001, 2007) and the Globe project (House et al., 2004). Reducing and absorbing uncertainty is essential for the design of socio-intercultural entrepreneurship strategies that is related to the propensity of individuals from a specific culture to accept a more entrepreneurial vision of the future. Absorbing the uncertainty related to socio-intercultural entrepreneurship requires a process of adaptation and implementation to the specific reality where it needs to be applied.

However, high level of uncertainty leads individuals to avoid risk and to have less initiative for entrepreneurial ventures. According to the model of the cultural dimensions of Hofstede (2001, 2007) and the Globe project (House et al., 2004) there are cultures with a higher degree of avoidance or aversion of uncertainty. This cultural trait is contradictory to the concept of entrepreneurship in the new environment (Urbano, Toledo & Ribeiro, 2010) that encourages social entrepreneurship (Dancin et al., 2011). Therefore, Dancin, Dancin & Tracey (2011), conclude that social entrepreneurship is related to the level of uncertainty in the environment to create value in society by solving social problems (Austin et al., 2006; Mair & Martí, 2006).

The entrepreneurship faces the uncertainty with innovation to make better decisions and contributing to the emergence of new products, services and companies while prolonging their lifecycle patterns in the markets (Cantarero, Gonzalez-Loureiro and Puig 2017). The feature of avoiding uncertainty as a consequence of economic, technological, social, political changes, etc., seems to be in contradiction to the spirit of entrepreneurial development, although it can rather be said that the entrepreneurial culture is changing (Urbano, Toledo & Ribeiro, 2010).

Future orientation is the capability to imagine and engage in future-oriented behaviors, contingencies and activities such as planning, setting goals, investing, formulate socio-intercultural dimensions of entrepreneurial initiatives, design strategies, etc. High level of future orientation leads to higher quality activities of entrepreneurship such as planning, interacting and documenting, resilience to risks and changes, etc. (Hayton et al., 2002, pp. 33–52).

SOCIO-INTERCULTURAL ENTREPRENEURSHIP CAPABILITY BUILDING AND DEVELOPMENT

Any investment in developing socio-intercultural competences and other diversity factors strengthens the entrepreneurial capabilities. Socio-intercultural competence and capability building involves socio-intercultural entrepreneurships skills development and learning from experiences, balancing support and challenge, absorbing uncertainty, reducing complexity, engaging ambiguity, reflection of values and life alignment etc. Building and developing some socio-intercultural business entrepreneurship capabilities

Capability Building and Development in Socio-Intercultural Entrepreneurship

requires to examine and engage in reflections about the assumptions, values, beliefs, expectations and other areas of personal life.

The notion of socio-intercultural competence has direct antecedents in the theoretical-methodological construct of cultural intelligence (Leung, Ang and Tan 2014) that in situations of complex interaction skills, interests, attitudes and values are implied. Socio-intercultural competencies of the small business entrepreneur and their negotiation skills in relation to the results of organizational performance.

Socio-intercultural entrepreneurship development as a competence involves *disregard-the-box* both and thinking in such a way that may be feasible to hold together two seemingly contrasting values and ideas at the same time to enhance creativity, innovation and synergy. The socio-intercultural relationships of the entrepreneur interaction such as the capacities and styles of negotiation (Mitchell, Busenitz, Bird, Gaglio, McMullen, Morse and Smith 2007; Artinger, Vulkan and Shem-Tov 2015) that suggest that there are positive and significant relationships between the socio-intercultural competencies of entrepreneurs as mediating variables of integrative negotiation systems and organizational performance (Sadler-Smith, Hampson, Chaston and Badger, 2003).

Socio-intercultural entrepreneurship competence is highly related to be situational context and environment-dependent on awareness and understanding of cultural differences, going beyond the unilateral to mutual accommodation between people doing international business. Therefore, the socio-intercultural awareness goes beyond unilateral accommodation. Socio-socio-intercultural awareness of entrepreneurship processes clearly enhances competences necessary in global and international business settings.

An entrepreneur has motivation and drives to create the knowledge and learning, develop the abilities, skills, competences, capacities, aptitudes and experience that results from the evolution through life and leading to embark on a specific project (Pablo, Begoña and Bueno, 2004p. 818). Individuals develop the capacities to acquire new attitudes, abilities and skills that make them entrepreneurs (Del Solar, 2010, p.12).

The formation of entrepreneurial competencies oriented to the construction of new realities is based on the capacity for creative thinking from understanding information, establishing relationships with other data and configuring new meanings (Del Solar Sepúlveda 2010, p.39-304). Divergent practices give support to socio-intercultural entrepreneurship that facilitate the implementation of programs for the development of socio-intercultural skills and competencies with orientations towards the participatory and comprehensive construction of individuals committed to the socio-economic development of communities. Socio-intercultural entrepreneurship practices based on socio-intercultural competencies like cultural bridging and reframing the issues to find more innovative and creative solutions to support transformative socio-intercultural entrepreneurial learning and development.

Entrepreneur socio-intercultural competencies are measured as the variable related to cultural intelligence (Ang et al. 2007). On this scale, socio-intercultural competencies are measured with integrative negotiation and organizational performance. Organizational performance depends on the entrepreneurial socio-intercultural competencies developed, which turn out to be a mediating factor for the management of the socio-interculturality of individuals in organizations and interest groups, vision, processes, organizational performance and the development of the performance.

Organizational performance depends on entrepreneurial competencies, considering that socio-intercultural competencies are a mediating factor in the integrative negotiation of individuals from different cultures in internationalization processes. Socio-intercultural competences to develop entrepreneurial activity are related to organizational performance in the international situational context and environment.

One of the important functions of universities is the transfer of knowledge considering the needs and interests of the regions, taking advantage of the methodologies that promote the training of professionals with entrepreneurial characteristics and attitudes, considering that scientific training must be complemented with business training. An effective development program in socio socio-intercultural entrepreneurship should develop analytical, critical and practical skills profiting from knowledge and learning from an innovative approach from social and human sciences, in tune with economics, management, marketing, etc.

Education for the development of entrepreneurship contributes to the generation of socially desirable attitudes in young people. Education is the means by which behaviors and attitudes are modified, so it can be specified that education is related to the training of entrepreneurs and, therefore, it can be concluded that entrepreneurs are formed and not born. The inclusion of the topic of entrepreneurship in study plans and programs plays a critical role in the training of entrepreneurs.

In this sense, Viera, Pérez and Paredes, (2008, p.47) argue that university professional training programs must incorporate teaching mechanisms for the development of entrepreneurial skills so that as graduates they promote their self-employment as intrapreneurs and become employers or entrepreneurs. A professional socio socio-intercultural entrepreneur must develop an autonomous and integrated entrepreneurship performance to incorporate initiatives and practices in diverse socio socio-intercultural situational contexts and environments, dealing with socio socio-intercultural situations, addressing the needs of people and improving the interactions between business cultures, leveraging economic growth, social development and sustainable environment.

Education develops entrepreneurship by promoting favorable psychological qualities for entrepreneurial activity, such as self-confidence, self-esteem, self-efficacy and the need for achievement (Howard Rasheed 2000, Formichella 2004). Entrepreneurs who emerge as apprentices are curious and open to what serendipity generates in high spirits to present certain prototypes quickly to find solutions that satisfy users (Slocum, 2004). The development of the entrepreneurial spirit requires that the apprentice discover for himself or herself the concepts, behaviors, attitudes, techniques, processes and tools to develop initiative, creativity, autonomy etc.

Professional practice in socio socio-intercultural entrepreneurship requires interactive, analogical, contrastive and critical approaches of culture, economy, socio-politics, management, languages, socio-intercultural communication etc., to be applied to specific socio-socio-intercultural groups and situational contexts and environments. University study programs should be oriented so that the professionals they train acquire entrepreneurial skills capable of becoming agents of change and generating their self-employment, which also promote the improvement of the quality of life of the entire population in their communities.

Entrepreneurial activities and socio-intercultural learning have a lot of things in common that connect and are considered both as socio-intercultural entrepreneurship development. Socio-intercultural learning is interaction with people from different cultural backgrounds. Socio-intercultural entrepreneurship is carried out in business situational contexts and environments by business men in need of business tools for practical applications of knowledge and experiences through meaningful interactions with other people to solve problems (Tomalin 2009:115) and to propose new business units, new ventures, new projects, new products, etc.

Socio-intercultural entrepreneurship is considered as a strategic tool of knowledge management for innovation and competitiveness that describes the attitudes, values, talents, abilities, skills and feelings that are intrinsic to the human being and that benefit from experience. Pro-entrepreneurial values serve

Capability Building and Development in Socio-Intercultural Entrepreneurship

as an incubator of entrepreneurship. As a movement that channels the participation of people, entrepreneurship strengthens social economies that meet the needs of society through actions with knowledge application tools.

Socio-intercultural knowledge may be the result of a personal learning facilitation process to growth and develop through personal opportunities such as the exposure to international education experiences, conversations with other people regarding the gender, ethnic, religious, etc., backgrounds. In the training of entrepreneurs, a constructivist approach centered on learning by doing by carrying out activities that define situations in conditions of uncertainty predominates, opportunities are identified in markets and the creation and development of companies are envisioned (Rusque, 2004, Viera, Pérez and Paredes 2008, p.48).

Research by Formichella, 2004, and Dehter 2002, confirmed that entrepreneur training programs exist only at the university level. From the perspective of a cognitive model of decision, Mitchell et al., (2000) have shown that mental schemes related to individual knowledge, skills, abilities and capacities, explain entrepreneurial decisions. However, using statistical modeling tools has found an indirect influence of the locus of control on the effect of level of studies on entrepreneurial behavior showing the relevance of knowledge resources available to the individuals and includes the internal control of individuals to invest on training.

CONCLUSION

Traditional culture is conceptually related to the values of collectivism, humane orientation and higher power distance while modern culture is related to future and performance orientations and uncertainty avoidance. Socio-intercultural entrepreneurship is described according to cultural diversify characteristics and categorized into value or dimensions of cultures. Entrepreneurial socio-interculturality is a dynamic situational variable dependent on the context and environment where people are motivated by the need to generate their own employment or company and convert it into an opportunity to satisfy all the economic sectors in production, distribution and commercialization of goods and services.

Learning, knowledge, interaction, and cultural exchange processes, all enhance socio socio-intercultural entrepreneurial behaviors understandings across socio cultural boundaries leading beyond the cultural economy to the creation of innovation, creativity and economic value. The relationship of education with entrepreneurship and employment as a transversal action is fundamental to understand the congruence with the satisfaction of human needs, mainly the needs of self-realization and subsistence of the subject based on the maximization of their potential. Socio-socio-intercultural entrepreneurship education should be practically designed for the future of global and international business, keeping in prospective the needs of people in mind.

The analysis of the cultural dimensions of Hofstede, the indicators indicate the existence of propitious situational contexts and environments for the development of social socio-intercultural enterprises in terms of social economies and cultural values proposed for the various cultures. However, it is important to consider the limitations of the indicators since the socio-culture variables are dynamic, in perpetual change. Moreover, professional profile of a socio socio-intercultural entrepreneurship articulates social and human sciences, history, politics, economic, management, communications, etc., required to become a proponent of socio socio-intercultural management as a strategic advantage, in diverse international cultural backgrounds.

REFERENCES

Acs, Z. J., Arenius, P., Hay, M., & Minniti, M. (2005). *Global Entrepreneurship Monitor. 2004 Executive Report*. Babson & London Business School.

Aldrich, H. E. (2012). The emergence of entrepreneurship as an academic field: A personal essay on institutional entrepreneurship. *Research Policy, 41*(7), 1240–1248. doi:10.1016/j.respol.2012.03.013

Alvord, S. H., Brown, L. D., & Letts, C. W. (2004). Social entrepreneurship and societal transformation, an exploratory study. *The Journal of Applied Behavioral Science, 40*(3), 260–262. doi:10.1177/0021886304266847

Ang, S., Van Dyne, L., Koh, D., Yee Ng, K., Templer, K., Tay, C., & Chandrasekar, A. (2007). Cultural intelligence: Its measurement and effects on cultural judgment and decision making, cultural adaptation and task performance. *Management and Organization Review, 3*(3), 335–371. doi:10.1111/j.1740-8784.2007.00082.x

Apetrei, A., Ribeiro, D., Roig, S., & Mas, A. (2013). El emprendedor social – una explicación socio-intercultural, CIRIEC-España. *C.I.R.I.E.C. España, 78*, 37–52. www.ciriec-revistaeconomia.es

Ardichvili, A.; Gasparishvili, A. (2003). Russian and Georgian Entrepreneurs and Non-Entrepreneurs: A Study of Value Differences. *Organization Studies,* 24(1), 29-46.

Artinger, S., Vulkan, N., & Shem-Tov, Y. (2015). Entrepreneurs negotiation behavior. *Small Business Economics, 44*(4), 737–757. doi:10.100711187-014-9619-8

Austin, J., Stevenson, H., & Wei-skillern, J. (2003). Social Entrepreneurship and Commercial Entrepreneurship: Same, Different, or Both? *Working Paper Series*, No. 04-029, Harvard Business School.

Baum, J. R., Frese, M., Baron, R. A., & Katz, J. A. (2007). Entrepreneurship as an area of psychology study: an introduction. *The Psychology of Entrepreneurship*, 1-18.

Begley, T.M.; Tan, W.L. (2001). The Socio-Cultural Environment for Entrepreneurship: A Comparison between East Asian and Anglo-Saxon Countries. *Journal of International Business Studie*s, 32(3), 537-553.

Bittán, M. (2017). El emprendimiento empresarial. *Disponible*. http://bit.ly/1R5erPv.

Brockhaus, R. H. (1980). Risk taking propensity of entrepreneurs. *Academy of Management Journal, 23*(3), 509–520. doi:10.2307/255515

Calderón, F., & Gamarra, E. (2004), Crisis, Inflexión y Reforma del Sistema de Partidos en Bolivia. Cuadernos de Futuro. La Paz, La Paz, Bolivia.

Cantarero, S., González-Loureiro, M., & Puig, F. (2017). Efectos de la crisis económica sobre el emprendimiento en empresas de economía social en España: un análisis espacial. *REVESCO. Revista de Estudios Cooperativos,* (125), 24-48. https://www.redalyc.org/articulo.oa?id=367/36754074002

Chen, G. (1997). A review of the concept of Intercultural Sensitivity. Bienal Convention of the Pacific and Asian Communication Association, Honolulu, Hawaii.

Capability Building and Development in Socio-Intercultural Entrepreneurship

Connelly, M., Gilbert, J., Zaccaro, S., Threlfall, K., Marks, M., & Mumford, M. (2000). Exploring the relationship of leadership skills and knowledge to leader performance. *The Leadership Quarterly*, *11*(1), 65–86. doi:10.1016/S1048-9843(99)00043-0

Cowling, M., & Taylor, M. (2001). Entreprenerurial Women and Men: Two Different Species? *Small Business Economics*, *16*(3), 167–175. doi:10.1023/A:1011195516912

Dancin, M. T., Dancin, D. A., & Tracey, P. (2011). Social Entrepreneurship: A Critique and Future Directions. *Organization Science*, *22*(5), 1203–1213. doi:10.1287/orsc.1100.0620

De la Garza Carranza, M. T., & Egri, C. (2010). Managerial cultural intelligence and small business in Canada. *Management Review*, *21*(3), 353–371. doi:10.1688/1861-9908_mrev_2010_03_dela-G

Dees, J. G. (2001). *The meaning of social entrepreneurship, Comments and suggestions contributed from the*. Social Entrepreneurship Funders Working Group.

Dehter, M. (2002). Problema conocido, no es más problema. *Justo Ahora*. http://www.justoahora.com/nws/v15.htm#1

Del Solar, S. (2010). *Emprendedores en el aula. Guía para la formación en valores y habilidades sociales de docen-tes y jóvenes emprendedores*. Fondo Multilateral de Inversiones del Banco Interamericano de Desarrollo.

Diario Correo. (2014). Crece la demanda por gimnasios. *Diario Correo*. https://diariocorreo.pe

Diario Gestión. (2015). El emprendimiento en el Perú: De la necesidad a la oportunidad. *Diario Correo*.

Earley, P. C., & Peterson, R. S. (2004). The elusive cultural chameleon: Cultural intelligence as a new approach to intercultural training for the global manager. *Learning and Education*, *1*(1), 100–115. doi:10.5465/amle.2004.12436826

Formichella, M. M. (2004). *El concepto de emprendimiento y su relación con la educación, el empleo y el desarrollo local*. Tres Arroyos.

Fornet-Betancourt, R. (2000). *Interculturalidad y globalización. Ejercicios de crítica filosófica intercultural en el contexto de la globalización*. DEI.

Fornet-Betancourt, R. (2005). Filosofía intercultural. In: Salas Astrain, Ricardo. (Coord.). (2005). Pensamiento crítico latinoamericano. Conceptos fundamentales. Ediciones Universidad católica Silva Henríquez (UCSH). (Chile).

Fornet-Betancourt, R. (2009). *Tareas y propuestas de la filosofía intercultural*. Editorial Mainz.

García, A.M.; García, M.G. (2007). Diferencias culturales y comportamiento emprendedor... *Revista Europea de Dirección y Economía de la Empresa*, *16*(4), 47-68.

Gartner, W. B. (1985). A conceptual framework for describing the phenomenon of new venture creation. *Academy of Management Review*, *10*(4), 694–706. doi:10.2307/258039

Goleman, D. (2005). *La Práctica de la Inteligencia Emocional*. 18va. Edición. Editorial

Hammer, M. R., Bennett, M. J., & Wiseman, R. L. (2003). *Measuring socio-intercultural sensitivity: The socio-intercultural development inventory.* International Inventory. *International Journal of Intercultural Relations, 27,* 421–443. doi:10.1016/S0147-1767(03)00032-4

Harmadyova, V. (1997). Occupational Mobility in the Transformation Process of Czech and Slovak Society, *Sociología, 29*(5), 505-536.

Hayton, J. C., George, G., & Zahra, S. A. (2002). National culture and entrepreneurship: A review of behavioral Research. *Entrepreneurship Theory and Practice, 26*(4), 33–52. doi:10.1177/104225870202600403

Hisrich, R., & Peters, M. (1992). *Entrepreneurship: starting, developing, and managing a new enterprise.* Irwin Publishing. doi:10.1002/jsc.4240040409

Hodgetts, R., & Kuratko, D. (2001). *Effective small business management.* Harcourt College Publishers.

Hofstede, G. (2001). *Cultures and Organizations. Software of the Mind.* McGraw-Hill.

Hofstede, G. (2007) *Geert Hofstede Cultural Dimensions.* Hofstede. www.geert-hofstede.com

House, R., Hanges, P., Javidan, M., & Dorfman, P. (2004). *Culture, Leadership and Organizations: the GLOBE Study of 62 Societies.* Sage Publications.

House, R., Javidan, M., Hanges, P., & Dorfman, P. (2002). Understanding cultures and implicit leadership theories across the globe: An introduction to project GLOBE. *Journal of World Business, 37*(1), 3–10. doi:10.1016/S1090-9516(01)00069-4

Ibrahim, N., & Masud, A. (2016). Moderating role of entrepreneurial orientation on the relationship between *entrepreneurial skills, environmental factors and entrepreneurial intention: A pls approach. Management Science Letters, 6*(3), 225–236. doi:10.5267/j.msl.2016.1.005

INEI. (2017). *Censos 2017.* Instituto Nacional de Estadística e Informática. www.censos2017.inei.gob.pe/red atam/

Jaén, I., & Fernandez-Serrano, J. & Liñan Francisco. (2013). Valores culturales, nivel de ingresos y actividad emprendedora. *Revista de Economía Mundial, 35,* 35–52.

Lachman, R. (1980). Toward measurement of entrepreneurial tendencies. *Management International Review,* 108–116.

Lee D Y and Tsang E W K. (2001). The Effect of Entrepreneur Personality, Background and Network Activities on Venture Growth, *Journal of Management Studies, 38*(4), pp 583-602.

Leung, K., Ang, S., & Tan, L. (2014). Intercultural competence. *Annual Review of Organizational Psychology and Organizational Behavior, 1*(1), 489–519. doi:10.1146/annurev-orgpsych-031413-091229

Levenson, H. (1974). Activism and powerful others: Distinctions within the concept of internal-external control. Journal of Personality Assessment, 38 (4), Light, P.C. (2009). Social entrepreneurship revisited. *Stanford Social Innovation Review, 7*(3), 21–22.

Mair, J., & Martí, I. (2006). Social entrepreneurship research: A source of explanations, prediction, and delight. *Journal of World Business, 41*(1), 36–44. doi:10.1016/j.jwb.2005.09.002

Maldonado, K. (2007). La socio-interculturalidad de los negocios internacionales Universidad del Rosario. *Empresa, Bogotá (Colombia), 6*(12), 261–291.

Martin, J. N., & Nakayama, T. K. (2010). *Intercultural Communication in Contexts* (5th ed.). McGraw-Hill.

Martin, R. L., & Osberg, S. (2007). Social entrepreneurship: The case for definition. *Stanford Social Innovation Review, 5*(2), 27–39.

McClelland, D. (1971). *The achievement Motive in Economic Growth Entrepreneurship and economic development*. P. Kilby.

Mitchell, R. K., Busenitz, L. W., Bird, B., Marie Gaglio, C., Mcmullen, J. S., Morse, E. A., & Smith, J. B. (2007). The central question in entrepreneurial cognition research 2007. *Entrepreneurship Theory and Practice, 31*(1), 1–27. doi:10.1111/j.1540-6520.2007.00161.x

Mitchell, R. K., Smith, B., Seawright, K. W., & Morse, E. A. (2000). Cross-cultural cognitions and the venture creation decision. *Academy of Management Journal, 43*(5), 974–993. doi:10.2307/1556422

Moriano, J. A., Trejo, E., & Palací, J. (2001). El perfil psicosocial del emprendedor: un estudio desde la perspectiva de los valores. Revista de psicología Social 2001, p. 230.

Pablo López, I., Begoña Santos, U., & Bueno Hernández, Y. (2004). *Las dimensiones del perfil emprendedor contraste empírico con emprendedores de éxito*. Universidad Autónoma de Madrid. https://www.uv.es/motiva/libromotiva/51PabloSantosBueno.pdf

Peredo, A. M., & Mclean, M. (2006). Social entrepreneurship: A critical review of the concept. *Journal of World Business, 41*(1), 56–65. doi:10.1016/j.jwb.2005.10.007

Pizzorno, A. (1985). *Sobre la racionalidad de la opción democrática, en CLACSO, Los límites de la democracia* (Vol. 2). CLACSO.

Porras, J., Oliveras, G., & Vigier, H. (2013). Probabilidades de éxito para la creación de empresas: Implicancias sobre la educación emprendedora. *Revista FIR, 2*(4), 42–48. doi:10.15558/fir.v2i4.45

Radziszewska Czestochowa, A. (2014). Socio-intercultural dimensions of entrepreneurship. *Journal of Socio-intercultural Management, 6*(2), 35–47. doi:10.2478/joim-2014-0010

Rauch, A., & Frese, M. (2007). Born to be an entrepreneur? Revisiting the personality approach to entrepreneurship. *The Psychology of Entrepreneurship*, 41-65.

Revista Andina (2017). Tacna: el futuro se escribe en el Sur. *Andina*. www.andina.pe

Rusque, A. M. (2004). *Reflexiones en torno a un programa emprendedor para universidades Latinoamericanas*. I Congreso Emprendedurismo y V Reunión Anual Red Motiva: El emprendedor innovador y las empresas de I+D+I. Universitat de Valencia.

Sadler-Smith, E., Hampson, Y., Chaston, I., & Badger, B. (2003). Managerial behavior, entreprenurial style and small firms performance. *Journal of Small Business Management, 41*(1), 47–67. doi:10.1111/1540-627X.00066

Sarasvathy, S. D. (2001). Causation and effectuation: Toward a theoretical shift from economic inevitability to entrepreneurial contingency. *Academy of Management Review*, 26(2), 243–263. doi:10.2307/259121

Sarasvathy, S. D. (2004). The questions we ask and the questions we care about: Reformulating some problems in entrepreneurship research. *Journal of Business Venturing*, 19(5), 707–717. doi:10.1016/j.jbusvent.2003.09.006

Shane, S., & Venkataraman, S. (2000). The promise of entrepreneurship as a field of research. *Academy of Management Review*, 25(1), 217–226. doi:10.5465/amr.2000.2791611

Shapero, A. (1975). The Displaced, Uncomfortable Entrepreneur. *Psychology Today*, 9(6), 83–88.

Shaver, K. G., & Scott, L. R. (1991). Person, process, choice: The psychology of new venture creation. *Entrepreneurship Theory and Practice*, 16(2), 23–45. doi:10.1177/104225879201600204

Slocum, J. (2004), *Comportamiento Organizacional*. Cengage Learning Editores.

Smith, B. R., & Stevens, C. E. (2010). Different types of social entrepreneurship: The role of geography and embeddedness on the measurement and scaling of social value. *Entrepreneurship & Regional Development: An International Journal*, 22(6), 575–598. doi:10.1080/08985626.2010.488405

Stevenson, H., & Wei-Skillern, J. (2003). Social Entrepreneurship and Commercial Entrepreneurship: Same, Different, or Both? *Working Paper Series, No. 04-029*. Harvard Business School.

Sullivan Mort, G., Weerawardena, J., & Carnegie, K. (2003). Social entrepreneurship: Towards conceptualization. *International Journal of Nonprofit and Voluntary Sector Marketing*, 8(1), 76–88. doi:10.1002/nvsm.202

Tomalin, B. (2009). Applying the principles: Instruments for intercultural business training. In A. Feng, M. Byram, & M. Fleming (Eds.), *Becoming interculturally competent through education and training* (pp. 115–131). Multilingual Matters. doi:10.21832/9781847691644-010

Tracey, P., Phillips, N., & Jarvis, O. (2011). Bridging institutiona lentrepreneurship and the creation of new organizational forms: A multilevel model. *Organization Science*, 22(1), 60–80. doi:10.1287/orsc.1090.0522

Urbano, D., Toledano, N., & Soriano, D. R. (2010). Analyzing social entrepreneurship from an institutional perspective: Evidence from Spain. *Journal of Social Entrepreneurship*, 1(1), 54–69. doi:10.1080/19420670903442061

Verheul, I., Van Stel, A., & Thurik, R. (2006). Ex-plaining Female and Male Entrepreneurship at the Country Level. *Entrepreneurship and Regional Development*, 18(2), 151–183. doi:10.1080/08985620500532053

Viera, A., Pérez, A., & Paredes, M. (2008). La pedagogía crítica y las competencias de emprendedurismo en estudiantes universitarios. *Pensamiento y Gestión*, (24), 43–62.

Vilá, R. (2006). La dimensión afectiva de la competencia comunicativa intercultural en la Educación Secundaria Obligatoria: Escala de Sensibilidad Intercultural. Revista de Investigación Educativa, 2, 353–372.

Walker, D. M. (2003). *Doing business internationally*. McGraw-Hill.

Capability Building and Development in Socio-Intercultural Entrepreneurship

Wang, C. K.; Wong, P.K. (2004). Entrepreneurial Interest of University Students in Singapore, *Technovation*, *24*(2), 163-172.

Weerawardena, J., & Mort, G. S. (2006). Investigating social entrepreneurship: A multidimensional model. *Journal of World Business*, *41*(1), 21–35. doi:10.1016/j.jwb.2005.09.001

Wennekers, S., Thurik, R., Van Stel, A. & Noorderhaven, N. (2010). *Uncertainty avoidance and the rate of business ownership across 21 OECD countries 1976-2004*. Springer Berlin Heidelberg.

Zaccaro, S., Mumford, M., Connelly, M., Marks, M., & Gilbert, J. (2000). Assesment of leader problem solving capabilities. *The Leadership Quarterly*, *11*(1), 37–64. doi:10.1016/S1048-9843(99)00042-9

KEY TERMS AND DEFINITIONS

Capability Building: Process of developing and reinforcing the skills, instincts, aptitudes, processes, and resources that organizations and communities require to survive, adapt, and excel in a rapidly changing world.

Development: Action and effect of developing or developing.

Entrepreneurial profile: The traits and personal characteristics of an entrepreneur considered as a person who detects a business opportunity and who organizes several resources to be able to operate one or more companies, assuming certain economic risks.

Entrepreneurship: Starting an activity that requires effort or work, or has some importance or scope.

Intercultural: From different cultures or related to them.

Interculturality: It refers to the presence and equitable interaction of diverse cultures and the possibility of generating shared cultural expressions,

Socio-intercultural: it is an event that notices the intimate relationship between nature, society, and culture. The deep relationship between man and nature is observable evidence that turns the human effort to adapt into a cultural work.

Chapter 4

The Role of SHRM in Navigating the Hospitality Sector During a Crisis

Dimitrios Belias
Hellenic Mediterranean University, Greece

Nikolaos Trihas
Hellenic Mediterranean University, Greece

ABSTRACT

The hospitality sector is a fragile sector. This means that it is very fragile when a crises hits, such as political, environmental, and financial crises. The operation of hotels relies a lot on the ability of the personnel to offer high quality services. Therefore, HRM plays a strategic role in the sustainability of the hospitality sector, especially during a crisis. For this purpose, the chapter has made not only a literature review into the overall use of SHRM for navigating the hospitality sector during a crisis, but also more precisely for the case of the COVID-19 crisis. Indeed, the related findings – deriving from the existing literature – indicate that there is limited research on this field.

INTRODUCTION

COVID-19 is an infectious disease caused by the recently discovered coronavirus (World Health Organization, 2020a). In December 2019, this new coronavirus (2019-nCoV) was isolated for the first time from three patients with acute pneumonia associated with acute respiratory disease in Wuhan, China (Kumar, 2020). In March 2020, The World Health Organization (WHO) has officially declared the coronavirus outbreak a global pandemic (World Health Organization 2020b). In response to the outbreak of COVID-19, countries around the world imposed strict protection measures, such as banning the movement of citizens for any purposes deemed unnecessary (lockdown) and travel restrictions, in order to curb the spread of the virus. The outbreak of coronavirus significantly affected the tourism sector and struck the global economy in general (World Tourism Organization, 2020).

DOI: 10.4018/978-1-6684-6055-9.ch004

The Role of SHRM in Navigating the Hospitality Sector During a Crisis

Covid-19 has affected the hospitality sector. The closure of hotels along with travel bans and restrictions had negative effect on the hospitality sector. One of the outcomes of this situation was the fact that the hotels had to decide on how they will handle their human resources and also how they would look after their wellbeing and safety when the tourist industry would start again its operations (Agarwal, 2021). This means that Human Resource Management (HRM) has a significant role concerning the resilience of the hospitality industry from the COVID-19 crisis (Belias & Trihas, 2022a) and its ability to recover and become fully operational, without jeopardizing the safety of the employees (Ngoc Su et al, 2021).

For this reason, this chapter will not only investigate how HRM can contribute to hospitality sector in order to cope with the consequence of COVID-19 crisis, but also how to handle the post COVID-19 situation. The topic is examined through an extended literature review, which means that it will investigate the current literature, with a focus on the latest papers, as well as it will rely on the existing theories. The aim is to produce a number of guidelines for future research which will help the academia and practitioners to better understand the examined issues

BACKGROUND

The aim of this chapter is to investigate how strategic HRM (SHRM) can help the hospitality sector to deal with the effects of COVID-19 crisis and to find ways to help the organizations in the tourist sector to meet their strategic goals. There is evidence that an effective Strategic HRM can have a positive effect on the resilience of the personnel towards the COVID-19 measures (Le and Phi, 2021; Belias & Trihas, 2022b). It is important to mention that hospitality relies on the provision of effective and quality-driven services delivered by the personnel (Chand, 2010). Therefore, an effective SHRM policy and strategy is expected to leverage the ability of a hotel to cope with the consequences of the COVID-19 crisis, though this is something new and the related research is pretty limited (Le & Phi, 2021). Hence, this chapter will help the academia and the practitioners to understand how Strategic HRM can leverage the hospitality sector during the COVID-19 crisis.

MAIN FOCUS OF THE CHAPTER

There is a plethora of research (Tsaur & Lin, 2004; Belias et al, 2018; Belias & Trichas, 2022; Belias, Vasiliadis & Mantas, 2020; Belias et al., 2020; Belias et al., 2017; Rossidis et al., 2021a, Rossidis et al., 2021b; Rossidis, Belias & Aspridis, 2020) which indicate that Strategic HRM has a positive impact on the performance of hotels. Nonetheless, what is important is to understand how Strategic HRM contributes on the hospitality sector during a crisis such as the case of the COVID-19 pandemic. Indeed, there is evidence that Strategic HRM can have a positive role for the leverage and the strengthening of the personnel's resilience during a crisis in the hospitality sector (Channa et al, 2019). Nonetheless, the case of COVID-19 is totally different from past crises. Till now humanity had dealt with major financial crises and health crises which had short-term effect such as the SARS crisis in SE Asia. However, COVID-19 is a major outbreak which had an effect on every aspect not only of the economies but also of the daily life of everyone living on this planet. This means that it needs special attention and a careful study on how to deal with such a health crisis. Despite of being a recent event, there is a number of researches (Cheng & Kao, 2022; Ahmed et al, 2021) which indicates that Strategic HRM can improve resilience of the employees by ensuring the sustainability of the jobs, the safety at work and through training which will help the employees to implement the necessary health protocols and make sure that they will protect their own health as well as the health or their guests (Belias and Trihas, 2022c; Ntalakos et al., 2022b), though the literature about this is very limited for the time being (Boiral et al, 2021). Therefore, there is a need to have a further investigation of the current literature and also to make suggestions for future research on this field, which will help the academia and the practitioners to better understand how strategic HRM is able to strengthen the resilience of the employees and their performance, with focus on the hospitality sector.

DEFINITION OF STRATEGIC HUMAN RESOURCE MANAGEMENT (SHRM)

Employees are regarded as the valuable resource of a business (Boselie, 2014) and the SHRM is one of the most important assets that a business can have (Barney & Wright, 1998). SHRM is a key factor to create a competitive advantage (Barney, 1995; Albrecht et al., 2015) and the main feature which differentiates successful businesses from unsuccessful ones (Marchington & Wilkinson, 2005). This fact is particularly evident in the services industry where employees are the main source of contact with customers, either through face-to-face interaction in the provision of service, either by phone and internet (Marchington & Wilkinson, 2005). However, it has been the subject of debate as to what SHRM really means, as argued by Marchington & Wilkonson (2005).

Nickson (2007) found that there is no common agreement on how the SHRM is rooted and provides a variety of possible concepts which makes the SHRM difficult to understand. Unfortunately, many are given the impression that SHRM is a simple title and that there is nothing special about it, or the fact that some people are taking advantage of the term SHRM to manipulate their employees. However, Nickson (2007) also lists the reasons why they are being harassed. SHRM as an effective practice with positive results. For example, SHRM can be seen as a charter that helps professionals in the field, to understand the concept of human resource management, while it is also a set of professional practices that can be used to ensure a professional approach to the management of employees.

Similarly, Collings et al. (2019) found both positive and negative perceptions of SHRM, such as that SHRM is considered a harmful aspect which will gain a remarkable place in business and contribute to administrative decisions only when it is proven that its implementation is ongoing.

For some time, SHRM has been a controversial topic in academic circles where it was said to promise more than it offers and that doing so is immoral (Armstrong, 2008). Employees, on the other hand, want the presence of SHRM. Workers run by SHRM practices are more motivated and feel more insecure and satisfied in their workplace (Armstrong, 2008). Boxall and Purcell (2016, p. 7) provide a more detailed definition and describe the SHRM as "the process through which management builds the workforce and tries to create in people representations that the organization needs". SHRM is the bridge between employers and employees (Vardalier, 2016) which focuses on the relationship between employee and business and is what contributes to its success in terms of increasing financial performance (Boselie, 2014). The role of SHRM is the development of policies and practical systems in a business in relation to strategic objectives that affect the behavior, attitude and performance of employees. In addition, the role of SHRM is to create an environment that encourages and motivates employees to make an effort in such a way as to benefit the business (Ulrich & Brockbank, 2005). This result can be achieved using the five basic practices of recruitment and selection of human resources, training and development, performance

The Role of SHRM in Navigating the Hospitality Sector During a Crisis

evaluation and management, compensation and employee participation (Boselie, 2014). To sum up, there is a no overall definition of SSHRM that adequately captures the complexity of the term. The perception of SHRM depends on the status of the person who analyzes it (academics, principals or employees).

THE ROLE OF HUMAN RESOURCE MANAGEMENT DURING A CRISIS

SHRM is referred to as a managerial function which is able to survive into different situations. As it is vulnerable to external factors such as economic conditions, the SHRM must constantly discover its role in order to gain legitimacy and power (Gudlaugsdóttir & Raddon, 2013). SHRM has its roots in the early 20th century when it emerged as a response to the industrial revolution whose purpose was to add value by improving the partnership between workers and machines and to settle revenue-related issues on terms of productivity (Ulrich & Dulebohn, 2015). During World War I, there was a shortage of labor due to immigration and many workers were called to the army. Thus, the companies recognized the need for SHRM, which appeared both as a personnel manager and as a profession designed to support the company, contributing to its objectives and adding value to it (Ulrich & Dulebohn, 2015). Its importance declined during the economic crisis of the 1930s, but this lasted only for a short time. During the post-war economic boom, the world was characterized by stability and experienced only slightly unexpected occurrences. As a result, the SHRM was only seen as an essential function which focused on administrative activities. It was not concerned as adding value to a business (Ulrich & Dulebohn, 2015).

The recession of the 1980s is often considered the actual birth of SHRM. Legge (1995) pointed out that changes in the market during this decade intensified competition and therefore provoked the emergence of SHRM. Ulrich and Dulebohn (2015) found that SHRM was transformed in the 1980s from an administrative maintenance function to a core business function that could contribute to organizational efficiency. Similarly, Vardalier (2016) argues that it appeared in the 1980s with a different content than what was hitherto known as personnel management.

Personnel management perceives the employees as an input in order to achieve a desired outcome determined by the top management, while the SHRM deals with training, skills development of employees, talent management or career planning (Vardalier, 2016). However, according to Gudlaugsdóttir and Raddon (2013), there seem to be contradictory views on whether the recession of the 1980s strengthened or weakened the role of the SHRM. Legge (as reported in Gudlaugsdóttir & Raddon, 2013) came to the view that, although there was a temporary increase in inflow and power, the recession of the 1980s did not significantly affect the role of the SHRM. Tyson and Witcher (1994), on the other hand, reported that the recession of the 1980s contributed to the SHRM gaining more value and power, despite the fact that the role of it turned into a more dynamic rather than a superstitious one.

During an outbreak of the SARS virus at the beginning of the new millennium, Lee and Warner (2005) found that the outbreak had a negative impact, both on employment and on SHRM, and that the HR practices adopted by hotels were of relatively low importance in their operation. SHRM was mainly involved in activities cost reduction, but mass layoffs were not widespread as one of the management's strategies aimed at reducing costs work without layoffs of workers. This particular paternalistic approach of the SHRM demonstrates concern about the need for workers to work together (Lee & Warner, 2005).

The next crisis after the SARS outbreak was the 2008 recession, which had a dramatic impact on businesses and the labor market as a whole. SHRM focused mainly on minimizing and acquiring as much as possible more with the minimum possible expense. An Irish study found that there were no dramatic role changes, but that SHRM managers gained strength in decision-making on cost-cutting measures to save the business (Roche & Teague, 2012). SHRM gained strategic power in implementing and communicating many cut methods and was involved in the early stages of decision-making processes. However, by assuming responsibilities outside its traditional boundaries and shifting other operational processes in the field of SHRM, while SHRM activities have been halted or postponed, the perception of SHRM as a key function was undermined. In the end, this event probably resulted in the weakening of the operation of SHRM (Gudlaugsdóttir & Raddon, 2013).

From the above it follows that the financial difficulty brings the know-how of the SHRM to the forefront, requiring the SHRM to formulate and carry out cost-cutting activities, which increases its importance. However, this increased power is often not long-term, as is the reaction to an acute economic need (Gudlaugsdóttir & Raddon, 2013). Nevertheless, it seems that a crisis is leading to an increase in the perception and awareness of the role of the SHRM.

Nowadays, it is argued that the role of SHRM is increasingly important in times of crisis than in the past. Vardalier (2016) found that HR managers are not only focused on managerial views, but that the SHRM has a strategic role when a crisis erupts and that the following possible outcomes occur after a crisis:

- Panic within the company
- Loss of significant staff and knowledge
- High turnover
- Low performance caused by a lack of prudence and motivation
- Cancellation of appointments
- Cancel a scheduled training

SHRM can help businesses prevent irreparable damage and reduce the above-mentioned negative impacts. At a time when a crisis breaks out, the creation of a crisis management team should be one of the first steps in its control, as it helps to reduce the cost of crisis management. The cancellation of recruitment and the loss of staff with a crucial role in the firm have the effect of reducing employees for the same work. While the classic approaches of SHRM design ways of organizing the project more effectively, modern practices human resources are focused on talents and supporting them mentally in order to create faith that will last throughout and after the crisis (Vardalier, 2016).

As for the high variation of workers during a crisis, the classic SHRM approaches did not seek to prevent turnover, but instead increased it by reducing jobs. Modern SHRM practices, however, propose the implementation of training programs in order to ensure flexibility and thus an easy and inevitable transition between responsibilities and tasks. Training activities are an important part, in the pre-crisis period, as also the development of human capital to deal with a crisis and manage it in a way that is beneficial to businesses (Pforr & Hosie, 2008, Vardalier, 2016). Situations such as panic, the loss of efficient workers and the high turnover of jobs will eventually lead to a lack of motivation and morale of workers with their low performance as a result. Classic SHRM approaches tend to have no formal policy to prevent it. Modern SHRM, on the other hand, supports the human side within a company and organizes under-performing - support programs for employees, such as training and mentoring programs, in order to promote and maintain employee morale and motivation (Vardalier, 2016).

The lack of effective communication between decision makers and subordinates in relation to visitor satisfaction and feedback seems to be another key reason why businesses fail to control a crisis and reduce its negatives impact (Mirzapour et al., 2019). Although social media can be used to misinform (Belias et al., 2020b; Tsiotas et al., 2020; Belias et al., 2022a), there is no way to limit their use (Skagias et al., 2022; Belias et al., 2022b; Belias et al., 2018; Varsanis et al., 2019). Businesses could therefore use them as communication channels to handle defamation when and if it occurs (Vardalier, 2016). It would be useful for modern SHRM to have a communication plan that prevents the spread of disinformation in a time of crisis, describing how communication between employees, customers as well as other members involved (Mirzapour et al., 2019).

SHRM has one of the most important roles for a company before, during and after a crisis. SHRM cares not only in the interest of the business, but also in the interests of its employees. Therefore, the key element in order to effectively prepare operations for crisis management is the SHRM (Mirzapour et al., 2019).

COVID-19 AND ITS IMPACT ON THE TOURISM AND HOSPITALITY INDUSTRY

COVID-19 is an infectious disease caused by the newly discovered coronavirus. It remained unknown until the outbreak began in Wuhan, China, in December 2019 (World Health Organization, 2020a). In March 2020, the World Health Organization (WHO) officially declared the coronavirus as a global pandemic (World Health Organization, 2020b). Since that time it has affected all of the major tourist destinations. An example is the case of Greece, where COVID-19 first appeared in Greece on February 26, 2020 and then spread rapidly (COVID-19 in Greece, 2020). Since July 2020 there has been a large spread of COVID-19 in the Balkan countries neighboring Greece, which after some retreat in September 2020 accelerated again almost uncontrollably in the period October - December 2020.The situation got better during the summer of 2021, while the prediction is that Greek tourism will fully recover in 2023 (Papadimitriou et al, 2022).

In response to the outbreak of the pandemic, countries around the world have imposed measures such as lockdowns and travel restrictions to control the spread of the coronavirus (Ntalakos et al., 2022). On 12 March 2020, the United States banned travel to 26 European nations (BBC News, 2020), and only a few days later, the European Union decided to close all SCHENGEN borders for 30 days (SCHENGEN Visa Information, 2020). The travel bans have therefore led to significant challenges for the tourism and the hospitality industry. The industry accounted for 10.4% of global GDP in 2018 and the WTTC noted that travel and tourism-related activities accounted for 319 million jobs, or 10% of jobs worldwide (World Travel & Tourism Council, 2019). However, the tourism and hospitality industry is one of the industries most affected, as they are based on the interaction between people who have been completely curtailed during the pandemic. Therefore, the World Tourism Organization (UNWTO) estimates a decrease of between 20% and 30% in global international tourist arrivals in 2020, which could turn into a loss of $30 to $50 billion in spending from international visitors (World Tourism Organization, 2020).

Apart from the great human suffering and the tens of thousands of deaths caused by the unprecedented COVID-19 pandemic, it also has a huge economic impact which in turn has led to the vertical reduction of travel and tourist traffic around the world. The duration and depth of the tourist downturn in 2020 depends on a number of factors that at this stage are impossible to quantify.

CRISES IN TOURISM

The tourism and hospitality industry is particularly vulnerable to political problems and economic cycles and can be negatively affected in periods of uncertainty. The global nature of the industry makes it prone to external incidents which cause fluctuations in tourism visits. The terrorist attack on 9/11, the war in Iraq and the outbreak of the SARS virus led to a drop in revenues in the hospitality industry (Glaesser, 2006). These exogenous factors reduced the number of international travelers and left uncertainty and instability in the tourism market (Bonham, Edmonds & Mak, 2006; Nickson, 2007).

In the literature, there is a consensus that the main feature of crises in tourism is that unforeseen events occur. The laws define a crisis in tourism as an exceptional event associated with increased media attention, economic losses and injuries or deaths, i.e. negative incidents that turn stable situations into critical ones (Glaesser, 2006). They happen without warning and with serious consequences and sometimes disastrous for the government and business communities; they are also, inevitably, episodic events that disrupt the industry on a regular basis and act as a shock to tourism and the hospitality industry. While concern about crisis management in the industry emerges over time, history shows that crises in tourism and hospitality are often not handled with proper administration (Pforr & Hosie, 2008).

Pforr and Hosie (2008) argue that because there is always a crisis somewhere in the world, tourism and the hospitality industry seem to be under a never-ending threat of yet another crisis that is on the way. Therefore, companies in the sector should prepare for potential risks that will affect their facilities. Basically, it is a task of crisis management to plan in tourism and hospitality, and to prepare for the conditions which the business has not experienced before. This plan can be divided into four stages. The first stage is the pre-crisis stage, where actions are needed to prevent the effects of a possible crisis. Every hotel, regardless of its size or location, must adequately understand how these crises are likely to affect the industry of tourism and hospitality in general and in particular its business. This will be achieved through a crisis management plan (Johnson Tew, Lu, Tolomiczenko & Gellatly, 2008).

The second stage, the stage of acute crisis, refers to the point in time at which the effects of a crisis are felt and the situation seems that is not easy to be under control. For tourism and hospitality enterprises it is necessary to take drastic measures to protect property, customers and employees. Emphasis should be placed at this stage on administrative responses, mobilization and the establishment of a crisis management mandate center. Also, this stage is usually accompanied by cost reduction strategies. The third stage, the time stage, is a period for self-analysis and recovery. This stage includes drawings investment development, advice to the victims of the crisis; including employees, and restoring customer trust. At the last stage, the review stage, the undertaking shall examine the crisis as a whole, including the works which were successfully handled and those in need of improvement (Johnson Tew et al., 2008).

Regarding crisis management planning in the tourism and hospitality sector, two main approaches have been identified. The first is the preventive approach in which a possible crisis is recognized in advance as a result of careful monitoring. Efforts are therefore being made to avoid the problem completely or at least to minimize the impact. The second approach is the reactionary approach after the crisis is over. The priority of the reactive approach lies in anything that involves harm and ensures that the business returns to stability. Businesses in the tourism and hospitality industry tend to use the reactive approach and give more importance in the post-crisis issue than in the period before it appears. It was found that the majority of tourist enterprises in Alpine destinations in Germany, Austria and Italy had only minimal planning and no crisis management plan followed in the most vulnerable sectors. Awareness of the risk was not high although there had been several avalanches in the area in the past which had as result hundreds of injuries and several deaths (Laws et al., 2007).

Although the literature on crisis management in the tourism and hospitality industry argues that the crises were treated the moment they appear, it would be more effective for tourism businesses to use the proactive approach to the passive reactive, which ensures better preparation and management when the crisis finally arises (Pforr & Hosie, 2008). While large enterprises have the ability to develop permanent crisis management teams, the smaller enterprises, which characterize the tourism and hospitality industry, are often unable to devote these resources in a similar way. However, tourism and hospitality businesses need to plan for the unexpected in order to achieve their goals effectively and therefore need to turn their attention from the reaction to a more preventive and long-term strategy for managing potential crises (Laws et al., 2007).

When it comes to health-related threats, such as COVID-19, history proves that the crises that are occurring due to a pandemic have severely affected the tourism and hospitality industry. The International Labour Organization estimated that countries facing an epidemic could lose a third of the travel and tourist employment. The outbreak of SARS in Asia, at the beginning of the new millennium, is an example of this kind of crisis. SARS is a contagious pneumonia, a disease for which we do not have much data, but it had as a fact extensive media publicity. The main argument was that travelers who carried the virus, which resulted in air transport, being considered particularly dangerous. The virus had spread mainly to Asia, China, Taiwan and Vietnam (Laws etc., 2007).

Figure 1. The evolution of the SARS crisis
(Laws et al., 2007)

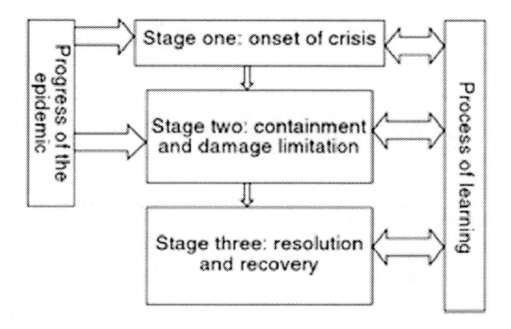

Figure 1 shows the evolution of the SARS crisis. The first stage, the onset of the crisis, was very short and the crisis was quickly transferred to the second stage, limiting the limits of damage. In the second stage, the WHO distributed information about the virus, issued travel warnings and proposed a health check for departing international passengers. They were also distributed information on how to handle possible infected persons as well as those with whom they had been in contact. Numerous departments were involved in the crisis, such as government and non-governmental agencies, national and local authorities, tourism and other businesses, managers and staff, and all accepted the need for cooperation and coordination (Laws et al., 2007).

The crisis entered the third stage, resolution, and recovery, when the region was declared SARS-free by the WHO about six months after the outbreak of the virus. National and international parties shifted from reactionary tactics in pre-active tactics, such as intensive advertising and special promotion of the area. When travel to Asia was considered safe again, a marketing plan for the region was launched with the aim of restoring trust and creating a collective Asian voice, using the means.

Despite the good intentions of a marketing campaign, industry observers were skeptical about the effectiveness of such action given the small size of the budgets, short-term time frame, broad geographical coverage and emulation (Laws et al., 2007).

Similarly, Gil-Alana and Huijbens (2018) found that the marketing campaign that Iceland had launched after the Eyjafjallajökull volcano erupted to address the perceived negative effects of the eruption was unfounded. The money allocated to the campaign could have been spent on more efficient practices in preparing the Icelandic infrastructure for the resumption of the incoming development of tourism as the effects of the volcanic eruption had diminished after history had shown that such exogenous factors affecting incoming tourism in Iceland never seemed to have a lasting effect. Once the effect of the shock itself, such as the interruption of air traffic in the case of the explosion of the Eyjafjallajökull, had been overcome, incoming tourist trends were likely to resume in Iceland (Gil-Alana & Huijbens, 2018). In addition, in 2009, Lonely Planet, a major travel guide publisher, had stated that Iceland is one of the most modern destinations for tourists. This combined with a favorable exchange rate for visitors led to a 10.4% increase in passengers in the first five months of 2009 (Jóhanesson & Huijbens, 2010).

Pforr and Hosie (2008) found that disasters do not tend to have a long-term impact as tourism flows and that most tourists will continue to travel when they feel the immediate threat of being over. However, the tourism and hospitality companies need to develop strategies that include crisis management and a future plan for minimizing the negative effects of a crisis. A well-developed plan helps the company to react quickly and effectively as soon as a crisis occurs (Johnson & Tew et al., 2008).

THE ROLE OF STRATEGIC HUMAN RESOURCE MANAGEMENT IN THE TOURISM AND THE HOSPITALITY INDUSTRY

When looking at SHRM in tourism, several authors show contradictions. Baum (2007 & 2015), Nickson (2007) and Saad (2013) have identified irrational HR practices in tourism businesses, such as the fact that businesses want to offer excellent services, but at the same time the majority of staff consist of employees with low and semi -professional competence. While it would be highly effective to provide adequate training, managers tend to stand idly by on this track due to high turnover rates in the industry (Saad, 2013).

The Role of SHRM in Navigating the Hospitality Sector During a Crisis

Further contradictory feature is the fact that managers in the industry tend to hire low-skilled staff in order to solve faster temporary problems, such as low productivity or turnover, than using HRM practices to achieve long-term positive results (Saad, 2013). Nickson (2007) pointed out that although the amount of jobs in the tourism industry is undeniable, the quality of many of them is of great concern. At the same time, he notes that although that the frontline staff is the one that serves the tourists, at the same time it is also the one that often holds the lowest positions in the business (Nickson, 2007).

Hence, Human Resource Management of companies associated with the hospitality industry should take into consideration the importance of the employees that they hire. For example, they could hire skilled personnel, with tourism-hospitality studies as well as hospitality work experience, and they could train them in order to handle not only everyday working conditions but also crises or risky situations that can occur unexpectedly by the external environment (Belias et al., 2022c). As a result, the employees would feel more secure and confident in their everyday working environment and this can have a positive impact to a plethora of their working aspects, such as job satisfaction, job commitment, work stress, emotional intelligence, workplace well-being, role conflict, team effectiveness, readiness for change as well as communication between employees (Belias et al., 2022d; Belias et al., 2022e; Belias and Trihas, 2022d; Koutiva et al., 2020; Ntalakos et al., 2022c; Ntalakos et al., 2022d, Ntalakos et al., 2022e; Belias et al., 2022f).

Baum (2007) discovered something paradoxical in the drastic growth of the world tourism over the last fifty years, on the way and conditions in which people offer tourism services and hosting. Baum (2007) succinctly states that while the industry has grown, the supply of services remains outdated, even though they are subject to notable changes. In a retweeting of his article, Baum (2015) found that although work in the tourism and hospitality sector has begun to change, the process is slow and many factors remain unchanged which prevents a clearer conclusion from being made compared to his first article. The nature of the work of tourism and hospitality does not provide a good work-life balance. In addition, this sector has a leadership deficit and there is a shifting power in the workplace in favor of the employer (Baum, 2015).

In general, tourism and the hospitality industry often struggle against a negative image of employment practices and conditions. Problems include low wages, overtime and shifting tasks, poor or nonexistent structures and limited opportunities for promotion, informal recruitment methods or high levels of staff turnover (Maroudas et al., 2008; Baum 2012). The response of administrative decisions to these challenges is often short-term which ultimately leads to a weak internal market. However, long-term decision-making and perspective could provide more growth and career opportunities for the existing employees (Nickson, 2007).

STRATEGIC HRM INSIGHTS FOR HELPING THE HOSPITALITY SECTOR TO DEAL WITH COVID-19 CRISIS

The COVID-19 crisis seems to be in a phase-out situation. However, there is still the question of what it may come next, since nobody can predict if the COVID-19 will be transformed from a pandemic to a lesser threat, which means that the hospitality sector and the economies overall will return back to normality or that a new variant may appear, which will create again anxiety and will not allow the fast recovery of the hospitality sector. Hence, there is a high level of uncertainty on this issue. In addition to this, this is a new phenomenon and this means that there is a limited amount of research.

It seems that SHRM has a crucial role on the COVID-19 and the post COVID-19 era for the hospitality sector. An important insight is that focus is given on training (Viterouli & Belias, 2021) and development. This is because the nature of work in the hospitality sector has changed. To be more precise, hospitality personnel is coming into a close encounter with the guests (especially those who work on the front office services). This means that there is a high threat of getting the virus since the personnel is exposed on this in a daily basis. Hence, research indicates that a key strategic function of HRM is to train the personnel so to protect themselves but also the guests (Huang et al, 2021). For this reason, SHRM can have a strategic role as function which will help the employees to learn by heart and implement the COVID-19 protocols (Park et al, 2022). Actually, to a large extent the sustainability of a hotel today depends a lot on its ability to prove that it is safe for the tourist and that it has reduced the risk factors related with COVID-19 (Baum & Hai, 2020). Hence, through training on health protocols it is possible to help the hotel and the personnel to cope with the crisis.

Another area where SHRM can valuable is the case of keep the morale of the personnel high. An empirical research made from Rivera et al (2021) has indicated that on hotels that the human resource department has taken care of the employees' resilience and have adopted policies to support them – financially and emotionally – during and after the COVID-19 crisis this had a payoff for the hotel since the resilience levels and job satisfaction increase with a positive effect on the performance of the hotel and its recovery from the crisis. This means that the HR managers would have to work hard in order to keep the morale high and also to find efficient ways to keep the employees satisfied in an era where many hotels were out of business and hence out of cash. This was a really difficult task to execute (Lai & Cai, 2022).

FUTURE RESEARCH DIRECTIONS

As it is stated on the previous pages the health crisis of COVID-19 is a new situation where the markets have to go through uncharted water. The fact that there is not any such unprecedented means that there is not any best practice to suggest or how to handle this crisis in a safe manner. The previous section indicated that there are two key issues that SHRM can be useful for helping a hospitality organization to navigate during this crisis. The first one is through training and helping the personnel to cope with the consequences of the crisis, including taking care of the health protocols and the second one is to leverage the emotional situation so to strengthen the resilience of the personnel and of course of the hospitality sector as a whole. This means that there is a need to investigate those two functions but also to investigate whether there are areas and functions of SHRM which can contribute on the resilience of the hospitality sector in the COVID-19 and post COVID-19 environment.

CONCLUSION

The chapter has made a literature review on issues related with SHRM and how it handle a crisis in the hospitality sector. SHRM can provide hospitality business with a plethora of key elements in order for them to be able to survive from an upcoming crisis. One of the most important elements that SHRM has to take into consideration is the implementation of training programs which can provide flexibility, awareness, and preparations skills to the employees of hospitality businesses. Human capital is the most

The Role of SHRM in Navigating the Hospitality Sector During a Crisis

important factor as far as the hospitality industry is concerned. During crisis, the morale and the motivation of the employees can be totally declined due to the anxiety and uncertainness that the employees feel. Thus, the role of SHRM is to promote and maintain employee motivation and morale through training and mentoring programs. When an employee feels comfortable in his/her working environment, this reflects to his/her attitude to the costumer. If a customer feels that the quality of service which was provided to him/her was very poor, then he/she would feel dissatisfied of the whole hospitality company. As a result of this dissatisfaction, the customer's feedback may be very negative. This can create negative results to the image of the hospitality industry.

During the analysis of literature review on the current paper, emphasis was given in the case of the COVID-19 crisis where the research is pretty limited. This opens the way for a future research with emphasis on issues of training and of emotional support on the employees. It is important to mention that the hospitality sector has suffered a lot from the COVID-19 crisis and even today many hotels do not operate in full capacity. This creates anxiety and uncertainty about the future of their operations and of course it affects the personnel of the hotels. For this reason, this chapter suggests that the direction for future research must be towards the training and the strengthening of the resilience of the employees so to cope with the multiple effects of the crisis. Also, it suggests to examine the possibility of any other direction related with SHRM.

REFERENCES

Agarwal, P. (2021). Shattered but smiling: Human resource management and the wellbeing of hotel employees during COVID-19. *International Journal of Hospitality Management, 93*, 102765. doi:10.1016/j.ijhm.2020.102765 PMID:36919177

Ahmed, E., Kilika, J., & Gakenia, C. (2021). Progressive convergent definition and conceptualization of organizational resilience: A model development. *International Journal of Organizational Leadership, 10*(4), 385–400. doi:10.33844/ijol.2021.60599

Albrecht, S. L., Bakker, A. B., Gruman, J. A., Macey, W. H., & Saks, A. M. (2015). Employee engagement, human resource management practices and competitive advantage: An integrated approach. *Journal of Organizational Effectiveness: People and Performance, 2*(1), 7–35. doi:10.1108/JOEPP-08-2014-0042

Armstrong, M. (2008). *Strategic human resource management. A guide to action* (4th ed.). Kogan Page.

Barney, J. B. (1995). Looking inside for competitive advantage. *The Academy of Management Executive, 9*(4), 49–61. doi:10.5465/ame.1995.9512032192

Barney, J. B., & Wright, P. M. (1998). On becoming a strategic partner: The role of human resources in gaining competitive advantage. *Human Resource Management, 37*(1), 31–46. doi:10.1002/(SICI)1099-050X(199821)37:1<31::AID-HRM4>3.0.CO;2-W

Baum, T. (2015). Human resources in tourism: Still waiting for change? A 2015 reprise. *Tourism Management, 50*, 204–212. doi:10.1016/j.tourman.2015.02.001

Baum, T., & Hai, N. T. T. (2020). Hospitality, tourism, human rights and the impact of COVID-19. *International Journal of Contemporary Hospitality Management, 32*(7), 2397–2407. doi:10.1108/IJCHM-03-2020-0242

BBC News. (2020). Trump's virus travel ban on Europe comes into force. *BBC News.* https://www.bbc.com/news/world-us-canada-51883728

Belias, D., Papademetriou, C., Rossidis, I., & Vasiliadis L. (2020). Strategic Management in the Hotel Industry: Proposed Strategic Practices to Recover from COVID- 19 Global Crisis. *Academic Journal of Interdisciplinary Studies, 9*(6), 130 – 138. . doi:10.36941/ajis-2020-0117

Belias, D., Rosidis, I., & Velissariou, E. (2018). Shapting the consumers' behaviour who are using Airbnb- The case of airbnb's users in Greece. In Katsoni V. and Velander K., (Eds.) The Cultural and Sustainability Synergies. Springer. doi:10.1007/978-3-030-12453-3_10

Belias, D., Rossidis, I., Lazarakis, P., Mantas, C. & Ntalakos, A. (2022d). *Analyzing organizational factors in Greek Tourism Services.* Corporate & Business Strategy Review.

Belias, D., Rossidis, I., Ntalakos, A., & Trihas, N. (2022b). Digital Marketing: The Case of Digital Marketing Strategies on Luxurious Hotels. *Conference Proceedings of Centeris – DTI4T22 – Workshop on Digital Transformation & Industry 4.0 technologies*, Lisboa, Portugal.

Belias, D., Rossidis, I., Papademetriou, C., & Lamprinoudis, N. (2020d). The Greek Tourism Sector: An analysis of Job Satisfaction, Role Conflict and Autonomy of Greek Employees. *Journal of Human Resources in Hospitality & Tourism.* doi:10.1080/15332845.2021.1959825

Belias, D., Rossidis, I., Papademetriou, C., Mantas C. (2020c). Job Satisfaction as affected by Types of Leadership: A Case Study of Greek Tourism Sector. *Journal of Quality Assurance in Hospitality & Tourism, 10*(3), 39 – 45. doi:10.1080/1528008X.2020.1867695

Belias, D., Rossidis, I., Papademetriou, C., & Mantas, C. (2022e). Job satisfaction as affected by types of leadership: A case study of Greek tourism sector. *Journal of Quality Assurance in Hospitality & Tourism, 23*(2), 299–317. doi:10.1080/1528008X.2020.1867695

Belias, D., & Trichas, N. (2022) Strategic HRM approaches as mediators to change management I the tourism industry: Potential and prospects for future research. *Proceedings of Academicsera International Conference*, Hamburg, Germany.

Belias, D., & Trichas, N. (2022c) Strategic HRM approaches as mediators to change management in the tourism industry: Potential and prospects for future research. *Proceedings of Academicsera International Conference*, Hamburg, Germany.

Belias, D., & Trihas, N. (2022a). The relationship of the change context with the resilience of hotels: Proposal for a Research Framework on Hotels during the Covid-19 crisis. *ECRM, 21st European Conference on Research Methodology for Business and Management Studies*, Aveiro, Portugal.

Belias, D., & Trihas, N. (2022b). Human Resource Training of front office employees and change management in hospitality sector during crisis. *4th International Conference on Finance, Economics, Management and IT Business*. Scite Vents.

Belias, D., & Trihas, N. (2022d). Investigating the Readiness for Organizational Change: A Case Study from a Hotel Industry Context/Greece. *Journal of Tourism & Management Research, 7*(2), 1047–1062. doi:10.5281/zenodo.7090337

Belias, D., Trivellas, P., Koustelios, A., Serdaris, P., Varsanis, K., & Grigoriou, I. (2017). Human Resource Management, Strategic Leadership Development and the Greek Tourism Sector. In V. Katsoni, A. Upadhya, & A. Stratigea (Eds.), *Tourism, Culture and Heritage in a Smart Economy. Springer Proceedings in Business and Economics*. Springer. doi:10.1007/978-3-319-47732-9_14

Belias, D., Vasiliadis, L., & Mantas, C. (2020). The human resource training and development of employees working on luxurious hotels in Greece. *Cultural and Tourism Innovation in the Digital Era*, 639-648.

Belias, D., Vasiliadis, L., & Velissariou, E. (2020b). Internal Marketing in Tourism: The Case of Human Resource Empowerment on Greek Hotels. In V. Katsoni & T. Spyriadis (Eds.), *Cultural and Tourism Innovation in the Digital Era. Springer Proceedings in Business and Economics*. Springer., doi:10.1007/978-3-030-36342-0_43

Bonham, C., Edmonds, C., & Mak, J. (2006). The impact of 9/11 and other terrible global events on tourism in the United States and Hawaii. *Journal of Travel Research, 45*(1), 99–110. doi:10.1177/0047287506288812

Boselie, P. (2014). *Strategic human resource management: A balanced approach* (2nd ed.). McGraw-Hill Education.

Boxall, P., & Purcell, J. (2016). *Strategy and human resource management* (4th ed.). Palgrave. doi:10.1007/978-1-137-40765-8

Chand, M. (2010). The impact of HRM practices on service quality, customer satisfaction and performance in the Indian hotel industry. *International Journal of Human Resource Management, 21*(4), 551–566. doi:10.1080/09585191003612059

Channa, N. A., Shah, S. M. M., & Ghumro, N. H. (2019). Uncovering the link between strategic human resource management and crisis management: Mediating role of organizational resilience. *Annals of Contemporary Developments in Management & HR (ACDMHR)*, 2632-7686.

Cheng, S. C., & Kao, Y. H. (2022). The impact of the COVID-19 pandemic on job satisfaction: A mediated moderation model using job stress and organizational resilience in the hotel industry of Taiwan. *Heliyon, 8*(3), 09134. doi:10.1016/j.heliyon.2022.e09134 PMID:35342829

Collings, D. G., Wood, G. T., & Szamosi, L. T. (2019). *Human resource management. A critical approach* (2nd ed.). Routledge.

COVID-19 Coronavirus Pandemic. (2020). WorldoMeters. https://www.worldometers.info/coronavirus/

Covid-19 in Iceland. (2020). Covid.com. https://www.covid.is/data

Gil-Alana, L. A., & Huijbens, E. H. (2018). Tourism in Iceland: Persistence and seasonality. *Annals of Tourism Research, 68*, 20–29. doi:10.1016/j.annals.2017.11.002

Glaesser, D. (2006). *Crisis management in the tourism industry*. Elsevier. doi:10.4324/9780080464596

Government of Iceland. (2020). Iceland implements Schengen and EU travel restrictions. Government of Iceland. https://www.government.is/diplomaticmissions/embassy-article/2020/03/20/Iceland-implements-Schengen-and-EU-travelrestrictions-/

Huang, A., De la Mora Velasco, E., Marsh, J., & Workman, H. (2021). COVID-19 and the future of work in the hospitality industry. *International Journal of Hospitality Management, 97*, 1–13. doi:10.1016/j.ijhm.2021.102986 PMID:34720330

Jóhanesson, G. T., & Huijbens, E. H. (2010). Tourism in times of crisis: Exploring the discourse of tourism development in Iceland. *Current Issues in Tourism, 13*(5), 419–434. doi:10.1080/13683500.2010.491897

Johnson Tew, P., Lu, Z., Tolomiczenko, G., & Gellatly, J. (2008). SARS: Lessons in strategic planning for hoteliers and destination marketers. *International Journal of Contemporary Hospitality Management, 20*(3), 332–346. doi:10.1108/09596110810866145

Koutiva, M., Belias, D., Nietos, I. F., & Koustelios, A. (2020). The Effects of Workplace Well-Being on Individual's Knowledge Creation Outcomes: A Study Research Among Hotel Employees. In A. Kavoura, E. Kefallonitis, & P. Theodoridis (Eds.), *Strategic Innovative Marketing and Tourism. Springer Proceedings in Business and Economics*. Springer. doi:10.1007/978-3-030-36126-6_118

Kumar, D. (2020). Corona Virus: A Review of COVID-19. *Eurasian Journal of Medicine and Oncology, 4*(6), 15–23.

Kusluvan, S. (2003). *Managing employee attitudes and behaviors in the tourism and hospitality industry*. Nova Science Publishers, Inc.

Lai, Y. L., & Cai, W. (2022). Enhancing post-COVID-19 work resilience in hospitality: A micro-level crisis management framework. Sage. https://journals.sagepub.com/doi/pdf/10.1177/14673584221075182

Laws, E., Prideaux, B., & Chon, K. S. (2007). *Crisis management in tourism*. Cabi., doi:10.1079/9781845930479.0000

Le, D., & Phi, G. (2021). Strategic responses of the hotel sector to COVID-19: Toward a refined pandemic crisis management framework. *International Journal of Hospitality Management, 94*, 102808. doi:10.1016/j.ijhm.2020.102808 PMID:34785839

Lee, G. O. M., & Warner, M. (2005). Epidemics, labour markets and unemployment: The impact of SARS on human resource management in the Hong Kong service sector. *International Journal of Human Resource Management, 16*(5), 752–771. doi:10.1080/09585190500083202

Legge, K. (1995). *Human resource management: Rhetorics and realities*. Macmillan Press LTD. doi:10.1007/978-1-349-24156-9

Lisi, D. & Malo, M. A. (2017). The impact of temporary employment on productivity. The importance of sectors' skill intensity. *Journal for Labour Market Research, 50*, 258–271.

Marchington, M., & Wilkinson, A. (2005). *Human resource management at work. People management and development* (3rd ed.). Chartered Institute of Personnel and Development.

Maroudas, L., Kyriakidou, O. & Vacharis, A. (2008). *Employees' motivation in the luxury hotel industry: the perceived effectiveness of human-resource practices*. Taylor and Francis.

Mirzapour, M., Toutian, S. S., Mehrara, A., & Khorrampour, S. (2019). The strategic role of human resource management in crisis management considering the mediating role of organizational culture. *International Journal of Human Capital in Urban Management, 4*(1), 43–50.

Ngoc Su, D., Luc Tra, D., Thi Huynh, H. M., Nguyen, H. H. T., & O'Mahony, B. (2021). Enhancing resilience in the Covid-19 crisis: Lessons from human resource management practices in Vietnam. *Current Issues in Tourism, 24*(22), 3189–3205. doi:10.1080/13683500.2020.1863930

Nickson, D. (2007). *Human resource management for the hospitality and tourism industries.* Elsevier. doi:10.4324/9780080469461

Ntalakos, A., Belias, D., & Koustelios, A. (2022e). *The relationship between Leadership Styles & Communication – Effect on Team Efficiency: The case of Greek Hotel Businesses' employees.* In IACUDIT 2022, Semantic Scholar.

Ntalakos, A., Belias, D., Koustelios, A., & Tsigilis, N. (2022). Effect of Covid-19 on the Tourism Industry: Opportunities and Threats in Covid-19 Era. In *Proceedings of the 4th International Conference on Finance, Economics, Management and IT Business,* (pp. 107-114). Research Gate.

Ntalakos, A., Belias, D., Koustelios, A., & Tsigilis, N. (2022c). Organizational Culture and Group Dynamics in the Tourism Industry. *Proceedings of the 5th International Conference on Tourism Research 2022,* (pp. 286-293). Research Gate.

Ntalakos, A., Belias, D., Trihas, N. (2022b). The Impact of Covid-19 on Hospitality and Tourism Industry in Greece. *International Journal of Science and Research Methodology, 21*(1), 190–200

Ntalakos, A., Rossidis, I., & Belias, D. (2022d). Trait Emotional Intelligence & Leadership: A study of managers and employees. *21st European Conference on Research Methodology for Business and Management Studies,* Aveiro, Portugal.

Papadimitriou, D. B., Rodousakis, N., & Zezza, G. (2022). *Is Greece on the Road to Economic Recovery (No. sa_3_22).* Levy Economics Institute.

Park, E., Kim, W. H., & Kim, S. B. (2022). How does COVID-19 differ from previous crises? A comparative study of health-related crisis research in the tourism and hospitality context. *International Journal of Hospitality Management, 103,* 103199. doi:10.1016/j.ijhm.2022.103199 PMID:36540129

Pforr, C., & Hosie, P. J. (2008). Crisis management in tourism. Preparing for recovery. *Journal of Travel & Tourism Marketing, 23*(2-4), 249–264. doi:10.1300/J073v23n02_19

Roche, W. K., & Teague, P. (2012). Business partners and working the pumps: Human resource managers in the recession. *Human Relations, 65*(10), 1333–1358. doi:10.1177/0018726712451282

Rossidis, I., Belias, D., & Aspridis, G. (2020). *Change Management and Leadership (Διαχείριση Αλλαγών και Ηγεσία).* Tziolas. (in Greek)

Rossidis, I., Belias, D., & Vasiliadis, L. (2021a). Strategic Hotel Management in the "Hostile" International Environment. In V. Katsoni & C. van Zyl (Eds.), *Culture and Tourism in a Smart, Globalized, and Sustainable World. Springer Proceedings in Business and Economics.* Springer. doi:10.1007/978-3-030-72469-6_21

Rossidis, I., Belias, D., & Vasiliadis, L. (2021b). Strategic Human Resource Management in the International Hospitality Industry. An Extensive Literature Review. *Culture and Tourism in a Smart, Globalized, and Sustainable World,* 337-346.

Saad, S. (2013). Contemporary challenges of human resource planning in tourism and hospitality organizations: A conceptual model. *Journal of Human Resources in Hospitality & Tourism, 12*(4), 333–354. doi:10.1080/15332845.2013.790246

Schengen Visa Info. (2020). *EU decides to close all Schengen borders for 30 days.* Schengen Visa Info. https://www.schengenvisainfo.com/news/breaking-eu- decides-toclose-all-schengen-borders-for-30-days/

Skagias, K., Belias, D., Vasiliadis, L., & Christos, P. (2022). Digital Tourist Marketing: The Latest Developments and Recommendations on How Mykonos Can Take Advantage of Digital and Influencer Marketing. In V. Katsoni & A. C. Şerban (Eds.), *Transcending Borders in Tourism Through Innovation and Cultural Heritage. Springer Proceedings in Business and Economics.* Springer. doi:10.1007/978-3-030-92491-1_60

Tsaur, S. H., & Lin, Y. C. (2004). Promoting service quality in tourist hotels: The role of HRM practices and service behavior. *Tourism Management, 25*(4), 471–481. doi:10.1016/S0261-5177(03)00117-1

Tsiotas, D., Niavis, S., Belias, D., & Sdrolias, L. (2020). What Can the TripAdvisor Tell Us About the Complaints Management Strategies? The Case of the Greek Hotels. In A. Kavoura, E. Kefallonitis, & P. Theodoridis (Eds.), *Strategic Innovative Marketing and Tourism. Springer Proceedings in Business and Economics.* Springer. doi:10.1007/978-3-030-36126-6_111

Tyson, S., & Witcher, M. (1994). Getting in gear: Post recession HR management. *Personnel Management, 26*(8), 19–23.

Vardalier, P. (2016). Strategic approach to human resources management during crisis. In Procedia - Social and Behavioral Sciences, *12th International Strategic Management Conference,* Antalya, Turkey.

Varsanis, K., Belias, D., Kakkos, N., Chondrogiannis, M., Rossidis, I., & Mantas, C. (2019). The Relationship Between Service Quality and Customer Satisfaction on Luxurious Hotels So to Produce Error-Free Service. In A. Kavoura, E. Kefallonitis, & A. Giovanis (Eds.), *Strategic Innovative Marketing and Tourism. Springer Proceedings in Business and Economics.* Springer. doi:10.1007/978-3-030-12453-3_8

Viterouli, M., & Belias, D. (2021). True Organizational Learning Culture as a key to unlocking Operational Performance: A Critical Review. *Proceedings of the 37th International Business Information Management Association (IBIMA),* Cordoba, Spain.

Vo-Thanh, T., Vu, T. V., Nguyen, N. P., Nguyen, D. V., Zaman, M., & Chi, H. (2021). COVID-19, frontline hotel employees' perceived job insecurity and emotional exhaustion: Does trade union support matter? *Journal of Sustainable Tourism,* 1–18.

World Health Organization. (2020a). *Q&A on coronavirus (COVID-19).* WHO. https://www.who.int/emergencies/diseases/novel- coronavirus2019/question-and-answers-hub/q-a-detail/q-a-coronaviruses

World Health Organization. (2020b). WHO timeline – COVID-19. WHO. https://www.who.int/newsroom/detail/27-04-2020-who-timeline---covid-

World Travel & Tourism Council. (2019). Travel & tourism economic impact 2019. World Travel & Tourism Council. https://wttc.org/Research/Economic-Impact

Chapter 5
Future of Sustainable Tourism:
Opportunities in Health, Sports, Alternative Tourism, and Analysis of How Sustainable Tourism Will Be Shaped Post COVID-19

Dimitrios Belias
University of Thessaly, Greece

Ioannis Rossidis
Hellenic Open University, Greece

Angelos Ntalakos
University of Thessaly, Greece

Nikolaos Trihas
Department of Business Administration and Tourism, Hellenic Mediterranean University, Greece

ABSTRACT

Tourism today is in a critical crossroad, not only due of the changes on the structure of the tourist industry where the focus has shifted from mass tourism to alternative tourism, but also the question on how the tourist industry will cope with the case of the Covid-19 crisis. Still, the tourist industry does not know what the future of the sector can be. Therefore, the purpose of this paper is to investigate and make suggestions on how the future will shape sustainable tourism. This is a literature review in an ongoing phenomenon which is the Covid-19 pandemic. Hence, this chapter will rely on both the existing literature review and on published scientific papers. Nonetheless, it is crucial to refer to the fact that there is a lack of research on this issue. For this reason, the authors will expand their research on articles and reports published on the internet so to have the latest updates on this issue.

DOI: 10.4018/978-1-6684-6055-9.ch005

Copyright © 2023, IGI Global. Copying or distributing in print or electronic forms without written permission of IGI Global is prohibited.

INTRODUCTION

Tourism is an economic activity which is affected by a number of factors found on the environment of the tourist industry (Belias et al., 2020; Belias et al., 2018; Belias et al., 2017; Koutiva et al., 2019; Rossidis et al., 2021; Rossidis et al., 2021b; Rossidis et al., 2019; Rossidis et al., 2019b; Belias and Trihas, 2022d; Belias and Trihas, 2022e; Belias and Trihas, 2022f; Ntalakos et al., 2022c; Ntalakos et al., 2022d; Belias et al., 2022; Belias et al., 2022b; Belias et al., 2022c; Belias et al., 2022d). During the past months the tourist industry, like every economic activity on this world has been affected by the pandemic of COVID-19 (Belias and Trihas, 2022a; Belias and Trihas, 2020b; Belias and Trihas, 2022c;). On many cases, demand for tourist services has collapsed or even disappeared (Polyzos et al, 2020). The pandemic has some unique characteristics that cannot be found on similar crises which affected the tourist industry, such as the 9/11. For example there is a high uncertainty and it is not easy to predict when tourism will be back in normal but also how this may happen (Gössling et al., 2020). Another feature is that there is not guarantee as on how tourists can be safe and what needs to be done so to ensure their safety, something that increases uncertainty among the tourists who are hesitating to travel when there are not travel bans due of the pandemic (Ghosh, 2020; Ntalakos et al., 2022; Ntalakos et al., 2022b; Belias et al., 2020b).

From the above it is understood that tourism has to face a severe crisis where there is not a guarantee blueprint to recovery. The tourist destinations and businesses must find ways to continue their operations during several crises (Belias et al., 2022a) but also to find ways to ensure not only the satisfaction but also the health of their guests. Romagosa (2020) claims that despite of the negative situation for the tourist industry, there are opportunities for sustainable and proximity tourism. For example, Fletcher et al (2020) argues that the current control and restrictions on the mobility of tourists, as it has been imposed by governments, indicates that where there is a will and a consensus from the society and the government to do so, hence it is possible to regulate the flows of tourists based on the sustainability of the destination something that before the pandemic was argued that it was not possible. Hence, the pandemic of COVID-19 can create new opportunities for sustainable tourism. However, there is a need to provide some investigation on this in order to conceptualize the different issues and factors which will determine on how there can be opportunities for sustainable tourism in the post-COVID 19 era. Therefore, the aim of this chapter is to investigate what are the opportunities for sustainable tourism in the post-covid 19 era and how to conceptualize them.

This chapter has great value since it can indicate on the academia and on professionals how sustainable tourism will develop after the pandemic and it can be the starting point for future empirical researches. It is a literature review which combines the existing theories on sustainable tourism with the latest publications on this issue. The material used has been retrieve from online search engines such as Scholar Google and EBSCO. It is important to note that the current literature is limited and there is a lack of empirical evidence which is the key limitation on this subject.

INTRODUCTION ON SUSTAINABLE TOURISM

Tourism is a process that requires a series of decisions taken by stakeholders to coordinate and organize strategic planning in order to achieve the long-term goals set (Azzone and Noci, 1998).

Future of Sustainable Tourism

In recent years, tourism has been directly linked to sustainable development and many areas are promoting alternative tourism (Belias et al, 2022c) in order to support development efforts while minimizing the negative effects that mass tourism has despite the investment and tourism demand it has with tourist accommodation based on mass (Liu, 2003). Tourist development as a concept was first introduced in 1980 by the U.N. (United Nations) where proposals were made for a series of changes in the approach to lifestyle and the promotion of the tourism product, while the proposals in the way of governance based on sustainability were also important. In addition, tourism and local development were re-examined in 1993 by the W.H.O. (World Tourism Organization) based on sustainability and a number of environmentally friendly practices were proposed in order to (Rahmafitria, et al, 2020):

- Reduce pollutant emissions, save water and use less energy
- Reduce the operating costs of hotel units
- Minimize the payback time of investments for hotels and tourism investments
- Increase the value of units and tourist accommodation
- Expand the customer base for tourism itself but also for the organization of days, conferences and business meetings as many of the aforementioned activities are now organized in hotels.

The environmental aspect has been taken into account as a component for development relatively recently (Belias et al., 2022b) because in previous decades tourism was linked to economic development and economic benefit was seen as a driving force for tourism entrepreneurship. On the other hand, sustainability has taken into account the satisfaction of the needs that the current generation; although this generation is guided by the environmental and social balance of the next generations through the rational use of natural resources which presupposes rational development (Azzone and Noci, 1998).

Sustainability in tourism and sustainability in general are two concepts that are considered almost identical. On the one hand, sustainability concerns the alternative ways of tourism development and the promotion of their ecological dimension; on the other hand, sustainability adopts the protection of the environment as the main concern of the tourist perspective and is based on attracting visitors along with the protection of natural and cultural resources of the country (Azzone and Noci, 1998).

Through sustainable development, the necessary conditions are created for every activity to be sustainable and sustainable, which leads to setting a limit on the exploitation of natural and cultural resources meant for development, so that entrepreneurship on the one hand is profitable and on the other hand is balanced ecologically (Gerlach, 2003). Sustainable development is directly related to tourism as both are based on the quality of the features of the product promotion through timelessness. According to the 1987 Brundland Report, sustainability takes into account the current needs of tourism, without ignoring the needs that will arise in the future and will need to be met through sustainable development, existing resources are maintained and strengthened while the needs of future generations are upgraded. As a result, the needs of today's tourists are met, while the needs of the future are enhanced through the preservation of cultural integrity, the support of essential ecological processes, the enhancement and protection of biodiversity, and the promotion of sustainable lifestyles (Middleton et al, 2009).

Through sustainable development, the products that will emerge no longer contribute to the disruption of the harmony of the environment, society and culture as the way of approaching the object by those involved in the process changes (Azzone and Noci, 1998). In addition, through this process, the quality of the products receives competitive advantages as the positive image of the projected areas contributes to the increase of business revenues and the increase of tourist traffic.

As for the main resources of the tourist areas that attract tourism, they are:

- Natural resources and the environment in general
- Cultural resources and monuments
- Social resources and benefits to the visitor

In addition, the tourist resources provided to visitors are:

- The provision of accommodation
- The organization of trips
- Catering facilities
- Transportation
- Leisure and entertainment
- Information and briefing
- The facilities and infrastructure provided to the visitor (Middleton et al, 2009).

Tourism is a sector that is constantly growing with international arrivals for 2019 reaching 1.5 billion tourists according to data collected by the World Tourism Organization. Tourism is projected to continue to grow, reaching 1.8 billion international tourists by 2030, although this number may be reconsidered due to the covid-19 pandemic (Rasoolimanesh et al., 2020).

International tourism, which receives a lot of attention, is in fact a domestic product that represents a large part of the market. The tourist trips that take place every year often exceed the world population (Gössling et al., 2016). Thus, global tourism contributes to the economy by more than $ 7 trillion or a total of 10.2% of world GDP.

Due to the fact that tourism is of great economic importance, it has been studied a lot and it is not surprising that its negative effects on the environment and society are often mentioned. Therefore, due to the fact that there is a lot of interest in the impact of tourism, sustainability is a key element that is further explored when we talk about tourism and the economy. It is therefore clear that even sporadic and non-systematic monitoring of the impact of traffic in places with low carrying capacity should be considered. Significant efforts are also being made to benchmark the impact of the indicators that highlight the sustainability of the implementation of tourism policies given the importance that these indicators have for the protection of a place. Thus, sustainable tourism development is a key element of the United Nations agenda that promotes sustainable tourism by monitoring and controlling the use of natural resources as tourism develops but also encouraging environmental protection and job creation efforts, both in culture and in the environment with the promotion of local products and marine elements that make many countries popular for their special tourist product. Therefore, these indicators mentioned above are a key focus for tourism and sustainable development (Hall et al., 2018).

The development of these indicators gradually leads to the strategic monitoring of places that receive large volumes of tourists and is considered as an integral part of assessing the progress towards a sustainable development of a place. At the same time, in this way the sustainability of the tourism product can be studied (Stoddard et al., 2012). For the measurement of sustainable tourism indicators, an important element is the effects of tourism itself, although many times these effects cannot be completely controlled. Thus, the importance of monitoring the indicators and the bearing capacity of a place for the balance that must exist between economy, society and environment is highlighted.

Future of Sustainable Tourism

In the light of today, there is an urgent need for entrepreneurship to benefit from the development of sustainability in tourism and to initiate a series of extensive structural changes in tourism that will give basis to its sustainability and environmental protection. This fact is especially important in the current era where criticisms are taking place mainly from the academic sector around the concept of sustainability, which emphasize the need to reconsider the carrying capacity of a place and the resilience of an area (Hall, 2018). For example, the current coronavirus season is a disaster for tourism where human activities are changing and therefore more emphasis is being placed on climate change and the unpredictable effects of the pandemic on the environment, which leads scientists to think about sustainability of the tourism industry and travel, in double, opening a debate that has begun a few years earlier to limit the uncontrolled growth of the international tourism sector. This shows that there should be a development strategy that will give weight to the environment, especially in areas that receive an excessive volume of tourism. Since the excessive reception of tourism has nothing to do with development, there should be a voluntary protection and a planned contraction towards the environment and society when we talk about tourism entrepreneurship (Rasoolimanesh et al., 2020).

Now, the authors and researchers point out that there should be restrictions and controls on the mobility of people, especially at a time when the coronavirus crisis prevails, so that the rules of health protection can be enforced with the help of a political consensus that can make these structural changes. Despite the fact that the current era creates a lot of uncertainty, the strengthening of tourism and environmental protection is considered imperative and should now be based on the fact that the tourist must first acquire social and environmental awareness (Lew, 2020).

Thus, after the crisis that prevails at this time, tourists should have learned to choose destinations that are safe and close to their homes, reducing their environmental footprint and at the same time strengthening the local economy. In this context of insecurity and uncertainty, nearby destinations should be highlighted and considered the least risky by the visitor while they can enable local economies to strengthen and positively affect the economic crisis, which prevails at the moment.

At the same time, this focus on nearby tourist destinations may affect the purchasing power of these areas, which today due to this crisis has decreased, while at the same time the total carbon emissions from the nearest trips will decrease, something that can align with the new reality by promoting a new sustainable model.

SUSTAINABLE TOURISM IN THE COVID-19 ERA

Coronavirus is a virus that has hit the world with the number of confirmed cases doubling rapidly and being linked to a series of extremely common symptoms that started in China and Japan and ended throughout the European Union such as Germany and Austria (Belias and Trihas, 2022a; Skagias et al., 2021; Belias et al., 2021). The rate of infection accelerated through the Member States of the European Union until April 15 and the confirmed cases reached 2 million cases with more than 125,000 deaths. This means that more than 200 countries were affected by the coronavirus (ECDC, 2020) with the true total number of cases still unknown as the cases identified were the cases that have been tested. Although countries are constantly testing for further cases, the world is currently without a vaccine to prevent the disease and medical interventions are quite limited so there is not much data available to treat the coronavirus. Isolation at home and voluntary quarantine is something that has greatly affected tourism

Future of Sustainable Tourism

as well as workplaces with entrepreneurship collapsing, dragging tourism and traffic to countries outside the place of residence (Gössling et al., 2020).

At the same time, many events which attract people, were postponed, such as large sessions and exhibitions, as well as concerts and festivals, and sports events such as the Olympic Games. At the same time, gatherings of people are prohibited, making it impossible for visitors interested in a state to get to know it up close as they cannot go there as a group. International regional and local travel restrictions have affected both the national economy and the tourism system as a whole as international travel has declined enormously at air, cruise and public transport (Gössling et al., 2020).

International air travel has slowed sharply as a result of the crisis and the borders have been closed so that the populations of the Member States can find themselves in quarantine periods that will significantly reduce cases. Thus, within a few weeks, tourism was severely affected and although many countries tried to return to normalcy, travelers were no longer interested in visiting the destination countries as the coronavirus transmission is particularly high. A typical case is the case of England where the country's foreign minister urged British citizens to return to their homeland, advising them not to travel by air or by boat, while it was decided to suspend flights and airports were closed with no exit and further restrictions that are necessary to reduce the phenomenon (The Foreign & Commonwealth Office, 2020).

At the same time, cases such as cruising soon became the worst case scenario for tourism as the transmissibility on cruise ships was extremely high. A typical case is the one of the Diamond Princess which was a cruise ship with many coronavirus infections that sailed on March 26, 2020 and which was forced to remain at sea as it could not find a port to anchor (Mallapaty, 2020).

Thus, an ideally safe sea environment turned into a huge trap with passengers being quarantined inside the ship in the cabins and facing challenges when they had to return home. At the same time, the coronavirus affected the hospitality in accommodation as a whole, while many events were canceled and many accommodations were left without customers, while there were also problems in the supply chain of the hotel sector. Unfortunately the hit in tourism was so hard that many companies, such as the British company Flybe, were forced to file for bankruptcy. Other companies, including companies such as the German TUI, have already requested compensation and assistance from the state (Gössling et al., 2020).

In the light of this particular health crisis due to the pandemic, a huge economic and social debate began in which many questions were asked about the impact that this pandemic has on tourism in the long run and in the short run. Given that this crisis is particularly widespread and has come as a surprise, the predictions that are being made are not yet quite realistic. However, there is a hope that many things will change at the socio-economic level which will have an impact on tourism and improve mobility as well as consumption patterns and leisure when the pandemic is over. However, so far, the coronavirus has negative dimensions in social life and based on the data available so far, the tourism sector is moving downwards and this affects the lives of travelers as a whole and in reality and their online communication (Yu et al., 2020).

Based on the precautionary measures that have been taken and the developments that prevail in Asia, the World Tourism Organization emphasizes that the decrease, which is found in 20% to 30% of tourist arrivals for 2020 compared to 2019, seems that the prevailing variability will create a new profile for the visitor in the coming years and is likely to enhance both cruising and hospitality due to the fact that tourists still have hopes for an improved and of better quality holiday season. However, it should be emphasized that the economic and social turmoil that exists so far is unprecedented (Romagosa, 2020)

Researchers today argue that tourism is a fairly resilient sector that has the ability to adapt to new data and can even recover from catastrophic phenomena. Although the ordeal that tourism is going through

Future of Sustainable Tourism

is very serious and difficult and often creates stress for travelers, it is a situation that will pass. Thus, many analysts argue that when the worst scenario is over, a timetable will gradually be set that will lead to a new normality and a situation that will be similar to the period before the coronavirus crisis. This is something that is expected by all entrepreneurs in the tourism industry who are still hoping for an improved situation and a recovery of tourism immediately after this difficult situation (Navarro Jurado et al., 2020).

CONCEPTUALIZATION OF THE OPPORTUINITIES FOR SUSTAINABLE TOURISM IN THE POST-PANDEMIC ERA

Currently there are many destinations with travel restrictions while none can ensure on whether 2021 will be the years that tourism will be back and how this will happen. Nonetheless, this chapter can develop a conceptual framework on the opportunities which may arise for sustainable tourism and what the practitioners need to do so to ensure that their travel business will be on the front line when tourism will be back. Therefore the following lines will examine a number of issues which will help to understand the opportunities created in the post-pandemic era. It will take the form of questions and answers in order to deliver the final output which is a model.

Which Tourist Development Model to Adopt?

An issue which was examined in detail the previous years was the shift of the tourist industry towards niche tourism which is related with sustainable tourism. Nonetheless, it is important to note the gap between what the theory claims and what is reality on the tourist industry. During the previous years many authors defended niche tourism and the shift from overcrowded tourism into a sustainable model where tourism relies on fewer inflows and on tourists from middle and upper social classes (Linca et al, 2013).

However, in practice many destinations tried to combined sustainable tourism but elements of mass tourism. Despite of the overall sentiment that mass tourism hurts the environment and it in the long term it has a negative impact on the destinations, the reality was that tourist businesses must make profit so to continue their operations; hence they need tourists and many cases they need the crowds, which contradicts what is said on many publications and theories (Gurso et al, 2010).

The mass vs niche tourism models have been contradicted from Weaver (2014) who referred on "enlightened mass tourism". The two dichotomous models of tourist development (mass and sustainable tourism) are challenged from an alternative model of tourist development. More precisely, the first generation of tourist development relied on mass tourism and on huge tourist development. The second generation came during the 1990's with the introduction of sustainable tourism. Hughes et al (2015) claim that both models are useful but also both models have some serious limitations and contradictions. As it has been said on the previous lines, a tourist business / destination surely need sustainability but also it needs tourist so to be financial viable and sustainable at the same time. Therefore both models are characterized from substantive contradictions that negate these claims – hence the stagnation. For this reason a "third generation" has been developed which is a synthesis of the previous two generations. Instead of the antithesis that the two models had developed between theme, the enlightened mass tourism is combing the benefits of both models and it reduces their limitations. (Hughes et al, 2015).

Future of Sustainable Tourism

While many authors, such as Hakim (2020), believe that the pandemic of COVID-19 doomed mass-tourism, there is a contradictive opinion from Jugănaru (2020) who argue that the post-covid19 tourist industry needs tourists so to have a rapid financial recovery and this can be made with enlightened mass tourism.

Therefore, the post-pandemic era surely will strengthen sustainable tourism but a pragmatic view is that the tourist industry will not have to snob mass tourism but to find a genuine way to combine mass and sustainable tourism under the concept of enlightened mass tourism. Of course, it is upon the decision makers on each destination and tourist business to decide which model of tourist development match better their post-pandemic operations.

Which Types of Alternative Tourism will Have Advantage in the Post-pandemic era?

One of the advantages of alternative tourism is that it has a plethora of activities which are adjust on the environmental and other resources that the destination can offer. For example a mountain resort can offer mountain tourism activities such as hiking, skiing etc. On the other hand, megacities offer other types of tourism including sport and event tourism. However, in the post-pandemic era the destinations cannot rely – or better say shall not rely at all – on mega events. It is well accepted that mega-events can bring a number of benefits for the destinations where mega events can be a vehicle for tourist development, while the infrastructure left (hotels, roads, transportation systems and the know-how on managing events and tourist crowds) can be the basis of the tourist development for many years (Tien et al, 2011). In the post-pandemic era this is not certain that it will happen. Actually, it may take several years to see again a mega event which will have a tourist impact. The fact that a sports event requires a significant number of athletes, fans etc. means that currently is impossible to think of any major event on packed stadiums (Mann et al, 2020).

At this point comes the question on which type of alternative tourism can be prolific in the post-pandemic era? What is sure is that the answer is not clear, and the related literature is limited. Higgins-Desbiolles (2020) argues that surely sustainable events which gather large crowds are out of question. For example, Tokyo's Olympic Games were postponed for 2021 and it is not sure if and how they will take place. Surely, a major sport event without fans will not bring any benefits. On the other hand, the pandemic offers are rare and invaluable opportunity for responsible and ethical tourism. Actually, tourism can make a restart where the community-centered tourist activities will take advantage. For example, major sport events can be postponed, but small-scale sport tourism events such as trail running can take place and benefit all of the stakeholders. Ludvigsen & Hayton (2020) argue that the types of sustainable sport tourism events which will benefit in the post-pandemic era are the events which will be in a safe environment for the participants, while Mann et al (2020) agree with that view. Ioannides & Gyimóthy (2020) implies that the tourist industry needs to forget any mass event and it needs to concentrate on alternative forms of tourism which will "greener" and with respect on local communities and on the health of tourists. Those activities may include mountain tourist activities, such as hiking, cultural tourism, religion tourism and similar forms of sustainable tourism. Actually, the forms for tourism which will benefit on the post-pandemic are the ones addressed for small groups and not on the urban environment. Hence, tourist activities such as city breaks probably will not benefit, while smaller cities and suburbs may benefit due to the fact that tourists will avoid overcrowded cities, while they would prefer destinations which have easy access on alternative activities such as biking (Jiricka-Pürrer et al, 2020).

Future of Sustainable Tourism

To sum up, it is not easy to justify which alternative tourism activities can benefit on the post-pandemic era. However, there are some speculations and assumptions which focus on emphasis on alternative types of tourist activity which include small or even no crowds with respect on local communities and the physical environment. On the other hand, alternative tourism activities related with events on the cities or events which gather crowds, including major sport events and city breaks are going to face difficulties in the post-pandemic era.

What will Determine Tourist Quality in the Post-pandemic era?

An important question is what the tourists will consider as "tourist quality" in the post-pandemic era. What is for sure is that it is not possible to "calculate" the impacts of the Covid-19 pandemic on the tourist industry nor to consider how the tourist's profile will be. However, there can be some thoughts on what factors will determine the tourist quality in the post-pandemic era.

The traditional models of tourist quality focus on issues how the services are delivered as they are promised to the customers, the empathy of the service provide towards the tourist (Budeanu, 2007), the value of money and the ability to handle with care the moments of truth (Zhang et al, 2019) and the feeling created among the tourists that their tourist activities do not have a negative effect on the social values and the physical environment of the destination (Yu et al, 2011).

All of the above are variables that for the post-pandemic sustainable tourist organization must be considered as well established. However, there are some new variables which will affect the perception that tourists will have about service quality. Those includes measures such as having strict regulations and follow by heart the health protocols so to ensure the guests' and the society's health (Jiricka-Pürrer et al, 2020). Santos-Roldán et al (2020) argue that the current crisis caused by COVID-19 can benefit sustainable tourism. Through empirical research Santos-Roldán et al (2020) argue that responsible tourism can be the key to success on the post-pandemic era. This means that tourist destinations should promote sustainability on less crowded destinations. This can favor social distancing along with a strict enforcement of health protocols that can ensure the success for sustainable tourism. The research made by Santos-Roldán et al (2020) indicates that sustainable tourist businesses which focus on health protocols are the most popular choices among sustainable-driven tourists, while health tourism for those who want to recover from COVID-19 will also have an important segment. Many of those tourists are willing to pay something extra in order to have a "covid-free" experience. Furthermore, Escobar et al. (2020) have made empirical research which indicates that wealthy women are more demand than men in terms of health measures taken on hotels. Also, innovation is considered an important aspect which will attract the interest of potential customers. For example, Wan et al (2020) have argued that the use of robots can ensure social distancing on several front-line services, while there is an overall sense that the use of robots increases service quality (Belias, 2020; Belias et al., 2021b; Belias and Vasiliadis, 2021; Belias and Vasiliadis, 2022).

Conceptualizing the Opportunities on Sustainable Tourism

The above paragraphs have described how sustainable tourism will shape in the post-pandemic era. It is important to express that the environment is unclear and hence it is not easy to make any certain prediction on how and when tourism will be back. However, this chapter is able to produce a model which will help the decision makers, the academia and the practitioners to consider a number of factor that will determine how sustainable tourism will shape in the post-covid19 era. These factors are presented on Table 1:

Table 1. Factors shaping the opportunities in the post-pandemic era

Factors shaping the opportunities in the post-pandemic era	Description	Related authors
Tourist development model	There are three tourist development models which have been discussed. The first one, which is mass tourism, is excluded due of the negative effects that it has on tourism development. The second model which is sustainable tourism which is the dominant model. Nonetheless, the third choice is the "enlightened mass tourism" which is a combination of the two other models. It is argued that the latter model shall be seriously considered in the light that tourist businesses need to fully recover and generate income but also to respect the environment. Hence, the second and the third choice shall be considered on how they can create opportunities for the tourist industry	Hakim (2020), Jugănaru (2020)
Which type of alternative tourist activity to consider?	There is a plethora of alternative modes of tourism that we can consider. However, it seems that the consumer's preference moves towards the less crowded types of tourism activity, "greener" activities and also those who are considered as being away from cities. For example, some modes of sports tourism can benefit, such as hiking and trail running games, but not mega events such as the Olympic Games.	Mann et al, (2020) Higgins-Desbiolles (2020) Ioannides & Gyimóthy (2020) Jiricka-Pürrer et al, (2020)
Determinants of tourism quality	Besides the traditional factors, opportunities can be created from the hygiene protocols, a promise for a covid-19 free tourist experience and measures to ensure social distancing such as the use of Robots. Though still it is not easy to portray the profile of tourists, it seems that wealthy women are the most demanding segments.	Santos-Roldán et al (2020) Escobar et al (2020) Wan et al (2020)

The above variables can create a model which will help to determine who sustainable tourism can create opportunities in the post-pandemic era. For instance, as it is described on Table 1, "the enlightened mass tourism" could be connected with "greener" alternative tourism activities (such as hiking) where the sport travel agencies as well as the mountain hospitality residences should apply all the hygiene protocols in order to make a safe relaxing healthy environment for the upcoming guests (tourists).

Of course, there is a need to further investigate this issue and examine the validity of this model so as to be further examined and developed in future research that will help the academia and practitioners to better understand what opportunities may appear in the post-pandemic era and how they can take advantage of those opportunities.

CONCLUSION

Currently the tourist industry tries to understand how the post-pandemic era will shape tourist operations, especially those related to sustainable tourism. By the existing literature it seems that some modes and types of sustainable tourism can benefit in the post-pandemic era. Of course, there is the fact that there is a high uncertainty and it is not sure when and how this crisis will end, and therefore the academia can make some suggestions but it needs to update them frequently. Overall, it seems that ethical modes of tourist activity along with the tourist activities taking place on rural areas which ensure health protocols may have the potential advantage.

This chapter has developed a number of factors shaping the opportunities in the post-pandemic era. This brings the need to examine these factors with a further research which will examine which factors are considered the most important regarding the tourist industry and whether there is a need to reconsider some of those factor or add some new ones as a result of a primary research and of examining the updates on the current literature.

REFERENCES

Azzone, G., & Noci, G. (1998). Seeing ecology and "green" innovations as a source of change. *Journal of Organizational Change Management, 11*(2), 94–111. doi:10.1108/09534819810212106

Belias, D. (2020). Research Methods on the Contribution of Robots in the Service Quality of Hotels. In *Strategic Innovative Marketing and Tourism* (pp. 939–946). Springer. doi:10.1007/978-3-030-36126-6_104

Belias, D., Papademetriou, C., Rossidis, I., Vasiliadis L. (2020b). Strategic Management in the Hotel Industry: Proposed Strategic Practices to Recover from COVID- 19 Global Crisis. *Academic Journal of Interdisciplinary Studies, 9*(6), 130 – 138. . doi:10.36941/ajis-2020-0117

Belias, D., Rossidis, I., Lazarakis, P., Mantas, C. & Ntalakos, A. (2022d). *Analyzing organizational factors in Greek Tourism Services.* Corporate & Business Strategy Review.

Belias, D., Rossidis, I., Papademetriou, C., & Lamprinoudis, N. (2020). The Greek Tourism Sector: An analysis of Job Satisfaction, Role Conflict and Autonomy of Greek Employees. *Journal of Human Resources in Hospitality & Tourism.* doi:10.1080/15332845.2021.1959825

Belias, D., Rossidis, I., Papademetriou, C., & Mantas, C. (2022b). Job satisfaction as affected by types of leadership: A case study of Greek tourism sector. *Journal of Quality Assurance in Hospitality & Tourism, 23*(2), 299–317. doi:10.1080/1528008X.2020.1867695

Belias, D., Rossidis, I., Papademetriou, C., & Valeri, M. (2022c). Destination Governance: The Role of Local Authorities in Greek Tourism Marketing. In Valeri M. (Ed.) New Governance and Management in Touristic Destinations, 1- 18. IGI Global.

Belias, D., Rossidis, I., Sotiriou, A., & Malik, S. (2022). Workplace Conflict, Turnover, and Quality of Services. Case Study in Greek Seasonal Hotels. *Journal of Quality Assurance in Hospitality & Tourism,* 1–24. doi:10.1080/1528008X.2022.2065655

Belias, D., Rossidis, I., & Valeri, M. (2022a). Tourism in Crisis: The Impact of Climate Change on the Tourism Industry. Valeri, M. (Ed.) Tourism Risk, Emerald Publishing Limited. Bingley. doi:10.1108/978-1-80117-708-520221012

Belias, D., Rossidis, I., Vasiliadis, L., & Papademetriou, C. (2021). Utilizing strategic tools in hotel industry in the era of pandemic. *Proceedings of the 37th International Business Information Management Association (IBIMA)*, Cordoba, Spain.

Belias, D., & Trichas, N. (2022b) Strategic HRM approaches as mediators to change management I the tourism industry: Potential and prospects for future research. *Proceedings of Academicsera International Conference,* Hamburg, Germany.

Belias, D., & Trihas, N. (2022a). The relationship of the change context with the resilience of hotels: Proposal for a Research Framework on Hotels during the Covid-19 crisis. *ECRM, 21st European Conference on Research Methodology for Business and Management Studies,* Aveiro, Portugal.

Belias, D., & Trihas, N. (2022c). Human Resource Training of Front Office Employees and Change Management in Hospitality Sector during Crisis. In *Proceedings of the 4th International Conference on Finance, Economics, Management, and IT Business.* Research Gate.

Belias, D., & Trihas, N. (2022d). Investigating the Readiness for Organizational Change: A Case Study from a Hotel Industry Context/Greece. *Journal of Tourism & Management Research*, 7(2), 1047–1062. doi:10.5281/zenodo.7090337

Belias, D., & Trihas, N. (2022e). How can we measure the "Resistance to Change?" An exploratory Factor Analysis in a sample of employees in the Greek Hotel Industry. In *IACUDIT 2022 Conference Proceedings*. Research Gate.

Belias, D., & Trihas, N. (2022f). How can we measure the "Success of Change Management?" An exploratory Factor Analysis in a sample of employees in the Greek Hotel Industry. *In IACUDIT 2022 Conference Proceedings*. Research Gate.

Belias, D., Trivellas, P., Koustelios, A., Serdaris, P., Varsanis, K., & Grigoriou, I. (2017). Human Resource Management, Strategic Leadership Development and the Greek Tourism Sector. In V. Katsoni, A. Upadhya, & A. Stratigea (Eds.), *Tourism, Culture and Heritage in a Smart Economy. Springer Proceedings in Business and Economics*. Springer. doi:10.1007/978-3-319-47732-9_14

Belias, D., & Vasiliadis, L. (2021). A Conceptual Study of Proposing a Model to Use Robots in Hospitality Industry based on the Empirical Evidences. *Journal of Tourism and Management Research.*, 6(1), 830–841. doi:10.26465/ojtmr.2018339544

Belias, D., & Vasiliadis, L. (2022). Robots on the Tourist Industry—A Review for Future Research Directions. In V. Katsoni & A. C. Şerban (Eds.), *Transcending Borders in Tourism Through Innovation and Cultural Heritage. Springer Proceedings in Business and Economics*. Springer. doi:10.1007/978-3-030-92491-1_23

Belias, D., Vasiliadis, L., & Rossidis, I. (2021b). The Intention and Expectations of Modern Robotic Technologies in the Hotel Industry. *Journal of Quality Assurance in Hospitality & Tourism.* doi:10.10 80/1528008X.2021.1995566

Belias, D., Velissariou, E., & Rossidis, I. (2018). The contribution of HRM on the development of effective organizational culture in hotel units—The case of Greek hotels. In Exploring smart tourism: The cultural and sustainability synergies. Springer.

Budeanu, A. (2007). Sustainable tourist behaviour–a discussion of opportunities for change. *International Journal of Consumer Studies*, 31(5), 499–508. doi:10.1111/j.1470-6431.2007.00606.x

Future of Sustainable Tourism

Escobar, A. L., López, R. R., Campos, A. M., & López-Felipe, T. (2020). Differences between women and men regarding the security measures required of the hotel sector to deal with COVID-19.

European Centre for Disease Prevention and Control (ECDC). (2020). *COVID-19 Situation update worldwide.* ECDC. https://www.ecdc.europa.eu/en/geographical-distribution-2019-ncov-cases [28/10/2020]

FCO (The Foreign & Commonwealth Office). (2020). *Foreign Secretary advises all British travelers to return to the UK now.* FCO. https://www.gov.uk/government/news/foreign-secretary-advises-all-british-travellers-to-return-to-the-uk-now [28/10/2020]

Fletcher, R., Murray, I. M., Blázquez-Salom, M., & Asunción, B. R. (2020). Tourism, degrowth, and the COVID-19 Crisis. POLLEN *Ecology Network.* https://politicalecologynet-work.org/2020/03/24/tourism-degrowth-and-the-covid-19-crisis/ [18/10/2020]

Gerlach, A. (2003). Sustainable entrepreneurship and innovation, Centre for Sustainability Management, University of Lueneburg. In *Conference Proceedings of Conference Corporate Social Responsibility and Environmental Management* (pp. 1-10). Springer.

Ghosh, S. (2020). Asymmetric impact of COVID-19 induced uncertainty on inbound Chinese tourists in Australia: Insights from nonlinear ARDL model. *Quantitative Finance and Economics, 4*(2), 343–351. doi:10.3934/QFE.2020016

Gössling, S., Ring, A., Dwyer, L., Andersson, A. C., & Hall, C. M. (2016). Optimizing or maximizing growth? A challenge for sustainable tourism. *Journal of Sustainable Tourism, 24*(4), 527–548. doi:10.1080/09669582.2015.1085869

Gössling, S., Scott, D., & Hall, C. M. (2020). Pandemics, tourism and global change: A rapid assessment of COVID-19. *Journal of Sustainable Tourism, 29*(10), 1–20.

Gursoy, D., Chi, C. G., & Dyer, P. (2010). Locals' attitudes toward mass and alternative tourism: The case of Sunshine Coast, Australia. *Journal of Travel Research, 49*(3), 381–394. doi:10.1177/0047287509346853

Hakim, L. (2020). COVID-19 and the Moment to Evaluate Tourism Euphoria, Indonesia. *Journal of Indonesian Tourism and Development Studies, 8*(2), 119–123. doi:10.21776/ub.jitode.2020.008.02.09

Hall, C. M., Prayag, G., & Amore, A. (2018). *Tourism and resilience: Individual, organizational and destination perspectives.* Channelview.

Higgins-Desbiolles, F. (2020). Socialising tourism for social and ecological justice after COVID-19. *Tourism Geographies, 22*(3), 610–623. doi:10.1080/14616688.2020.1757748

Hughes, M., Weaver, D., & Pforr, C. (2015). *The practice of sustainable tourism: resolving the paradox.* Routledge. doi:10.4324/9781315796154

Ioannides, D., & Gyimóthy, S. (2020). The COVID-19 crisis as an opportunity for escaping the unsustainable global tourism path. *Tourism Geographies, 22*(3), 624–632. doi:10.1080/14616688.2020.1763445

Jiricka-Pürrer, A., Brandenburg, C., & Pröbstl-Haider, U. (2020). City tourism pre-and post-covid-19 pandemic–Messages to take home for climate change adaptation and mitigation? *Journal of Outdoor Recreation and Tourism, 31*(1), 1–6. doi:10.1016/j.jort.2020.100329

Jugănaru, I. D. (2020). Mass Tourism during the Coexistence with the New Coronavirus. The Predictable Evolution of the Seaside Tourism in Romania. Ovidius University Annals. *Series Economic Sciences*, *20*(1), 171–179.

Koutiva, M., Belias, D., Flabouras, I., & Koustelios, A. (2019). The Effects of Workplace Well-being on Individual"s Knowledge Creation Outcomes. A Study Research among Hotel Employees. *International Conference on Strategic Innovative Marketing and Tourism*. Springer.

Lew, A. (2020). How to create a better post-COVID-19 World. *Medium*. https://medium.com/new-earth-consciousness/creating-a-better-post-covid-19-world-36b2b3e8a7ae

Linca, A. C., Stanciulescu, G. C. J., & Bulin, D. (2013). The importance of niche tourism in sustainable development. *Calitatea*, *14*(2), 385.

Liu, Z. (2003). Sustainable tourism development: A critique. *Journal of Sustainable Tourism*, *11*(6), 459–475. doi:10.1080/09669580308667216

Ludvigsen, J. A. L., & Hayton, J. W. (2020). Toward COVID-19 secure events: Considerations for organizing the safe resumption of major sporting events. *Managing Sport and Leisure*, *25*(6), 1–11.

Mallapaty, S. (2020). What the cruise-ship outbreaks reveal about COVID-19. *Nature*, *580*(7801), 18–28. doi:10.1038/d41586-020-00885-w PMID:32218546

Mann, R. H., Clift, B. C., Boykoff, J., & Bekker, S. (2020). Athletes as community; athletes in community: Covid-19, sporting mega-events and athlete health protection. *British Journal of Sports Medicine*, *54*(18), 1071–1072. doi:10.1136/bjsports-2020-102433 PMID:32303522

Middleton, V. T., Fyall, A., Morgan, M., & Ranchhod, A. (2009). *Marketing in travel and tourism*. Routledge.

Navarro Jurado, E., Ortega Palomo, G., & Torres Bernier, E. (2020). *Propuestas de reflexio_n desde el turismo frente al COVID-19. Incertidumbre, impacto y recuperacio_n*. Universidad de Malaga. https://www.i3t.uma.es/wp-content/uploads/2020/03/Propuestas-Reflexiones-Turismo-ImpactoCOVID_i3tUMA.pdf [28/10/2020]

Ntalakos, A., Belias, D., & Koustelios, A. (2022c). The relationship between Leadership Styles & Communication – Effect on Team Efficiency: The case of Greek Hotel Businesses' employees. In *IACUDIT 2022 Conference Proceedings*. Springer.

Ntalakos, A., Belias, D., Koustelios, A., & Tsigilis, N. (2022). Effect of Covid-19 on the Tourism Industry: Opportunities and Threats in Covid-19 Era. In *Proceedings of the 4th International Conference on Finance, Economics, Management and IT Business*. SciTePress.

Ntalakos, A., Belias, D., & Trihas, N. (2022b). (in press). The Impact of Covid – 19 on Hospitality and Tourism Industry in Greece. International Journal of Science and Research Methodology. *Human Journals*.

Ntalakos, A., Belias, D., & Tsigilis, N. (2022d). Leadership Styles and Group Dynamics in the tourism industry. In *IACUDIT 2022 Conference Proceedings*. Research Gate.

Future of Sustainable Tourism

Polyzos, S., Samitas, A., & Spyridou, A. E. (2020). Tourism demand and the COVID-19 pandemic: An LSTM approach. [23/10/2020]. *Tourism Recreation Research*, 1–13. https://www.tandfonline.com/doi/full/10.1080/02508281.2020.1777053

Rahmafitria, F., Pearce, P. L., Oktadiana, H., & Putro, H. P. (2020). Tourism planning and planning theory: Historical roots and contemporary alignment. *Tourism Management Perspectives, 35*, 1–9. doi:10.1016/j.tmp.2020.100703

Rasoolimanesh, S. M., Ramakrishna, S., Hall, C. M., Esfandiar, K., & Seyfi, S. (2020). A systematic scoping review of sustainable tourism indicators in relation to the sustainable development goals. *Journal of Sustainable Tourism*, 1–21. doi:10.1080/09669582.2020.1775621

Romagosa, F. (2020). The COVID-19 crisis: Opportunities for sustainable and proximity tourism. *Tourism Geographies, 22*(3), 1–5. https://www.uab.cat/doc/article_turisme_postcovid_francesc_romagosa.pdf. doi:10.1080/14616688.2020.1763447

Rossidis, I., Belias, D., Papailias, S., Tsiotas, D., Niavis, S., & Vasiliadis, L. (2019). The Use of Customer Relations Management's Digital Technologies from Greek Hotels. In A. Kavoura, E. Kefallonitis, & A. Giovanis (Eds.), *Strategic Innovative Marketing and Tourism. Springer Proceedings in Business and Economics*. Springer. doi:10.1007/978-3-030-12453-3_9

Rossidis, I., Belias, D., Varsanis, K., Papailias, S., Tsiotas, D., Vasiliadis, L., & Sdrolias, L. (2019b). Tourism and Destination Branding: The Case of Greek Islands. In A. Kavoura, E. Kefallonitis, & A. Giovanis (Eds.), *Strategic Innovative Marketing and Tourism. Springer Proceedings in Business and Economics*. Springer. doi:10.1007/978-3-030-12453-3_11

Rossidis, I., Belias, D., & Vasiliadis, L. (2021). Strategic Human Resource Management in the International Hospitality Industry. An Extensive Literature Review. In V. Katsoni & C. van Zyl (Eds.), *Culture and Tourism in a Smart, Globalized, and Sustainable World. Springer Proceedings in Business and Economics*. Springer. doi:10.1007/978-3-030-72469-6_22

Rossidis, I., Belias, D., & Vasiliadis, L. (2021b). Strategic Hotel Management in the "Hostile" International Environment. In V. Katsoni & C. van Zyl (Eds.), *Culture and Tourism in a Smart, Globalized, and Sustainable World. Springer Proceedings in Business and Economics*. Springer. doi:10.1007/978-3-030-72469-6_21

Santos-Roldán, L., Castillo Canalejo, A. M., Berbel-Pineda, J. M., & Palacios-Florencio, B. (2020). Sustainable Tourism as a Source of Healthy Tourism. *International Journal of Environmental Research and Public Health, 17*(15), 53–59. doi:10.3390/ijerph17155353 PMID:32722271

Skagias, K., Vasiliadis, L., Belias, D., & Papademetriou, C. (2021). From mass tourism and mass culture to sustainable tourism in the post-covid19 era: The case of Mykonos. In V. Katsoni & C. van Zyl (Eds.), *Culture and Tourism in a Smart, Globalized, and Sustainable World. Springer Proceedings in Business and Economics*. Springer. doi:10.1007/978-3-030-72469-6_23

Tien, C., Lo, H. C., & Lin, H. W. (2011). The economic benefits of mega events: A myth or a reality? A longitudinal study on the Olympic Games. *Journal of Sport Management, 25*(1), 11–23. doi:10.1123/jsm.25.1.11

Wan, L. C., Chan, E. K., & Luo, X. (2020). Robots Come to Rescue: How to reduce perceived risk of infectious disease in Covid19-stricken consumers? *Annals of Tourism Research*. https://www.ncbi.nlm.nih.gov/pmc/articles/PMC7550303/pdf/main.pdf [28/10/2020]

Weaver, D. B. (2014). Asymmetrical dialectics of sustainable tourism: Toward enlightened mass tourism. *Journal of Travel Research*, *53*(2), 131–140. doi:10.1177/0047287513491335

Yu, C. P., Chancellor, H. C., & Cole, S. T. (2011). Measuring residents' attitudes toward sustainable tourism: A reexamination of the sustainable tourism attitude scale. *Journal of Travel Research*, *50*(1), 57–63. doi:10.1177/0047287509353189

Zhang, T., Chen, J., & Hu, B. (2019). Authenticity, quality, and loyalty: Local food and sustainable tourism experience. *Sustainability*, *11*(12), 34–37. doi:10.3390u11123437

Chapter 6

Lego® Serious Play®:
Design Thinking as a Tool to Teach the Value Proposition Concept to Promote the Regional Development of Creative Industries

Miguel Angel Ponce-Camacho
CETYS Universidad, Mexico

Josue Aaron Lopez-Leyva
CETYS Universidad, Mexico

ABSTRACT

This chapter describes the experience of a group of graduate students using Lego® Serious Play® (LSP) and design thinking as tools to learn the value proposition concept to promote the regional development of creative industries. The use of LSP encourages teamwork, co-creation, and motor skills, transporting individuals to a play space, where each opinion has equivalent importance through the use of their hands, learning and reinforcing what they have learned through the techniques of teaching others, practicing doing it and group discussion. LSP facilitates in a short time the experience of creative freedom and the exercise of empathy with the client which refers to one of the phases of the design thinking method, as well as the creation of a conceptual prototype as a metaphor for the value proposition for the client. As a result, a business model canvas, and a value proposal canvas were generated, which help the innovation of the real service analyzed, as well as serve as an innovative tool in the process of teaching-learning for graduate students in the area of innovation.

DOI: 10.4018/978-1-6684-6055-9.ch006

Copyright © 2023, IGI Global. Copying or distributing in print or electronic forms without written permission of IGI Global is prohibited.

INTRODUCTION

In particular, the competitiveness of companies in any sector has always been an aspect that is sought by all means. Said aspect is related to the business's capacity to continue offering its products and services to its client segment over time, which is understood as sustainable competitiveness, that is, competitiveness that remains despite time, considering particular actions to promote business competitiveness in the short, medium and long term (Komarova and Ustyuzhanin, 2017: Yoshino et al., 2021; D'yakonova et al., 2020). Now, considering a broader analysis, companies in the same sector make up a specific industrial cluster, and the various clusters make up a regional industrial sector or cluster. In general, this cluster of regional companies must also promote regional sustainable competitiveness, for which various strategies can be carried out for the comprehensive sustainable growth of the region based on good practices of closed and open innovation (participating both the sector private, public, academic, among others), in accordance with the specific capabilities of each region (de Paulo et al., 2017; Paiva et al., 2020; Yoon et al., 2020).

However, sometimes the strategy for sustainable regional development focuses on the industrial or business sectors with the greatest economic impact in the study region, for example, companies in the energy sector, production, and transformation of metals, agriculture, livestock, among others. This means that other developing business sectors are not fully considered in the design and deployment of strategies for sustainable regional development. Such is the case of the creative and cultural industries, which have become important around the world due to their variety of activities and a much broader market segment than other business sectors.

In the particular case of Mexico, the Creative and Cultural Industries (CCI) have proven to be an important sector for the Mexican economy since in 2015 they represented around 7% of the Gross Domestic Product (GDP) according to estimates made by the Mexican Institute for Competitiveness (Instituto Mexicano para la Competitividad in Spanish). The main reason for the significant contribution to GDP is, among other aspects, the national cultural wealth, which has allowed Mexico to position as the country with the most exports of creative products and services in Latin America. However, despite their clear importance in the economic sector, CCIs have had a relatively small growth rate at the national level according to Mexican Institute for Competitiveness. This is due to the lack of support received by the creators and authors of the works involved in the sector, among other factors (Valdivia, 2018; Benita, 2019).

Now, it is important to note that creative industries have different approaches and definitions around the world, but everyone agrees on a single argument, CCIs are knowledge-intensive, based on individual creativity and talent, while generating economic and social development indispensable for the welfare state, likewise, they are indispensable for the preservation of the identity, culture, and values of a nation (Loots, et al., 2021; Mäe, 2016). In general, it is possible to find differences that some countries make between some of the activities that belong to the creative or cultural industries. To understand the reason for the differentiation of the term, many authors point out that the countries of the southern European continent usually retain the term cultural industries because they have an abundant cultural and artistic heritage that has gradually been capitalized; on while the countries of northern Europe adopt the term creative industries since they are more oriented towards the knowledge economy and Information and Communication Technologies (ICT) (Lazzeretti et al., 2008; Innocenti & Lazzeretti, 2019; Boix et al., 2016). Once the commercial activities covered by the CCIs have been identified, various

Lego® Serious Play®

proposals seek to harness the economic potential of this sector through a comprehensive public policy to raise the contribution of the CCIs to GDP, in the case of Mexico, up to 12% of GDP. In particular, in Mexico, CCIs are considered to be those companies that are related to advertising, architecture, arts and antiques, handicrafts, design, fashion design, cinema, different types of software, music, performing arts, publishing, radio. and television, cuisine, and regional beverages, among others. Although it is important to note that in other countries, such as the United Kingdom, Germany, Spain, and France, the classification and terminology can vary over time (Consulting, 2010; Bednar & Grebenicek, 2012; Matiza, 2020; Higgs et al., 2008).

Considering the above, the design and implementation of actions within the framework of a strategy that allows regional development for various business sectors have been supported by various innovation methodologies and activities such as hackathons, design thinking, lean startup, Forth innovation method, blue ocean strategy, among others. However, sometimes these methodologies require other techniques or secondary methods that allow accelerating the understanding and result of the competitiveness and innovation of companies. After a review of the literature, no reported works were found in Mexico regarding the implementation of primary and secondary methodologies in the Creative and Cultural Industries that allow supporting the strategies of sustainable regional development. Therefore, this work contributes to the body of national and international knowledge regarding the contribution of primary and secondary innovation methodologies in support of the Creative and Cultural Industries.

This chapter is organized in the following manner. Firstly, the theoretical basis of the Value Proposition Concept, Lego® Serious Play®, and Design Thinking Methodologies is presented. Afterward, the student experience related to the application of these methodologies to make a value proposition for a local company is detailed. The general qualitative results are presented below, as well as the challenges associated with said methodologies and the value proposition as a boost and promotion for the regional development of creative and cultural industries. Finally, the conclusions, limitations, and future work are presented.

THEORETICAL BACKGROUND

Value Proposition Concept

In particular, a value proposition is a summary of how a product or service benefits the customers (e.g., the business highlights) (Frow & Payne, 2011; Winkler & Dosoudil, 2011). Even though it's extremely challenging to determine or define the company's services down into one concise sentence. Normally, the value proposition can include literary or graphic support, for example, a headline, a paragraph of text, photographs, graphics, among others (Ghandour, 2019; Baker, 2015; Hassan, 2012; Harrington & Trusko, 2017). Surprisingly, not all companies have a well-defined effective value proposition (i.e., approximately 2.3% of companies have an effective and useful value proposition). Even with this, the creation of companies, particularly in the field of the creative and cultural industry, sometimes responds to a potential vocation of the owner without having a well-defined value proposition. The foregoing can be a parameter that significantly affects the success of the business since a well-defined value proposition can be an important advantage over the competitors. In this way, it is very likely that a customer prefers another competitor because he does not understand the value proposition of a company. Therefore, the benefits that a company has when it has a clear and direct proposition value are diverse, such as creating a strong differential between the competitors, improving customer understanding and engagement, Attracts the right prospects, and increases not only the quantity but the quality of prospective leads, among others (Gander, 2018; Porfírio et al., 2016). Figure 1 shows the value proposition canvas used in this project.

Figure 1. Value proposition canvas

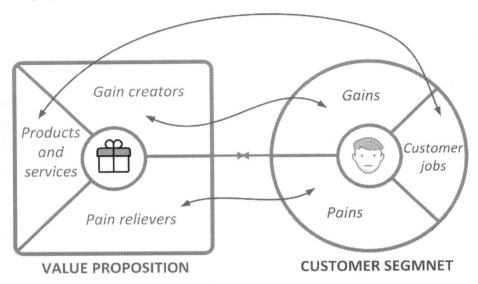

Lego® Serious Play®

Lego® Serious Play® (LSP) is a methodology that uses LEGO blocks as a means to facilitate teamwork in problem-solving. In particular, it uses four stages coordinated by a facilitator (someone who assistances to bring about an outcome, such as knowledge, productivity, communication, among others, by providing indirect or unobtrusive assistance, guidance, or supervision) to lead a group of individuals in the construction of visual models, i.e., LPS is based on "thinking with their hands". This playful activity is in a dimension in which the game is the trigger for creativity, taking a group of adult students to a "universe" where there are no cultural differences or hierarchical positions. In addition, it places individuals in a scenario where their intellectual and emotional expressions cease to be an obstacle to become a strength, that is, a creative space where all opinions are relevant (Hayes & Graham, 2020; Zenk et al., 2021; Kranawetleitner et al., 2020; Peabody & Turesky, 2018; Wheeler, et al., 2020). In this way, people generate a wide variety of ideas and an endless number of possible solutions through a three-dimensional physical model (using the physical pieces of Lego® Serious Play®) built by themselves in the same space and time. In particular, LSP contemplates the following stages: 1) the facilitator declares a seed or trigger question, and directs the workgroup so that, through the game, "thinking with their hands", 2) they build visual models as answers to the question in a limited time, for later, 3) the participants tell their story around the elaborated visual model, and finally, 4) express a reflection to the group (Wengel, 2020; Wengel et al., 2020; McCusker, 2020; Cerezo-Narváez et al., 2019).

Lego® Serious Play®

However, in the present work, the four-step method was modified. In particular, individual work was changed to teamwork (6-7 students). Within each working group, one person was asked to participate as a hypothetical client. The facilitator asks the working groups to build a visual model of a value proposition according to the requirements defined by the client. The concept of value proposition is a principle defined by Alexander Osterwalder in his book, Bussines model generation, in which a board (canvas) is described (Ostewalder and Pigneur, 2010) made up of nine sectors, such as key partners, key resources, key activities, value propositions, customer relationships, channels, customer segments, cost structure, and revenue streams. In this tool, the construction of a value proposition for the client is established as a starting point. Thus, the value proposition is based on customer expectations, looking for attributes of a product or service that meet one or more of the following characteristics; a) client's pains, b) client's gains, and c) common activities performed by the client.

Design Thinking Methodology

In general, Design Thinking is based on the logic, imagination, intuition, and systematic reasoning of people to explore the possibilities of defining a potential need for a client and then propose the creation of services and products. that meet the needs of the client through complete satisfaction. In this manner, Design Thinking seeks to find potential solutions beyond conventional business paradigms. The structure and stages of the Design Thinking methodology are simple and widely discussed, but in particular, the stages are: 1) Empathize (research the users' needs), 2) Define (clearly state the users' needs and problems), 3) Ideate (challenging assumptions and creating ideas), 4) Prototype (start to create solutions), and 5) Test (try the solutions out) (Pande & Bharathi, 2020; Auernhammer & Roth, 2021; Dunne, 2018; Razzouk & Shute, 2012).

In particular, the Design Thinking methodology with the modifications made in this work is described below. The methodology uses empathy (as a first stage) with the customer to direct the design and construction of an initial prototype (related to a product or service) that meets customer expectations. The methodology clarifies that the client's requirements are not necessarily represented by what the client explicitly expresses as a need, but warns the work team that it is their responsibility to investigate based on a personal approach with the client, that is, to seek what the client really requires (i.e. empathize with the client). In addition, the methodology does not follow a specific sequence but is a process in constant transformation, in which it is possible to return to any of its phases, at any time. However, it is important to emphasize that the starting point is always empathy with the customer. After the empathize stage, the Define stage follows, where the real needs of the client are established. These real needs of the client constitute the raw material for the Ideating stage the innovative service or product that gradually or disruptively solves the client's need. Next, the Prototyping stage allows materializing of a proposal that adds value to the client's activities, that is, that said proposal seeks to solve the client's need. In these first four stages, the Lego® Serious Play® methodology is present to support the Design Thinking method. The last stage is Evaluate, to obtain feedback on the opinions and customer satisfaction degree concerning the product and service proposal (Elsbach & Stigliani, 2018; Prud'homme, 2017; Dym et al., 2006).

Lego® Serious Play® and Design Thinking: Experience of Students

Pedagogical Experience - Hypothetical Customer

Considering the theoretical foundation presented in the previous sections, the modified Lego® Serious Play® - Design Thinking technique was used with a group of students from the academic program, Master in Engineering and Innovation, particularly within the framework of the subject, Innovation & Developing. In particular, a local company was chosen, Mexicali Beer Garden By Porter House, which is classified as a creative and cultural company due to its contribution to the gastronomic culture of the region. Actually, there are 650 companies in Mexico related to the production and commercialization of craft beers, and around 10,000 companies worldwide. In addition, the company's business model is distinctive in its customer segment, since the company does not obtain its income from the direct consumer of the product, that is, its customers are local craft beer producers. To clarify the business model, it can be said that the company has several beer racks that are rented to local brewers, who directly serve the consumer. In this way, Mexicali Beer Garden currently offers brewers a place to sell their products so that they become known in the locality, acquire customers, and have direct interaction with them.

Figure 2. Creativity room at CETYS University (CETyS, 2016)

Before going to the client's facilities, the group of students tested the value proposition concept in the classroom (see Figure 2) using the Lego® Serious Play® - Design Thinking methodology as the basis for the regional development strategy. The group of students (with the help of the facilitator of the methodology) was organized into 4 groups of between 6 and 7 people. Next, the facilitator asked each team to choose one of their members to represent the hypothetical client. This role is very important since the pedagogical experience is based on the creation of a value proposition for potential clients based on the Lego® Serious Play® - Design Thinking methodology.

Figure 3. A pilot test with postgraduate students to learn the concept of the customer value proposition

Figure 3 shows a group of postgraduate students rehearsing the development of a physical model built with LEGO blocks to represent a value proposition for the hypothetical client whom they interviewed during the dynamic to find out their requirements in a fictitious scenario using the Lego ® Serious Play® - Design Thinking methodology. Thus, each team developed a different visual model with LEGOs to meet the expectations of the hypothetical client in a controlled academic setting. In this exercise of immersion in the proposed methodology, the concept of empathy with "the other" is relevant, since the concept of innovation is based on the creation of added value not as an act of creativity for the individual himself, but to fulfill with the expectations of another individual or organization. Afterward, the group of students went to the premises of the aforementioned company to begin the Empathy stage in a real and direct way.

Real Experience - Real Customer

Figures 4 and 5 show the group of students and the teacher in various locations of the company talking individually and in groups with the owners of the company. In this way, the group seeks empathy and awareness regarding the problem, and in turn, defines real problems and needs of the company and then proceeds to devise, as a group, proposals for solutions.

Finally, Figure 6 shows a group of students and the main partner of the company in the fourth stage of Design Thinking, with which a prototype of the idea is generated that will add value to the service through Lego® Serious Play®.

Figure 4. The class students go to the company locations to raise awareness about the problem

Figure 5. The students and teacher (facilitator) talk with the company's partners (clients) as part of the stage of empathy, definition, and ideation of the design thinking methodology

Overall Results and Discussions

First of all, it is important to point out that this document does not intend to show results in the business framework, rather, it tries to show how postgraduate students can learn entrepreneurship concepts and techniques in real cases in an innovative way. Also, due to confidentiality issues, it is not allowed to show the company's particular results. In this fashion, the general results of said promotion of regional competitiveness and development are related to the innovative design of the business model canvas using Lego® Serious Play® within the framework of Design Thinking. In general, a large number of arguments were obtained that could strengthen the business model canvas, due to the large number of students who participated. However, the most empathic arguments between the innovation team and the client were selected and synthesized, and said the technical report was delivered to the client.

Figure 6. Postgraduate students formed a work team with the main partner (center) of the company to develop value proposals for the Mexicali Beer Garden by Porter House company

Thus, the use of Lego® Serious Play® - Design Thinking allowed, through strategic management, to document an existing business model and then propose an innovative improvement to the existing business model. Afterward, a canvas value proposal was made in which feelings and situations of the client were detected, which served as a basis to provide an option for improvement and competitiveness to the client.

Therefore, the use of Alex Osterwalder's value proposition canvas is innovative as an educational tool because it implicitly forces the student to immerse himself in a general problem of a particular company. The classification of the functions in the entrepreneurship scheme into nine sections without exhaustive descriptions focuses the student's attention on logically constructing an answer for each section. In this way, in the analysis of Alexander Osterwalder's canvas for the business model, as well as for the value proposition canvas, the student makes a diagnosis of the entrepreneurship, fluidly, in a single session of knowledge of the business, as well as with a single interview to the main partner of the company.

As part of the discussion, it was possible to appreciate qualitatively that for some companies and individuals, it is still very difficult to work on an innovation project focused on the promotion of sustainable regional development through well-defined innovation methodologies, as well as in the open innovation framework (Ollila & Elmquist, 2011; Raya et al., 2021; van de Vrande et al., 2009). The foregoing implies that, although open innovation has multiple benefits (e.g., it can lead to reduced costs, greater efficiency, create new products and services, innovate old products and services, build a strong network and community of people who are engaged with their work, keeping your employees engaged, new revenue streams, innovation risk reduction), there is still a convincing effort for all parties involved. This is probably due to maximizing the disadvantages of an open innovation framework, such as the possibility of revealing information not intended for sharing, the potential for hosting organizations to lose competitive advantages as a consequence of revealing intellectual property, the increased complexity of controlling information, the regulating how contributors affect a project, the devising means to properly incorporate and identify innovation, the realigning innovation strategies to extend beyond to get the full benefit from the innovation on the external side of things, among others (Khan & Arshad, 2019; Heimstädt & Friesike, 2021; Mahdad et al., 2020).

Challenges to Promote the Regional Development of Creative Industries based on Lego® Serious Play®: Design Thinking

The innovation methodologies mentioned have had their development in other fields of knowledge and industries, mainly in the development of industrial products. Therefore, the use of Lego® Serious Play® - Design Thinking is not yet as widespread in other business sectors. Such is the case in the creative industries. One of the main reasons is not so much related to the methodologies themselves, but rather the creation, development, and strengthening of cultural and creative industries. The foregoing implies that this concept has not been expanded in society, therefore, there are not so many actions to promote it. In fact, considering the classification of creative industries referred to in the introduction section, even today, many companies in the sector do not know that they belong to this particular category. In this way, there is a transversal challenge for the promotion of these industries that must be addressed by various disciplines of knowledge.

In particular, some of the main challenges are 1) knowing and facing new business models to adapt to the new behaviors of consumers, mainly consumers of different generations, 2) The limited experience in the development of projects in cooperation, either with companies in the same sector or with companies from other sectors. The above should be addressed through collaborative work of the public, private, and government sectors 3) Industrial globalization since the said market is large but with other levels of demands that it is difficult for a micro-business sector to address, 4) The training of cultural professionals, since there must be a human resource prepared to face a strategic process with business guarantees, 5) Financing problems, both internally or business level, and externally through other entities or organizations, and finally, 6) intellectual property, its valuation and the value of businesses. On the other hand, individual methodologies (Lego® Serious Play® and Design Thinking) have their challenges that must be addressed.

CONCLUSION

The present work shows the activities of postgraduate students in innovation in the framework of the use of Lego® Serious Play® - Design Thinking, testing the concept of value proposition in the classroom and the experience of the students in a case study for the company Mexicali Beer Garden by Porter House. This process was characterized by development both in the understanding of the opportunities for innovation in the company's processes, and in the development of a visual model, in which at the same time that they worked together with the representatives of the company, empathizing with them, a space of free creativity was created both for the value proposition for the client, as well as a playful environment that allowed fluidity in a short time to deliver innovative ideas for improvement to create added value in the company's processes. In this fashion, the group of students demonstrated the benefits of using Lego® Serious Play® - Design Thinking in a simultaneous and complementary way by promoting the construction of objective proposals in a collaborative framework based on involvement, awareness, commitment, and trust.

Lego® Serious Play®

In addition, the innovative teaching activity allowed the self-knowledge of each student, because Lego® Serious Play® - Design Thinking allows finding hidden knowledge or opinions in the participants, which, without a doubt, allows visualize unconventional scenarios and strategies, thus helping to generate innovative decision making. As objective results, two examples of evaluation of the business model for Mexicali Beer Garden by Porter House are presented using the Business model canvas generation, as well as the value propositions canvas of Alexander Osterwalder and Yves Pigneur. In addition, the proposed binomial, Lego® Serious Play® - Design Thinking, proved to be an important help in raising student awareness, so that the teaching sector expands, from knowledge of conventional science and technology to procurement of a generation of true social impact in the implementation of the knowledge and techniques acquired by students in their academic training. Finally, the innovative learning experience shown allowed, in general, to increase the active and quality participation of each student in a collaborative framework, predetermined effectiveness through the correct use of the methodologies used, and due to the methodological foundation, it allows a change significant in the way of analyzing innovation problems that could be sustainable over time and reproducible by students in the institutions and/or companies where they work. In particular, our work presents some limitations related to the adequacy of innovation methodologies for various companies in the creative industries sector. However, adjustments and various actions are currently being carried out for the mapping of creative industries in the region that would allow for improving sustainable regional competitiveness.

REFERENCES

Auernhammer, J., & Roth, B. (2021). The origin and evolution of Stanford University's design thinking: From product design to design thinking in innovation management. *Journal of Product Innovation Management, 38*(6), 623–644. doi:10.1111/jpim.12594

Baker, R. J. (2015). *Pricing on Purpose: Creating and Capturing Value. Pricing on Purpose: Creating and Capturing Value*. Wiley Blackwell. doi:10.1002/9781119201366

Bednar, P., & Grebenicek, P. (2012). Mapping Creative Industries in the Zlin Region. *Journal of Competitiveness, 4*(1), 20–35. doi:10.7441/joc.2012.01.02

Benita, F. (2019). On the performance of creative industries: Evidence from Mexican metropolitan areas. *Papers in Regional Science, 98*(2), 825–842. doi:10.1111/pirs.12403

Boix, R., Capone, F., De Propris, L., Lazzeretti, L., & Sanchez, D. (2016). Comparing creative industries in Europe. *European Urban and Regional Studies, 23*(4), 935–940. doi:10.1177/0969776414541135

Cerezo-Narváez, A., Córdoba-Roldán, A., Pastor-Fernández, A., Aguayo-González, F., Otero-Mateo, M., & Ballesteros-Pérez, P. (2019). Training competences in industrial risk prevention with lego® serious play®: A case study. *Safety (Basel, Switzerland), 5*(4), 81. doi:10.3390afety5040081

Consulting, B. (2010). Mapping the Creative Industries: A Toolkit. *Creative and Cultural Economy series, 2,* 1–33. https://www.britishcouncil.org/mapping_the_creative_industries_a_toolkit_2-2.pdf

D'yakonova, I. I., Kravchuk, A. V., Sheliuk, A. A., & Haber, J.-E. (2020). Quantitative methods estimation of the competitiveness of insurance companies in the context of sustainable development. *Financial and Credit Activity Problems of Theory and Practice*, *3*(34), 366–380. doi:10.18371/fcaptp.v3i34.215575

de Paulo, A. F., De Oliveira, S. V. W. B., & Porto, G. S. (2017). Mapping impacts of open innovation practices in a firm competitiveness. *Journal of Technology Management & Innovation*, *12*(3), 108–117. doi:10.4067/S0718-27242017000300011

Dunne, D. (2018). Implementing design thinking in organizations: An exploratory study. *Journal of Organization Design*, *7*(1), 16. doi:10.118641469-018-0040-7

Dym, C. L., Agogino, A. M., Eris, O., Frey, D. D., & Leifer, L. J. (2006). Engineering design thinking, teaching, and learning. *IEEE Engineering Management Review*, *34*(1), 65–90. doi:10.1109/EMR.2006.1679078

Elsbach, K. D., & Stigliani, I. (2018). Design Thinking and Organizational Culture: A Review and Framework for Future Research. *Journal of Management*, *44*(6), 2274–2306. doi:10.1177/0149206317744252

Frow, P., & Payne, A. (2011). A stakeholder perspective of the value proposition concept. *European Journal of Marketing*, *45*(1), 223–240. doi:10.1108/03090561111095676

Gander, J. (2018). Competing in the creative and cultural industries. In *Strategic Analysis* (pp. 9–28). Routledge. doi:10.4324/9781315644592-2

Ghandour, A. (2019). Crafting a web-unique value proposition using the concept analysis technique. *Global Business and Economics Review*, *21*(1), 14–25. doi:10.1504/GBER.2019.096853

Harrington, H. J., & Trusko, B. (2017). *Maximizing Value Propositions to Increase Project Success Rates*. *Maximizing Value Propositions to Increase Project Success Rates*. Productivity Press. doi:10.1201/b16786

Hassan, A. (2012). The Value Proposition Concept in Marketing: How Customers Perceive the Value Delivered by Firms– A Study of Customer Perspectives on Supermarkets in Southampton in the United Kingdom. *International Journal of Marketing Studies*, *4*(3). doi:10.5539/ijms.v4n3p68

Hayes, C., & Graham, Y. (2020). Understanding the building of professional identities with the LEGO® SERIOUS PLAY® method using situational mapping and analysis. Higher Education. *Skills and Work-Based Learning*, *10*(1), 99–112. doi:10.1108/HESWBL-05-2019-0069

Heimstädt, M., & Friesike, S. (2021). The odd couple: Contrasting openness in innovation and science. Innovation. *Organization and Management*, *23*(3), 425–438. doi:10.1080/14479338.2020.1837631

Higgs, P., Cunningham, S., & Bakhshi, H. (2008). Beyond the creative industries: Mapping the creative economy. *Nesta*. https://www.nesta.org.uk/publications/reports/assets/features/beyond_the_creative_industries

Innocenti, N., & Lazzeretti, L. (2019). Do the creative industries support growth and innovation in the wider economy? Industry relatedness and employment growth in Italy. *Industry and Innovation*, *26*(10), 1152–1173. doi:10.1080/13662716.2018.1561360

Khan, Y. K., & Arshad, A. S. M. (2019). Innovation Ecosystem in the Small and Medium Enterprises. *Journal of Management Info*, 6(1), 51–54. doi:10.31580/jmi.v6i1.461

Komarova, I. P., & Ustyuzhanin, V. L. (2017). Problems of companies' sustainable competitiveness. *Espacios, 38*(62).

Kranawetleitner, T., Krebs, H., Kuhn, N., & Menner, M. (2020). Needs Analyses with LEGO® SERIOUS PLAY®. In Lecture Notes in Computer Science (including subseries Lecture Notes in Artificial Intelligence and Lecture Notes in Bioinformatics) (pp. 99–104). Springer Science and Business Media Deutschland GmbH. doi:10.1007/978-3-030-61814-8_8

Lazzeretti, L., Boix, R., & Capone, F. (2008). Do creative industries cluster? Mapping creative local production systems in Italy and Spain. *Industry and Innovation, 15*(5), 549–567. doi:10.1080/13662710802374161

Loots, E., Neiva, M., Carvalho, L., & Lavanga, M. (2021). The entrepreneurial ecosystem of cultural and creative industries in Porto: A sub-ecosystem approach. In *Growth and Change* (Vol. 52, pp. 641–662). John Wiley and Sons Inc., doi:10.1111/grow.12434

Mäe, R. (2016). The Creative Industries: A discourse-theoretical approach. *International Review of Social Research*, 5(2), 78–87. doi:10.1515/irsr-2015-0007

Mahdad, M., De Marco, C. E., Piccaluga, A., & Di Minin, A. (2020). Harnessing adaptive capacity to close the pandora's box of open innovation. *Industry and Innovation*, 27(3), 264–284. doi:10.1080/13 662716.2019.1633910

Matiza, V. M. (2020). The Role of Creative Industries in Economic Development: The Human Factor Development Approach. *African Journal of Inter/Multidisciplinary Studies, 2*(1), 50–61. doi:10.51415/ajims.v2i1.833

McCusker, S. (2020). Everybody's monkey is important: LEGO® Serious Play® as a methodology for enabling equality of voice within diverse groups. *International Journal of Research & Method in Education*, 43(2), 146–162. doi:10.1080/1743727X.2019.1621831

Ollila, S., & Elmquist, M. (2011). Managing open innovation: Exploring challenges at the interfaces of an open innovation arena. *Creativity and Innovation Management*, 20(4), 273–283. doi:10.1111/j.1467-8691.2011.00616.x

Osterwalder, A., & Pigneur, Y. (2010). *Business Model Generation - A handbook for visionaries, Game Changers and challengers striving to defy outmoded business models and design tomorrow's enterprises. The Medieval Ous: Imitation.* Rewriting, and Transmission in the French Tradition. http://0-search. ebscohost.com.library.uark.edu/login.aspx?direct=true&db=mzh&AN=1996055971&site=ehost-live

Paiva, T., Ribeiro, M., & Coutinho, P. (2020). R&D collaboration, competitiveness development, and open innovation in R&D. *Journal of Open Innovation*, 6(4), 1–18. doi:10.3390/joitmc6040116

Pande, M., & Bharathi, S. V. (2020). Theoretical foundations of design thinking – A constructivism learning approach to design thinking. *Thinking Skills and Creativity*, 36, 100637. doi:10.1016/j.tsc.2020.100637

Peabody, M. A., & Turesky, E. F. (2018). Shared Leadership Lessons: Adapting LEGO® SERIOUS PLAY® In Higher Education. *International Journal of Management and Applied Research*, *5*(4), 210–223. doi:10.18646/2056.54.18-015

Porfírio, J. A., Carrilho, T., & Mónico, L. S. (2016). Entrepreneurship in different contexts in cultural and creative industries. *Journal of Business Research*, *69*(11), 5117–5123. doi:10.1016/j.jbusres.2016.04.090

Prud'homme van Reine, P. (2017). The culture of design thinking for innovation. *Journal of Innovation Management*, *5*(2), 56–80. doi:10.24840/2183-0606_005.002_0006

Raya, A. B., Andiani, R., Siregar, A. P., Prasada, I. Y., Indana, F., Simbolon, T. G. Y., Kinasih, A. T., & Nugroho, A. D. (2021). Challenges, open innovation, and engagement theory at craft smes: Evidence from Indonesian batik. *Journal of Open Innovation*, *7*(2), 121. doi:10.3390/joitmc7020121

Razzouk, R., & Shute, V. (2012). What Is Design Thinking and Why Is It Important? *Review of Educational Research*, *82*(3), 330–348. doi:10.3102/0034654312457429

Valdivia, M. (2018). Cultural and creative industries in Mexico: The role of export-oriented manufacturing metro areas. In *Creative Industries and Entrepreneurship: Paradigms in Transition from a Global Perspective* (pp. 262–282). Edward Elgar Publishing Ltd. doi:10.4337/9781786435927.00021

van de Vrande, V., de Jong, J. P. J., Vanhaverbeke, W., & de Rochemont, M. (2009). Open innovation in SMEs: Trends, motives and management challenges. *Technovation*, *29*(6–7), 423–437. doi:10.1016/j.technovation.2008.10.001

Wengel, Y. (2020). LEGO® Serious Play® in multi-method tourism research. *International Journal of Contemporary Hospitality Management*, *32*(4), 1605–1623. doi:10.1108/IJCHM-04-2019-0358

Wengel, Y., McIntosh, A., & Cockburn-Wootten, C. (2020). A critical consideration of LEGO® SERIOUS PLAY® methodology for tourism studies. *Tourism Geographies*, *23*(1–2), 162–184. doi:10.1080/14616688.2019.1611910

Wheeler, S., Passmore, J., & Gold, R. (2020). All to play for: LEGO® SERIOUS PLAY® and its impact on team cohesion, collaboration and psychological safety in organisational settings using a coaching approach. *Journal of Work-Applied Management*, *12*(2), 141–157. doi:10.1108/JWAM-03-2020-0011

Winkler, M., & Dosoudil, V. (2011). On Formalization of the Concept of Value Proposition. *Service Science*, *3*(3), 194–205. doi:10.1287erv.3.3.194

Yoon, J., Sung, S., & Ryu, D. (2020). The role of networks in improving international performance and competitiveness: Perspective view of open innovation. *Sustainability (Switzerland)*, *12*(3), 1269. Advance online publication. doi:10.3390u12031269

Yoshino, N., Taghizadeh-Hesary, F., & Otsuka, M. (2021). Covid-19 and Optimal Portfolio Selection for Investment in Sustainable Development Goals. *Finance Research Letters*, *38*, 101695. Advance online publication. doi:10.1016/j.frl.2020.101695 PMID:32837379

Zenk, L., Primus, D. J., & Sonnenburg, S. (2021). Alone but together: Flow experience and its impact on creative output in LEGO® SERIOUS PLAY®. *European Journal of Innovation Management*, *25*(6), 340–364. doi:10.1108/EJIM-09-2020-0362

Chapter 7
Sustainable Growth Strategies for Entrepreneurial Tourism:
A Link Between Entrepreneurial Growth and Regional Development

Eliza Sharma

Symbiosis International University, India

ABSTRACT

The present study seeks to develop a model that can establish a structural association between development of entrepreneurial tourism, and development of socially-backward communities as well. Keeping in view the promising growth of the tourism sector, and huge opportunities for the entrepreneurs in this sector, this current study will aim to answer the followings research questions: RQ1: What can be the different sustainable growth strategies for the entrepreneurial tourism? RQ2: How different stakeholders can be involved for the sustainable growth of tourism sector? RQ3: How growth of entrepreneurial tourism can be linked to regional development?

INTRODUCTION

The multi-billion-dollar tourism industry of today exhibits huge direct and indirect sway over a country's economy and overall development. It has the power to transform entire cities and communities, especially in developing countries. The tourism industry has immense growth potential; it not only generates employment, but it can also develop social, cultural and educational values among people. Thus, the development of modern tourism industry is no longer limited to merely economic perspectives; its social impact has attracted significant attention from governments, NGOs, and private organizations (Ghasemi and Hamzah, 2014). Over the years, tourism has evolved from favouring solely those areas which offered countryside escapes or scenic beaches and hills. The modern tourist is not just tempted by the promise of scenic beauty, but also by the lure of exotic cultural gifts like heritage sites, traditional food, and eco-conscious experiences (Barett, 2008). Hence, the tourism industry is now open to exploration of

DOI: 10.4018/978-1-6684-6055-9.ch007

Copyright © 2023, IGI Global. Copying or distributing in print or electronic forms without written permission of IGI Global is prohibited.

areas that were previously deemed unlikely to be tourist destinations due to their lack of natural scenic landscapes. This shift has brought new areas to attention where tourism can be promoted for achieving social and economic development. As per the report of United Nations (2020), around 60 percent of the world's population shall reside in urban areas by the year 2030[1]. The tourism sector consists of a highly segmented and imperative arena in the economy of modern nation states. In a global economy, the tourism sector acts as a major determinant of the resources that a country can showcase against its competitors whilst also using the same to bring in ample finance. Several strands of thought are invested in the development of tourism theories and the identification of key issues that problematize the efficiency of the tourism sector. Hence, a holistic analysis of this particular sector requires that we undertake a comparative historical analysis of the development of the tourism sector in various economies over time and also consider micro-arenas where impact-evaluation can take place. Tourism has already had an impact on the development of developing economies (Ashley et al., 2007), which also explains its highly competitive and globalized all-inclusive nature, consisting of entities ranging from small sector enterprises to global mass-production chains. In this context, the present paper seeks to analyse the role of the tourism sector in development of national economies and how sustainable growth can be ensured for entrepreneurial tourism. To begin with, the definitions of certain key concepts need to be undertaken.

The landscape of the tourism sector, as has already been mentioned above, has continuously changed to incorporate more elements which can be relied on in the long run. The concept of sustainable tourism emerges in the 1960's with understandings of environmentalism and ecological goals coming to the forefront of tourism discourse (Sagasti and Colby, 1993). This resulted in the Stockholm Conference on Humans and the Environment (1972) which focussed more on industry-specific issues that needed to be addressed on lines of environmental degradation, cultural specificities and geographical adversities. Driml (1996) has defined 'sustainable development X' as the pattern of linking industry sectors with the concept of sustainable development. In this context, sustainable tourism emerges as one of the several industries that attaches itself with sustainable developmental governance. Such definitions also include categories such as 'new tourism' that focus on preservation of towns, non-exceeding of carrying capacities, enhancement of heritage and environmental values and education of tourists about sustainable growth in micro-sectors (Rosenow and Pulsipher, 1979). Such concepts have also been formalized- an example being the *Our Common Future* project (WCED, 1987) that emphasized six challenges and coherent solutions including conservation of places outside protected areas, incorporating small-scale and environmentally-sensitive tourism with aboriginal communities, and wildlife-based protective tourism. Hence, the common ground for sustainable tourism has been laid.

Tourism enterprises have a hand in contributing to the welfare of various communities. The socio-economic and political mobilization of communities can also take place along touristic lines, which requires that touristic enterprises on or within that community be formed in the first place. This can be done through policy development that has on-ground positive managerial implications (Koh, 1996). Hence, the role of entrepreneurial activity on tourism development needs to be assessed. By definition, tourism entrepreneurship is the 'creation of a touristic enterprise with the motive to make profit or not but with the intention to pursue a market opportunity through legal means or otherwise' (Koh and Hatten, 2005). Thus, the creation and operation of legal touristic ventures is the avenue of tourism entrepreneurship. Tourism entrepreneurs can be classified into inventive, imitative, marginal, social, lifestyle and closet, each differing in their methods of management and area of investment.

Sustainable Growth Strategies for Entrepreneurial Tourism

Hence, this paper seeks to explore the intersection of tourism entrepreneurship and sustainable tourism, and devise various methods through which regional development can be undertaken in sustainably touristic senses.

Table 1. Strategy for sustainable tourism development (Polnyotee and Thadaniti, 2015)

Tourism	Description	Promotional strategies	Impacts on society	Citations
Sustainable tourism	The tourism that is directed towards ensuring a long-term viable mode of tourism. It is the opposition of conventional mass tourism practices and aims to protect environment, wildlife and natural resources from tourism's side effects. The development of tourism must also be of immediate and long-term benefit to backward communities.	-Sustainable alternative destinations (Malaysia) - Green Hotel practices (Japan) -Natural resources for energy and fuel (Sweden) - Organic farming experiences (Italy) -Corbett Wildlife Reserve Park (India)	-Encourages environment-conscious behaviour - Preserves and protects local flora and fauna - Reduces income inequality in backward areas - Provides social support for disadvantaged communities	Pan et al., 2018; Paner-Krause, 2019; Lane, 2004; Sharpley, 2000

Polynotee and Thadaniti (2015) presents a model that seeks to adapt community-based tourism to promote sustainable tourism and provide solutions to environmental, social, and economic problems of the area. The model proposes five kinds of strategies to bring development for the people in the area. Firstly, political strategies include the empowerment of local people by participation in decision-making, campaigning, and knowledge and power to manage natural resources in the area. Secondly, environmental development strategies ensure the sustainability of resources through raising community awareness and adequate waste disposal. Thirdly, social development strategies focus exclusively on raising the quality of life of the people, providing security and fair distribution of roles and responsibilities among various sections. The model also emphasizes the need to build community management organizations. Fourthly, cultural development strategies advocate the fostering of respect and cultural exchange activities through history and art. Lastly, economic development strategies seek to directly benefit the local community by raising funds for community development and by the creation of new jobs and businesses in the area. This model provides a wide perspective towards approaching tourism with the intent to bring sustainable development in an area. While the model provides multifaceted strategies to uplift the local community, it has given guidelines for the development of the community as a whole. The strategies suggested by the model aim solely at the relationship between the community and the local administration, and do not include the influence of local businesses or industries. There is a lack of specific attention to socially-marginalized groups within the community, such as ostracised women, orphans, or disabled people. These groups require dedicated plans and policies that target their growth and gradual acceptance into society.

The present study seeks to develop a model that can establish a structural association between development of entrepreneurial tourism, and development of socially-backward communities as well. Keeping in view the promising growth of the tourism sector, and huge opportunities for the entrepreneurs in this sector, current study will aim to answer the followings research questions:

RQ1: What can be the different sustainable growth strategies for the entrepreneurial tourism?
RQ2: How different stakeholders can be involved for the sustainable growth of tourism sector?
RQ3: How growth of entrepreneurial tourism can be linked to the regional development?

Methodology: The study was based on the mix method approach where more than one data collection method was used:

1. Informal interview method to record the opinions of the entrepreneurs in the tourism sector towards the concept of sustainable tourism, regional development, how and up to what extent they are contributing to the regional development through tourism business. What kind of strategies they are using in line to the sustainable growth of the tourism sector.
2. Qualitative analysis method used to analyse the data collected from the websites of the tourist agencies, and government to understand the business models for sustainable growth of tourism sector, strategies adopted by tourism companies to involve the stakeholders.

For data collection through informal interview method, tourism companies, agencies, and agents from all the major states of India which are contributing highly to the tourism sector included. These states are mainly; Uttarakhand, Himachal Pradesh, Gujarat, Madhya Pradesh, and Jammu & Kashmir. Total sample of 100 tourism companies taken which comprises 20 respondents from each of the five states. While, for the qualitative analysis data of major South Asian countries has been collected. Text analytics and content analysis were major methods to analyse the data.

Followings are the answers of the research questions based on the content analysis of the data collected through informal interview to record the opinions of the entrepreneurs in the tourism sector towards the concept of sustainable tourism, regional development, how and up to what extent they are contributing to the regional development through tourism business.

Sustainable Growth Strategies for Tourism

Sustainability is important to the tourism sector due to several reasons. For instance, tourism is the one industry that sells the environment in both its physical and human form as a product. Hence, sustainable conservation and development of the environment is in the best interest of the stakeholders in the tourism sector. Defining sustainable development in this regard is important- as per the Our Common Future (1987) agenda, it is the kind of development that meets the needs of the present without hindering the ability of the future to do so. Hence, a more ecologically inclusive approach is taken to economic development based on older ideas of stewardship and conservationism. The international conference organized by the United Nations in 1992 in Rio De Janerio focussed primarily on protecting the earth's environment and fostering developmental strategies for nations which were less harmful to the environment. However, much scholarly work has been devoted to noting that the actual progress made in this sector has been extremely limited (Murphy and Price, 2005: 167).

It has been estimated that climate change would be the most significant factor affecting the tourism sector worldwide through 2030, owing to the trickle-down effects of it in multiple areas (Croce, 2018: 225). Tourism itself has been considered to be a victim and vector of climate change worldwide (Cabrini et al., 2009). Some tourism sectors specifically contribute to the process of global warming, including desertification, rising sea levels, deforestation etc. In this context, it is imperative that the policymaking

Sustainable Growth Strategies for Entrepreneurial Tourism

apparatus take into account these factors and formulate legislation designed specifically to address issues on the growing impact on and contribution of the tourism sector in climate change. For instance, the European Commission has studied the impact of climate change on this sector (Amelung and Moreno, 2009) and has provided support for various state-funded initiatives as well as intra-state initiatives such as the European Destinations of Excellence Programme. Regardless, World Bank Report (2016) notes that there is a substantial gap between the data available on climate change and it use in policy-making and decision-making at the level of civil society and state, which prevents nations from adopting a more responsible and environment-friendly tourism consumption practices.

Several approaches can be taken to improve the sustainability of tourism practices in various economies. For example, weakness-threats (WT) have been suggested to be incorporated by Mondal (2017), in his study of the tourism sector of a developing economy like that of Bangladesh, which utilizes various strategies like ensuring the safety of tourists at a particular tourist spot, planning adequately for the implementation of sustainable economic benefits, implementing environmental regulations for the sustainability of local ecology and ensuring proper mechanisms for the development of environmental infrastructure. Several weaknesses have to be identified prior to these measures being taken- such as, improper management of tourism in economies, business designs which are motivated towards making high profits, *threats* such as lack of awareness and tourism mismanagement etc. Identification of the issues and a proper weakness-threats analysis will lead to policymakers creating more effective solutions to the aforementioned problems, especially for economies in the developing world. Pro-poor strategies can also be adopted to increase sustainability practices in economies. These are more suited to developing countries of Asia where considerable growth for the tourism sector is possible due to the following reasons: first, Asia has a rich reserve of natural and cultural heritage which are considerable as juxtaposed against their western counterparts; and secondly, Asia has an increasingly mobile population with higher income capacities that allows it have a large internal tourist cohort in the form of domestic tourists (Lin and Guzman, 2007: 2). Pro-poor tourism would encourage the development of small and medium-sized enterprises (SMEs), much of which are primarily owned by poor communities, and this would benefit businesses from marginalized backgrounds thrive. Opportunities for SMEs would also rise considering that the various sectors of local economies such as agriculture, telecommunications and transportation would substantially input and link with each other. This would also, in turn and as a trickle-down effect, generate cash income for women and other disadvantaged groups (ABD, 2005). It has since been noted that tourism of multiple sorts depend on the participation of the poor, and pro-poor tourism would be sustainable as it would increase the chances of the natural and cultural resources of the poor to be protected through the official policymaking apparatus (Roe and Urquhart Khanya, 2001). Additionally, as has been noted, local tourism brings about with it increased local pride and improved local communications (Roe et al., 2002), which means that the local communities benefit both materially and psychologically from local tourism that is sustainable in nature.

The concept of eco-tourism has also been focussed on as an enabler of sustainability in the tourism sector. The term can be defined as 'responsible travel to natural areas with the intention of low-impact travel and preserving the natural and cultural features of the environment through interpretation and education (Fennel, 2017; Ghosh et al., 2020; Fletcher, 2014). Through methods of sustainable integration concerning fragile ecosystems, community participation and social conscience can be ensured alongside enhancing cultural sensitivity (Prakash, 2020). What needs to be considered are also the ecological costs of tourism, the expectations of tourists and the needs of the host community. In many cases, however, a need to bring synchronization between the needs of the service providers and the service-takers is required, more often than not there being a discord between the two. In this context, the formation of eco-parks, eco-spots etc., may include four basic tenets as has been pointed out by Prakash et al. (2017):

- Activity-based Segmentation (ABS)
- Four-I model (Involvement, Investment, Infrastructure and Integration)
- Product Diversification
- Industry Destination Partnerships (IDP)

Additionally, the role of eco-tourism entails product diversification, conservation of nature, stakeholders' participation, community development and a benefits-sought promotional strategy.

On the other hand, it has also been observed that growth in tourism is itself harmful to sustainability, i.e., development of tourism causes more damage than the formation of sustainable tourism. 'Slum tourism' and child exploitation have been found to be a major moral deficiency in the tourism sector which feeds off healthy tourism practices and hinders sustainability for tourism practices among vulnerable groups of populations (Higgins-Desbiolles, 2018). What has been recommended is that lives in home communities be made more sustainable so that tourism necessities are decreased and travel declined, to accommodate lesser involvement with tourism. What has been proposed is the incorporation of tourism into a structural management of mobilities approach, which focusses on the identification of imbalanced priorities in the tourism sector and international tourism management.

Hence, there are several approaches to the idea of sustainable development within the tourism sector. To come to a holistic approach requires integrating several elements from the various approaches and formulating custom-made frameworks for region-specific and ecosystem-specific needs.

Inclusive Stakeholder's Model for Sustainable Growth Strategies of Tourism Sector

The incorporation of policies based on sustainable goals should also include the interests of the various stakeholders involved in the process. In this light, it is imperative that we define the nature of stakeholders that we are trying to incorporate as well as the nature of relationships that they form both amongst themselves and the concerned policymaking bodies.

Issue-based stakeholder networks can be defined as 'a set of interdependent actors that are affected by some common socio-economic issue and are a relevant source of creation of organizational values' (Sachs and Ruhli, 2011; Svendsen and Laberge, 2005). According to stakeholder theorists, value-creation is embedded in the relational contributions among the stakeholders and the central organization. In this model, the capacity of a business organization to generate profit and wealth depends on the relationship it holds with its critical stakeholders (Post et al., 2002: 89). Alternatively, the organization has been made a focal stakeholder among critical stakeholders by Rowley (1997) as a means of wealth-generation. Overall, it can be inferred that the stakeholder theory addresses issues and challenges created by an increasingly globalized and interconnected society. Hence, it is in the best interests of any organization to create as much value as possible for the stakeholders involved with it, whereas incorporating the interests of the stakeholders in the value-creation process can enhance the organization's capacities to deal with the challenges that business in a globalized society poses (Freeman et al., 2010). Additionally, what is valuable in a stakeholder-organization dynamic differs from stakeholder to stakeholder and must be clarified with each individually (Harrison and Wicks, 2013). Hence, including stakeholders in the decision-making

Sustainable Growth Strategies for Entrepreneurial Tourism

process of various organizations, including the formulation of policies by policymaking bodies, increases the value that is generated by these organizations. As a consequence, stakeholders benefit directly.

In this context, the inclusion of various stakeholders in the policymaking process concerning sustainable development of the tourism sector is primary. Stakeholder cooperation has been deemed to be a primary factor in stakeholder inclusion and analysis when it comes to making policies relevant to sustainable tourism (Miocic et al., 2016). It has been advocated that in terms of destination management (as a cohort of primary stakeholders and resources), multi-stakeholder management should include the interests of individuals and other influential groups who are involved in tourism management as well as planning. Conversely, the negative effects on the local communities in the form of environmental degradation, as well as their socio-economic needs should be taken into consideration. In fact, the issues around tourism management revolve primarily around the complexities that arise out of ecological degradation of host communities that results from tourist practices. Sustainable development ensures that the tourism sector develops in a controlled manner using various resources but also preserving those resources for use by the next generations (UNWTO, 2011).

Since the declaration of 2017 as the international year of sustainable development of the tourism sector and attainment of Sustainable Development Goals (SDGs), several efforts have been made in various nation-states to incorporate sustainable objectives in policymaking. Regardless, there have been lapses in the incorporation of trust, social capital, justice, power and participation in the tourism governance frameworks of countries like South Africa (Siakwah, 2019). The shift of the state as a 'provider' to an 'enabler' comes along as complementary to the formation of the neoliberal state itself and subsequent collaborative policymaking (Vernon et al., 2005: 327). Additionally, a top-down approach of the state has been replaced by the bottom-up approach that focusses more on decentralization than centralized planning systems (Hall, 2000), through which businesses take up more responsibility for management. It is in this light that the importance of community engagement in sustainable tourism development can be understood, with local communities acting as stakeholders in the process. It has been suggested that when studying the role of local communities in tourism management, the economic, social and political processes within the community can hardly be separated from one another (Hall, 2003). Interdependence among the various stakeholders within the communities, and not just communities as stakeholders, further complicate the planning issues that already exist in tourism destination settings (Jamal and Getz, 1999). If we consider community participation from an urban planning perspective, stakeholder inclusion only adds to being fundamentally fair and representative in a democratic decision-making environment (Mahjabeen et al., 2009). The basic understanding is that when local communities are engaged in the decision-making/ policymaking process, stakeholder engagement happens and in turn brings about local forms of knowledge, information and skills together. However, for stakeholder participation to be effective in the case of tourism management and sustainable tourism, the local populace needs to be aware that their participation will bring about affirmative changes to already existing tourism arrangements (Byrd, 2007: 8). The challenges arise primarily because of diverging interests of the local communities, visiting individuals, investors, the state, governmental and non-governmental organizations (Richins and Pearce, 2000). However, different destinations face a different set of problems and challenges (Laws, 1995).

It is through conflict resolution that policies and actions in sustainable tourism development are undertaken. There are many goals that are always in conflict but there are also goals that are shared (McCool, 2009). Planning personnel need to take into account the stakeholders' interests to formulate plans that have desirable outcomes for them, through appropriate dialogue-creation and preparability for uncertainty (2009: 138). Mair and Reid (2007) have suggested that several factors need to be taken into account including deciding the components that should be in place for sound community-based tourism planning. Hence, conflict resolution adds to stakeholder inclusion in sustainable tourism management.

Entrepreneurial Tourism and Regional Development

It has been noted that tourism has potential for the development of large areas, especially in the rural areas, which can enhance the process of regional development (Dana and Lasch, 2014). Especially in the case of rural communities, the concentration of agricultural activities, migration of younger people to more urban spaces and the springing up of more efficient farms have transformed the nature of life in peripheral areas (Anderson, 2000). In this context, tourism development of marginal areas can bring about significant changes to the community life and environment- including stress and work-life balance, population flows, income levels, seasonality of specific occupations and work stress (Pearce et al., 2010).

In the more negative sense, mass tourism can cause environmental degradation owing to the vandalism of heritage sites, depletion of natural heritages, degeneration of local community culture owing to influx of outside elements, rural exodus that comes about as a result of inclusionary and exclusionary practices, increased demand for public services, as well as the increase in cost of living of the host communities which comes about as a result of real estate speculation (Calado et al., 2011: 161-62). It has been observed that there is no comprehensive framework to prevent these from happening; rather, the specific needs of local communities should be taken into account to counter practices that are debilitating to local culture and resources in terms of tourism management (Gaddefors and Cronsell, 2009).

On the other hand, a paradigm shift from the tourist destination as 'space' to the tourist destination as 'place' helps characterise local rural communities as fit for entrepreneurial activity (Hudson, 2001). Places can be defined as areas where people of a particular community engage in meaningful social life and contribute to socialization and cultural acquisition (Johnstone and Lionais, 2004: 219). The role of tourism in this is dubious- a change in the agricultural and craftmanship abilities of local communities has the capability to disrupt meaning-making and cultural faculties of that community, and hence, alter its social fabric (Dana, 1999). As is often the case, in-migrant entrepreneurs develop new activities without consideration for local knowledge systems or the willingness to decipher local meanings and behaviour (Bosworth and Farrell, 2011). As such, economic activities that generate pressure outpacing the general flow of local life can degenerate local community and social identity of members by threatening to alienate them from their own cultures. In more extreme instance, local identity can be entirely destroyed by market forces and be replaced by more consumer-oriented patterns that, in the long run, are not sustainable and threaten to destroy social and moral fabric of a local tourism community.

Hence, entrepreneurship in terms of tourism management can be a complicated field requiring specialized deliberation of policy. Market forces present a different kind of threat- even if entrepreneurialism brings about economic change. In an effort to marketize tourist destinations, local communities may be entirely uprooted of their cultural moorings, while creating a façade of cultural heritage that serves not the interests of the local communities themselves but the interests of tourism entrepreneurs, which may create an artificial paraphernalia of heritage not native to the host community but created through interaction with a neoliberal market (Anderson and McAuley, 1999).

Concepts of marginality are also inherent in discussions around regional development. However, policies differ in the way they address marginality and vulnerability, especially when it comes to the same in the tourism sector. It also depends on the nature of the policy environment that the vulnerable communities or peripheral locations exist (Hall, 2007:23). Additionally, various approaches can define

Sustainable Growth Strategies for Entrepreneurial Tourism

peripheral and urban areas differently based on the kind of audience it woos and the faculties it provides. For instance, Christaller (1963) defines peripheral areas as those which are primarily geared towards pleasure activities and urban areas as those where business transactions are preponderant. Turner and Ash (1975) have hinted on the possibility of 'pleasure peripheries' that focusses more on a core-periphery binary model than a simple econometric categorization. More recently, peripheral areas have become the site of study in and of themselves, owing to economic and political restricting of certain areas, especially in the European context. Hence, definitional categories, in discursive terms, have made possible wider explanations of the tourism development of peripheral areas to include those activities which have traditionally not been associated with tourism in the first place, through a complicated nexus of core-periphery relations in a globalized economy.

CONCLUSION

Sustainable development goals have long been integrated in the development of several sectors, including that of entrepreneurial tourism. This study has explored several areas that link developmentalist strategies with entrepreneurial tourism in contexts of sustainability. Several key insights have been made in this arena. Firstly, local socio-cultural contexts need to be considered to develop sustainable entrepreneurial tourism which involves the local people of the region as stakeholders (Kisi, 2019). This ensures that community development at the local level is undertaken through sustainably exploiting the resources of the region and enabling the people of the community to take part in the entrepreneurial process through commercial or State channels. Secondly, entrepreneurial tourism is also a political issue in many instances that leads to its development in certain constricted manners (Goodwin, 2017). Interventions to ensure that positive headway is made in the direction of benefit for the local population, thus, have to be framed. Thirdly, resource allocation is a major factor in the development of entrepreneurial tourism. Hence, sustainable entrepreneurial tourism development strategies need to consider the 'carrying capacity' of region which is contextual in nature. Overall, the study has explicated on the diverse nature of sustainable entrepreneurial tourism and paves the way for the development of strategies that enhance its potential. In conclusion, the confluence of entrepreneurial tourism and regional development harps on the intersection of various stakeholders as well as definitional categories that change over time. It is in these intersections that economic linkages can be traced to ensure that policymaking focusses more on the needs and aspirations of the local communities rather than handing over entrepreneurial responsibility entirely to market forces.

IMPLICATIONS

Theoretical implications: The study will add a new element to the existing literature in the form of "Entrepreneurial Tourism and Regional development". The study will also highlight the importance of Entrepreneurial Tourism growth and how inclusive growth can be achieved in the tourism sector. A comprehensive research paradigm invokes that adequate addressing of theoretical problems be undertaken. In this context, this study explores the intersection of sustainable development and tourism entrepreneurship, including the theoretical complications that arise from the same. Considering that there are areas which overlap between the two, developing a holistic theory around addressing challenges of sustainable entrepreneurial tourism requires that hybrid methods like SWOT (strengths, weaknesses, opportunities and threats) be adopted. This study adds to the conceptualization of new measures that considers all these factors, hence leading to the creation of methods that can be applied in context-specific cases.

Practical implications: The study will focus on developing an inclusive stakeholder's model which can be used by the government, policy makers, or the corporate sector for sustainable growth in the tourism sector, by involving the multiple stakeholders. Study will also suggest the different ways where the tourism sector can promise the growth the regions, along with its own growth. Considering that tourism has become one of the most important sources of foreign revenue for States (Clayton, 2002), there is an increasing need to deal with the environmental crises that several face, especially developing economies, which constricts their social development. The paper has explored ideas around 'carrying capacity' (the amount of population that a specific geographical area can hold against the resources that are within it), which can be used to develop specific policies catering to entrepreneurial tourism. For instance, policies can be framed to regulate tourism that puts pressure on the natural resources of particular sector or even use the same to further the generation of more resources through public participation. The study will also enable specific intervention nodes to be identified for collaborative participation to be initiated.

REFERENCES

Amelung, B. and Moreno, A. (2009). Impacts of climate change in tourism in Europe, PESETA-tourism study. *JRC Scientific and Technical Reports EUR, 24114.*

Anderson, A. R. (2000). Paradox in the Periphery: An Entrepreneurial Reconstruction? *Entrepreneurship and Regional Development, 12*(2), 91–109. doi:10.1080/089856200283027

Anderson, A. R., & McAuley, A. (1999). Marketing Landscapes: The Social Context. *Qualitative Market Research, 2*(3), 176–188. doi:10.1108/13522759910291680

Bosworth, G., & Farrell, H. (2011). Tourism Entrepreneurs in Northumberland. *Annals of Tourism Research, 38*(4), 1474–1494. doi:10.1016/j.annals.2011.03.015

Byrd, E. T. (2007). Stakeholders in sustainable tourism development and their roles: Applying stakeholder theory to sustainable tourism development. *Tourism Review, 62*(2), 6–13. doi:10.1108/16605370780000309

Cabrini, L., Simpson, M., & Scott, D. (2009). *From Davosto Copenhagenandbeyond:advancingtourism's response to climate change.* SDT. www.sdt.unwto.org

Calado, L., Rodrigues, A., Silveira, P., & Dentinho, T. (2011). Rural Tourism Associated with Agriculture as An Economic Alternative for the Farmers. *European Journal of Tourism, Hospitality and Recreation, 2*(1), 155–174.

Christaller, W. (1963). Some considerations of tourism location in Europe: The peripheral regions – underdeveloped countries – recreation areas. *Regional Science Association Papers, 12*, 95–105.

Croce, V. (2018). With growth comes accountability: could a leisure activity turn into a driver for sustainable growth? *Journal of Tourism Futures.*

Croce, V., & Maggi, R. (2007). From the ideal to the real destination: tourists' location choice for holiday experience. In T. Bieger & P. Keller (Eds.), *Productiveness in Tourism* (pp. 69–81). ESV.

Dana, L. P. (1999). The Social Cost of Tourism: A Case Study of Ios. *Cornell Hospitality Quarterly*, *40*(4), 60–63. doi:10.1177/001088049904000414

Fennell, D. A. (2017). *Eco-Tourism* (4th ed.). Routledge.

Fletcher, R. (2014). Romancing the wild. In *Romancing the Wild*. Duke University Press.

Gaddefors, J., & Cronsell, N. (2009). Returnees and Local Stakeholders Co-Producing the Entrepreneurial Region. *European Planning Studies*, *17*(8), 1191–1203. doi:10.1080/09654310902981045

Ghosh, R. N., & Siddique, M. A. B. (Eds.). (2017). *Tourism and economic development: Case studies from the Indian ocean region*. Routledge. doi:10.4324/9781315235981

Hall, C. M. (2003). Politics and place: An analysis of power in tourism communities. In S. Singh, D. J. Timothy, & R. K. Dowling (Eds.), *Tourism in destination communities* (pp. 99–114). CABI. doi:10.1079/9780851996110.0099

Harrison, J. S., & Wicks, A. C. (2013). Stakeholder theory, value, and firm performance. *Business Ethics Quarterly*, *23*(1), 97–124. doi:10.5840/beq20132314

Higgins-Desbiolles, F. (2018). Sustainable tourism: Sustaining tourism or something more? *Tourism Management Perspectives*, *25*, 157–160. doi:10.1016/j.tmp.2017.11.017

Hudson, R. (2001). *Producing Places*. Guilford.

Jamal, T., & Getz, D. (1999). Community roundtables for tourism-related conflicts: The dialetics of consensus and process structures. *Journal of Sustainable Tourism*, *7*(3&4), 290–313. doi:10.1080/09669589908667341

Johnstone, H., & Lionais, D. (2004). Depleted Communities and Community Business Entrepreneurship: Revaluing Space Through Place. *Entrepreneurship and Regional Development*, *16*(3), 217–233. doi:10.1080/0898562042000197117

Laws, E. (1995). *Tourist destination management: Issues, analysis and policies*. Routledge.

Lin, T., & De Guzman, F. D. (2007). *Tourism for pro-poor and sustainable growth: Economic analysis of tourism projects*. Asian Development Bank.

Mahjabeen, Z., Shresha, K. K., & Dee, J. A. (2009). Rethinking community participation in urban planning: The role of disadvantaged groups in Sydney metropolitan strategy. *Australasian Journal of Regional Studies*, *15*(1), 45–63.

McCool, S. (2009). Constructing partnerships for protected area tourism planning in an era of change and messiness. *Journal of Sustainable Tourism*, *17*(2), 133–148. doi:10.1080/09669580802495733

McCool, S. F. (2009). Constructing partnerships for protected area tourism planning in an era of change and messiness. *Journal of Sustainable Tourism*, *17*(2), 133–148. doi:10.1080/09669580802495733

Mondal, M., & Haque, S. (2017). SWOT analysis and strategies to develop sustainable tourism in Bangladesh. *UTMS Journal of Economics (Skopje)*, *8*(2), 159–167.

Parmar, B. L., Freeman, R. E., Harrison, J. S., Wicks, A. C., Purnell, L., & De Colle, S. (2010). Stakeholder theory: The state of the art. *The Academy of Management Annals*, *4*(1), 403–445. doi:10.5465/19416520.2010.495581

Pearce, P. L., Filep, S., & Ross, G. F. (2010). *Tourists, Tourism and the Good Life*. Routledge. doi:10.4324/9780203845868

Post, J. E., Preston, L. E., & Sauter-Sachs, S. (2002). *Redefining the corporation: Stakeholder management and organizational wealth*. Stanford University Press. doi:10.1515/9781503619692

Prakash, K. B., & Reddy, M. P. S. (2020). Eco-tourism-the enabler and enhancer of sustainable growth. *Innov. Econ. Policy Res.*, *1*(1), 16–23.

Richins, H., & Pearce, P. (2000). Influences on tourism development decision making: Coastal local government areas in eastern Australia. *Journal of Sustainable Tourism*, *8*(3), 207–225. doi:10.1080/09669580008667359

Rowley, T. J. (1997). Moving beyond dyadic ties: A network theory of stakeholder influences. *Academy of Management Review*, *22*(4), 887–910. doi:10.2307/259248

Sachs, S., & Rühli, E. (2011). *Stakeholders matter: A new paradigm for strategy in society*. Cambridge University Press. doi:10.1017/CBO9781139026963

Siakwah, P., Musavengane, R., & Leonard, L. (2020). Tourism governance and attainment of the sustainable development goals in Africa. *Tourism Planning & Development*, *17*(4), 355–383. doi:10.1080/21568316.2019.1600160

Svendsen, A. C., & Laberge, M. (2005). Convening stakeholder networks: A new way of thinking, being and engaging. *Journal of Corporate Citizenship*, *2005*(19), 91–104. doi:10.9774/GLEAF.4700.2005.au.00013

Turner, L., & Ash, J. (1975). *The Golden Hordes: International Tourism and the Pleasure Periphery*. Constable.

Vernon, J., Essex, S., Pinder, D., & Curry, K. (2005). Collaborative policymaking: Local sustainable projects. *Annals of Tourism Research*, *32*(2), 325–345. doi:10.1016/j.annals.2004.06.005

ENDNOTE

[1] Available at: https://sustainabledevelopment.un.org/index.php?page=view&type=255&nr=19645(Accessed 27 February 2021).

Chapter 8

Traditional Music and Tourism Identity in Cyprus:
A Strong Means Strategy to Strengthen Cultural Tourism

Stalo Georgiou

Neapolis University, Cyprus

ABSTRACT

Music provides an important and emotional narrative for tourists as an expression of culture, a form of heritage, and a significant place. Indeed, it is becoming increasingly difficult to imagine tourism in silence. Music defines and transcends the boundaries of destinations, while emphasizing and even challenging the concepts of tradition and helping to define the identity of visitors. Traditional music is part of the identity of each region and a global artistic language, while its wide appeal enables it to nurture the richest dialogues between different cultures. As a symbol of cultural identity in relation to the past, traditional music is used by many cultural groups and individuals, including nation states, for political empowerment and cultural diplomacy. The cultural tourist identity of a country includes traditional music, traditional dances, improvised street entertainment, tours in concerts, watching music festivals; these are what accompany the visitor-tourist.

INTRODUCTION

Culture is a point of reference for collective identity, as it simultaneously performs basic functions for society as a whole, such as recognition, integration and participation. Through it the members of a group or larger groups are recognized and acquire their collective identity. Every cultural identity is hybrid and dynamic, as it incorporates a variety of diverse elements and determines the basis of a claim for difference rather than a timeless and absolute differentiation (Paschalidis, 2002). The elements that make up a cultural identity can be real, ideological or symbolic or a combination of multiple elements from the

DOI: 10.4018/978-1-6684-6055-9.ch008

Copyright © 2023, IGI Global. Copying or distributing in print or electronic forms without written permission of IGI Global is prohibited.

cultural space. In addition, cultural identities and heterogeneities are two-way systems adopted by the individual in a particular group or group of groups. Cultural identity also includes artistic identities, such as dance and music. Music, song and dance at the level of identity play an important role, as they are used by members of a group or a wider group, such as the nation, as a means of promoting their cultural identity (Anholt, 2010).

Goal of the Article

The aim of the article is to assess the connection between traditional music and identity and how these two can be used as a strong strategic means for enhancing the cultural tourism experience.

Methodology

The article makes use of the descriptive review of the literature, which aims to investigate the issue under consideration through different perspectives, and to try to assess the overarching questions keeping in mind the future research perspectives and the application in practice.

Definition of Terms

National identity: The inhabitants of a state who share common myths, common historical memories, common language, common geographical place, are defined according to Smith (1991) as persons with a common national identity. These concepts have turned the interest of the social sciences in clarifying national identity. Individuals perceive themselves as members of a national group where everyone has in common, their national identity

Cultural tourism: Cultural tourism is one of the special and alternative forms of tourism (Kokkosis and Chartas, 2001). One of the oldest forms of travel, it is today emerging as one of the most important and rapidly growing fields of the tourism phenomenon (Krajnović and Gortan-Carlin, 2018).

Traditional music: Traditional music is the music of a people, a nation or a region which is spread orally, evolving through the variation of melodies created by the people themselves (Smith, 2000)

LITERATURE REVIEW

The Cultural Heritage

Since the Renaissance and, mainly, since the Enlightenment, societies have been in a search for the remnants of the past, material and intangible, in order to be able to establish their historical origin, legitimizing both their cultural and national identity (Sbonias, 2002: 129). According to the definition of ICOMOS (1999) the concept of cultural heritage includes in its contents both the natural and the cultural environment. The broader concept includes landscapes, archaeological or historical sites, sites and settlements, architectural, natural or geological monuments and biodiversity. It also includes elements of tradition and identities, such as beliefs, knowledge, experiences, social relationships and behaviours, but also other spiritual, moral or aesthetic values. The promotion of tangible and intangible cultural heritage supports

Traditional Music and Tourism Identity in Cyprus

the creation of infrastructure for the preservation of cultural heritage in the areas where it develops, as it offers the opportunity to the local community, on the one hand to preserve its cultural heritage and to develop infrastructure capable of receiving cultural visitors (Kokkosis - Chartas, 2001: 79).

The Intangible Cultural Heritage and the Musical Tradition of a Place

The Intangible Cultural Heritage focuses on the culture of everyday life and ordinary people, on customary practices, knowledge, practices, and traditions, which, being rooted in time, determine both our individual and collective self-knowledge as well as our collective memory and identity (Kallimopoulou, 2009).

The Greek state, in the context of work on the drafting of the UNESCO Convention, adopted in 2002 the term "intangible cultural property" for those elements of cultural heritage that were described as "traditional and modern popular culture". Intangible cultural assets are myths, oral traditions, customs, dances, events, music and songs or other elements that are evidence of traditional or learned culture. The main feature of intangible cultural heritage is that it changes, transforms. In particular, as far as the musical tradition is concerned, it encompasses both the musical creation and the songs and the dance, and is the creation of a long process, where the original element can remain as it is. or to be processed and adapted in the context of individual factors, such as language, place and people (Virvidakis, 2003: 60).

The musical tradition as an intangible heritage was passed down from generation to generation orally and was adapted to the particular cultural environment of a community or transcended local boundaries and spread to a greater extent. In the context of multinational and multicultural empires, the loss of natural borders between peoples and nations allowed the spread of music (Grapsas, 2003: 219). Similarly, it allowed songs to be adapted to different languages that were popular or activated the emotional element of the listeners. There is, in fact, the phenomenon of maintaining the music and the rhythm itself and adapting the song to the needs of the language (Grapsas, 2003: 202-205). As an intangible heritage, traditional songs are of great importance for the oral history of a place or a group, as they include elements from local myths, customs and traditions, local heroes, historical events, battles, squats, love affairs, births, while inheriting to the next generation elements that preserve historical memory and strengthen identity. Individual elements of the musical tradition, such as dances, are evidence of the origin and dispersion of members of a community (Grapsas, 2003: 202-205). In the dipole tradition-heritage, the meaning of tradition goes back to the distant past and to the oral elements that are transmitted from generation to generation keeping the tradition alive in the present, while the word heritage refers directly to the past and the role it plays in the present (Sbonias, 2002: 129).

The cultural heritage of a place in many cases becomes a pole of attraction for international tourists and the main source of financial income, while it is an important pillar of sustainable tourism development (Prentice, & Andersen, 2013). In any case, it is important that the physical, mental and emotional access to cultural heritage is done within a reasonable framework and with appropriate handling, since both cultural and natural heritage are unique and non-renewable resources, important for the understanding of cultural heritage. identity of a social group or a wider whole. The uncontrolled and rapid development of tourism can cause damage to the cultural heritage and alter its character and significance (Kokkosis - Chartas, 2001: 164) The relationship between cultural heritage and tourism is a dynamic one, as culture needs funding for preservation and creation of goods and products of culture, while tourism needs the quality and the extended environment offered by culture(Kostakis,2003: 3).

There is something deeply human in music, but also deeply cultural (Savage, 2019), as there are many different types of music, as well as languages. But unlike language, music, as a vehicle of culture, does not require a code to lead to the understanding of a message or the expression of an emotion. People understand, feel and are moved by the music they listen to, even though the language that accompanies it means nothing to them, while at the same time, to another people and their culture, this music is an important part of history, of culture and its own identity. And this power of music to move is used by people to create cultural identity, to create unity among members of the community (Pachoulidis, 2007).

Today is more characterized than ever by multicultural societies (Rogerson 2006). This fact leads us to see music and culture from many angles. For example, through a single cultural perspective, we assume that we can use the same practices, patterns, and patterns to create music. However, from a multicultural perspective, we realize that there are many different approaches and musical practices that reflect the different cultures of the world (Rogerson 2006). It is this diversity that enriches our lives, expands our understanding of the world around us and increases respect for diversity and a willingness to research in order to get to know our own music and our own culture better. This is because, through different musical paths and other areas, we learn more, our horizons expand and so we try to get to know better what concerns our own place, to find out what is behind these sounds, what is their history. and what is their origin in order to better understand our own identity (Ruud, 2009).

Music, Sociability, and Identity

Social scientists who have studied music and song as social practices in the Aegean region have demonstrated the special importance of musical performances for local identity and gender identity. Music and song are dominant symbols and vehicles of sociability in community events, in life cycle events, but also in homosexual gatherings, in which the sexes are formed as social entities. In male groups, singing is often the core of sociability. Women are a key player in the collective memory of local cultural expressions and their participation in the rituals of death, through collective mourning, gives them a special role in the ritual management processes of the community (Richards, 2003). The improvisational character of the song at the local festivities creates a special plasticity in the expression through the song, providing an important framework for dealing with key social issues for the life of the local communities, such as immigration, alienation, changing living conditions, new conditions created by tourism in the islands (Richards, 2003).

In areas where improvised song flourishes, such as Karpathos, local music and dance expressions function as symbolic equivalents of the place, transforming the party into a "symbolic village". Music and dance expressions are also becoming fields of intense controversy and political expression of the new social data of the community (Avdikos, 2014).

In recent years, there has been a strong movement in the Aegean region to revive local cultural practices that had begun to decline in the post-war period, a time when the phenomenon of permanent migration prevailed in the islands, both inside and outside. From the mid-1970s onwards, with the regular return of immigrants to their birthplaces, music and song became the focus of cultural practices at the local level, experiencing a new flourishing, through revived or even newly established cultural performances, such as the diverse events of local clubs. These events formed a wave of revival of "tradition" at the local level, which relied on music, but also had a decisive influence (Avdikos, 2014).

Traditional Music and Tourism Identity in Cyprus

The Composition of the Tradition

The "traditional" music in the Mediterranean today is largely determined by the demands of the record industry and the increased demand for "authentic" cultural products. These two tendencies sometimes have a complementary relationship and sometimes contradictory and inconsistent results. The commercialization of music on a nationwide scale has formed a new category of fantasy music, the so-called "island song", which originates from the Mediterranean area, but comes to systematically simplify the ideal characteristics of the music of the Mediterranean area, and weakly completely marginalizing local peculiarities and peculiarities. In a later stage, the "island" song and its actors merged with other aspects of the Greek and Cypriot music industry, producing musical osmosis of local, folk and pop elements, which are reintroduced into local communities to meet the growing and constantly renewed needs for " traditional music (Theologou, 2007).

Our ideas for the unity of the musical idiom of the Aegean come equally from our knowledge of the history of the area, but also from other sources, less official and "valid", such as the iconology of tourism and exoticism that accompanies it. The search for "traditional" Aegean music today must also be seen, to some extent, in parallel with the discovery of "Mediterranean music", which in recent years has been a key aspect of the "world music" current. The local idioms of Karpathos, Amorgos, Naxos, Chios, Mytilene and other islands do not form a single "tradition", except to the extent that we are determined to invent it and give it specific characteristics. In such a movement, the common features of the various musical expressions of the Aegean area are no longer important for determining the unity of the region by the broader historical, economic, and social factors, but also the cultural policies that construct the unity of the Mediterranean (Theologou, 2007).

Cultural Tourism: Conceptual Definition and Effects

The most known and popular definition of cultural tourism was given by Richards (1996: 23), who noted that cultural tourism refers to the movement of people away from the place they live in order to engage to cultural activities and to participate in events that aim to satisfy and enhance their cultural needs. Based on a definition provided by Silberberg (1995), cultural tourism is defined as the visits of individuals outside their local community, influenced in whole or in part by the interest in the historical, scientific or cultural sources of a community, region or institution (Stevenson, 2007).

Music, as a product of the human spirit, seems to be completely intertwined with the daily life of people as it is the one that can accompany their joys and sorrows, to frame their dances and celebrations, to help them communicate with each other. even in their communication with God or with what they consider sacred, to rest them, to help them escape, to unite them, to encourage them, to give them rhythm and command, to help them to express themselves for love even give them the opportunity through it to challenge, to claim, to revolt. In previous years it seems that music was more connected with sociality and with the moments when the older societies found reasons to gather their members in common actions, such as celebrations, festivals, etc. but also in a common place. Music represents an admirable meeting point of the private and public space, providing self-determination meetings with a collective identity (Hesmondhalgh, 2008). Music, then, that accompanies all aspects of human life, always seems to accompany travel but also to be one of the first motivations of people, along with the mood for contact with other arts and cultures, when in the 17th century the first voyages began, the famous Gran tour.

Gran tours were trips organized by the elite of the time, mainly to Britain, with the aim of the off-spring of wealthy families to come in contact with other cultures and various forms of high art such as literature, architecture, painting and of course music, or listening music in various recitals or acquiring the same skills in music, studying a musical instrument. For this reason, these trips are considered as the beginning of modern tourism (Gibson and Connell, 2007). Until the middle of the 18th century, these trips became fashionable for the rest of the world, while with the development of spas there is a movement of travellers to spa resorts and later with the development of railways and the emergence of a working class that followed the construction of railways, seaside. Resorts become a tourist attraction. In this context, music always accompanied the free time of travellers, while later in the 18th and 19th centuries it would be an even stronger motivation to make a trip since people chose to attend, theatre or music-related festivals. The idea of music tourism - to travel to listen to music - is a historical phe-nomenon related to industrialization and modernism; in the nineteenth century differentiation began to appear between classical music and popular music as those who belong to Europe's elite rush to listen to composers at various festivals while the working class travels to enjoy popular songs in large halls (Lashua, et al 2014). The rise of music tourism, however, has taken music from being just an expected, or occasionally unexpected, holiday supplement and given it a central role (Connell and Gibson, 2004).

People now travelled to listen to music, to meet their favourite artist, to attend concerts or festivals that lasted for days. On the other hand, the places that organized activities related to music such as concerts or festivals or had a long musical history such as e.g. Milan or New Orleans began to become a tourist attraction, as did places that even seemed to be associated with music or an artist, such as locations that appeared on a music album cover or the lyrics of a song spoke of these or even the places where a band was active became especially important to some music fans. Such synapses, combined with the powerful emotional role of music in consumer energies, create forms of demand that translate into new local cultural economies, as debates about authenticity and uniqueness are mobilized against markets of all scales and become means of transforming places (Gibson and Conell, 2003). Even the places that had a special folk music tradition, were a pole of attraction for scholars or people who showed interest in coming in contact with different sounds while at the same time gaining the opportunity for rebirth and stimulating the sense of pride of their inhabitants for history and their identity. So it seems that the music acts as a motivation for making a trip but also to be connected to the place in a special way since through it or because of it the place becomes a tourist destination. Music is both a core cultural industry and a field through which places can be made known and represented by providing a new source of im-ages and sounds to promote tourism (Gibson and Connell, 2003).

From the middle of the last century, however, as technology gained ground, so music was heard ev-erywhere and not only in specific places or on specific occasions, or people chose to get in touch with it by watching e.g. a concert or listening to a record - or not, since it was no longer heard on the radio, on the computers, on the cell phones anywhere else, e.g. in places like malls or supermarkets, in any activities like sports, social, cultural (Lashua et . al, 2014). The music that is heard often seems to be imposed by the music industry since from a very early age the industry realized the power that music had in influencing but also imposing standards and ideas on the masses. The commercialization of music from the last century is an aspect that we can not overlook. However, musical genres are products of human culture that are worshiped for their aesthetic value but it is also a place of questioning of mean-ing and purpose throughout history from one side of the earth to the other (Lashua et al., 2014). Music, in addition to the serenity or intensity that its sound can create, can also have a catalytic effect on the lyrics and convey meanings, ideas and even political positions in a very crucial way and function as a

Traditional Music and Tourism Identity in Cyprus

means of expression of an entire society. It is an inexhaustible source of emotions, artistic expression and creation, social and personal expression, creation and acquisition of identity, whether personal, collective or national. Above all, because music is related to the feeling of people, it creates a feeling of nostalgia for people, situations, experiences and places, even a sense of intimacy even with situations or places with which there was no direct contact and a possibility of personal and collective narration.

This is why the paradoxical phenomenon is observed that an increasing percentage of people are not content with the commercialized form of music but to look for new forms, to look for older ones, to discover traditional sounds that are offered for new readings, to seek to connect with one of their own a special way for music to acquire an identity in the era of globalization and for this reason to travel more and more because of music. This fact is also reflected in the literature, since the issue of music and tourism is increasingly of concern to tourism studies. The 2014 issue of Tourist Studies attempts to explore certain important aspects between music and tourism, such as how music turns specific places into tourist hotspots or whether music is another 'resource' that the tourism industry can exploit for consumption. tourist masses (Lashua et. al, 2014). In the aftermath of their work (Gibson and Connell, 2003) a large conference was held in 2012 in Liverpool, England, Soundracks: Music Tourism and Travel, where lectures were given that explored music in relation to old and new movements, the musical pilgrimage, the flows of travellers and musicians, cultural and economic policies related to tourism, festivals and performances for tourists, the ethnography of tourist meetings with music as a tourist destination, the role of music in the creation of tourist discussions, narratives and memories. Thus the subject of music and tourism seems to occupy a number of sciences, not only tourism, but anthropology and sociology, musicology, management geography.

Traditional Music and the Case of Cyprus

The Cypriot folk music, as an integral part of the Greek Culture, had the same general origins as the Greek traditional music, survived, over time, in similar traces as those of the other Greek regions and in similar historical challenges. Nevertheless, it managed and cultivated its own peculiarities. The musical wealth of Cyprus has been kept alive and unscathed through the centuries and is the quintessence of the soul of its people. The Cypriot folk heritage, in adverse conditions of centuries of slavery, slavery, and oppression was the support of the inhabitants of the island for national survival, keeping the Greek spirit standing, until today. Through the centuries, it was inextricably linked to the musical tradition of metropolitan Greece, the music of Byzantium and the Greek islands and was naturally influenced by a number of foreign conquerors who passed through the island through the centuries.

The Frankish occupation was one of the most important historical periods, which left many monuments and influenced parts of the Cypriot culture. Exclusively French or French-influenced pieces of music are included in the Cypriot-French manuscript J.II.9. Its content offers music and material in general for all the religious, liturgical and other activities of a French court and its nobles in Nicosia. What characterizes many of the melodies of the manuscript is the melodic line that follows a descending direction within the tropical medieval scale. The ways in which these melodies were used in the pieces show that the practice of medieval Europe was followed.

There are many examples of early folklore recordings that are accompanied by interpretations that focus on proving the linear continuity of the Greek Cypriot with the ancient Greek culture. One such example is the Greek Cypriot folklore performance of the Tsiatista to the ancient Greek rhapsodists. As Papadakis (1988) observes, the competitive construction of rhyming verses is the result of a wider cultural interaction of the surrounding area, since it is found in various regions such as Greece, Turkey, Malta and Jamaica. Similar efforts were made to establish a cultural connection between Cyprus and Greece for dances such as karsilamas, tsifteteli and zebekikos, whose names come from Turkish words. As far as the musicological aspect is concerned, the same goal was pursued through the westernized transcripts and the western type harmonization of the local melodies that gradually dominated. The transliteration into a Western European stave had in itself eliminated any tropical element that referred to oriental musical traditions. In addition, intervals of Monday increased and color transitions reminiscent of microtones of oriental origin were very often replaced in transcription with other intermittent intervals.

It is in the context of this intense music and cultural activity that the work of important Cypriot composers who laid the foundations of classical music creation in Cyprus is projected. In addition, between 1920 and 1930, a strong musical development is presented and the foundations are laid for the subsequent promotion of art music in Cyprus, with the rise of Cypriot music producers (operas, oratorios, etc.). The intense musical activity of this period laid the foundations for the creation of the first Orchestras (Betelian Symphony Orchestra, "Olympic" String Orchestra (1934), "Olympic" Symphony Orchestra and Mixed Choir (1935), Mozart Orchestra (1938). The "Mozart" Orchestra was an important nucleus of music development until 1963. These orchestras find a worthy continuation of the orchestral music tradition, the Cyprus State Orchestra and the Cyprus State Youth Orchestra.

Despite the complex identity of Cyprus, its musical tradition is an important element for its understanding. Communication through music overcomes all kinds of "conflicts" between Greek Cypriots and Turkish Cypriots. There are many songs that are considered "genuine" Cypriot traditional but there are also in the Turkish version from the Turkish Cypriot side. This is justified, considering how many years the Turkish Cypriots have settled in Cyprus. This is how the fact is understood that the chronic coexistence of Greek Cypriots and Turkish Cypriots influenced the Cypriot tradition musically. Cypriot songs and Cypriot dances which are adopted by both communities, have taken such a formation today due to the fact that musicians take the role of mediator of culture from one place to another (Albayrak, 2017, p. 327).

As the modern representations of the Cypriot traditional music vary, they end up becoming "folklore", which are most often presented as so-called "collective memories" of social groups of the various regions of the whole island. Thus, what is presented is a standardization of the Cypriot music tradition, which is full of repetitions and continuous references to the past space-time, where everything is considered "genuine" and "authentic". As Iliadou (2010, p. 41) states, "" folk "music, cut off from its functional context, is crystallized in a standardized form, which favors homogeneity". However, at the present time, people are composing shared memories through various sources of information. In Cyprus, the various, common experiences that most people have for the musical tradition of their place, are formed mainly through the media. After the 20th century, with the technological development, music becomes the "companion" of people every day in any place and time.

Due to this, Cypriots have the opportunity to listen to many different types of music with the help of new technological means, choosing the musical styles of their choice which, however, usually take most of them away from the traditional music of their country. However, today, with the transformation of the Cypriot tradition from the media, a large number of young people with little to no "traditional listening" know the music of their place through the mediation of the media. As a result of the above, the music of the past is not transmitted by word of mouth but by televisions, radios, etc., projecting the traditional as a "national repertoire".

CONCLUSION

The contribution of music to cultural life is enormous and forms the bonds of a people with its roots, strengthening human nature and drawing moral supplies and moral forces. Music and song can be considered as the mirror of the psychosynthesis of a people, the indisputable presumption of its cultural and cultural level, traditions and history. They are also a reference point for origin and memory, a symbol of ancient civilization, an element of identity, a code of communication and consolation, in difficult times, historically and over time.

Culture and art can be combined and give the most positive image in a city that before had bad memories as long as the projects that will be implemented are acceptable to the citizens, are necessary for the city itself and have development, that is not to stand still just for hosting a cultural activity. Thus, the dynamics of the city will change and will attract more and more tourists who will be interested to know the city itself for the identity it promotes and then to tour its cultural resorts.

REFERENCES

Anholt, S. (2010). *Places Identity, Image, and Reputation*. Palgrave Macmillan Hampshire.

Avdikos, V. (2014). *The cultural and creative industries in Greece*. Epikentro Publications.

Connell, J., & Gibson, C. (2004). World Music: Deterritorializing Place and Identity. *ERA, 2010*(3), 28. doi:10.1191/0309132504ph493oa

Fyall, A., & Garrod, B. (1996). Sustainable heritage tourism: Achievable goal or elusive ideal? In M. Robinson, N. Evans, & P. Callaghan (Eds.), *Managing cultural resources for tourism* (pp. 50–76). British Education Publisher.

Grapsas, N. (2003). Absurdities, acritics, radicals, historical elements. In D. Lekkas (ed.), Arts II Overview of Greek Music and Dance. Patras: E.A.P.

Hesmondhalgh, David. (2008). *Cultural and Creative Industries*. Sage. . doi:10.4135/9781848608443.n26

Hollinshead, K. (1988). First-blush of the Longtime: The Market Development of Australia's Living Aboriginal Heritage. Tourism Research: Expanding Boundaries. In *Proceedings of the 19th annual conference of the Tourism Research Association*, Lake City: University of Utah.

Kallimopoulou, E. (2009). *Paradosiaka Music, Meaning and Indetity in Modern Greece*. Ashgate Publishing.

Kokkosis, C. & Tsartas, P. (2001), Sustainable tourism development and environment. *Athens: Review*

Lashua, B., Spracklen, K., & Long, P. (2014). Introduction to the special issue: Music and Tourism. *Tourist Studies, 14*(1), 3–9. doi:10.1177/1468797613511682

Lekkas, D. (2003). Theories of Greek traditional music. In D. Lekkas (Ed.), *Arts II Overview of Greek Music and Dance* (Vol. III, pp. 151–346). EAP.

Pachoulidis, K. (2007). *The national identity of Greek Cypriots: a socio-psychological genetic approach.* [Unpublished doctoral dissertation, Panteion University of Social and Political Sciences].

Paschalidis, G. (2002) Introduction to Culture, Volume A. Patra: EAP Publications

Poria, Y., Butler, R., & Airey, D. (2001). Clarifying Heritage Tourism. *Annals of Tourism Research, 28*(4), 1047–1049. doi:10.1016/S0160-7383(00)00069-4

Prentice, R., & Andersen, V. (2013). Festival as creative destination. *Annals of Tourism Research, 30*(1), 7–30. doi:10.1016/S0160-7383(02)00034-8

Richards, G. (2003). What is Cultural Tourism? A. van Maaren, A. (Ed.), Erfgoed voor Toerisme. Weesp: Nationaal Contact Monumenten.

Rogerson, C. (2006). Creative Industries and Urban Tourism: South African Perspectives. *Urban Forum,* (17), 149-166.

Rudd, M. A., & Davis, J. A. (1998). Industrial Heritage Tourism at the Bingham Canyon Copper Mine. *Journal of Travel Research, 36*(3), 85–89. doi:10.1177/004728759803600310

Sbonias, K. (2002). Cultural approaches and interpretations of the Past. In K. Sponias (ed.), The concept of culture, aspects of Greek culture. Patras: E.A.P.

Smith, A. D. (2000). National identity. (trans. E. Peppa). Athens: Odysseus.

Stevenson, D. (2007). *Cities and Urban Cultures* (I. Pentazou, Trans.). Critical Scientific Library Publications.

Theologou, K. (2007). The Value of Memory for a Society. *Intellectum3*, 1-17. https://www.intellectum.org/articles/issues/intellectum3/ITL03P053069_H_aksia_tis_mnimis.pd

Virvidakis, S. (2003). Problems of defining the concept of folk creation. In D. Lekkas (ed.), Arts II overview of Greek music and dance. Patras: E.A.P, 59-66

Waitt, G. (2000). Consuming heritage: Perceived historical authenticity. *Annals of Tourism Research, 27*(4), 835–862. doi:10.1016/S0160-7383(99)00115-2

Zeppal, H., & Hall, C. (1991). Selling Art and History: Cultural Heritage and Tourism. *Tourist Studies, 2*, 47–55.

Chapter 9
Digital Protection of Traditional Villages for Sustainable Heritage Tourism:
A Case Study on Qiqiao Ancient Village, China

Yixin Zuo
The University of Hong Kong, Hong Kong

Apple Hiu Ching Lam
The University of Hong Kong, Hong Kong

Dickson K. W. Chiu
The University of Hong Kong, Hong Kong

ABSTRACT

Similar to the plight of other traditional villages, Qiqiao Ancient Village is declining under the impact of urbanization and the devastation of modernization. Qiqiao is chosen as the case study as it is the second-largest settlement of Confucian descendants, with a rich cultural heritage. In recent years, the local government has taken measures such as cultural heritage restoration and tourism development to protect their traditional village, but the result is unsatisfactory. By field observation and interviewing three groups of stakeholders, the protection project manager, villagers, and tourists, this research analyzed the current situation of Qiqiao and digital protection applications for its heritage tourism to reveal some recent problems. Considering the local economic and technological conditions, this research suggested digital solutions for similar traditional villages in protection projects for sustainable heritage tourism.

DOI: 10.4018/978-1-6684-6055-9.ch009

Copyright © 2023, IGI Global. Copying or distributing in print or electronic forms without written permission of IGI Global is prohibited.

INTRODUCTION

Traditional villages are the heritage of historical development and agricultural civilization, carrying much human historical information, and are essential for traditional cultural history. In China, agrarian society has lasted for thousands of years, with numerous precious tangible and intangible cultural heritage embedded in traditional villages.

With rapid urbanization over several decades causing the gradual decline of the countryside (Fuguitt, 1965), the magnificent cultural heritage in traditional villages has been damaged or even destroyed. This phenomenon has not received enough attention worldwide until the 1930s and much later in China. Since the 1960s, archaeology, architecture, environmental science, and sociology experts have taken the lead in saving, restoring, and protecting traditional villages (Halpern & Halpern, 1972; King, Hickman & Berg, 1977). In the 20th century, some positive results appeared in cultural heritage conservation, as heritage restoration and conservation procedures have adopted advanced and innovative digital technologies for more possibilities to improve effectiveness and efficiency (Wong & Chiu, 2023). So, it is meaningful to explore digital methods and strategies for better preserving traditional villages, as in many other protection projects widely used in various village conditions (Stanco, Battiato & Gallo, 2011).

In this study, Qiqiao Ancient Village (漆桥古村落), listed in "The List of Chinese Traditional Villages" in 2013, was chosen as the case. Qiqiao locates near Nanjing, a provincial capital city in middle China, and was previously China's capital. As the second-largest settlement of Confucian descendants in China, many historical sites and unique folk customs are well retained, recording the brilliance of Chinese Confucian culture. Besides as an ancient commercial hub, this village also documented commercial culture and practice development in southern China's history. However, most cultural heritage there has been severely damaged by experiencing the devastation of war and the impact of urbanization. In recent years, the local government has carried out cultural heritage restoration and protection projects for this traditional village and developed heritage tourism to retain its traditional culture. However, the results of these measures appear to be unsatisfactory. Therefore, this study explores digital protection methods to solve Qiqiao's problems during the protection projects for the following objectives:

- To investigate the current situation of heritage restoration in Qiqiao Ancient Village, focusing on digital technology applications and tourism development (Chiu & Ho, 2022a; 2022b).
- To discover the problems in these efforts focusing on sustainable heritage tourism development.
- To suggest digital solutions for overcoming the problems in such a development project.

LITERATURE REVIEW

Problems of Traditional Villages

"Traditional Village" has been emphasized in China's unique cultural environment and Chinese context in the 1980s, similar to the "historic town, historic village, small-town" in Western studies. In 2012, Chinese official organizations published a relatively complete definition of traditional villages as having established early, abundant traditional resources and specific historical, cultural, scientific, artistic, social, and economic values that should be protected. Thus, traditional villages still have much value in modern society, but their survival and development are not optimistic, as cities have been developing and expanding rapidly. This phenomenon is even more apparent in China, where society has changed dramatically. In 2000, China had 3.6 million villages, but by 2010, only 2.7 million were left: 900,000 villages disappeared silently in 10 years. According to the "relics facts" statistics, the total number of traditional villages with historical, ethnic, regional culture, and architectural art value was 9,707 in 2004 and decreased to 5,709 in 2010, meaning 1.6 traditional villages disappeared every day (Hu, 2012). Many small towns and historic villages are also disappearing in the United States and Europe, while others have grown into large towns. Residents' traditional living habits and customs have also changed, and cultural heritage is losing.

Researchers generally believe that urbanization's erosion is the main reason for traditional villages' decline or destruction in two aspects. Materially, urbanization is often achieved by reconstructing rural landscapes. Cities occupy large areas of high-quality farmland in the suburbs, destroying the ecological environment and transforming the more rural area into the reserve landscape of urban expansion (Duan & Lei, 2014). Modern buildings have replaced ancient architecture in villages, and the traditional village layout has also changed into an urban pattern. In the non-material aspect, many traditional villages are experiencing a spontaneous transformation of "modernization." The local self-construction activities in the vast rural areas gradually abandoned the craftsmanship, customs, symbols, and even the aesthetic taste of the classical era. In addition, urbanization and the adjustment of rural industrial structure also make the rural labor flow into the city, leaving fewer people to inherit traditional crafts or develop their villages and significantly accelerating the disintegration of traditional villages.

In addition to urbanization erosion, excessive or inappropriate tourism development has become an essential factor endangering traditional villages. Duan and Lei (2014) argued that over-exploitation, such as building some antique-style architecture or renovating unnecessary ancient buildings, has damaged the historical memory of traditional villages. Chen (2015) believed that if tourists and the management are not aware of environmental protection, they will probably do something harmful to the village environment. Moreover, many people may change the physical environment around the heritage, such as temperature and humidity, accelerating the aging of the tangible heritage.

PRESERVING TRADITIONAL VILLAGES

Facing the rapid decline of traditional villages, Europe has started to conserve traditional villages by first preserving their cultural heritage. Around the 1960s, European countries began incorporating protection rules into the law. For example, the United Kingdom promulgated the Urban Civilization Act in 1967, incorporating traditional villages with artistic research, architecture, and historical commemorative value into protected areas. At the same time, some countries in Asia also began to preserve their traditional village by making relevant laws. In 1960, Korea promulgated the Invisible Cultural Heritage Protection Law crucial in preserving and renovating traditional Korean villages.

In continuous exploration, the conservation of traditional villages not only focuses on preserving tangible heritage but also everything about the villages constitutes the conservation objective. For example, in 1971, French museologists put forward the ecological museum theory to protect traditional villages (Jiang, 2012). They regard the whole traditional village as a living museum that preserves the ancient buildings and historical relics, together with the village's natural features, traditional folklore, culture, and art.

Regarding specific protection methods, experts in different fields have proposed various preservation methods from different angles. Using the spatial analysis method, Xu (2015) analyzed traditional Chinese villages' spatial distribution characteristics and spatial autocorrelation and proposed ways to protect the village structure and improve the village environment by rationally arranging the village space. From the cultural heritage conservation perspective, Zhang (2013) advocates establishing cultural heritage archives of traditional villages and evaluating cultural heritage from three aspects: material structure, visual landscape, and social function. From a sociological perspective, Hanh (2016) emphasizes villagers' importance in protecting urban cultural heritage, community participation, and training to become competent managers. Davis (2004) suggested tourism development encourages people to repair traditional buildings and ruins to establish protected areas and preserve traditional artisanal art and customs as cultural products. This way can increase local revenue, indirectly promoting investment in village protection as a sustainable strategy.

APPLICATION OF DIGITAL TECHNOLOGIES AND TOURISM IN TRADITIONAL VILLAGES CONSERVATION

Today, digital technology has been widely applied to all aspects of cultural preservation (He et al., 2022; Jiang et al., 2019; 2023; Lo et al., 2019; Mak et al., 2022; Sun et al., 2022). The achievements of digital technology in preserving cultural heritage and tourism show that digital technology has great potential to conserve traditional villages, especially with the rise of the mobile Internet facilitating self-drive tourists and online travel agencies (Gong et al., 2017; Ni et al., 2022; Chan & Chiu, 2022). The application of digital technology in heritage conservation basically covers three areas: digitization of cultural heritage, digital management in cultural heritage preservation, and restoration techniques for tangible heritage.

Digitization of cultural heritage refers to digitalizing cultural heritage information for long-term preservation and dissemination over websites and social media, which can sustainably reduce running costs (Mak et al., 2022; Sun et al., 2022). Common technologies used include digital photography, video, 3D laser scan technology, Geographical Position Systems (GPS), Remote Sensing (RS), Geographical Information Systems (GIS), a 3D reconstruction based on 2D Images, and terrain generation technology (Zhou et al., 2012). After collecting and creating digital information, a heritage information system is also necessary to preserve and prepare it for use (Santana & Addison, 2007). Alternatively, open-access catalogs may provide minimum searching and accessing functions (Chung et al., 2016; Sun et al., 2022).

Digital management of heritage preservation includes information visualization, virtual analysis, spatial geographic information system, data mining, knowledge discovery, non-immersion virtual reality, and other technologies. These technologies provide more sophisticated information and conservation of cultural heritage and are also useful for professional research (Lo et al., 2019; Suen et al., 2020).

Digital restoration techniques can save much cost and time in restoring antiquities. Spectral imaging and reproduction technologies contribute to classifying relic fragments. Professional software employing radio-based functions and the moving least square method can help repair the hole in the photos to effectively restore paintings, like repairing their creak and color (Giakoumis & Pitas, 1998; Pappas & Pitas, 2000).

On the other hand, developing tourism is one of the strategies to preserve traditional villages (Ni et al., 2022). In the past ten years, many traditional villages in China have commissioned heritage tourism development. Digital technology application in the tourism industry focuses on displaying and

Digital Protection of Traditional Villages for Sustainable Heritage Tourism

disseminating information, and virtual reality (VR) technology is a primary engaging means of general interest (Lo et al., 2019; Suen et al., 2020). VR practically reproduces scenes and landscapes through data collection, processing, and modeling, effectively showing realistic and vivid traditional villages. It can be applied to traditional village landscape creation, virtual tourism product development, digital museum construction, and cultural preservation combined with 3D printing (Lo et al., 2019; Zhang et al., 2017; Cho et al., 2017).

Ubiquitous Internet access has changed the information habits of people, especially the younger generation (Yu et al., 2022a; Ding et al., 2021; Ezeamuzie et al., 2022; Yip et al., 2021; Yao et al., 2023; Zhang et al., 2021; Lau et al., 2017; 2020). The Internet also provides a broad platform for disseminating tourism information, especially the low-cost and widely available mobile Internet in China, which facilitates self-service and self-drive tourists during their tours (Chiu et al., 2009; Gong et al., 2017; Ni et al., 2022). Further, digital photos, audio, and video can serve as effective promotional materials through the Internet and social media (Cheung et al., 2023; Lam et al., 2023; Wang et al., 2022; Deng & Chiu, 2023; Liu et al., 2023; Li et al., 2023). With adequate promotion arousing public interest, volunteer helpers in preservation, activity participants, and visitors can be attracted and engaged sustainably (Mak et al., 2022; Wang et al., 2022). Other Internet-related digital technologies, such as big data and cloud storage, also provide technical support for optimizing tourism design and enhancing the tourism experience, thus helping traditional villages to develop tourism (Gao et al., 2021; He et al., 2022).

Research Gap

As most studies focus on the tangible cultural heritage of villages, scant studies cover intangible heritage such as traditional festival celebrations, crafts, folk customs, operas, or other traditional arts. Further, scant studies focus on the digital protection of traditional villages, which various factors, such as cultural atmosphere and economic conditions, could restrict. From the perspective of digital preservation, this study chooses a village in China as a case for in-depth study, comprehensively considering the current situation of the village as well as their conditions of using digital technology to provide appropriate digital solutions with a combined strategy of cultural heritage preservation and tourism development. Notably, scant studies cover the digital protection of traditional villages for sustainable heritage tourism in China and East Asia written in English (though some in Chinese).

METHODOLOGY AND DATA COLLECTION

The decline of traditional villages is a common phenomenon worldwide. Although different villages own their unique traditions and customs and grew up in different environments and histories, the reasons why these villages were vanishing are similar. This case study can usefully provide detailed descriptions of the complexities of this situation and thus contribute to the understanding of a greater phenomenon (Rossman, 2011). Qiqiao, a traditional village with abundant cultural heritage, was chosen for this case study. Through field investigation in this village, this study analyzed the problems in their protection project to suggest sustainable digital solutions to address these problems, providing a reference for other traditional villages.

This study adopted qualitative methods to look into the current conservation and application of digital technology in Qiqiao. The observation method covered the old and new areas of Qiqiao, with emphasis on the "Qiqiao Old Street" and the vicinity of "Nanlingguan" (南陵关), to obtain the following information:

1. The appearance and layout of this village;
2. Current situation of the tangible heritage in this village;
3. The situation of digital facility establishment; and
4. Rough visitor flow rate of this village.

The interview method was adopted for three stakeholders, i.e., the project manager, villagers, and tourists, for more detailed information to explore the following:

1. Current situation of intangible cultural heritage;
2. People's evaluation of current preservation effect;
3. People's attitude toward the application of digital technology;
4. Detailed information about the local protection policy and plan.

Observation and interviews were conducted in Qiqao village. For the interviews, nine interviewees participated, and according to their identities, the interviewees were divided into three groups:

Group 1: Mr. Kong, who is the director of Qiqiao Old Street Development Office
Group 2: four local residents
Group 3: four tourists

Mr. Kong was chosen as an interviewee because he is one of the directors of Qiqiao's protection and development project and is also a descendant of Confucius. He is familiar with the work content and process of the protection and development project and knows well about the history and culture of the village as a member of the Confucian family.

During the interviews, people in different groups were asked different questions. For the Project Manager, 23 questions were asked, covering four themes (see Appendix 1): preservation program and methods, development and promotion, public participation, and plans. For villagers, ten questions were asked to know their evaluation of the protection project and their attitude toward digital conservation methods and strategies (see Appendix 2). Ten questions were asked for tourists' assessment of tourism development and their perceptions toward applying digital technology in local tourism (see Appendix 3).

FINDINGS AND DISCUSSIONS

Culture Heritage Preservation

Although there are rich cultural heritage resources in Qiqiao, not all have been restored and preserved well. The local government has invested 530 million RMB (1USD=6.5RMB approximately) in the an-cient architecture renovation project since 2012, but only some dangerous houses along the streets have been repaired so far. The Qiqiao Old Street was still severely damaged, with frequent broken walls and

Digital Protection of Traditional Villages for Sustainable Heritage Tourism

ruins. Some houses had tilted, with large cracks in the walls, and the walls well supported by wooden poles in the renovation area were just around one-tenth of them. Many other historical sites and relics, such as Confucian Temple and Niangniang Temple, have not been restored.

However, much intangible cultural heritage was not well-protected. For example, Confucius' family rules and sacrificial activities, not well-known but representative of local culture and history, were not recorded in cultural heritage archives. As fewer people are familiar with these folk customs, they will likely disappear soon. According to the interview results in Table 1, villagers and tourists also expressed their negative assessments of the conservation outcome. The renovation scope was too limited, and the project's progress was slow.

Table 1. Villagers' and tourists' evaluation of cultural heritage preservation

Subject	Themes	Extracted quotations
Villagers	How do you feel about the effect of the cultural heritage protection project Qiqiao?	● + *It's OK. You can see that the environment here is much better. It used to be the same old road. It's not easy to walk. The bare houses on this site have been repaired for several years. You can go to the square over there and see how well it's built there.*
		● - *Many ancient buildings, such as the Confucian Temple, have not been repaired. So, I think it's not good enough.*
		● - *It's not very well in my opinion, because I went to Yangliu village, another traditional village in Nanjing, this village was better protected.*
		● - *I still can see some ruins in the village. I came here with my father a year ago, and I didn't find any changes here. It's still many broken architectures.*
Tourists	Do you think the cultural heritage in Qiqiao has been protected well? Why?	● - *No, because many historic buildings are still in ruins.*
		● - *No, because Qiqiao Old Street was reformed into a modern business street. It's a little like "Master Temple" in Nanjing, you know, it's a business street. Qiqiao Old Street lost its initial charm.*
		● - *It's hard to say, actually. We cannot see a lot of heritage in these places, apart from historical relics, so it's hard for tourists to get more information about the culture or history of this village.*
		● + *Yes, because the local government is preparing to rebuild Confucius' temple*

("+" means "Positive," "-" means "Negative")

The most basic application of digital technology in preserving cultural heritage is to build digital archives of cultural heritage. According to the project manager's response in the interview, Qiqiao has created electronic archives of the local cultural heritage for long-term preservation. However, they did not choose appropriate methods to record all of them. For example, everything was recorded in text or pictures and could not reflect the most authentic content of dynamic cultural heritage, which is more appropriate with digital video for every authentic detail coherently with synchronous sound and pictures, such as drama and craftsmanship.

Table 2 shows the digital methods they utilized in their cultural heritage. Besides digital archives, another digital technology applied was digital GIS, which marked the water system, streets, and important buildings of Qiqiao in digital maps. This system enabled easy searches for geographical information and recorded geographical changes, providing heritage information and a vital reference for restoring old streets and buildings.

Digital Protection of Traditional Villages for Sustainable Heritage Tourism

Table 2. Cultural heritage in Qiqiao and their digital preservation methods

Intangible Heritage	Subject	Digital preservation methods
Folklore	Legend of Prime Minister Ping building Qiqiao (平丞相造漆桥传说), Legend of TuoWei Dragon (脱尾龙传说)	Digital archive (text)
Literary Works	Five Poems by Yang Wanli in Southern Song Dynasty, e.g., 《发孔镇,晨炊漆桥道中纪行十首》	Digital archive (text)
Traditional Sports and Athletics	Stone lock (石锁), Exercise on a horizontal bar (盘杠子)	None
Time-honored Business	Fuchang Wuyang Store (福昌五洋商店), Qiantai Dyeing House (谦泰染坊), Yongchang Wuyang Store (永昌五洋商店), Zhenqin Business Association (震秦商社)	Digital archive (text, picture)
Festival and Celebrations	Celebrations on Lantern Festival (正月十五跳马灯), Dragon Boat Rowing on the Qiqiao River on June 6(六月初六漆桥河划龙船)	Digital archive (text, picture)
Clan's culture	Confucius' family discipline and worship ceremony	None
Traditional Opera	Puppet Show(小戏玲玲), Gaoqiang Opera (高腔剧)	Digital archive (text, picture)
Folk Handicraft	Local Architectural Skills, Drawing ink painting on the wall	Digital archive (text, picture)

Tangible Heritage	Subject	Digital protection methods
Historical and Cultural Sites	Kong Deqiu's residence (孔德秋民宅), Kong Jinlai's residence (孔来金民宅), Confucius temple (孔氏迎六公祠), Lacquer bridge(漆桥)	Digital archive (text, picture)
Immovable Historical Relics	29 immovable cultural relics discovered in the third national cultural relics census, such as Kong Xinhua's residence	Digital archive (text, picture)
Historical Water System	Qiqiao River (漆桥河), Pingjia Pond (平家池), Niangniang Pool (娘娘塘), Zhajia Pool (查家塘), Xinlian Pool (新连塘), Sanjiao Pond (三角池), Chenjia Pond (陈家池) and other anonymous water systems	Digital archive (text, picture), Digital GIS
Historic Street	South Street, North Street, and other 24 historical streets	Digital archive (text, picture), Digital GIS
Old Well	Baoan Well (保安井), Baoping Well (保平井)	Digital archive (text, picture)
Stone Inscription	Record of repairing Lacquer Bridge on a tablet (民国重修漆桥碑记), Merit steles in the gram-management office (桥南粮管所围墙内各功德碑)	Digital archive (text, picture)
Ancient Tree	31 ancient trees such as Ginkgo biloba and Elm	Digital archive (text, picture)
Port and Wharf	16 ports and wharfs	Digital archive (text, picture) Digital GIS

HERITAGE TOURISM DEVELOPMENT

Proper development of the rural heritage tourism industry is also a strategy to conserve traditional villages. In Qiqiao, the local government has begun to develop the heritage tourism industry in the old rural area as a "leisure tourism spot" to promote the cultural image of the Gaochun district (where Qiqiao is situated). Qiqiao Old Street has been renovated as a business block and food court for sustainable income, focusing on displaying the local traditional commercial culture.

Qiqiao Old Street maintained its appearance and charm in the Qing Dynasty, paved with bluestone a century ago and still preserved well today, and shops renovated from ancient buildings. However, the field investigation found that most stores sold modern products, and there were even western-style cafes. Most old shops sell industrial goods as traditional crafts, while genuine traditional handcrafts have

Digital Protection of Traditional Villages for Sustainable Heritage Tourism

been abandoned for a long time. Thus, the government renovated Old Street in a modern commercial atmosphere. In the interview, a villager said, "at the beginning of the tourism development program, the government used cement to cover the ancient bluestone slab road to make the road less bumpy. But it was a kind of destruction, and the villagers vehemently opposed this. Then the government removed the cement from the road, and the ancient street emerged." This showed that the government's initial tourism development planning lacked conservation consideration. Although Old Street was renovated to preserve traditional commercial culture, it focuses too much on economic interests, resulting in many commercial acts contradicting heritage conservation.

When asked about tourists' experience in Qiqiao, all respondents also mentioned the problem of over-commercializing local tourism development (see Table 3). They thought the business streets could not show the particular traditional culture of this village. In addition, the lack of tourist attractions and the difficulty of obtaining local tourism information also affected tourists' experience. On the other hand, the beautiful ecological environment, the convenient geographical location of this village in the city's suburbs, and being less crowded were the reasons for their pleasant experiences.

Table 3. Tourists' reasons and experiences for visiting Qiqiao ancient village

Themes	Coding	No. of responses
Why did you come to Qiqiao for tourism?	This village is on the city's outskirts, so getting there is easy.	2
	It's not a popular tourist destination. It's not crowded.	1
	There are some historic architecture and relics in this village.	1
	It is a newly developed tourist attraction.	1
How was your experience of traveling in Qiqiao?	There are not so many tourist spots.	2
	Tourism development is too commercialized.	3
	Qiqiao Old Street is similar to other commercial streets and has no unique characteristics.	2
	There are few tourists and not crowded here.	2
	The food here is delicious.	1
	The environment here is beautiful and pleasant.	1

Qiqiao Government also has utilized some digital platforms to promote their heritage tourism. In the interview, the project manager said that the Qiqiao government cooperated with online media, such as "Xinlang News" and "Sohu" to publish articles about Qiqiao's heritage tourism online. Local merchants also cooperated with some travel websites to provide information about the village's accommodations and attractions for tourists. More people knew about Qiqiao and its history from these websites, and more tourists were attracted by such tourism information.

However, these digital publicity activities were still not enough. Table 4 shows that only 25% of the visitor respondents learned about the tourism information of the village through tourism applications. Most said they learned about Qiqiao through recommendations from relatives, friends, and colleagues. All visitor respondents got little information about the village on social media like Weibo or WeChat even if they searched the relevant information online: just a few articles or brief introductions about this village could be found. As the local government did not explore enough digital channels for promotion, and few people knew about Qiqiao, the heritage tourism industry developed slowly.

Table 4 shows 87.5% of the villager respondents could use mobile Internet and hoped to receive relevant information about Qiqiao on popular Chinese social media such as WeChat and Weibo. They could use digital information to learn about Qiqiao's protection and tourism development anytime, anywhere, which also arouses their enthusiasm to participate in protection projects. Villager respondents also expressed their willingness to participate in the recording of local oral history and cultural promotion videos. In particular, short video promotion is trendy and attractive for younger tourists (Cheng et al., 2023; Lam et al., 2023; Chan et al., 2020).

For tourists, information on social media and travel websites was more likely to attract their attention (Cheung et al., 2023). Moreover, 3D restoration models, digital voice guides, and digital interactive display activities made the presentation more interesting and greatly facilitated tourists' access to target information (Lo et al., 2019; Chin & Chiu, 2023; Cheung et al., 2021; 2022; Dai & Chiu, 2023). Therefore, all tourist respondents hoped that Qiqiao could adopt more digital technologies.

Table 4. Views of villagers and tourists on digital technology applications

Subject	Themes	Coding	No. of responses
Group 2: Villagers	Would you like to take part in making a documentary about Qiqiao and the recording of oral history?	Yes	3
		No	1
	Do you use the Internet? Do you have Weibo or WeChat accounts? Can Qiqiao's history and culture be promoted on these platforms?	I use the Internet and use Weibo or WeChat accounts. I hope the history and culture of Qiqiao can be promoted on these platforms.	3
		I don't have Weibo or WeChat account.	1
Group 3: Tourists	How did you get all kinds of information about Qiqiao?	From the recommendation of relatives, friends, and colleagues	3
		From travel APP	1
	Would you like more information about Qiqiao on Weibo, WeChat, or other digital platforms?	Yes	4
	Will the digital restoration model of ancient architecture appeal to you?	Yes	4
	Do you think it is necessary to add digital information facilities or services to the tourism development of Qiqiao? (e.g., electronic map, electronic tour guide, digital display, digital interaction, etc.)	Yes	4

DISCUSSION AND SUGGESTIONS

Based on the situation of local heritage conservation and tourism development, as well as the application of digital technology in these two kinds of preservation measures, this research found the following problems in Qiqiao Ancient Village's protection project.

Digital Protection of Traditional Villages for Sustainable Heritage Tourism

1. The conservation scope of cultural heritage was relatively limited, the preservation of intangible cultural heritage was neglected, and only a small part of the material cultural heritage in the village was restored and protected.
2. Advanced digital technology was seldom used to restore ancient buildings and monuments, and the progress of restoration was slow.
3. Intangible cultural heritage was not recorded appropriately and would face difficulties in its future usage and preservation.
4. Local tourism development was over-commercialized, neglecting to show the local featured traditional culture sustainably.
5. The lack of digital promotion resulted in few tourists.
6. There was a lack of communication channels among the government, villagers, and tourists. So, it would be difficult for the three stakeholders to exchange their views timely and accurately.
7. The traditional exhibit and service modes used in scenic areas were unattractive to tourists.

Qiqiao's financial stress and limited technical support led to these problems regarding sustainability. During the interview, the project manager said their funds for the protection project came from three different parent departments and external commercial investment. Most of these funds were used for infrastructure construction, environmental improvement of the village, and restoration and preservation of the most critical heritage. Therefore, the limited funding could not support all cultural heritage renovations, and they perceived no need to renovate the low-value cultural heritage. The project manager also indicated that their protection team did not have an independent technical department and just relied on the provincial technical department's digital technology support. Therefore, the local government did not introduce or apply advanced digital technology according to village conservation and development needs. The following possible sustainable digital solutions are suggested to solve these problems.

First, various newer technologies, such as three-dimensional laser scanning, digital photo analyzing, and modeling technology, can be applied to renovate ancient architecture (Kuzminsky& Gardiner, 2012). These technologies are widely used in architecture prospection and modeling in first- and second-tier Chinese cities to save the workforce and material resources needed by traditional surveying and avoid the conventional labor damage surveying to historic sites. Digital photo analysis and 3D modeling technology can also help preserve the village panorama, allowing sustainable heritage preservation and development. Even if the ancient buildings or low-value relics will not be renovated or rebuilt in the future, they can also retain their real and comprehensive information through these technologies.

Next, recording intangible cultural heritage through digital video and audio recordings can comprehensively preserve the dynamic information, particularly for intangible cultural heritage (Lo et al., 2019; Mak et al., 2022), such as opera, crafts, and festival celebrations. Adding these digital films and recordings to cultural heritage archives can better preserve the heritage. Further excerpts and selected recordings can serve as engaging promotional materials on social media and other digital means (Cheng et al., 2020; Cheung et al., 2022; 2023). Further, such content can also serve as educational materials for various culture, history, and sustainability subjects (Chung et al., 2020; Jiang et al., 2023; Mak et al., 2022; Chen et al., 2018), applying digital recordings to several aspects of the projects and attempting to achieve cost-effectiveness.

Then, inviting villagers to participate in the production of digital video or audio can also arouse villagers' enthusiasm to participate in protection projects so that more local people pay attention to village protection (Jiang et al., 2023; Mak et al., 2022). They can opine on various aspects of the protection projects concerning the local culture, facilitating sustainable heritage tourism development of satisfying tourists' needs without exploiting the cultural heritage's environment and local communities. With more interest aroused, crowdsourcing platforms and mechanisms can be employed for wider and deeper media creation (Au et al., 2022; Zhuang et al., 2015).

Social media is a leading media for modern information dissemination and promotion (Lam et al., 2023; Zeng, 2014). WeChat, Weibo, and QQ are contemporary China's most popular social media platforms (Dong et al., 2021; Ni et al., 2022). Publishing tourism information on these three platforms can expand the scope of tourism information dissemination, let more people know about Qiqiao, and increase potential tourist visits, especially with increasing self-drive and self-service tourists (Gong et al., 2017; Ni et al., 2022; Xu et al., 2023). As tourism websites still provide essential references for tourists to understand and decide on destinations (Gong et al., 2017; Ni et al., 2022), publishing online travel guides with traffic information, scenic spot introduction, accommodation, and education regarding traveling and protecting cultural heritage on well-known tourism websites in China remains crucial for the sustainable heritage tourism development.

Next, the government should establish electronic communication channels with villagers and tourists.

Although Qiqiao has its government website, there is little information about village conservation and tourism development. Villagers cannot readily know the progress of the village protection and development projects or relevant policies to participate in these projects. Timely conservation progress updates on government websites or public accounts of protection projects on social media can provide evaluation and feedback, help villagers know the scope and progress of preservation work, and let villagers participate in the conservation, tourism, planning, and supervision work sustainably as maximization of the information flows to all possible stakeholders can facilitate sustainable heritage tourism development through better communication (Risteskia et al., 2012). Regarding tourists, they can also reflect on their evaluations and perceptions about travel more quickly and conveniently through the above-mentioned electronic platforms (Gong et al., 2017; Ni et al., 2022). They can better safeguard their rights as consumers of the over-commercialization of local tourism development (e.g., non-authentic products and poor services) and enable the government to deal with tourist disputes more effectively (Xu et al., 2014). This approach may ensure sustainable heritage development by minimizing tourism impact, i.e., over-commercialization, on the local communities and environment (cultural heritage). Such tourist feedback also can improve tourism development planning according to tourists' needs (Risteskia et al., 2012).

Adding digital displays, interaction, and services in tourism areas can increase visitor engagement and information availability on-site (Deng et al., 2022; Lo et al., 2019). Digital displays and interactive activities such as holographic projection, interactive projection, and digital cinema have been widely used in the tourism industry and museums for heritage reconstruction (Lo et al., 2019; 2021). These digital displays and interactive technologies can optimize the tourist experience. However, due to the limited local government funds and the high cost of these technologies, the local government should consider cooperating with outside investment and educational institutions to achieve these digital projects (Chan & Chiu, 2023). As a digital museum is an ideal combination of science, technology, and cultural industry, establishing a digital museum is an excellent choice for the local government to attract investments (Marty, 2010). The museum can use 3D projection technology to display historical buildings such as Confucius Temple, use virtual reality technology to let tourists explore the whole village in the virtual world, and play movies about the village's history and legends, showing the history and culture of the village to tourists sustainably in a new way (Lo et al., 2019).

Lastly, mobile apps running on visitors' mobile phones, such as voice guides, electronic maps, and educational and promotional videos and audio creations for cultural heritage (the village), provide convenience and ease for tourists, especially self-service and self-drive tourists, and simplify the management of the tourism area (Chan et al., 2023). At the same time, such service systems can also record various usage data accurately, providing data for future optimization design of scenic spots (Zhuang et al., 2014).

CONCLUSION

By analyzing the observation and interviews in Qiqiao Ancient Village, this research found that digital technologies have not been well adopted in heritage renovation and tourism development projects. This resulted in limited protection scope, slow project progress, less participation of the public, over-commercialization of tourism, and fewer tourists. Various digital solutions for sustainable heritage tourism and protection have been suggested to solve these problems. As the current situations of many traditional villages in China are similar to Qiqiao, we hope these suggestions can also be applied to a wider scope.

Although this research has explored current problems in their protection project and put forward some digital solutions, there are still some limitations. Due to the limited sample size, that might not be sufficient to adequately represent the general opinions of the government, villagers, and tourists. Surveys and focus groups can be conducted to obtain more information. Secondly, many factors may influence digital technology applications in protection projects. Further feasibility and user perceptions studies are necessary. Besides, the special rural environment should consider more general political, economic, and cultural conditions. We are interested in the problems and recovery of tourism and public services due to the COVID-19 pandemic (Huang et al., 2021; 2022; 2023; Meng et al., 2022; Yu et al., 2022b) and the impact of the pandemic to information consumption (Yi & Chiu, 2023; Sung & Chiu, 2022; Ho & Chiu, 2022a; 2022b).

REFERENCES

Au, C. H., Kevin, K. K. W., & Chiu, D. K. W. (2022). Managing users' behaviors on open content crowdsourcing platform. *Journal of Computer Information Systems*, *62*(2), 1125–1135. doi:10.1080/0 8874417.2021.1983487

Chan, M. M. W., & Chiu, D. K. W. (2022). Alert driven customer relationship management in online travel agencies: Event-condition-actions rules and key performance indicators. In A. Naim & S. Kautish (Eds.), *Building a brand image through electronic customer relationship management* (pp. 286–303). IGI Global. doi:10.4018/978-1-6684-5386-5.ch012

Chan, T. T. W., Lam, A. H. C., & Chiu, D. K. W. (2020). From Facebook to Instagram: Exploring user engagement in an academic library. *Journal of Academic Librarianship*, *46*(6), 102229. doi:10.1016/j. acalib.2020.102229 PMID:34173399

Chan, V. H. Y., & Chiu, D. K. W. (2023). Integrating the 6C's motivation into reading promotion curriculum for disadvantaged communities with technology tools: A case study of Reading Dreams Foundation in rural China. In A. Etim & J. Etim (Eds.), *Adoption and use of technology tools and services by economically disadvantaged communities: Implications for growth and sustainability*. IGI Global.

Chan, V. H. Y., Chiu, D. K. W., & Ho, K. K. W. (2022). Mediating effects on the relationship between perceived service quality and public library app loyalty during the COVID-19 era. *Journal of Retailing and Consumer Services*, *67*, 102960. doi:10.1016/j.jretconser.2022.102960

Chen, R. (2015). The impact of tourism development on traditional village style. *Journal of Lanzhou Institute of Education*, *31*(9), 57–58.

Chen, Y., Chiu, D. K. W., & Ho, K. K. W. (2018). Facilitating the learning of the art of Chinese painting and calligraphy at Chao Shao-an Gallery. *Micronesian Educators*, *26*, 45–58.

Cheng, W., Tian, R., & Chiu, D.K.W. (2023) Travel vlogs influencing tourist decisions: Information preferences and gender differences. *Aslib Journal of Information Management*. doi:10.1108/AJIM-05-2022-0261

Cheng, W. W. H., Lam, E. T. H., & Chiu, D. K. W. (2020). Social media as a platform in academic library marketing: A comparative study. *Journal of Academic Librarianship*, *46*(5), 102188. doi:10.1016/j.acalib.2020.102188

Cheung, L. S. N., Chiu, D. K. W., & Ho, K. K. W. (2022). A quantitative study on utilizing electronic resources to engage children's reading and learning: Parents' perspectives through the 5E instructional model. *The Electronic Library*, *40*(6), 662–679. doi:10.1108/EL-09-2021-0179

Cheung, T. Y., Ye, Z., & Chiu, D. K. W. (2021). Value chain analysis of information services for the visually impaired: A case study of contemporary technological solutions. *Library Hi Tech*, *39*(2), 625–642. doi:10.1108/LHT-08-2020-0185

Cheung, V. S. Y., Lo, J. C. Y., Chiu, D. K. W., & Ho, K. K. W. (2023). Predicting Facebook's influence on travel products marketing based on the AIDA model. *Information Discovery and Delivery*, *51*(1), 66–73. doi:10.1108/IDD-10-2021-0117

Chin, G. Y. L., & Chiu, D. K. W. (2023). RFID-based robotic process automation for smart museums with an alert-driven approach. In R. Tailor (Ed.), *Application and adoption of robotic process automation for smart cities*. IGI. Global.

Chiu, D. K. W., & Ho, K. K. W. (2022a). Special selection on contemporary digital culture and reading. *Library Hi Tech*, *40*(5), 1204–1209. doi:10.1108/LHT-10-2022-516

Chiu, D. K. W., & Ho, K. K. W. (2022b). Editorial: 40th anniversary: Contemporary library research. *Library Hi Tech*, *40*(6), 1525–1531. doi:10.1108/LHT-12-2022-517

Chiu, D. K. W., Yueh, Y. T., Leung, H. F., & Hung, P. C. (2009). Towards ubiquitous tourist service coordination and process integration: A collaborative travel agent system with semantic web services. *Information Systems Frontiers*, *11*(3), 241–256. doi:10.100710796-008-9087-2

Digital Protection of Traditional Villages for Sustainable Heritage Tourism

Cho, A., Lo, P., & Chiu, D. K. W. (2017). *Inside the world's major East Asian collections: One Belt, One Road, and beyond.* Chandos Publishing.

Chung, A. C. W., & Chiu, D. K. W. (2016). OPAC usability problems of archives: A case study of the Hong Kong Film Archive. [IJSSOE]. *International Journal of Systems and Service-Oriented Engineering, 6*(1), 54–70. doi:10.4018/IJSSOE.2016010104

Chung, C., Chiu, D. K. W., Ho, K. K. W., & Au, C. H. (2020). Applying social media to environmental education: Is it more impactful than traditional media? *Information Discovery and Delivery, 48*(4), 255–266. doi:10.1108/IDD-04-2020-0047

Dai, C., & Chiu, D. K. W. (2023). (in press). Impact of COVID-19 on reading behaviors and preferences: Investigating high school students and parents with the 5E instructional model. *Library Hi Tech.* doi:10.1108/LHT-10-2022-0472

Davis, J. S., & Morais, D. B. (2004). Factions and enclaves: Small towns and socially unsustainable tourism development. *Journal of Travel Research, 43*(1), 3–10. doi:10.1177/0047287504265501

Deng, S., & Chiu, D. K. W. (2023). Analyzing Hong Kong Philharmonic Orchestra's Facebook community engagement with the Honeycomb Model. In M. Dennis & J. Halbert (Eds.), *Community engagement in the online space* (pp. 31–47). IGI. Global. doi:10.4018/978-1-6684-5190-8.ch003

Deng, W., Chin, G. Y.-l., Chiu, D. K. W., & Ho, K. K. W. (2022). (in press). Contribution of literature thematic exhibition to cultural education: A case study of Jin Yong's Gallery. *Micronesian Educators, 32*.

Ding, S. J., Lam, E. T. H., Chiu, D. K. W., Lung, M. M., & Ho, K. K. W. (2021). Changes in reading behavior of periodicals on mobile devices: A comparative study. *Journal of Librarianship and Information Science, 53*(2), 233–244. doi:10.1177/0961000620938119

Dong, G., Chiu, D. K. W., Huang, P.-S., Lung, M. M., Ho, K. K. W., & Geng, Y. (2021). Relationships between research supervisors and students from coursework-based Master's degrees: Information usage under social media. *Information Discovery and Delivery, 49*(4), 319–327. doi:10.1108/IDD-08-2020-0100

Duan, W., & Lei, N. (2014). Zhangjiatong Village, Tiantai, Zhejiang Province: Protection and renewal of traditional villages based on micro-intervention strategy. *Beijing Planning and Construction, 2014*(5), 50–57.

Ezeamuzie, N.M., Rhim, A.H.R., Chiu, D.K.W., & Lung, M. M.-W. (2022). Exploring gender differences in foreign domestic helpers' mobile information usage. *Library Hi Tech.* doi:10.1108/LHT-07-2022-0350

Fuguitt, G. V. (1965). The growth and decline of small towns as a probability process. *American Sociological Review, 30*(3), 403–411. doi:10.2307/2090721

Gao, W., Lam, K. M., Chiu, D. K. W., & Ho, K. K. W. (2021). A big data analysis of the factors influencing Movie Box Office in China. In Z. Sun (Ed.), *Handbook of research on intelligent analytics with multi-industry applications* (pp. 232–249). IGI Global. doi:10.4018/978-1-7998-4963-6.ch011

Giakoumis, I., & Pitas, I. (1998, May). Digital restoration of painting cracks. *Proceedings of the 1998 IEEE International Symposium on Circuits and Systems* (Cat. No. 98CH36187) (Vol. 4, pp. 269-272), IEEE.

Gong, J. Y., Schumann, F., Chiu, D. K. W., & Ho, K. K. W. (2017). Tourists' mobile information seeking behavior: An investigation on China's youth. [IJSSOE]. *International Journal of Systems and Service-Oriented Engineering*, *7*(1), 58–76. doi:10.4018/IJSSOE.2017010104

Halpern, J. M., & Halpern, B. K. (1972). *A Serbian village in historical perspective*. Holt, Rinehart and Winston.

Hanh, V. T. H. (2006). Canal-side highway in Ho Chi Minh City (HCMC), Vietnam – Issues of urban cultural conservation and tourism development. *GeoJournal*, *66*(3), 165–186. doi:10.100710708-006-9024-1

He, Z., Chiu, D. K. W., & Ho, K. K. W. (2022). Weibo analysis on Chinese cultural knowledge for gaming. In Z. Sun (Ed.), *Handbook of research on foundations and applications of intelligent business analytics* (pp. 320–349). IGI Global. doi:10.4018/978-1-7998-9016-4.ch015

Hu, B. (2012). Present situation and protection of traditional villages and their cultural relics in China. *Guangming Daily*, *1*(15), 7.

Huang, P. S., Paulino, Y., So, S., Chiu, D. K. W., & Ho, K. K. W. (2021). Editorial - COVID-19 pandemic and health informatics (Part 1). *Library Hi Tech*, *39*(3), 693–695. doi:10.1108/LHT-09-2021-324

Huang, P.-S., Paulino, Y. C., So, S., Chiu, D. K. W., & Ho, K. K. W. (2022). Guest editorial: COVID-19 pandemic and health informatics part 2. *Library Hi Tech*, *40*(2), 281–285. doi:10.1108/LHT-04-2022-447

Huang, P.-S., Paulino, Y. C., So, S., Chiu, D. K. W., & Ho, K. K. W. (2023). Guest editorial: COVID-19 pandemic and health informatics part 3. *Library Hi Tech*, *41*(1), 1–5.

Jiang, L. (2012). *Study on the gains and losses of the early eco-museum and its continuation in China* [Master's thesis]. Chongqing Normal University.

Jiang, T., Lo, P., Cheuk, M. K., Chiu, D. K. W., Chu, M. Y., Zhang, X., Zhou, Q., Liu, Q., Tang, J., Zhang, X., Sun, X., Ye, Z., Yang, M., & Lam, S. K. (2019). 文化新語:兩岸四地傑出圖書館、檔案館及博物館傑出工作者訪談 (New Cultural Dialog: Interviews with Outstanding Librarians, Archivists, and Curators in Greater China). Hong Kong: Systech publications.

Jiang, X., Chiu, D. K. W., & Chan, C. T. (2023). Application of the AIDA model in social media promotion and community engagement for small cultural organizations: A case study of the Choi Chang Sau Qin Society. In M. Dennis & J. Halbert (Eds.), *Community engagement in the online space* (pp. 48–70). IGI Global. doi:10.4018/978-1-6684-5190-8.ch004

Jones, K. B. (2012). The transformation of the digital museum. In P. F. Marty & K. Jones (Eds.), *Museum informatics* (pp. 25–42). Routledge.

King, T. F., Hickman, P. P., & Berg, G. (1977). *Anthropology in historic preservation: Caring for culture's clutter*. Academic Press.

Kou, H., & Zhang, S. (2015). Changes in the protection of traditional villages under the background of new rural construction. *Chinese Cultural Heritage*, *2015*(001), 12–17.

Kuzminsky, S. C., & Gardiner, M. S. (2012). Three-dimensional laser scanning: Potential uses for museum conservation and scientific research. *Journal of Archaeological Science, 39*(8), 2744–2751. doi:10.1016/j.jas.2012.04.020

Lam, A. H. C., Ho, K. K. W., & Chiu, D. K. W. (2023). Instagram for student learning and library promotions? A quantitative study using the 5E Instructional Model. *Aslib Journal of Information Management, 75*(1), 112–130. doi:10.1108/AJIM-12-2021-0389

Lau, K. P., Chiu, D. K., Ho, K. K., Lo, P., & See-To, E. W. (2017). Educational usage of mobile devices: Differences between postgraduate and undergraduate students. *Journal of Academic Librarianship, 43*(3), 201–208. doi:10.1016/j.acalib.2017.03.004

Lau, K. S. N., Lo, P., Chiu, D. K. W., Ho, K. K. W., Jiang, T., Zhou, Q., Percy, P., & Allard, B. (2020). Library, learning, and recreational experiences turned mobile: A comparative study between LIS and non-LIS students. *Journal of Academic Librarianship, 46*(2), 102103. doi:10.1016/j.acalib.2019.102103

Li, S., Chiu, D. K. W., & Ho, K. K. W. (2023). Social media analytics for non-governmental organizations: A case study of Hong Kong Next Generation Arts. In Z. Sun (Ed.), *Driving socioeconomic development with big data: Theories, technologies, and applications* (pp. 277–295). IGI Global.

Liu, Y., Chiu, D. K. W., & Ho, K. K. W. (2023). Short-form videos for public library marketing: Performance Analytics of Douyin in China. *Applied Sciences (Basel, Switzerland), 13*(6), 3386. Advance online publication. doi:10.3390/app13063386

Lo, P., Chan, H. H. Y., Tang, A. W. M., Chiu, D. K. W., Cho, A., Ho, K. K. W., See-To, E., He, J., Kenderdine, S., & Shaw, J. (2019). Visualising and revitalising traditional Chinese martial arts – Visitors' engagement and learning experience at the 300 years of Hakka KungFu. *Library Hi Tech, 37*(2), 273–292. doi:10.1108/LHT-05-2018-0071

Lo, P., Hsu, W.-E., Wu, S. H. S., Travis, J., & Chiu, D. K. W. (2021). *Creating a global cultural city via public participation in the Arts: Conversations with Hong Kong's leading arts and cultural administrators.* Nova Science Publishers.

Mak, M. Y. C., Poon, A. Y. M., & Chiu, D. K. W. (2022). Using social media as learning aids and preservation: Chinese martial arts in Hong Kong. In S. Papadakis & A. Kapaniaris (Eds.), *The digital folklore of cyberculture and digital humanities* (pp. 171–185). IGI Global. doi:10.4018/978-1-6684-4461-0.ch010

Marty, P. F. (2010). Museum informatics. In Encyclopedia of library and information sciences (3rd ed., pp. 3717-3725).

Ni, J., Chiu, D. K. W., & Ho, K. K. W. (2022). Exploring Information search behavior among self-drive tourists. *Information Discovery and Delivery, 50*(3), 285–296. doi:10.1108/IDD-05-2020-0054

Pappas, M., & Pitas, I. (2000). Digital color restoration of old paintings. *IEEE Transactions on Image Processing, 9*(2), 291–294. doi:10.1109/83.821745 PMID:18255399

Risteskia, M., Kocevskia, J., & Arnaudov, K. (2012). Spatial planning and sustainable tourism as basis for developing competitive tourist destinations. *Procedia: Social and Behavioral Sciences, 44*, 375–386. doi:10.1016/j.sbspro.2012.05.042

Rossman, G. B., & Rallis, S. F. (2011). *Learning in the field: An introduction to qualitative research*. Sage.

Santana-Quintero, M., & Addison, A. C. (2007, September). Digital tools for heritage information management and protection: The need of training. In T. G. Wyeld, S. Kenderdine, & M. Docherty (Eds.), Lecture notes in computer science: Vol. 4820. *Virtual Systems and Multimedia* (pp. 35–46). Springer. doi:10.1007/978-3-540-78566-8_4

Stanco, F., Battiato, S., & Gallo, G. (Eds.). (2011). *Digital imaging for cultural heritage preservation: Analysis, restoration, and reconstruction of ancient artworks*. CRC Press.

Suen, R. L. T., Tang, J., & Chiu, D. K. W. (2020). Virtual reality services in academic libraries: Deployment experience in Hong Kong. *The Electronic Library*, *38*(4), 843–858. doi:10.1108/EL-05-2020-0116

Sun, X., Chiu, D. K. W., & Chan, C. T. (2022). Recent digitalization development of buddhist libraries: A comparative case study. In S. Papadakis & A. Kapaniaris (Eds.), *The digital folklore of cyberculture and digital humanities* (pp. 251–266). IGI Global. doi:10.4018/978-1-6684-4461-0.ch014

Sung, Y. Y. C., & Chiu, D. K. W. (2022). E-book or print book: Parents' current view in Hong Kong. *Library Hi Tech*, *40*(5), 1289–1304. doi:10.1108/LHT-09-2020-0230

Tse, H. L., Chiu, D. K. W., & Lam, A. H. C. (2022). From reading promotion to digital literacy: An analysis of digitalizing mobile library services with the 5E Instructional Model. In A. Almeida & S. Esteves (Eds.), *Modern reading practices and collaboration between schools, family, and community* (pp. 239–256). IGI Global. doi:10.4018/978-1-7998-9750-7.ch011

Wang, J., Deng, S., Chiu, D. K. W., & Chan, C. T. (2022). Social network customer relationship management for orchestras: A case study on Hong Kong Philharmonic Orchestra. In N. B. Ammari (Ed.), *Social customer relationship management (Social-CRM) in the era of Web 4.0* (pp. 250–268). IGI Global. doi:10.4018/978-1-7998-9553-4.ch012

Wong, A. K.-k., & Chiu, D. K. W. (2023). Digital Transformation of museum conservation practices: A value chain analysis of public museums in Hong Kong. In R. Pettinger, B. B. Gupta, A. Roja, & D. Cozmiuc (Eds.), *Handbook of research on the digital transformation digitalization solutions for social and economic needs* (pp. 226–242). IGI. Global. doi:10.4018/978-1-6684-4102-2.ch010

Xu, C., Lam, A. H. C., & Chiu, D. K. W. (2023). Antique bookstores marketing strategies as urban cultural landmark: A case analysis for Suzhou Antique Bookstore. In M. Rodrigues & M. A. M. Carvalho (Eds.), *Exploring niche tourism business models, marketing, and consumer experience*. IGI Global.

Xu, H., Wan, X., & Fan, X. (2014). Rethinking authenticity in the implementation of China's heritage conservation: The case of Hongcun Village. *Tourism Geographies*, *16*(5), 799–811. doi:10.1080/1461 6688.2014.963662

Xu, Y. (2015). Discussion on the protection and renewal of public space in traditional villages - Taking Cangtai Village, Jianshui County, Honghe Prefecture as an example. *Value Engineering*, *34*(14), 203–205.

Yao, L., Lei, J., Chiu, D. K. W., & Xie, Z. (2023). Adult learners' perception of online language English learning platforms in China. In A. Garcés-Manzanera & M. E. C. García (Eds.), *New approaches to the investigation of language teaching and literature*. IGI Global.

Yi, Y., & Chiu, D.K.W. (2023). Public information needs during the COVID-19 outbreak: A qualitative study in mainland China. *Library Hi Tech*. doi:10.1108/LHT-08-2022-0398

Yip, K. H. T., Chiu, D. K. W., Ho, K. K. W., & Lo, P. (2021). Adoption of mobile library apps as learning tools in higher education: A tale between Hong Kong and Japan. *Online Information Review*, *45*(2), 389–405. doi:10.1108/OIR-07-2020-0287

Yu, H. Y., Tsoi, Y. Y., Rhim, A. H. R., Chiu, D. K. W., & Lung, M. M. W. (2022a). Changes in habits of electronic news usage on mobile devices in university students: A comparative survey. *Library Hi Tech*, *40*(5), 1322–1336. doi:10.1108/LHT-03-2021-0085

Yu, P. Y., Lam, E. T. H., & Chiu, D. K. W. (2022b). *Operation management of academic libraries in Hong Kong under COVID-19*. Library Hi Tech. doi:10.1108/LHT-10-2021-0342

Zeng, B., & Gerritsen, R. (2014). What do we know about social media in tourism? A review. *Tourism Management Perspectives*, *10*, 27–36. doi:10.1016/j.tmp.2014.01.001

Zhang, H., Luo, Y., Liu, H., Wang, Y., Chen, Q., & Tan, X. (2017). Research status and prospect of digital protection technology for traditional villages in China. *Resource development and market*, *33*(08), 912-915.

Zhang, S. (2013). Protection and inheritance of intangible cultural heritage as a cultural ecology: Theoretical thinking and problem analysis of China's conservation practice. *Journal of Tongji University: Social Science Edition*, *2013*(5), 58–66.

Zhang, X., Lo, P., So, S., Chiu, D. K. W., Leung, T. N., Ho, K. K. W., & Stark, A. (2021). Medical students' attitudes and perceptions towards the effectiveness of mobile learning: A comparative information-need perspective. *Journal of Librarianship and Information Science*, *53*(1), 116–129. doi:10.1177/0961000620925547

Zhou, M., Geng, G., & Wu, Z. (2012). *Digital Preservation Technology for Cultural Heritage*. Springer. doi:10.1007/978-3-642-28099-3

Zhuang, Y., Zhu, F., Chiu, D. K. W., Ju, C., & Jiang, B. (2014). A personalized travel system based on crowdsourcing model. In X. Luo, J. X. Yu, & Z. Li (Eds.), Lecture notes in computer science: Vol. 8933. *Advanced Data Mining and Applications* (pp. 163–174). Springer. doi:10.1007/978-3-319-14717-8_13

KEY TERMS AND DEFINITIONS

Digital management of cultural heritage: comprises information visualization, virtual analysis, spatial geographic information system, data mining, knowledge discovery, non-immersion virtual reality, and other technologies.

Digital restoration: employing digital imaging and reproduction technologies to visualize the original image or structure of the cultural heritage for effective and time-saving restoration.

Digital technologies: electronic tools, devices, resources, and systems processing or storing data, such as social media for marketing and promotion, mobile applications for leisure, promotion, and education, and 3D technologies for geographical surveying, etc.

Digitization of cultural heritage: digitally transferring cultural heritage information, for example, collecting and creating digital information of the cultural heritage via advanced digital technologies, for long-term preservation.

Heritage preservation/conservation: protecting tangible or intangible things being parts of the culture of a particular society, for instance, the craftsmanship, customs, and symbols, from decaying or destruction.

Heritage tourism: traveling to the destinations to experience the attractions, artifacts, and activities telling the authentical stories and people in the past.

Intangible cultural heritage: is recognized as nonmaterial practices, expressions, skills, knowledge, and even people associated with the physical artifacts ("the producer"), such as performing arts, traditional skills, and oral traditions.

Sustainable heritage tourism development: tourism development that meets the present needs of tourists with minimal environmental impacts on the local attractions and communities.

Tangible cultural heritage: is defined as physical artifacts with cultural significance undergoing maintenance and intergenerational transmission in a society, for instance, buildings, monuments, and paintings.

Traditional village: an early-established village with substantial traditional resources and specific protective values in its history, culture, science, arts, society, and economy, for instance, the village's natural features, traditional folklore, culture, arts, and architecture.

Digital Protection of Traditional Villages for Sustainable Heritage Tourism

APPENDIX 1 - INTERVIEW QUESTIONS FOR THE PROJECT MANAGER

Conservation Plan and Methods

1. In 2013, Qiqiao Ancient Village was listed in the *"List of Chinese Traditional Villages."* What plans have the state and local governments made to protect this village?
2. What are the sources of funds for the conservation of Qiqiao? What protection projects are these funds used for? Are there enough funds?
3. We know that in 2018, the "Nanjing Qiqiao Ancient Village (Protection) Plan (2017-2030)" was issued. What is the focus of this plan? (Is it the conservation of tangible cultural heritage, such as historical architecture, or intangible cultural heritage, such as folk customs? Or both?) This project mainly invests money in what kinds of work? (e.g., In the restoration of historical buildings)
4. What measures did you take to preserve tangible cultural heritage, such as ancient buildings and cultural relics?
5. Have you created archives for tangible cultural heritage? What forms of archives have been created? (paper? Electronics? Is there a special database for these archives?)
6. What measures did you take to preserve intangible cultural heritage, such as festivals, traditional crafts, and traditional operas?
7. How did you record the intangible cultural heritage? Has it been archived? What forms of archives have been established? (video? Picture? Text description? Oral Recording?)
8. Numerous descendants of Confucius live in this village. Their family rules, ancestral rituals, and other living habits are also the embodiment of Confucian culture. Have these customs been recorded? If it is recorded, how is it recorded?
9. Has the protection program received technical support from national or local IT departments or IT-related enterprises?
10. We know that the office of protection and development program was established in 2011. Are there any IT departments or IT professionals in this office?
11. Has digital technology been used in conservation? (e.g., 3D laser scanning technology, digital photography and video technology, digital storage technology, etc.) If so, what digital technologies are used?

Promotion and Development

12. In addition to restoring and preserving cultural heritage, will the government publicize and utilize them? How does the government promote and use such cultural heritage? (e.g., developing tourism)
13. Are the historic sites and heritage tourist attractions of Qiqiao marked on electronic maps commonly used by the public?
14. Has digital technology been used in the process of publicity and development? (For example, making documentaries, displaying 3D restoration models of buildings, publicizing on the internet platform, etc.)

Public Participation

15. Are local villagers involved in protection projects and activities? Are they actively participating in the conservation of Qiqiao?
16. According to our survey in 2017, young local villagers pay less attention to the conservation of Qiqiao. Has this been any change in recent years? Will you consider using more digital conservation methods to attract more young residents' attention and participation?

Problems and Challenges

17. What are the major problems you encountered during the protection projects? What problems are still unsolved?
18. Do you think digital technology can help solve these problems?
19. The government started its protection program in 2011, but 8 years have passed, and there is still a lot of protection work that has not been completed. What is the reason for the slow progress of protection work?
20. The government only plans to renovate parts of ancient buildings along the Gaochun old street. So why only part of the ancient buildings will be renovated but not all of them? Is digital restoration considered for some cultural heritage difficult to repair or expensive to repair? (e.g., 3D restoration technology, etc.)

Future Plans

21. Do you think it necessary to increase investment in digital conservation in the future? Why?
22. Are there plans to use more digital technologies to protect Qiqiao in the future?
23. Do you think Qiqiao can adopt digital and information technology for conservation? Or what problems may exist in practice? (e.g., technical, financial, etc.)

APPENDIX 2 - INTERVIEW QUESTIONS FOR VILLAGERS

1. Have you seen or felt the actions taken by the government to preserve the Qiqiao? Tell me more specifically.
2. What aspects of your life are related to Qiqiao's protection project? What impact does it have on your life?
3. How do you feel about the effect of the protection project implemented so far in Qiqiao?
4. Have you noticed that the number of villagers who know and participate in traditional folk activities is decreasing? Are you worried that these traditional cultures will decline and perish?
5. Do you think retaining these traditional cultures with digital technologies such as recording, video recording, and electronic restoration is necessary and effective? What is your attitude towards preserving history and folklore in digital form?
6. As a descendant of Confucius, what memories do you still have about your family culture or family customs?

Digital Protection of Traditional Villages for Sustainable Heritage Tourism

7. Would you like to participate in making a documentary about Qiqiao and the recording of oral history?
8. Do you use the Internet? Owning and using Weibo or WeChat accounts? Do you hope that the history and culture of Qiqiao can be promoted on the network platform?
9. What do you think is the lack of protection projects undertaken by the government and the plans for protection?
10. Do you think more digital conservation methods should be adopted? Why?

APPENDIX 3 – INTERVIEW QUESTIONS FOR TOURISTS

1. Why did you visit Qiqiao Ancient Village for tourism?
2. Do you think Qiqiao has been preserved well? And why?
3. Do you know what intangible cultural heritage there has after touring Qiqiao? (e.g., traditional crafts, operas, folklore, village-related literature, etc.)
4. Do you know that Qiqiao is the gathering place of the descendants of Confucius? Do you want to know more about Confucian culture?
5. Can cultural documentaries or oral historical videos about this village attract you?
6. How did you get all kinds of information about Qiqiao?
7. Would you like to see more information about Qiqiao on Weibo, WeChat, or other network platforms?
8. Do you think that Qiqiao should repair all ancient architecture? Will the digital restoration model of ancient architecture appeal to you?
9. How was your experience of traveling in Qiqiao?
10. Do you think it is necessary to add digital information facilities or services to the tourism development of Qiqiao? (e.g., electronic map, electronic tour guide, digital display, digital interaction, etc.)

Chapter 10
Saving Heritage in War Zones:
The Case Study of Ukraine

Stavros Christodoulou
Neapolis Univeristy, Pafos, Cyprus

ABSTRACT

The events of the last days after the invasion of Russia by the Russian troops raise concerns not only about the humanitarian crisis that Ukraine and Europe are facing, but also about the preservation and preservation of the Ukrainian cultural heritage. Thousands of museums across Ukraine store important works of art by Ukrainian and Russian artists; Byzantine artefacts; and paintings, among others by Bellini, Goya, and David; according to a report by the Indian Express. In Ukraine there are seven UNESCO World Heritage Sites. As a result, UNESCO asks for implementation of international humanitarian law, notably the 1954 Hague Convention for the Protection of Cultural Property in the Event of Armed Conflict, and its two (1954 and 1999) Protocols, to ensure the prevention of damage to cultural heritage in all its forms.

INTRODUCTION

The events of the last months after the invasion of Russia by the Russian troops raise concerns not only about the humanitarian crisis that Ukraine and Europe are facing, but also about the preservation and preservation of the Ukrainian cultural heritage.

But what is cultural heritage? According to Unesco "Heritage is the cultural legacy which we receive from the past, which we live in the present and which we will pass on to future generations. With the 1972 Convention concerning the Protection of the World Cultural and Natural Heritage, UNESCO established that certain places on Earth have "exceptional universal value" and belong to humanity's common heritage," (Khan Academy, n.d.), such as the Pyramids of Egypt, the Hosios Loukas Monastery, and the Parthenon. According to ICOMOS "Cultural Heritage is an expression of the ways of living developed by a community and passed on from generation to generation, including customs, practices, places, objects, artistic expressions and values. Cultural Heritage is often expressed as either Intangible or Tangible Cultural Heritage" (ICOMOS, 2002), (Feather, 2006), (Thurley, 2005).

DOI: 10.4018/978-1-6684-6055-9.ch010

Copyright © 2023, IGI Global. Copying or distributing in print or electronic forms without written permission of IGI Global is prohibited.

Saving Heritage in War Zones

"Nonetheless, cultural heritage is not limited to monuments and collections of objects. It is also comprised of living expressions inherited from our ancestors, such as oral traditions, performing arts, social manners, rituals, festive events, knowledge and practices related to nature and the universe, and knowledge and techniques linked to traditional crafts. Despite its fragility, intangible cultural heritage or living heritage is an important factor in maintaining cultural diversity," (Τμήμα, Δ., 2009).

For UNESCO, the concept of cultural heritage is proving to be vital for culture and the future because it not only constitutes the "cultural potential" of today's societies, but it also contributes to the evaluation and re-evaluation of cultures and cultural identities, as well as the transmission of experiences and knowledge from one generation to the next. Heritage is one of the main sources of inspiration for creativity and innovation, two of the key features of contemporary and future cultural products. The cultural heritage as a springboard strengthens the sense of individual and collective belonging, the preservation of social and territorial cohesion. In addition, cultural heritage is proving to be economically beneficial for tourism[1].

CASE STUDY: UKRAINE UNDER ATTACK

In December 1991 the Soviet Union dissolves and in the referendum to ratify the Act of Declaration of Independence the vast majority, 92.3% of Ukrainian voters, vote in favor. Since then, Ukraine has become an independent state. However, separatist tendencies toward Russia in the east of the country continued for many years. It was the end of November 2004 when the "Orange Revolution" broke out. A wave of protests has rocked the country, reacting to widespread corruption and fraud during the presidential election. For the first time in Ukraine there is an attempt to secede from Russia at all levels. Then, in 2013, follows the "Maidan Revolution", also known as the "Dignity Revolution". The then Ukrainian leadership decides, under the presidency of Viktor Yanukovych, to withdraw from the association agreement with the European Union, strengthening ties with Moscow. This decision immediately sparked protest rallies, which turned into a movement (Euromaidan).

However, this action provoked the Russian invasion of Crimea and the annexation of the peninsula, as well as the outbreak of a war in the Donbas region, in the east of the country. More than 14,000 people lost their lives in the battles that destroyed Donbass, the industrial heart of Ukraine in the east. "Imperial" Moscow never actually accepting Kyiv's independence or Ukraine's removal from its sphere of influence. More than 100,000 Russian troops are already on standby in the event of an invasion, while the Pentagon has deployed 8,500 US troops in case it needs to send them to Eastern Europe. At the same time, NATO is sending ships and fighter jets to strengthen the region's defenses.

It is clear that the Russian President has found the right opportunity not only to re-enter the geopolitical game but also to lead his country to the revival of Soviet greatness. For Russia, Ukraine's accession to NATO is a red line, while another demand is the withdrawal of American forces from the territories of the countries of the former Soviet Union. According to Russian diplomacy, military tension in Europe will decrease if NATO withdraws its forces from Eastern European countries.

According to Sotirios K. Serbos (Associate Professor of International Politics at the Democritus University of Thrace)"Russia's biggest problem is not Ukraine but the US". The renewed crisis in Russia's relations with Ukraine is part of the Kremlin's systematic effort (mainly after 2014) to reclaim the historic and later lost buffer zones in order to regain vital and high-value strategic depth over of the West.

Since the spring of 2021, the concentration of military forces on the border between the two countries is used as a tool to Russia create an atmosphere of crisis to draw America's attention to its own needs and demands on regional issues. (See proximity abroad) and maintain a credible leverage to start negotiations between Washington and Moscow. Thus, tension-instability is a precondition for moving forward (if at all possible) to a new and less unpredictable period of stability. We see, then, that Russia's biggest problem is not Ukraine (although it was the brightest gem in the crown of imperial Russia) but the United States. If Moscow had approved a major military invasion and occupation operation, it would have already done so and would have left no time for the West to prepare military retaliation. You attack using all your tactical advantages on the field and you certainly do not let time pass so that your opponent is better prepared.

On the contrary, in the context of diplomatic preparation for a new, even partial high-level consultation with your opponent, it makes sense to record many and consecutive threats. On the other hand, if diplomacy fails, one should not rule out a limited Russian operation in eastern Ukraine, moving further south to fully fill the positions of the Russian fleet in the Sea of Azov, achieving greater reach in the Black Sea and maintaining a permanent threat to southern Ukraine. Of course, the Americans risked responding with Ukraine's accession to NATO[2].

This is a decision that the Russian President will take, assessing the situation that will develop in five years and whether it is ultimately in his interest to move from now on or to wait[3].

Of course, such an invasion or a war has multiple function against the social, financial sectors, but it has definitely consequences against the cultural sector. The protection of the Ukrainian cultural heritage is considered necessary and the ways of its protection is the subject of this publication.

CULTURAL HERITAGE AT RISK OF DESTRUCTION

Thousands of museums across Ukraine store important works of art by Ukrainian and Russian artists, Byzantine artefacts, and paintings among others by Bellini, Goya and David.

The Museum of Freedom in Kyiv has a collection of around 4000 objects. Most of these record Ukraine's pre-democracy movement and are at the risk of being destroyed by the Russian forces. The Odessa National Fine Arts Museum houses more than 10,000 pieces of art, is at risk too. It includes more than 10,000 pieces of art and some of them are works by the best-known Russian and Ukrainian artists from the 16th century, (REF/RL, 2023).

Moving collections out of Ukraine is not only complicated, but under these circumstances impossible; an important reason is the fact that state museums need government permission, something that will definitely take time. Kyiv's Museum of Freedom -founded in 2014- as a memorial museum for the pro-democracy movement. Now is working to find a secure storage place somewhere in the Kyiv's city. "Our museum is evidence of Ukraine's fight for freedom," director Ihor Poshyvailo told the New York Times. "Of course, I'm fearful, (Πανταζόπουλος, 2022).

The Museum of Freedom is just one of institutions in the city, which are now under threat. At the National Museum of the History of Ukraine, also in Kyiv, workers had moved objects into storage, while on the Black Sea, the Odessa Fine Arts Museum hid art in the basement.

International museums have also scrambled to recall loans to Ukraine, like artifacts related to Russia's 2014 annexation of Crimea that had been touring the country and some of them left Ukraine, but more than 300 remain in Kyiv. Olesia Ostrovska-Liuta, general director of Kyiv's Mystetskyi Arsenal National Culture, Arts and museum Complex, reacted to Russian President Putin's announcement of the invasion by implementing the museum's safety plan[4].

Saving Heritage in War Zones

"We should be preparing now the 'Book Arsenal' to be held in May, exhibitions, and cross-sectoral projects—instead, our team focuses the efforts to ensure the safety of our staff, our families, as well as to guard our collection,". "By escalating their eight-year-long aggression with these horrid and disgusting actions against Ukraine, by invading the territory of Ukraine, Russia is attacking the basic, fundamental principles of international peace and security, the pillars of the UN, the very existence of the Ukrainian state."

In Ukraine there are seven UNESCO World Heritage Sites. As a result, "UNESCO calls for respect for international humanitarian law, notably the 1954 Hague Convention for the Protection of Cultural Property in the Event of Armed Conflict and its two (1954 and 1999) Protocols, to ensure the prevention of damage to cultural heritage in all its forms.

This also includes the obligations under the United Nations Security Council Resolution 2222 (2015) on the protection of journalists, media professionals and associated personnel in situations of conflict, to promote free, independent and impartial media as one of the essential foundations of a democratic society, and which can contribute to the protection of civilians. UNESCO also calls for restraint from attacks on, or harm to, children, teachers, education personnel or schools, and for the right to education to be upheld, (Mystetskyi Arsenal, n.d.), (Ostrovska, 2022).

But also, various Ukrainian member organizations had been in contact with the Museum Watch Committee, a branch of CIMAM (the International Committee for Museums and Collections of Modern Art), in order to offer practical support, (FP Explainers, 2022).

The St Sophia Cathedral in Kyiv (11th century A.D.) and Kyiv-Pechersk Lavra (the Kyiv Monastery of the Caves, founded in 1051) and the old quarter of Lviv (13th century), which is also a world heritage site, are in danger too. And last, but not least, the city of Kharkiv has been under heavy attack by Russian forces, has an important number of museums and cathedrals, (Lifestyle Desk, 2022).

What Has Been Lost So Far

The Ukrainian Foreign Ministry wrote on Twitter on February 28 that the Ivankiv Historical and Local History Museum had been completely burnt down after the Russian attack. In addition, 25 paintings by the famous Ukrainian artist Maria Prymachenko were burned. Picasso himself had said of the Ukrainian artist: "I bow before the artistic marvel of this brilliant Ukraine," (BBC News, 2022).

As a result of the demolition of some radio and television towers under the Russian air raid on Kyiv, the Holocaust memorial at Babyn Yar in Kyiv was hit. It is a monument to the massacre of more than 33,000 Jews by Nazi forces in 1941 during World War II. On the occasion of the above catastrophes, the President of Ukraine Volodymyr Zelenskyy wrote on Twitter that the catastrophes that took place in World War II are repeated,

Due to the Ukranian "cultural catastrophe" after the ongoing invasion Russian forces a huge number of priceless artworks, artefacts and monuments is at risk of being destroyed. Paul Getty Trust, a global arts organization, stated that the Russian forces have "deliberately burned to the ground" the Ivankiv Museum north of Kyiv, which housed precious Ukrainian folk art, (O'Keefe, 2006).

But it's not only this! Ukraine's cultural heritage is being destroyed, a cultural heritage that represents centuries of history from Byzantine to the Baroque period.

Until nowadays none of the UNESCO World Heritage Site appears to have been damaged. Which guarantees their future, as they are in war zones. The destruction of monuments and historic buildings may seem insignificant compared to the growing number of injuries and deaths in Ukraine, but for each

Saving Heritage in War Zones

country culture and heritage can play a critical role. Deliberate targeting of religious and cultural sites is also prohibited by the 1954 Hague Convention, although perpetrators have rarely been punished[5].

The head of the satellite program of cultural heritage monitoring in Ukraine is the famous Smithsonian Institution Cultural Rescue Initiative. The database is housed in the Virginia Museum of Natural History in Martinsville. Ukraine, meanwhile, is doing all it can to protect its treasures by hiding gold Scythian treasures, Byzantine icons and manuscripts underground, or by secretly transferring some exhibits to supporting foreign museums. The program in Virginia is based on the know-how of curators from America and Europe and is led by archaeologist Hayden Bassett. "We are on alert 24 hours a day," he told the Washington Post recently, (McGlone, 2022). "Although we may not look at a screen at 3 in the morning, our satellites reflect what was happening at 3 in the morning." Brian Daniels, an anthropologist working with the team in Virginia, told the Observer: "Violence is now focused on civilian infrastructure, and that means that museums and cultural heritage are being targeted in this scorched earth policy, (Thorpe, 2022).

Ukrainian officials accused the Russian forces of confiscating "more than 2,000 works of art" from museums in the occupied city of Mariupol and transporting the works to areas of the Russian-controlled Donbas region. "The conquerors 'liberated' Mariupol from its historical and cultural heritage. "They stole and transported more than 2,000 unique exhibits from Mariupol museums in Donetsk," the Mariupol city council said in a statement posted on its Telegram channel. The collection includes many original works by Arkhip Kuindzhi and the Russian painter Ivan Aivazovsky. Kuindzhi paintings are in the collections of the Metropolitan Museum of Art in New York and the Tretyakov Gallery in Moscow. "The Mariupol municipal council is preparing material for law enforcement agencies to initiate criminal proceedings and to appeal to Interpol," the council added. According to the Mariupol city council, the works came from three local museums, including the Kuindzhi Art Museum, which was severely damaged during a Russian air raid on March 21, 2022. The seizure of works of art in Mariupol marks the first known case of mass cultural looting by Russian forces since the start of the war, (CBC Radio, 2022).

Ukraine has been rushing to protect its artefacts and monuments since the outbreak of the war, as many feared that Moscow would specifically target the country's cultural heritage, a war crime under international law. Ukraine's fears about its cultural property have been exacerbated by a series of public speeches by Russian President Vladimir Putin in which he rejected Ukraine's independent identity, language and traditions. Olesia Ostrovska-Liuta, director of the Art Arsenal Cultural Center in Kyiv, described culture as "at the core of this war", saying that Russia's attempt to erase Ukraine as a separate entity was "genocide" and that the war was in fact an "extreme attack on civilization". Ostrovska-Liuta said the Russian Federation therefore had a "very clear, unambiguous cultural policy" in its invasion, including targeting cultural workers, objects and institutions. The redefinition of Ukrainian culture as Russian; and the appropriation of cultural objects. He said there had been reports of "organized looting by the state" of museum collections by the Russian army in the cities of Mariupol and Melitopol[6].

MEASURES TAKEN TO REDUCE DISASTERS

According to The Guardian, four museums in Vinnytsia, Zhytomyr, Sumy and Chernihiv managed to "download and protect their main exhibitions. In Vinnytsia, the museum building is now partly used for internally displaced people, i.e., as a shelter. However, it is not yet known whether any of the aforementioned museums have been looted or attacked. Of course, Fedir Androshchuk, director of the National

Saving Heritage in War Zones

History Museum of Ukraine in Kyiv, has said that efforts are being made to protect the museum from attacks or looting.

"The museum is in the middle of a rich cultural heritage close to three churches, but also close to some potential targets (the Ukrainian security service and the border forces)," he wrote in an email to a Swedish academic, according to The Guardian.

Other measures, which possibly could help are the preparation of a RED LIST for endangered cultural property of Ukraine at European level immediately. It will be particularly important, as it will make a significant contribution to preventing and combating their illicit trafficking. Take also a European initiative to set up a platform for gathering information on looting and theft of cultural property in Ukraine and attempts to smuggle and market them. In the same context, inform the customs authorities of the EU countries, so that there is vigilance and increased control over the movement of cultural goods coming from Ukraine. In collaboration with UNESCO, to organize an information campaign aimed at art dealers. Immediate initiatives to take ad hoc legal and institutional measures to protect Ukraine's cultural heritage, if necessary, with the assistance of international cultural organizations.

Especially for the destruction of the monuments, Ms. Mendoni reiterated the political will of the Greek government "to participate in the restoration of the Ukrainian cultural heritage by sending experts and conservators to record and evaluate the damage to the monuments of the country and especially the wider area of Mariupol, where the Greek community lives. A European Ministry of Culture for example can provide the Ministry of Culture of Ukraine with assistance in the preparation of studies and the execution of rescue and restoration works of immovable and movable monuments.

The National Museum of Contemporary Art welcomed children and their teachers from the Ukrainian Educational and Cultural Center Bereginia. A cooperation with the Ukrainian community in European countries, can utilize a special platform for recording and announcing available jobs in the cultural sector (private and public), which could be made available to refugee Ukrainian artists.

"On the next day of the war," Ms. Mendoni noted, "one of the key issues is, of course, the restoration of damage to cultural heritage and cultural infrastructure." It would be appropriate to explore the possibilities of taking initiatives to finance programs for the restoration and restoration of injured monuments in Ukraine, from the budget of the European Union. The cultural heritage of a people is not only its history and culture, but also the means of healing its wounds as well as the vehicle for its mental uplift and its socio-economic recovery and return to a peaceful, a constructive and sustainable future. We must, therefore, defend and support it with all our might," (Ρόκου, 2022).

Legal Protection

"Is there no protection then?" You may think after seeing the umpteenth ruined temple. The answer is positive but requires nuance. Where heritage used to be seen as spoils of war, a major step forward has been taken in the 20th century, and especially in the aftermath of World War II. Today, wartime cultural heritage is protected by a treaty adopted by UNESCO in 1954: the Cultural Goods Convention. This convention prohibits, among other things, the attacking of cultural heritage and the use of such sites for military purposes. Yet we notice that the destruction of cultural heritage has not exactly decreased since 1954[7]. Why then does this protection not seem to work at all?

Issues

One of the main reasons why the protection is ineffective, is because the Cultural Goods Convention has a number of weaknesses. For example, there is an exception to the prohibition against attacking cultural heritage: where "military necessity" - a term not defined anywhere - so requires, the sites may still be targeted. This imprecise exception, of course, provides a great deal of leeway for parties in a conflict to destroy disturbing heritage.

Another major weakness of the convention is its sanctions regime, which is very vague and general. The non-binding nature of the provision has ensured that no Member State has adopted legislation based on this treaty, which ultimately results in a fall back on already existing national criminal law. The usefulness of the sanctions regime of the Cultural Goods Convention is therefore rightly questioned.

UNESCO was aware of these issues and therefore adopted a protocol to the Convention in 1999. This protocol – a kind of addendum – contains a better sanctions regime and considerably limits the possibility of exception, so a major improvement. However, the new instrument suffers from a lack of ratifications, with many states finding it too far-reaching and thus refusing to sign it. As long as this is the case, the defective and outdated Cultural Goods Convention will remain the most important protection instrument, with all the associated consequences.

SOLUTIONS

How can the protection of cultural heritage be improved? A number of short-term solutions are conceivable. The first is obvious: to get more states to ratify the 1999 protocol. This could be achieved by generating political pressure; many people have never heard of the Cultural Goods Convention or the protocol and there is therefore no immediate incentive for governments to become a party to it. A campaign could tackle this publicity problem and increase social awareness. When people are faced with the fact that their governments see no need to ratify the treaty or protocol, public opinion can exert the power to subvert this hard-to-defend position.

Another concrete improvement opportunity is to take inspiration from MINUSMA, the peace operation that the UN Security Council sent to Mali in 2013 during the civil war. For the first time, attention was also paid to the protection of cultural heritage by adding a clause to that effect to the mandate of the military personnel sent to the site. The good work that is still being done in the African country by MINUSMA could serve as an example for future peace missions. In this way, the care for heritage is given a more prominent place in conflicts.

Finally, we can look at the recent case law of the International Criminal Court in The Hague. In 2016, for the first time in history, this tribunal convicted someone solely for the destruction of cultural heritage (in previous sentences, the crime was always combined with other cases such as murder and torture). It is therefore a historic ruling that greatly benefits the protection of cultural heritage and also puts the International Criminal Court forward as the most suitable place to enforce the heritage treaties. The only problem with this statement is that only nationals of countries that have accepted the jurisdiction of the Court can be prosecuted for it. However, certain key countries such as the US, Russia and Syria have not done so, making this solution less valuable. However, this is also difficult because the permanent members of the Council (US, Russia, France, UK and China) may never agree to refer conflicts in which they have interests, such as that in Syria, to a court and thus expose their own military personnel

Saving Heritage in War Zones

to potential persecution. So, it is important to work for the Court's acceptance of jurisdiction so that it can build on historical precedent, (Blake, 20010).

Polish Cultural Solidarity: Food for Thought

With the help and guidance of the Ukrainian Museum Aid Committee, Polish cultural institutions are trying to establish a mechanism for the protection of cultural heritage in Russian-occupied Ukraine.

Poland was a country that suffered extensive cultural property destruction during World War II. "No nation or state should suffer such losses again," the commission said in a statement. "Unfortunately, this is unlikely to happen in Ukraine today, (International Council of Museums, 2022).

According to Pawel Ukielski, deputy director of the Warsaw Rising Museum and co-founder of the post-attack initiative, the extensive damage to Poland's cultural heritage in the past was not just a result of the war, but a "deliberate disaster," he said. in DW.

It is possible that Vladimir Putin has similar intentions, given that "since there is no Ukrainian nation, there is no Ukrainian identity" - which automatically implies that tangible and intangible cultural heritage could very easily be the target of catastrophic of mania in order not only to prove his point, but also to possibly carry out the plans of his expansionist policy, as an imitation of Hitler.

The purpose of the commission is to provide support to all museums and cultural institutions in Ukraine both for the preservation and for the safety and relocation of their collections. Ukielski said a first shipment of special materials for the protection of museum collections would be sent to the Lviv region. This example could be followed by the other countries bordering Ukraine or even the member states of the European Union. One possible solution would be to house works of art and exhibits in European museums until the end of the war, while in the case of archeological sites the highest economic sanctions in Russia in the event of partial or total destruction could act as a deterrent.

The Ukrainian Museum Aid Committee also plans to assist in the documentation, digitization and inventory of the collections and welcomes international partners to participate in the effort[8].

The creation of a digital register of cultural property could greatly contribute to the process of protection of Ukraine's cultural heritage, including the case of museum looting.

CONCLUSION

Protecting cultural heritage is a complex task, especially when groups like I.S.I.S. or other military groups deliberate attack. No law or court can match that. Nevertheless, there are a number of options for compensating for the shortcomings of the Cultural Goods Convention. Ratification of the protocol, a broader mandate for peacekeeping missions and acceptance of the jurisdiction of the International Criminal Court can each contribute in their own way to better protection. A protection that is also desperately needed for post-conflict reconstruction and stabilisation, not only to be able to continue to cherish a shared culture and history, but also to maintain a certain economic potential. Without these elements, achieving lasting peace becomes a lot more utopian. And let a lack of peace be the greatest threat to cultural heritage[9].

The first official project was the law passed in 1666 in Sweden for the protection of cultural heritage. Since then, have followed more, with the 1954 Hague Convention still the crowning achievement of conventions on what it calls the "Protection of Cultural Heritage in the Event of Armed Conflict," along with the two Additional Protocols that followed in 1954. and 1999 respectively. Other conventions were subsequently voted on, either to amend existing provisions or to supplement gaps in matters not covered by the Hague Convention and the Protocols, such as the UNIDROIT Convention on Cultural Property, (Raaij, 2016).

During the Second World War, the existing Conventions and institutions were not and are not able - even today - to prevent the destruction of the World Cultural Heritage. The above was understood, since the end of the last century in the context of armed conflicts, numerous monuments were destroyed both as collateral losses and deliberately. The deliberate destruction of the enemy's cultural monuments served as a basic propaganda weapon of war in order to weaken his morale, as well as his cultural annihilation[10].

The reasons why the Contracts appeared to be ineffective vary. The contracts up to the Second Protocol did not concern non-international internal conflicts, without specifying, by some definition, what exactly is included in this term.

Studying the cases of the above war conflicts, one realizes that it is difficult for the conventions to be applied to them. For example, in the case of the war in the former Yugoslavia, the impossibility of implementation lies in the fact that this conflict was considered an internal conflict. In other cases, such as ISIS, the perpetrators of the disasters were usually parastatals and unrecognized state entities. The latter were not parties to the existing conventions and therefore had no obligation to comply with them, nor could they be penalized, (BBC News, 2014), (Auwera, 2013).

Apart from this serious problem, there are two more serious reasons that make existing contracts ineffective. First, the term military necessity, which essentially means that if a position (even of cultural value) is a military target, the adversary can move against it, invoking the term and thus not be penalized. In fact, the fact that the concept is still not defined in a specific context gives an even greater possibility to invoke it in order for a member to avoid sanctions. The term military necessity is one of the most vulnerable points of the Hague Convention and no major amendment has yet been made to remove it, despite efforts to limit the use of the term to the provisions of the Second Protocol.

In addition, there are no sanctioning bodies and the prosecution of the perpetrators is left to the jurisdiction of each state in which the catastrophe unfolds. This naturally has many problems, as the law of each country is different. At the same time, the international community must have a say in such issues, which affect human rights, if we are talking about world heritage sites and not national ones, (Neumann, 2022).

REFERENCES

Amnesty. (2022). Η ιστορία της Οικουμενικής Διακήρυξης των Δικαιωμάτων του. Ανθρώπου.

BBC News. (2022). *'Ukraine war: On the front line of the battle for Kharkiv'. BBC News.* BBC.

BBC News. (2022). *'Syria Crusader castle Krak des Chevaliers has war scars', BBC News.* BBC.

BBC News. (2022). *'Syria Crusader castle Krak des Chevaliers has war scars', BBC News.* BBC.

Blake, J. (2015). *International Cultural Heritage Law.* Oxford University Press. doi:10.1093/acprof:oso/9780198723516.001.0001

Saving Heritage in War Zones

Bowma, M., Davies, P. G. G., Redgwell, C., & Lyster, S. (2010). *Lyster's International Wildlife Law*. Cambridge University Press. doi:10.1017/CBO9780511975301

CBC radio. (2022). *This museum director is staying in Kyiv as Ukrainian culture comes under fire*. CBD Radio.

D W. (2022). *Ukraine calls Putin's passport plan 'criminal*. Deutsche Welle.

ICOM. (2022). *ICOM Call for Donations to Support Museums and Museum Professionals in Ukraine*. ICOM.

International Council of Museums. (n.d.) *Κώδικας Δεοντολογίας του ICOM για τα Μουσεία. ΔΙΕΘΝΕΣ ΣΥΜΒΟΥΛΙΟ ΜΟΥΣΕΙΩΝ ΕΛΛΗΝΙΚΟ ΤΜΗΜΑ*. ICM. http://icom-greece.mini.icom.museum/wp-content/uploads/sites/38/2018/12/code-of-ethics_GR_01.pdf

Johannot-Gradis, C. (2015). Protecting the past for the future: How does law protect tangible and intangible cultural heritage in armed conflict? *International Review of the Red Cross*, 97(900), 1253–1275. doi:10.1017/S1816383115000879

McGlone, P. (2022). A lab in rural Virginia is racing to preserve Ukraine's cultural heritage. *Washington Post*.

Neumann, T. W. (2022). Heritage legilsation, the introduction of: disciplining through law. In Encyclopaedia of Global Archaeology. Springer.

O'Keefe, R. (2006). *The Protection of Cultural Property in Armed Conflict*. Cambridge University Press. doi:10.1017/CBO9780511494260

O'Keefe, R., Péron, C., Tofig, M., & Ferrari, G. (2016). *Protection of Cultural Property, Military Manual*. Manual.

Ρόκου, Τ. (2022). Δράσεις υπέρ προστασίας του ουκρανικού πολιτισμού ζήτησε στην ΕΕ η Λ. Μενδώνη. *Travel Daily News*.

Raaij, B. V. (2016). *Jihadist krijgt 9 jaar cel voor vernieling cultureel erfgoed*. De Volkstrant.

RFE/RL. (2022). *Live Briefing: Russia Invades Ukraine. Radio Free Europe*. .

Πανταζόπουλος, Τ. (2022). *Γιατί ηχούν «τύμπανα πολέμου» στα σύνορα Ουκρανίας - Ρωσίας*. Lifo.

Rokou, T. (2022). Δράσεις υπέρ προστασίας του ουκρανικού πολιτισμού ζήτησε στην ΕΕ η Λ. Μενδώνη. *Travel Daily News*.

Τμήμα, Δ. (2009). Κώδικας Δεοντολογίας του ICOM για τα Μουσεία. New York Times (2022). Russia attacks Ukraine. *The New York Times*. .

Mysteskyi Arsenal. (2002). *Exhibitions*. Mysteskkyi Arsenal.

Ostrovska, O. (2022). *The Invasion of Ukraine Is a War Against All Democratic States. As We Fight for Our Liberty, Here Are 5 Ways the Art World Can Help*. Artnet.

Thorpe, V. (2022). Crimes against history: mapping the destruction of Ukraine's culture. *The Guardian*.

Thurley, S. (2005). Into the future. Our strategy for 2005-2010. In *Conservation Bulletin* [English Heritage] (pp. 49). https://content.historicen gland.org.uk/i mages-books/publications/conservation-bulletin- 49/cb4926-27.pdf/

U. a. (2022). What Happened on Day 94 of the War in Ukraine. *The New York Times.* .

Cascone, S. (2022). *Hiding Art in Basements, Returning Loans, Reopening as Bomb Shelters: How Ukraine's Museums Are Handling the Russian Invasion.*

Explainers, F. P. (2022). *Museums, memorials, and monuments under attack: The cultural catastrophe in Ukraine.* Firstpost.

Lifestyle Desk. (2022). *Who is Maria Prymachenko, the Ukrainian artist whose artworks were nearly destroyed at a museum.* The Indian Express.

UNESCO. (2022). *UNESCO's statement on the recent developments in Ukraine.* UNESCO.

UNESCO. (1995). *The 1954 Hague Convention for the Protection of Cultural Property in the Event of Armed Conflict and its two (1954 and 1999) Protocols.* UNESCO.

Franchi, E. (2022). What is cultural. *Khan Academy. ICOMOS. (2002). International Cultural Tourism Charter. Principles And Guidelines for Managing Tourism at Places of Cultural and Heritage Significance.* ICOMOS International Cultural Tourism Committee. .

Feather, J. (2006). Managing the documentary heritage: issues from the present and future. *Preservation management for libraries, archives and museums,* 1-18.

Van der Auwera, S. (2013). International Law and the Protection of Cultural Property in the Event of Armed Conflict: Actual Problems and Challenges. *The Journal of Arts Management, Law, and Society, 43*(4), 175–190. doi:10.1080/10632921.2013.841114

Zelensky, V. (2022). *Twit* [Status update]. Twitter.

Chapter 11

Aspects of Total Quality Management:
An "Excellence in Quality" Path to a Long–Term Impact of Effective Teaching in Tourism Education

Despina Konstantinides
Neapolis University, Pafos, Cyprus

ABSTRACT

The aim of this chapter is to identify dimensions of total quality management (TQM), which are related to excellence in quality. The identified dimensions are expected to lead to a successful implementation of techniques and customer focus approaches and to teacher effectiveness. In favor of this purpose, the authors have chosen a qualitative and quantitative research approach. The research participants were teachers of general secondary education and teachers at vocational technical schools that include fields of hotel management and professions which belong to the field of tourism education. The importance of this study is revealed through research findings which highlight perceptions of quality with respect to the teaching environment. Teacher involvement in quality improvement educational activities will make them more effective in teaching and school practices. Quality can create an environment where all members of the school community work jointly together to provide students with the resources they need to meet up present and prospect academic and societal requirements.

INTRODUCTION

Being in times of undergoing education reform, the educational system of Cyprus seems to be seeking ways to strengthen teacher effectiveness through practices that trigger motivation, so that teachers will be able to arise and develop further. Lack of teacher quality policy formulation might disorientate teachers from achieving their mission. Quality teachers are able to implement the national education policy effectively and will strive to achieve their school's mission and vision (Shahril, 2005). Taking

DOI: 10.4018/978-1-6684-6055-9.ch011

Copyright © 2023, IGI Global. Copying or distributing in print or electronic forms without written permission of IGI Global is prohibited.

into consideration that teachers' duties are expanded, they consist of the most important human factor in education systems and are meant not only to carry out the knowledge; they serve the country by playing a vital part in students' personality formation. Teachers take the first step in training of human resources and are responsible for training of future human society (Ghaderi, Rigi and Salimi, 2015).

According to Mergen and Stevenson (2002) TQM is related to the philosophy of seeking to meet customer needs, constantly improving quality, and improve performance. One of the most important elements in the success of TQM, in various fields, is the measurement of quality performance (Benzaquen et al., 2019; Prajogo, 2005; Prajogo & Sohal, 2006). It has been considered as an approach to improve the effectiveness, flexibility and competitiveness of enterprises to meet customer requirements (Oakland, 1993). By focusing on the customers' needs, the operational practises are performed in line with the requirements of excellence. This might be the reason that TQM has been recognised as a viable way to achieve excellence, acquire efficient business solutions and enchant customers and suppliers (Mohanty & Behera, 1996).

Excellence in quality could be reflected in teaching practices, which have the power to generate outputs, namely student learning outcomes, and improve the quality of the provided education. Qualitative research on secondary school teachers' motivation has found that teacher inspection for evaluation constitutes an intrinsic motivator, which suggests that the power that energizes teachers to invest commitment into their job is internal, i.e. inside the teacher self (Konstantinides-Vladimirou, 2013; 2015).

Conceptualizing over the *excellence in quality* as a part of TQM, this chapter initiates a goal-setting perspective in a teacher evaluation process, which (perspective) is being examined via qualitative and quantitative research that has been conducted for teacher evaluation, in the context of secondary education in Cyprus (Konstantinides, 2021). At the research took part teachers of Secondary Schools and Secondary Technical and Vocational Education Schools that teach courses in the field of Management of Hotel Units and Hotel and Catering Professions.

Thus, this chapter aims to identify the dimensions of *excellence in quality* in tourism education through teachers' eyes, the impact of influence on their practices, as well as to analyse the extent to which this relationship occurs. Can such an approach enhance teacher effectiveness and student learning? May it work positively in developing schools as professional learning communities? By serving the aim of the chapter and exploring how beneficial such an impact would be, a model of *excellence in quality* teacher practice is adopted (Diagram 3).

In order to achieve the objectives of this study, basic strategic steps signpost the structure of the chapter:

- To discuss the linkage between TQM and tourism education.
- To create a research question that would investigate the dynamics of 'excellence in quality'.
- To construct a hypothesis over how a perspective through *excellence in quality* can affect teacher effectiveness.
- To test the hypothesis via qualitative and quantitative research experiment.
- To extract the conclusions and recommendations of the study through a discussion that indicates the empowerment effects of an excellence centred and school-based teacher practice on teacher effectiveness in the field of tourism education.

Aspects of Total Quality Management

BACKGROUND: THE LINKAGE BETWEEN TQM AND TOURISM EDUCATION

Lack of elements related to measurement of quality as a part of TQM, can be located upon the education system's inadequacy to actually contribute to the development and growth of teachers, which would motivate them towards effectiveness, through student- centered practices. Once established in the school context, school-based practices which favor the sharing of teacher knowledge, the giving of feedback on teacher performance, and the exchange of ideas would promote teacher growth and professional learning through conversation and connection, for 'Learning depends on making connections' (Stoll and Seashore Louis, 2007). Apart from lack of such practices, the multidimensional activity of the teachers who are distinguished from others thanks to their high professional commitment, exhibited at the school level, does not seem to be taken into serious account in terms of advancement. What mainly determines teachers' promotion is seniority, i.e. the years of teaching experience (MOEC, 2019), which was found to be a dispensation that favours the older teachers (Konstantinides-Vladimirou, 2015).

Implementation of TQM necessitates adherence, discipline and constant employee effort, it includes everything and is dependent on everyone. TQM is a system which guarantees the systematic and continual enhancement of all work processes. In such processes a cycle of quality is applied. This cycle is a complicated process that includes planning of quality, quality realization, control and evaluation of the achieved quality and quality improvement (Holjevac, 1996). There have been a limited number of empirically researched studies of TQM in tourism fields, like the hotel industry. It has been identified by Breiter and Kline (1995) that leadership, customer focus, vision and values of TQM in hotel industry, is followed by training communications, empowerment, alignment of organizational systems and implementation (Al-Ababneh, 2021).

Existing definitions of leadership indicate the need to set objectives and influence the behavior of employees, including their motivation (Shackleton and Wale, 2002). Quality objectives are meant to improve processes and set directions for continuous improvement (Varela and Pacheco, 2018). Aspects of customer focus practices deal exclusively with the motivational function of quality objectives. Sila and Ebrahimpour (2003) tested the Malcolm Baldridge National Quality Award, in order to investigate TQM practices in US luxury hotels and concluded that two main factors most often integrated by hotels through their TQM programs are leadership and customer focus.

If we consider the school as a kind of business, the "customers" in such a business are the students and the parents. In this case who might be the entrepreneurs? The student is the primary customer of education (Sallis, 1993; Zairi, 1995; Ho and Wearn, 1995). According to Gunter and Fitzerald, the school is transformed into a business that has customers-parents-consumers and teachers become professional in education by performing the role of entrepreneur who must meet the requirements of the customer (Zairi, 1995). Students are described as customers and education as a product (Craig, et al., 1999). The student is the recipient of service, acquiring knowledge/information. In such a way the education is conducted on the basis of rationalization, competition, autonomy and the student is guided as an educated person "by the rules of market" (Lynch, 2014).

The main factor of success in quality management is maintaining good relationship with students who are the school's main customers (Zhang, Waszink and Wijngaard 2000). This kind of relationship might be implemented by identifying the students' needs and receiving students' feedback to meet their needs and increase their satisfaction with the school (Flynn, Schroeder and Sakakibaba, 1994). Education is more viewed as an investment by "customers" who search the world for the best product available and students expect a pay-off from their investment (Lawrence and Sharma, 2002).

Through our research, an attempt is detected to identify the dynamics that consist of teaching quality frame, to figure out the extent according to which these criteria could be transformed to motivators, as per increasing teacher effectiveness and, consequently student learning. A few criteria of teacher evaluation are: Teacher professional training; Organisation, management and human relationships; and General behaviour and activity. Through a goal setting perspective, it is a challenge to investigate quality as a means of variable for teacher performance and effectiveness. Goals are an annual part of Cyprus education system. General goals are the ones set by the Ministry of Education annually or diachronically. Specific goals are set by each school after a diagnosis of the school's needs, performed at the beginning of the school year.

TQM practices enable organizations to achieve long-term goals, improving the organization's ability to respond more efficiently to customer demand in terms of quality, innovation and price, while also allowing for more accurate handling of the adversity of markets (Antunes, et al., 2017; Madanat & Khasawneh, 2017). According to findings of a research that has been conducted for teachers' evaluation performance based on TQM, process improvement is emphasis on methods which involve job performance to increase teachers' efficiency and consequently, improve the quality of education. The same research reveals that there is a strong need to improve teachers' job process quality and education system improvement.

The use of TQM according to the education system goals increases the effectiveness of human and material resources in organizations (Shahmohammadi, 2017). Contemplating about the need for teachers' engagement in a TQM centered process, a research question has been shaped to investigate the motivational dynamics of quality; What is defined as "excellence in quality" by teachers of tourism education through a "goal setting" mode and how can this quality approach motivate them towards effectiveness?

THE RESEARCH QUESTION: HOW ASPECTS OF TOTAL QUALITY MANAGEMENT RELATED TO *EXCELLENCE IN QUALITY* CAN LEAD TO TEACHING EFFECTIVENESS?

The research question is explored through literature review in this chapter, in order to excavate the *excellence in quality* in education and the way it can lead teachers to effectiveness, considering the TQM features.

Parameters of Total Quality Management (TQM)

Though it is quite difficult to introduce a single universal definition of TQM (Lau and Anderson, 1998), generally most of the definitions of TQM are focused on TQM as a philosophy of management that fosters an organizational culture committed to customer satisfaction throughout continuous improvement (Al-Ababneh, 2021). TQM must be viewed as a long-term process, the vision to continually looking into the future, not only to have to meet short term target, organization must plan for their existence in the future (Rogers, 2013).

A significant dimension of TQM is related to excellence in goal achievement. A TQM approach is focusing to improve effectiveness of the processes and the responsiveness in meeting the customer requirement as part of organization excellence goals in achieving customer satisfaction (Ramlawati and Putra, 2018). Successful TQM implementation is often linked with the CSFs which are responsible

Aspects of Total Quality Management

for achieving business excellence (Talib and Rahman, 2010). TQM practices have been classified by authors as hard and soft phase; some practices are considered to be hard elements of TQM (i.e. less human factors involved, like quality control, quality measurements, etc.), while others are considered as soft elements of TQM (i.e. human factors are involved, like quality control, quality measurement, etc.) (Ali, et al., 2018). Thus, it is very important to look carefully at the type of elements of TQM that while implementing in education sector measure indeed effectively.

Writing about the appropriate dimensions of TQM, it should be noted that theories of motivation referring to goals need to be taken into consideration. According to Vroom's theory it is assumed that achieving first-level results might increase the likelihood of success in the case of second level results. However, according to Locke's theory specific and difficult goals may lead to higher performance (Foster, 2003). His conclusions consisted of specific and challenging goals being more motivational than vague and easy ones, then with Gary Latham they developed five fundamental principles behind effective goal setting (Locke and Latham, 1990). Effects of better achievement of goals that exceed skills are more easily visible when easier tasks are carried out (in this case the speed and accuracy of task performance matters) (Gilliland and Landis, 1992).

Goal setting in educational practices has the power to increase teachers' task performance especially when goals involve a high level of difficulty, i.e. they are 'high' or 'hard, because those goals energise a person to work harder so as to gain a higher sense of satisfaction (Locke & Latham, 2006). Teachers' task performance relates to four characteristic practices: instructional delivery which is effective when teachers deliver teaching in an explicitly active way (Hattle, 2009); classroom management which was linked, through research, to an increase of 20% in student achievement when classroom rules and procedures were applied systematically (Hattle, 2009); formative assessment, which is developed through feedback, the vehicle towards the improvement of students' performance (Hattle, 2009); and personal competencies, such as enthusiasm, energy, love for teaching which have been defined as motivation (Konstantinides-Vladimirou, 2015). Those competencies may develop when teachers engage in a process of goal setting that encourages the externalisation of their views, ideas and practices, and when the process develops through constructive dialogue in the school context.

In favour of a goal setting TQM approach is a strategy needed? Strategy is defined by Hinterhuber (2004) as a way of using resources and capabilities of an organization, in the context of business management field. According to a research that aimed to examine the relationship between critical success factors (CSFs) of TQM, strategic goals and organizational performance in India TQM practices have a significant impact on financial and operational performance (Kumar & Mishra, 2020). Performance should not be considered as an objective, it is orientated by the efficiency of the outcomes of well-organized strategic goals. In school context some teachers become true performers (Jeffrey and Troman, 2011), in the sense that they have internalised performative ideas as "natural ingredients" of what it means to be a teacher (Wilkins, 2011). Therefore, when formulating quality objectives, the ideas, opinions and suggestions of those who are closest to the students should be considered; the teachers who are involved in the performance of daily school tasks and operations.

Total Quality Management and *Excellence in Quality*

In 1980 the notion of TQM was considered as a strategic policy which had been implemented by focusing all the resources of an organization to achieve quality excellence (Benavides-Velasco, et al., 2014). Companies have adopted this side of TQM in their attempt to move forward towards quality. According to a study *quality* is defined by the production worker and classified as *poor quality* which is related to loss of the business, and perhaps of his work and *good quality* that is related to the survival of the company in the business world (Deming, 1986).

TQM is an outward customer-based approach (Zairi, 1995) and has been considered to be "a management approach that ensures mutual cooperation of everyone in an organisation and associated business processes to produce products and services that meet, and hopefully exceed the needs and expectations of customers" (Dale, 2003). TQM has become an essential management philosophy used for improving quality and productivity in organizations (Karia and Asaari, 2006) and is the process of changing the basic culture of an organization and forwarding it towards advanced product or service quality (Gaither, 1996). TQM rapidly became a top priority in many organizations due to the globalization age and highly competitive environment forcing customers to search for better products and services (Thiagaragan, Zairi and Dale, 2001). It helps in creating a culture of trust, participation, team-work, quality mindedness, enthusiasm for continuous improvement, constant learning and as a result, a working culture that contributes towards a firm's success and existence (Yusuf and Aspinwall, 2000).

TQM is a measurement of Value (Zairi, 1995), it is about a strategic, integrated management system that focuses on achieving Customer Satisfaction and seeking Continuous Improvement of processes (Schulz and Masters, 1997). The most important dimensions of Customer-focused performance are Service Quality, Customer Value and Customer Satisfaction (Wang and Lo, 2003). Customer Satisfaction should be made the goal and the measure of Service Quality (Milakovich, 1995). An academic institution with the help of TQM would be able to build up its own description of quality, benchmark, and quality improvement practices in the view of customers' need (Saxena, 2021). Students are increasingly seeing themselves as customers and behaving accordingly (Davies, et al., 2001), thus greater emphasis should be placed on school institutions as part of educational industry and those who are expected to be the "service mediators" of education quality; the teachers.

Aspects of *Excellence in Quality* and Education

The commitment to TQM originates at the chief executive level in a business and it is promoted in all human activities (Pike and Barnes, 1996). Applicability of aspects of TQM in education could be considered as an important factor in producing goals and values, that guide the continuous teacher performance improvement considering the fulfilment of students' needs.

The involvement of teachers in quality improvement educational activities will have benefits in terms of quality, making them more effective in teaching practices and various school issues. Teachers' involvement in quality management can change their behavior in school and could be an inspiration in quality improvement in schools (Juran and Gryna, 1993). Quality can create an environment where educationalists, parents, government officials, community representatives, and business leaders work jointly to deliver students with the resources they need to meet up present and prospect academic, business, and societal requirements (Arcaro, 1995). According to many researchers it is supported that education and training are important elements in the successful implementation of quality management (Rahman, Nor and Wahab, 2020; Mann, 1992), while it has been also stated that education can be made superior by quality management (Tribus, 1993).

TQM is a general management philosophy and a mix of various tools which induce educational institutions to pursue a description of quality and the means to achieve it (Murad and Rajesh, 2010). According to a study (Rahman, Nor and Wahab, 2021) teachers' quality refers to the quality of teach-

Aspects of Total Quality Management

ers' personal and professional quality and these aspects are measured through teachers' professionalism, teachers' knowledge and understanding as well as teaching and learning skills in order to improve students' achievement and performance. Teacher goal achievement is linked to professional growth, as achievement and growth often appear together in Herzberg's (1968) theory of motivation. Growth, being associated with the feeling of perceived progress in professional life, can lead to advancement, also a motivator, as an outcome of evaluation emergent from progress, rather than seniority, for advancement is identified as promotion. Professional growth may result from a creating new knowledge practice, a practice that should be pursued by school headteachers who promote the development of their schools as professional learning communities, and by the educational system through a policy that favours formative teacher evaluation. Research findings showed that the job performance of teachers based on total quality management components (process design, management, process improvement, public participation, and focus on customer) was more than expected mean, the continuous increase of teachers and administrators' awareness (employees' empowerment) will not be effective as long as they are not professional, capable, and expert in their works; the teaching-learning process will remain ineffective (Shahmohammadi, 2017).

According to a TQM model of academic excellence (Sakthivel, et al., 2005), the five TQM variables are: commitment of top management; course delivery; campus facilities; courtesy and customer feedback and improvement. If we need to detect the variables in terms of teacher and teaching process, *course delivery* is related to the expertise in knowledge that equals with the expertise in transmitting the knowledge, *courtesy* refers to the positive and emotive attitude to the students, which is beneficial for the effective learning environment and *customer feedback and improvement* is closely related to the continuous feedback from the students, which effects on improvement in learning process leading to excellence.

According to a research that aimed to evaluate teachers' job performance based on TQM model, the quality is a factor affecting the development of industry, commerce and education and it is one of the most importance factors in organizational competitiveness and success in global markets, therefore, the use of TQM according to education system goals increases the effectiveness of human and material resources in organizations (Shahmohammadi, 2017). On the other hand, some researchers believe that TQM has effect on education to some extent and that higher education institutions are not like companies, but, some of the basic principles and tools can be applicable, as these are instruments at the service institutions and their governance and management boards subject to the institution's academic mission, goals and strategies (Dill, 1995; Harvey, 1995). On a literature review level, it is argued that TQM principles are not universally applicable across all contexts, but are contingent on contextual factors (Brinbaum and Deshotels, 1999; Brinbaum, 2000) and that the way the definition of quality is given based on the customers' needs and expectations in business and industry environments is not at all appropriate for education (Houston, 2008). Therefore, generally speaking, the term *quality* is needed to be fine tuned while putting in aspects of education, so that complex situations are not produced; components of TQM might be well-suited with education.

THE HYPOTHESIS

A hypothesis over how a perspective surrounded by *excellence in quality* might be blended in teacher practices is constructed. The hypothesis is tested through a qualitative and quantitative research that aimed to examine the term of *excellence in quality* through the eyes of teachers.

Quality Implementation: Goal Setting Practice

The hypothetical background is expected to construct recommendations that highlight the empowerment effects of an *excellence in quality* school-based model based on teacher effectiveness.

Goal setting aims at goal achievement, a highly motivating factor, which according to the achievement motivation theory, can be reached through teachers' yearning to achieve success, and avoid failure (Owen, 1997). For success to be achieved, teachers need to invest effort, time and love in teaching, the work itself, which, like achievement, is identified by Herzberg (1968), in his two-factor theory, as a motivator, but also to rid themselves of feelings of failure. Feelings of failure might deter teachers from engaging in a goal setting process, for such feelings are likely to give rise to feelings of doubt about their ability to attain successful performance, and ultimately direct them to apathy (Konstantinides-Vladimirou, 2015).

The strong relationship between motivation and evaluation releases the expectation that achievement goal constructs (e.g. effective task performance), may energise teachers to set goals of achieving high competence, which would be evaluated in an achievement context. Teacher competence indicates teachers' effectiveness, aptitude, adequacy and accomplishment (Brooks and Shell, 2006). Therefore, the goals that teachers set are not abstract ideas, but specific strategies that embody an orientation to the task, and encompassed in the goal orientation are their 'beliefs about purposes, competence, success, ability, effort, errors, and standards (Pintrich, 2000, p. 94).

The motivational power of goal setting, being uncovered through its relationship with teacher performance, teacher achievement, and teacher leadership, leads to a hypothesis. The hypothesis is predicated upon the need for student centered school-based practices that include goal setting in a way that would actively engage teachers in the externalisation of internalised goals, and in strategic planning about how to achieve them. The perspective of the recommended goal-setting teacher evaluation hypothesis is discussed below.

Underpinning the hypothesis is the concept that goals can be internal and external, and the two terms: internal' and 'external' are discussed here in order to clarify the mindset underpinning their usage. Internal goals are set by an individual as thoughts and ideas through a thinking process that happens in the teacher's inner world. External goals are voiced, i.e. they are externalised, via a thinking process that happens outside the teacher self. Since a teacher's thoughts and ideas which relate to the teaching job constitute knowledge, the externalised perceptions refer to explicit knowledge. The act of making knowledge explicit is considered, in this study, to be motivational because it is conversational, and being so, it satisfies teachers' need for communication and belongingness (Konstantinides-Vladimirou, 2015; Maslow, 1954).

In order to act as guidelines, teachers' goals need to be written on paper, be measurable, time-bound, and hard but attainable, rather than static. They should be revisited and reviewed, and be oriented to the expected outcomes, which are identified through the extent to which they contribute to the attainment of organisational principles (Konstantinides, 2021).

THE QUALITATIVE RESEARCH EXPERIMENT: TESTING THE *EXCELLENCE IN QUALITY* HYPOTHESIS IN TOURISM EDUCATION

The goal-setting side of teacher evaluation is part of the qualitative research conducted for Ph.D. thesis that aimed to examine teachers' point of view on their evaluation, from an *excellence in quality* perspective

Aspects of Total Quality Management

in the context of Secondary Education and Secondary Technical and Vocational Education Schools in Cyprus that include also fields of Management of Hotel Units and Hotel and Catering Professions which belong to the sector of tourism education. The research required educators to put down, via a reflective tool, the goals that they would have set at the beginning of the school year and at a second section they were expected to set the actions they would take in order to achieve them (their goals). For these actions specific dynamics were mounted as an axis according to which their actions would be implemented. The dynamics are mostly equivalent to the values: *excellence in quality*, *student-centeredness* and *correspondence*. In order to serve the purpose of this study only the data collected for the part concerning the value of *excellence in quality* are examined, underpinning that requirement was to identify the areas of teachers' focus that can be rated as indicators of factors measuring teacher effectiveness towards this value.

This part of the research used a reflective tool and collected data from 35 educators (teachers and assistant headteachers) of different subject matter from different secondary schools (Gymnasiums, Lyceums and Technical Schools). The qualitative data were analysed through a content analysis which found the following indicators: differentiation, learning objectives, critical thinking, vocational training, learning outcome, discipline, adequacy, reward, collaboration, syllabus detailed program, knowledge adequacy, improvement. Resulting from the data analysis, the diagram below 'Value of Excellence in Quality. Factors leading to teacher effectiveness' (Diagram 1) shows the number of research participants, who revealed the side of *excellence in quality* through the actions they need to take in order to achieve the goals they had set at the beginning of the school year 2019-2020, and the concepts dominating those, which are described as factors leading to teacher effectiveness.

Figure 1. Value of excellence in quality. Factors leading to teacher effectiveness

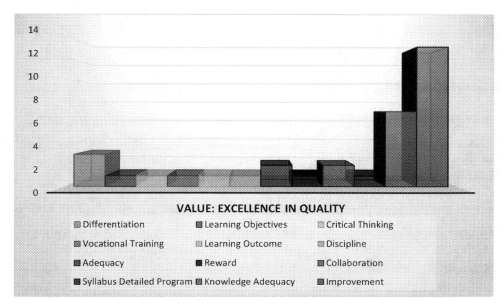

Improvement

Most of the answers of the research participants show that *excellence in quality* in teaching is enhances through the factor of improvement. "Improving vocational training", "improving learning outcomes", "improving student discipline" define how teachers feel they can achieve excellence in education. "The development of an action plan will contribute to the improvement of the school unit, the paving of an effective action plan will serve as a means of preventing and dealing with violence and delinquency in school", as well as "it is important enough to design a unit to cover all needs by channelling confidence and enthusiasm for the creation and offering satisfactory results". Therefore, we are talking about: a) individual level improvement concerning teachers and students, b) improvement at school unit level.

Knowledge Adequacy, Syllabus Detailed Program, Vocational Training

Excellence in the quality of education, according to teachers, means to possess "substantial global knowledge in all scientific matters, excellent knowledge of the subject itself, competence in scientific knowledge", as well as "adequacy of knowledge leads to the adequacy of learning, through quality educational material, which proves that in order to achieve goals quality in education and quality in the curriculum are implemented".

DIFFERENTIATION, LEARNING OUTCOME, LEARNING OBJECTIVES, COMPETENCE

"As teachers we are closer to excellence when we apply differentiated teaching, when we modify to achieve the learning goals we set". That it is, when the teacher adjusts the teaching process, so that it is addressed to all students, who (students) differ from each other in terms of skills, abilities, level of learning, it is possible for teachers and students to get closer to excellence.

Reward, Collaboration

Collaboration between both teachers and students is considered a driving force. "Collaboration at work has a positive contribution to the smooth and quality operation of the school" and "we strive for the best through dialogue, cooperation and strategic planning", as through the interactive method and cooperation many goals are achieved. We need method and targeted moves". Rewarding, but also acceptance by colleagues seem to play an ancillary role for teachers, so that they continue to strive for the best. "During a class in co-teaching, the colleague praised me for my contagiousness as a teacher, from that day I have more confidence in my teaching work and this is manifested during the lesson". However, the reward also has an important role for the students, "we have to reward students who showed excellence results, while rewarding those who show improvement".

Aspects of Total Quality Management

Critical Thinking, Discipline

"As a teacher of Greek subjects, I believe that I will reach educational excellence when I lead students to develop historical critical thinking and the study of literary texts". Critical thinking against teachers is what results from applications of educational excellence.

Figure 2. The indices of teachers' answers in the section of the reflective tool. Value: excellence

THE QUANTITATIVE RESEARCH: TESTING THE *QUALITY* HYPOTHESIS IN TOURISM EDUCATION

The need for quantitative research with a questionnaire as research tool arose as an indicator of confirmation, support or refection of the data that the majority of the sample of the qualitative tool consider as very important components of teacher evaluation in terms of *excellence in quality*. The second research method can be an indicator of consent or non-consent with conclusions extracted from the analysis of the data of the first research tool. The population of the quantitative research consisted of 203 teachers who worked in public schools in provinces of Cyprus during the school year 2020-2021. Schools of Technical and Vocational Education were included at the research, taking into consideration that the

Aspects of Total Quality Management

technical schools have teachers of different programs, different directions and generally different character that is connected directly and indirectly with tourism sector. For the purpose of this chapter, the results related to the question "When you set goals in relation to your role as a teacher you thing that you are contributing to: a) prioritization of actions related to your educational work, b) improving the quality of your educational work, c) empowerment and effectiveness of your role, d) improve and in general professional development" are brought to the surface, in order to unfold aspects of teachers' thoughts on what they consider as "quality" in their educational work.

Figure 1 shows that relative frequency distribution for the question "When you set goals in relation to your role as a teacher do you think you are contributing to:". It is observed that many teachers (46.5%) stated that they consider the prioritization of actions related to their educational work to be quite important, were 39.6% stated that this criterion is very important for the goal setting. In addition, the majority of teachers (61.1%) considered that the criterion of improving the quality of educational work is very important, with 35.0% of teachers considering this criterion quite important.

Furthermore, the majority of teachers (55.7%) stated that they consider the goal setting to contribute greatly to the empowerment and effectiveness of the teacher's role, with 39.9% stating that they consider this aspect quite important in the light of the goal setting. In addition, it was stated by many (48.0%) teachers that when they set goals they consider that they contribute a lot to their improvement and professional development in general, while 42.1% of teachers consider that they contribute a lot and 7.9% moderate.

Table 1. Allocation of relevant frequencies for the question "When you set goals in relation to your role as a teacher do you think you are contributing to"

	Not at all	Moderate	Enough	Too much
Prioritization of actions related to your educational work	2,0%	11,9%	46,5%	39,6%
Improving the quality of your educational work	0,0%	3,9%	35,0%	61,1%
Empowerment and effectiveness of your role	0,5%	3,9%	39,9%	55,7%
Improve and in general professional development	2,0%	7,9%	42,1%	48,0%

CONCLUSION AND RECOMMENDATIONS

Applicability of aspects of TQM in tourism education in terms of *excellence in quality* could be considered as an important factor that guides the continuous teacher performance improvement, considering the fulfilment of students' needs, while simultaneously assists in producing goals and values.

The involvement of teachers in quality improvement educational activities will make them more effective in teaching practices and various school issues. It can change their behavior in school and could be an inspiration in quality improvement in schools (Juran and Gryna, 1993). Quality can create an environment where all members of the school community work jointly to deliver students with the resources they need to meet up present and prospect academic and societal requirements. Education and training are important elements in the successful implementation of quality management (Rahman, Nor and Wahab, 2020; Mann, 1992); education can be better in favor of quality management (Tribus, 1993).

Educational quality refers to the quality of teachers' personal and professional quality and these aspects are measured through teachers' professionalism, knowledge and understanding, as well as teaching and

Aspects of Total Quality Management

learning skills, in order to improve students' achievement and performance (Rahman, Nor and Wahab, 2021). Teacher's goal achievement is linked to professional growth, as achievement and growth often appear together in Herzberg's (1968) theory of motivation. Growth, being associated with the feeling of perceived progress in professional life, can lead to advancement, also a motivator, as an outcome of evaluation emergent from progress, rather than seniority, for advancement is identified as promotion.

An educational frame based on TQM model, that takes into account the quality as a factor affecting the development of education, increases the effectiveness of human resources in schools. The strong relationship between motivation and evaluation releases the expectation that achievement goal constructs (e.g. effective task performance), may energise teachers to set goals of achieving high competence, which would be evaluated in an achievement context. Teacher competence indicates teachers' effectiveness, aptitude, adequacy and accomplishment (Brooks and Shell, 2006). *Excellence of quality* in tourism education rotates around the parameters: improvement; vocational training; learning objectives; reward, collaboration; critical thinking and goal setting.

Improvement

Excellence in education can be achieved with the power of improvement. Improvement is related to individual and school unit level. Improving vocational training, learning outcomes and student discipline define, according to teachers, lead to excellence in education. An organized action plan contributes to the improvement and covers all needs by channelling confidence and enthusiasm for the creation and offering satisfactory results.

Vocational Training

Excellence in the quality of education, according to teachers, means to possess substantial global knowledge in all scientific matters, excellent knowledge of the subject itself, competence in scientific knowledge. Adequacy of knowledge leads to the adequacy of learning through quality educational material.

Learning Objectives

Teachers believe that they are closer to excellence when differentiated teaching process is applied and when modification tools are used in order to achieve the learning goals they set.

Reward, Collaboration

Collaboration between teachers and students is considered as a driving force, it has a positive contribution to the smooth and quality operation of the school. Teachers strive for the best through dialogue, cooperation and strategic planning; through the interactive method and cooperation goals are achieved. Rewarding and acceptance by teachers seem to play a vital part, so that they continue to strive for the best.

Critical Thinking

Teachers reach educational excellence when they lead students to develop critical thinking.

Goal Setting and Quality

When teachers set goals they believe they contribute to the improvement of the quality of educational work.

This study recommends that mentioned above values should guide teachers of tourism education, in order to develop practices that could establish this theory in the tourism educational school context. The adoption of TQM excellence elements corroborates to effective evaluation and has the impetus to lead to teacher effectiveness, to effective student learning, and ultimately to the development of schools as professional learning communities.

Figure 3. Tourism Educational frame of an excellence in quality goal-setting model in aspects of TQM

REFERENCES

Al-Ababneh, M. M. (2021). The implementation of Total Quality Management (TQM) in the hotel industry. *International Journal of Tourism and Hospitality*, *1*(1), 25–34. doi:10.51483/IJTH.1.1.2021.25-34

Ali, S.R., Sweis, R.J., Saleh, F.M. and Sarea, A.M. (2018). Linking soft and hard Total Quality Management practices: Evidence from Jordan. *International Journal Business Excellence*, *14*.

Antunes, M. G., Texeira, Q., & Justino, M. R. (2017). The relationship between innovation and total quality management and the innovation effects on organizational performance. *International Journal of Quality & Reliability Management*, *34*(9), 1474–1492. doi:10.1108/IJQRM-02-2016-0025

Arcaro, J. (1995). *Quality in Education: An Implementation Handbook*. St. Lucie Press.

Benavides-Velasco, C. A., Quintana-García, C., & Marchante-Lara, M.Velasco, B. (2014). Total quality management, corporate social responsibility and performance in the hotel industry. *International Journal of Hospitality Management*, *41*, 77–87. doi:10.1016/j.ijhm.2014.05.003

Aspects of Total Quality Management

Benzaquen, J., Carlos, M., Norero, G., Armas, H., & Pacheco, H. (2019). Quality in private health companies in Peru: The relation of QMS & ISO 9000 principles on TQM factor. *International Journal of Healthcare Management*, 1–9.

Breiter, D., & Kline, S. F. (1995). Benchmarking quality management in hotels. *FIU Hospitality Review*, *13*(2), 45–52.

Brinbaum, R. (2000). *Management Fads in Higher Education: Where They Come from, What They Do, Why They Fail*. Jossey-Bass Inc.

Brinbaum, R., & Deshotels, J. (1999). Has the Academy Adopted TQM? *Planning for Higher Education*, *28*, 29–37.

Craig, Clarke, F. L., & Amernic, J. H. (1999). Scholarship university business schools Cardinal Newman, Creeping corporatisation and farewell to the "disturber of the peace". *Accounting, Auditing & Accountability Journal*, *12*(5), 510–524. doi:10.1108/09513579910298453

Dale, B.G. (2003). Managing Quality.

Davies, J., et al. (2001). Leadership in higher education. *Total Quality Management*, *12*(7 and 8), 1025-1030.

Deming, W.E. (1986). *Out of the Crisis*. Massachusetts Institute of Technology Centre for Advanced Engineering Study.

Dill, D. (1995). Through Deming's Eyes A Cross-National Analysis of Quality Assurance Policies in Higher Education. *Quality in Higher Education*, *1*(2), 95–110. doi:10.1080/1353832950010202

Flynn, B. B., Schroeber, R. C., & Sakakibaba, S. (1994). A framework for quality management research and an associated measurement instrument. *Journal of Operations Management*, *11*(4), 339–366. doi:10.1016/S0272-6963(97)90004-8

Foster, J. J. (2003). Motywacja w miejscu pracy. In N. Chmiel (Ed.), *Psychologia Pracy I Organizacjii*. GWP.

Gaither, N. (1996). *Production and Operations Management*. Duxbury Press.

Ghaderi, M., Rigi, A., & Salimi, J. (2015). Investigation of present teaching performance assessment system problems and preposition of an appropriate model by technology: Sciences classrooms. *International Journal of Educational and Psychological Researches*, *1*(2), 179–185. doi:10.4103/2395-2296.152257

Gilliland, S. W., & Landis, R. S. (1992). Quality and quantity goals in a complex decision task: Strategies and outcomes. *The Journal of Applied Psychology*, *77*(5), 672–681. doi:10.1037/0021-9010.77.5.672

Harvey,L.(1995).BeyondTQM.*QualityinHigherEducation,1*(2),123–146.doi:10.1080/1353832950010204

Hinterhuber, H. H. (2004). *Strategische Unternehmensführung: I. Strategisches Denken* (Vol. 7). Walter de Gruyter.

Ho, S. K., & Wearn, K. (1995). A TQM Model for Higher education and training. *Training for Quality*, *3*(2), 25–33. doi:10.1108/09684879510087503

Holjevac, I. A. (1996). Total quality management for the hotel industry and tourism. *Tourism and Hospitality Management, 2*(1), 67–80. doi:10.20867/thm.2.1.8

Houston, D. (2008). Rethinking Quality and Improvement in Higher Education. *Quality Assurance in Education, 16*(1), 61–79. doi:10.1108/09684880810848413

Jeffrey, B., & Troman, G. (2011). The construction of performative identities. *European Educational Research Journal, 10*(4), 484–501. doi:10.2304/eerj.2011.10.4.484

Juran, J. M., & Gryna, F. M. (1993). *Quality Planning and Analysis: From Product Development through Use.* McGraw-Hill.

Karia, N., & Asaari, M. H. A. H. (2006). The effects of total quality management practices on empoyees' work-related attitudes. *The TQM Magazine, 18*(1), 30–43. doi:10.1108/09544780610637677

Konstantinides, D. (2021). *Comparative approach to the evaluation of secondary school teachers with elements and influences from the private sector.* Neapolis University Pafos.

Konstantinides, D. D., & Reppa, A. (2021). Adopting an approach of entrepreneurial excellence to teacher evaluation in Greece and Cyprus during the first twenty years of the 21st century. *Educational Cycle, 9*(2), 49–65.

Konstantinides-Vladimirou, K. (2013). *Mid-career teacher motivation and implications for leadership practices in secondary schools in Cyprus.* University of Nottingham: School of Education.

Konstantinides-Vladimirou, K. (2015). Cypriot secondary school teachers' professional life phases: A research-informed view of career-long motivation. *International Journal of Multidisciplinary Comparative Studies, 2*(1-3), 33–55.

Kumar, R., & Mishra, R. (2020). Linking TQM Critical Success Factors to strategic goal: Impact on Organizational Performance. *Journal of Mechanical and Civil Engineering, 17*(3), 1–13.

Lau, R. S. M., & Anderson, C. A. (1998). A three-dimensional perspective of total quality management. *International Journal of Quality & Reliability Management, 15*(1), 85–98. doi:10.1108/02656719810199277

Lawrence, S., & Sharma, U. (2002). Commodification of education and academic labour: Using the balanced scorecard in a university setting. *Critical Perspectives on Accounting, 13*(5-6), 661–677. doi:10.1006/cpac.2002.0562

Locke, E. A., & Latham, G. P. (1990). *A theory of goal setting and task performance.* Prentice-Hall, Inc.

Locke, E. A., & Latham, G. P. (2006). *New Directions in Goal setting. Current directions in psychological science.* SAGE Publications.

Lynch, K. (2014). New managerialism: The impact on education. *Concept, 5*(3), 1–11.

Madanat, H., & Khasawneh, G. (2017). Impact of total quality management implementation on effectiveness of human resource management in the jordanian banking sector from employee's perspective. *Academic Strategy Management Journal, 16*, 114–148.

Mann, R. S. (1992). *The development of a framework to assist in the implementation of TQM*. [PhD Thesis, University of Liverpool, UK].

Mergen, E., & Stevenson, W. (2002). Sowing the seeds of quality: Quality at the source. *Total Quality Management, 13*(7), 1015–1020. doi:10.1080/0954412022000017085

Milakovich, M. E. (1995). *Improving Service Quality*. Lucie Press.

MOEC - Ministry of Education, Culture, Sport, and Youth (2019). *New system of teacher evaluation*. MOEC.

Mohanty, R. P., & Behera, A. K. (1996). TQM in the service sector. *Work Study, 45*, 13–17.

Murad, A., & Rajesh, K. S. (2010). Implementation of Total Quality Management in Higher Education. *Asian Journal of Business Management, 2*, 9–16.

Oakland, J. S. (1993). *Total Quality Management: The Route to Improving Performance*. Butterworth-Heinemann.

Pike, J., & Barnes, R. (1996). *TQM in Action: A practical approach to continuous performance improvement*. Chapman and Hall.

Prajogo, D. I. (2005). The comparative analysis of TQM practices and quality performance between manufacturing and service firms. *International Journal of Service Industry Management, 16*(3), 217–228. doi:10.1108/09564230510601378

Prajogo, D. I., & Sohal, A. S. (2006). The integration of TQM and technology/R & D management in determining quality and innovation performance. *Omega: The International Journal of Management Science, 34*(3), 296–312. doi:10.1016/j.omega.2004.11.004

Rahman, M. R. A., Nor, M. Y. M., & Wahab, J. L. A. (2020). Does Total Quality Management Influence Teacher Quality? An empirical analysis. *International Journal of Academic Research in Business & Social Sciences, 11*(1), 250–260.

Ramlawati, & Putra, A.H.P.K. (2018). Total Quality Management as the Key of the Company to Gain the Competitiveness, Performance Achievement and Consumer Satisfaction. *International Review of Management and Marketing, 8*(5), 60-69.

Rogers, R.E. (2013). *Implementation of Total Quality Management A Comprehensive Training Program*. The Haworth Press, Inc.

Sakthivel, P. B., Rajendran, G., & Raju, R. (2005). TQM implementation and students' satisfaction of academic performance. *The TQM Magazine, 17*(6), 573–589. doi:10.1108/09544780510627660

Sallis, E. (1993). *TQM in Education*. Kogan Page.

Saxena, M. M. (2021). Obstacles in accomplishing Total Quality Management in Higher Education. *International Research Journal of Education and Technology, 2*(2), 33–41.

Schulz, S. A., & Masters, R. J. (1997). Total quality management: The Deming food processing connection. *Journal of Food Products Marketing, 4*(1), 61–70. doi:10.1300/J038v04n01_06

Shackleton, V., & Wale, P. (2002). Przywództwo I zarządzanie. In N. Chmiel (Ed.), *Psychologia Pracy I Organizacji*. Gdańskie Wydawnictwo Psychologiczne.

Shahmohammadi, N. (2017). The Evaluation of Teachers' Job Performance Based on Total Quality Management (TQM). *International Education Studies, 10*(4), 58–64. doi:10.5539/ies.v10n4p58

Shahril, M. (2005). Amalan pengajaran guru yang bekresan: Kajian di beberapa sekolah menengah di Malaysia. *Jurnal Fakulti Pendidikan Universiti Malaya*, 1-14.

Sila, S., & Ebrahimpour, M. (2003). Examination and comparison of the critical factors of total quality management (TQM) across countries. *International Journal of Production Research, 41*(2), 235–268. doi:10.1080/0020754021000022212

Stoll, L., & Seashore Louis, K. (2007). *Professional learning communities: divergence, depth and dilemma*. Open University Press.

Talib, F., & Rahman, Z. (2010). Critical success factors of TQM in service organizations: A proposed model. *Services Marketing Quarterly, 31*(3), 363–380. doi:10.1080/15332969.2010.486700

Thiagaragan, T., Zairi, M., & Dale, B. G. (2001). A proposed model of TQM implementation based on an empirical study of Malaysian industry. *International Journal of Quality & Reliability Management, 18*(3), 289–306. doi:10.1108/02656710110383539

Tribus, M. (1993). Why Not Education: Quality Management in Education. *Journal for Quality and Participation, 16*, 12–21.

Varela, B., & Pacheco, G. (2018). Comprehensive evaluation of the internal and external quality control to redefine analytical quality goals. *Biochemia Medica, 28*(2), 1–11. doi:10.11613/BM.2018.020710 PMID:30022885

Wang, Y., & Lo, H. (2003). Customer-focused performance and the dynamic model for competence building and leveraging: A resource based-view. *Journal of Management Development, 22*(6), 483–526. doi:10.1108/02621710310478486

Wilkins, C. (2011). Professionalism and the post-performative teacher: New teachers reflect on autonomy and accountability in the English school system. *Professional Development in Education, 37*(3), 389–409. doi:10.1080/19415257.2010.514204

Yusuf, S. M., & Aspinwall, E. (2000). TQM Implementation Issue: Review and Case Study. *International Journal of Operations & Production Management, 20*(6), 634–655. doi:10.1108/01443570010321595

Zairi, M. (1995). Total Quality Education for superior performance. *Training for Quality, 3*(1), 29–35. doi:10.1108/09684879510082238

Zhang, Z., Waszink, A., & Wijngaard, J. (2000). An instrument for measuring TQM implementation for Chinese manufacturing companies. *International Journal of Quality & Reliability Management, 17*(7), 730–755. doi:10.1108/02656710010315247

Chapter 12
Boutique Hotel by HCH:
A New Tourism Trademark as a Tool for the Development of Small Hotels

Aimilia Vlami
Agricultural University of Athens, Greece

ABSTRACT

This chapter examines the purpose and effectiveness of a new tourism trademark, the "Boutique hotel" project, which has been designed and implemented by the Hellenic Chamber of Hotels. The scope is to encapsulate the efforts of the last five years to lay the institutional groundwork for a professionally operated accommodation system of boutique hotels, a relatively new form of accommodation in Greece. This chapter will analyse the goals, terms, and conditions for defining this tourism brand and its operating system. Also, it examines in detail the structural characteristics of boutique hotels in Greece, as they resulted from a survey of the 178 hotels that had received this certification. Boutique hotels in Greece are a successful example of the resilience of hospitality businesses during the periods of both the financial crisis and, subsequently, of the COVID-19 pandemic, given that the very nature of their services and products, enables them to immediately respond and adapt to new situations and cater for evolving consumer needs, ultimately striving for survival and for the return to a new reality of sustainable tourism development.

INTRODUCTION

In the late 2000s, Greece entered a period in which the debt crisis dictated sharp cuts in budget expenditure. The deep recession resulted in labour market disruptions. In this context and mainly caused by political uncertainty, there was a short-term decline in international arrivals at Athens airport, which combined with a downward trend in international tourist arrivals led to a hotel industry crisis (see figure 1). However, according to the WTTC (2020), currently, as tourism becomes more and more resilient, the average time required for tourist arrivals to return to pre-crisis levels is usually 19.4 months. Therefore,

DOI: 10.4018/978-1-6684-6055-9.ch012

Copyright © 2023, IGI Global. Copying or distributing in print or electronic forms without written permission of IGI Global is prohibited.

Greek tourism managed to survive and cope with the crisis in the best possible way, thus contributing and supporting the economic structure of the country and playing a primary role in the bid for growth of the Greek economy.

Figure 1. Trends in international tourist arrivals (million), 1950-2019

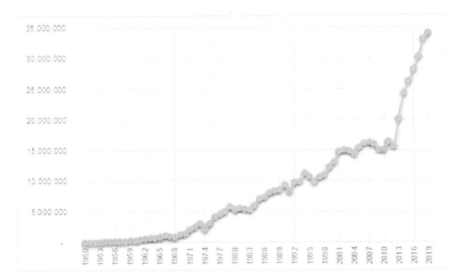

The period 2010-2019, as shown in figure 2, is characterized by increased investment activity in terms of the establishment of units of the three highest categories, but also the conversion of old or listed buildings into tourist accommodation. More specifically, 86% of the commissioned units were of the 3 highest hotel categories (91% in terms of rooms). On the other hand, 70% of the units that ceased to operate belonged to the 2 lowest categories (54% in terms of rooms). This points to a fundamental restructuring of the hotel industry in Greece, whereby the majority of beds currently belong to 3* to 5* star category hotels, which account for 73% of the total accommodation capacity.

This significant increase of the number of 5* hotels, in particular, goes hand in hand with a decrease in their average size (in 2019 it was 302 beds, against 326 beds in 2010). This fact indicates that hotels of this category are being transformed from large and impersonal buildings to smaller units that provide their guests with personalized contact and upgraded services (Research Institute for Tourism 2020). The development of 4* and 5*star hotels seems to be linked both to a hotel capital centralization trend with the establishment of mixed-use hotel schemes between foreign operators and big domestic chains in the form of mergers and acquisitions, as well as to the increase of the number of boutique hotels.

Taking into account the above evolutionary path of the Greek hotel sector in the years of the financial crisis, this paper will analyse the goals, terms and conditions for defining this national tourism brand, the operating system and the results of the first five years since its implementation. Especially, in mid-2022, 2,5 years after the onset of the pandemic Covid-19, discussion focuses on the form of all the components of tourism and the hotel industry in the sector's transition to an improved state of sustainable development. From this perspective, boutique hotels could play a key role in the endeavour to strengthen the hotel sector, as they involve small hotels of distinctive design and high specifications that, above all, are operationally flexible. Thus, assisted by their main professional objective, which is the development of personal connection and homelike warmth and comfort as a major aspect of hotel production, the assurance of health that will be sought after in the years to come will emerge in the best way possible.

Figure 2. Hotel unit evolution in terms of star categories, 1960-2022

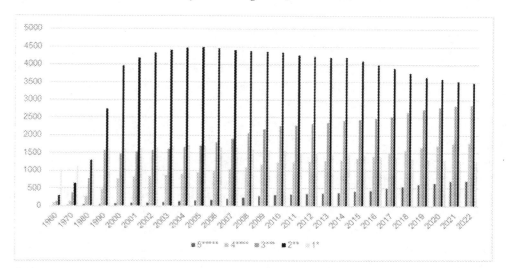

In essence, the establishment of tourism trademark in the hotel sector acquires greater importance in an era characterised by new consumer behaviours, new needs and emerging trends (such as the digital transformation brought to the fore by the pandemic). The Greek hospitality industry ultimately managed to survive during emergency conditions and intervening periods with the state's support and direct interventions. However, during the long-term recovery phase, it is becoming clear that normalisation, combined with the opportunity to improve the state of things, is a slow process with considerable challenges for the hotel industry, especially in light of the negative impacts of the Ukrainian crisis on inflation and the cost of energy. In this process, the "Boutique hotel" project and the certified hotels can serve as the flagship to usher in an improvement in the sector.

BACKGROUND

It is difficult to provide a clear and straight forward definition of the term "accommodation" as its connotation varies depending on the perspective of the researcher and on how tourists perceive the term based on their needs and desires. According to WTO's definition, "hotels and related establishments" are enterprises that provide sleeping facilities, have a specified minimum number of rooms, are managed by a single operator, offer a wide range of services and amenities, and are classified according to the services they provide (Todd & Mather, 1995). Walterspiel (1969) highlights the importance of hotel units defining them as "enterprises that provide authentic or original services directly dependent on the presence of tourists-consumers". There are two distinctive features that differentiate hotel undertakings from other service providers (Georgiadou, 1981; Chytiris, 1996):

- Firstly, the physical presence of customers is required for the provision of hotel services.
- Secondly, hotels are capital-intensive enterprises since their construction and operation requires significant capital investments.

At the same time, however, hotels are also labour-intensive enterprises, as their status as "service providers" implies the provision of personalized customer services, thus turning hotels into "experience" providers. In fact, tourist services are provided and consumed at the same time whereby there is a one-to-one service connection between hotel employees and hotel customers (depending on hotel's quality category). This implies that the production and provision of "hotel accommodation" services as a distinct final product, requires both the necessary number of employees and expertise (Pavlidis, 2000; Shaw & Williams, 2004; Herstein et.al., 2018). In other words, hotels are labour-intensive production units, or, to put it precisely, personality-intensive units, since one of the determinants of the tourist-consumer's satisfaction is the provision of personalized services.

In this context, the hospitality sector, and especially the hotel industry, are a rapidly evolving market, where the current main focus is on "experience-based differentiation". The period of the 70s and 80s was an era of intensive homogenization and standardization for the so-called hotel product (Freund de Klumbis & Munsters, 2005; Teo & Chang, 2009). During that period, the global hospitality industry developed according to the Ford model of production. In fact, in the context of a process of "McDonaldization" of their production (Aliukeviciute, 2012), hotels aimed at satisfying large numbers of tourists at small profit margins. The development of differentiated hotel products, which dates back to the mid-1980s, is directly linked to the gradual transition of the hotel industry to a more flexible production model, where the added value of accommodation service providers lies in offering personalized accommodation services (Poon 1989; Urry, 1994; Ioannides & Debbage, 1997; Judd, 2006; Rogerson, 2010). For many researchers (Freund de Klumbis & Munsters, 2005; Aggett, 2007; Timothy & Teye, 2009; Khosravi, et. al., 2014), the hotel product differentiation is dictated by changes in tourist behaviour, given that, nowadays, a hotel is promoted as a holistic experience, rather than as an unidimensional accommodation space.

Therefore, destinations and tourism accommodation focus on distinctiveness by using local attributes in the launching of innovative, new products and brands, which can help establish a more unique selling proposition (Haven-Tang & Jones 2006). Also, the service concept, quality level, sensitivity of the enterprise in terms of cleanliness and hygiene are also evidence of the extent to which the payment can be received. Goods and services produced by businesses should be of a quality that satisfies customers. Standards have been developed to ensure the said quality. In order to gain the trust of customers and to gain competitive advantage, businesses need to certify their compliance with standards (Akbulaev, 2021). For example, the tourism industry uses ecolabels (ecoseals or environmental awards) as ''trademarks or logos'' to communicate the environmental credentials of a lodging, with the hopes that customers develop positive attitudes toward their product. In the marketplace, this type of strategy can give hotels a differential advantage over their competitors (Sasidharan, et.al. 2002, Middleton & Hawkins, 1998). Certification can be beneficial for hotels to display their differentiated design, unique services, etc and simultaneously to embody and the history, culture, geography, cuisine and similar values of the destination in which they operate, in the tourism promotion activities they will develop, in the exhibitions and organizations they will participate in, in terms of providing an effective competitive advantage (Yildirgan & Zengin, 2014 as ref. Akbulaev, 2021).

Hence, in the context of a world-wide customer driven economy, hotels are increasingly adopting new trends in their product offering, in order to appear credible in a highly competitive market. Nowadays, in the early 2020s, there is no doubt that the hotel industry is becoming more and more focused on the tourist-consumer. It is the latter that shapes demand and hotel market segmentation given that digital technologies have shifted the bargaining power to consumers. According to current forecasts, Millennials, a generation of people who have grown up in a digital environment and who seek local, authentic experiences are expected to monopolize market interest well into the 2030s (Hein, 2015). The differentiated design and the way in which services are offered in a hotel environment is what makes a hotel experience high-quality and unique. International hotel chains play an important role, given their tendency to address tourist-consumers in a multitude of ways, using the power of their brand. At the same time, however, guests tend to make detailed future plans, due, among others, to the financial difficulties they experienced after the 2008 crisis. Hotels are constantly creating opportunities to satisfy their current and future customers, using such tools as mergers and strategic alliances with other economic activities, mainly in the tourism industry, including airlines, travel agencies, restaurants, etc (Jana & Chandra, 2016).

At the same time, boutique hotels have strongly penetrated the hotel market and are now developing in all host countries. The complex nature of boutique hotels has led to a multitude of definitions, although none of them is currently widely accepted. This is because boutique hotels stand out for their diversity in terms of design, services, and even, the way in which they go about serving their customers. Rabotu & Niculescu (2009) have noted that the BH concept refers to small size units, located in places with distinctive features, non-standardised, and designed to provide a warm, family-like atmosphere. In addition, thanks to BH small size, boutique hotel operators are acquainted with their guests and are able to propose services tailored to their needs and preferences (for the various approaches around the definition of boutique hotels, compare: Callan & Fearon, 1997; Teo et. al. 1998; Albazzaz et. al., 2003; Horner & Swarbrooke, 2005; Victorino et. al., 2005; Drewer 2005; Van Hartesvelt, 2006; Erkutlu & Chafra, 2006; Aggett, 2007; Lim & Endean, 2009; McNeill, 2009; Rogerson, 2010; Aliukeviciute, 2012; Jones et. al., 2013; Khosravi, et. al., 2014; Ahmad et. al., 2017; Malcheva, 2018; Hussein et. al., 2018; Kadir et. al., 2019; Loureiro et. al., 2020). The Boutique & Lifestyle Hotel Association (BLLA), in the context of its initiative to formulate a generally accepted definition for boutique hotels, has ended up with the following definition: "Boutique hotels (BHs) are small-size accommodations, which seek to offer an authentic cultural experience to the visitor, through the provision of upgraded services" (Jones et. al., 2013). Specifically, the main findings of this research effort are the following:

- They are small hotel units which stand out for their unique architecture and the decoration of their interior spaces, they are housed either in recently constructed buildings with modern decor, or in transformed historical and listed buildings.
- Transformations that correspond to modern lifestyles, respecting, however, the architectural characteristics and identities of the buildings, the goal being for guests to experience a "uniquely authentic" experience.
- Units that offer tailored services, aiming at producing the feelings of "intimacy" and "warm hospitality" in tourists - consumers.

According to the international literature, the four main characteristics of boutique hotels are: (a) their small size, (b) their location, (c) their unique design concept, (d) their upgraded amenities & tailored services, and (d) their focus on specific target markets. In general, BHs seem to attract guests from all age groups. In fact, boutique hotels cater for guests ranging from just above their 20s to their mid-50s depending on the design concept of the accommodation. Also, the elderly are an important target market, especially for 5-star boutique hotels. Research shows, however, that their target market is mainly people with a high level of education and moderate to high income. Essentially, these are design-aware tourists, whose expectation is to be key-participants, rather than simple observers of a unique experience, which is increasingly becoming emotion-focused (MacNaghten & Urry, 2000; Prentice, 2001; Crouch & Desforges, 2003; Loureiro et. al., 2020).

In summary, it is ascertained that the term boutique hotel refers to small hotels, at which the authenticity of the experience is the main concern. The main goal is to create a unique identity which is difficult to copy, by capitalising on its location, taking advantage of technology, and promoting local cultural heritage; by combining comfort with personal services, so that the tourist - consumer feels "like they are home", namely, that they are not a "faceless number" behind a closed door on a long hallway; that they are, instead, a visitor in a hospitable environment.

"BOUTIQUE HOTEL" PROJECT

It was in the late 2000s that Greek hotel industry professionals discovered that the best way to create value is to combine quality with innovation. In this context, in 2006, the Hellenic Chamber of Hotels set up for the first time a Working Group, which was assigned the task of creating the operating framework for a new type of hotel hospitality: Boutique Hotels. A year later, the Hellenic Hoteliers Federation published the "Study on the Upgrading of Existing Hotel Units", one of the key findings of which is the necessity to extend the tourist season by adding new products to the dominant "sun and sea" tourism development model, with an emphasis on tourists-consumers who are looking for hotels and destinations capable of providing a holistic experience. In this context, the study proceeded to group together new tourism products, including high-end hotels, and especially boutique hotels, since, as the study pointed out, their main characteristic is upgraded infrastructure and high-quality services, rather than their star classification. Despite the growing interest in Greece, at the end of the 2000s, in the identification of boutique hotel operating features, it is obvious that it took almost ten years for this first movement to mature and result, through a structured process, in the consolidation of a quality operating standard for boutique hotels in Greece.

During the economic crisis specifically, the Ministry of Tourism, in compliance with the mandates of the economic adjustment programmes, instituted a number of structural reforms aimed at increasing the flexibility of the tourism market and strengthening tourism development in Greece, mainly by lifting restrictions, simplifying procedures and allowing the hotel sector to become self-regulating. As part of this effort, the approval of Law 4276/2014 designated the HCH as the competent body for rating the main hotel accommodations and assigning star categories. With this institutional framework, for the first time in Greece, the permit process was split off from the rating process and the Chamber, as the institutional representative of all hotel undertakings in the country and legislative advisor to the state on tourism issues, acquired an active role in assigning hotel star-based classification, by issuing rating certificates.

Boutique Hotel by HCH

The HCH set as a primary goal the quality of service provided by all types of tourist accomodations. With that in mind, it planned and implemented two innovative programmes of national tourism brands, aiming to provide practical support for Greek hoteliers and help them to successfully keep up with the times and challenges of the 21st century as they continue to improve their product, given that the global hospitality economy demands vigilance and constant adaptation to new requirements. Specifically, in early 2010, it developed the national "Greek Breakfast" brand, the objective of which was to enrich the breakfast offered at Greek hotels with typical Greek agro-dietary products as well as with traditional foods and viands from various destinations of Greece. The challenge for Greek tourism authorities and businesses is to create innovative products, in order for the country to become a successful player in the global tourism market and to provide long-lasting solutions for structural problems of sustainable tourism development. The "Greek Breakfast" utilizes the cultural— gastronomic wealth of the country to connect tourism, local communities and local production, in order to enrich tourist experiences, diversification hotels' product and achieve multiple positive social and economic benefits in all sectors. (Kontis & Goumas, 2017)

In 2015, having refined its expertise, the HCH decided to design and develop the second tourism brand, "Boutique hotel", which essentially establishes the official professional institution of boutique hotels in Greece. The goal was to define the tourist products that support both the seasonality of demand and the qualitative improvement of Greek tourism. The demand for more distinctive tourist accommodations, such as boutique hotels, emerged in the 1980s on a global level, while in Greece, interest in these intensified in the early 21st century, in specific geographical areas. It peaked during the 2010s in urban centres and island tourist destinations, and was met by the ad-hoc creation of boutique-type lodgings. This outcome was not addressed in a timely fashion and caused the term "boutique hotel" to become appropriated by many accommodations including it in their names, but without possessing the principal traits of this new type of hospitality product. For this reason, the HCH in September 2015 moved to trademark the collective "Boutique hotel" seal with the Secretariat-General for Commerce and Consumer Protection of the Ministry of Economy and Development. Trademarking the designation was essentially the beginning of organising all of the hotel accommodation in Greece meeting boutique specifications into a collective professional base. According to Pippirs & Steckenbauer (2022) these types of considerations usually lead to two challenges that the partners have to face in a specific project being addressed: first, the development of a common value system, as the basis of a brand, and second, the question of how cooperation between the various partners can be organised and how the individual brands can be brought into harmony.

The generally held belief of bodies exercising tourism policy in Greece is that the key line of defence, the bulwark of the licensed hospitality sector against catalytic developments and international and unfair domestic competition is to upgrade the hotel product with an emphasis on quality. The result of these endeavours was to create a standardization for boutique hotels, which was transformed into an integrated ecosystem of acceptance, certification and promotion for small hotels in Greece offering a distinctive type of hospitality and having multiples aims:

- The certification of forward-thinking planning and development of innovative hospitality services.
- The protection of consumers from arbitrarily named boutique hotels, i.e. from hotels without a design concept or upgraded services, which usually fail to fulfil the expectations they create.
- The promotion of boutique hotels through planning and implementing an integrated marketing strategy with a customer-centred concept. The current efforts have focused on increasing the ac-

ceptability and usability of the "Boutique hotel HCH" at national as well as international level, through a complete nexus of digital marketing actions that target different groups of interest.

To achieve this purpose, two key objectives were set: a) to create a qualitative model of operation and certification of small hotels in Greece with distinctive design and b) embed the standard in the minds of visitors as a stamp of quality for the exceptional amenities and services of boutique hotels. The focus of the national "Boutique hotel" brand is a hotel certification with criteria and procedures, in order to create security for the guest, but also to strengthen the reputation and quality of the Greek hotel industry and thus hotel marketing.

Based on the results of a research, planned and carried out by the HCH in 2016, on selected members whose product has boutique hospitality features and by applying the triangulation of quantitative and qualitative research methods, it was finally possible to outline the concept of boutique hotels operating in Greece (Vlami, 2021; Flick U., 2006). More specifically, the survey revealed that BHs in Greece are very small and small-sized hotels, which differ from their competitors mainly in terms of their architectural aesthetics that inspire homely warmth and, at the same time, generate a feeling of personal space and comfort. These hotels meet the specifications of their star category and feature a holistic design concept (a story), which defines all sections and aspects of the accommodation, and makes it "unique" compared to its competitors.

In fact, for very small and small-sized hotels to be defined "Boutique Hotels", they should meet two conditions:

a. a unique design concept, consistently applied to the hotel's aesthetics, facilities and all aspects of operation, and
b. the provision of a variety of upgraded amenities and services to their guests that make these accommodations unique compared to their competitors.

The main prerequisites for the certification of hotel accommodations as "Boutique Hotels" are the following (HCH, 2019):

- a license or notification of operation for a main hotel accommodation or a hotel operating in an architectural heritage building.
- a star classification of 5*, 4* or 3*. Many believe that due to the uniqueness of BHs, it is not feasible to rate or classify these accommodations (Callan & Fearon, 1997). A number of researchers, however, argue that BHs should be ranked at least in the three-star category (Teo et. al., 1998; Van Hartesvelt, 2006; Aggett, 2007; Lim & Endean, 2009; Rogerson, 2010; Aliukeviciute, 2012). This is confirmed by the above mentioned research results, according to which 83% of all self-proclaimed boutique hotels were in the 5-3 star category.
- moreover, their maximum, overall capacity should not exceed 60 beds. This takes into account both the assumption of the Research Institute for Tourism that small hotels in Greece have a maximum of 50 beds and the results of the above mentioned research, according to which BH in Greece are usually 4*and 3* units with a maximum of 50 beds, while 5* boutique hotels appear to have a little bigger size.

Boutique Hotel by HCH

As regards main hotel units operating in architectural heritage buildings, the minimum star classification required is 4*, as the established star classification system is more lenient for these units, in terms of the minimum qualifications with regard, for example, to their operating specifications (due to the limitations and special conditions governing designated traditional/listed buildings).

The procedure of "Boutique hotel" certification is electronic and interactive with two consecutive evaluation phases (www.boutique-hotel.gr):

The **first phase** concerns the evaluation of the hotel's design concept (which should be clearly stated, unique and present in all aspects of the accommodation's operation). To this end, and in an effort to ensure the diversity of BHs, selection is based on a wide range of specifications. There are, in fact, three thematic specification clusters:

- Architectural Design Concept: the exterior of the building and the configuration of the surrounding space.
- Interior Design Concept: the main design and decoration concept of the hotel's interior and the way it is expressed by the hotel's overall operation.
- Other specifications: the hotel corporate design and, in particular, whether the accommodation's organizational culture and branding are inspired by its main design concept.

In the **second phase**, the hotel is evaluated to ensure that it provides its guests with a minimum of upgraded amenities and services, depending on its star classification. The evaluation is based on a check list of criteria for upgraded services, which groups in the following 9 thematic clusters:

1. Common areas & Reception
2. Rooms / Apartments
3. Bathrooms and toilets
4. Food service
5. Entertainment– sport – recreation
6. Other services
7. Special certifications
8. Staff
9. Cleanliness – hygiene

The vast majority of the criteria relate to the main spaces and services of a boutique hotel. More specifically: 25% concerns room amenities and services, 19% amenities and services in common areas, and the rest is equally divided (12%) between the remaining categories: bathroom amenities, other services, special certifications and entertainment and recreation. Food services and catering accounts for 9% of the total criteria, although the existence of a restaurant is not mandatory for 3-star hotels (while in 5* and 4* accommodations it is mandatory based on the classification requirements). All the more, since according to the above mentioned questionnaire research, the existence of catering, recreation and entertainment areas (e.g. gym, wellness and beauty centres, etc.), despite being a frequent feature of boutique hotels, is not a precondition for the BH certificating. It is important that these amenities' operation is also aligned with the BH concept, i.e. standing out aesthetics, unique products and personalized services, in accordance with the accommodation overall concept.

From the beginning an emphasis was given to the development of communication strategy for the effective promotion of the "Boutique hotel HCH" as a seal of small hotels in our country, which have invested on offering a unique accommodation experience. For this reason, a priority of the BH project was to create a critical mass of certified boutique hotels, in order for the project to achieve practical usage and integrated capacity. The BH communication strategy, firstly, addressed mainly to domestic b2b participants. The certified boutique hotels obliged to display the "Boutique hotel" sign in a visible place in the reception area and "Boutique hotel" logo in their website. At the same time, aiming at receive acceptance and recognition of "Boutique hotel" certification at national and international levels, the programme has focused on designing a comprehensive customer driven communication strategy inspired by the most effective methods of advertising, promoting and doing PR in favour of BHs in Greece and abroad, such as:

- B2B Boutique Hotels Forum,
- Reputation management,
- Promotional action plan for our members via Digital campaign & Social media,
- Curated, annual digest of certified Boutique Hotels
- Participation in specialized workshops, international tourism exhibitions, etc..

The communication strategy includes all the necessary actions not only for the enterprises (B2B), but also for tourists-consumers (B2C). Especially, aiming at the development and promotion certified hotels, HCH organizes the Boutique Hotels Forum, an annual B2B Forum, which gives the opportunity, through scheduled meetings of fixed time, to meet and create cooperation opportunities, by communicating "face to face" the key persons of certified by HCH boutique hotels in Greece with major representatives of Greek & European travel agencies who handle Leisure, Luxury, FIT & Alternative market. Also, for the distribution of information regarding the project uses extensively internet and social media (website, mobile applications, social media campaigns, etc.). Finally, an integrated web-based system (www.boutique-hotel.gr) has been designed for the constant evaluation of the implantation process by collecting and analyzing primary and secondary data.

BOUTIQUE HOTELS STRUCTURAL CHARACTERISTICS

This section examines in detail the structural characteristics of boutique hotels in Greece, as they resulted from a survey of the 178 hotels that by December 2021 had received (or were about to receive) the BH certification.

Accommodation Type & Size

The majority of BHs operating in Greece are classic hotel accommodation (160 out of 178 units, or 90% of the total). The number of self-catering hotel accommodation with a BH certification is much smaller. Greek boutique hotels are usually small independent units, whose owner or manager (frequently the same person) is the main person responsible for the organization and management of the accommodation. The average capacity of boutique hotels in Greece is, in fact, 25 rooms (or 50 beds). To be more specific, their average size varies according to their star classification, as follows:

- the average size of 5* BHs is 33 rooms,
- the average size of 4* BHs is 25 rooms,
- the average size of 3* BHs is 19 rooms.

In fact, the research indicates that the average Greek 3-star boutique hotel have invested more in the creation of a small number of spacious rooms (average room number: 19 rooms) with upgraded infrastructure, equipment and personalized services, than in dining and recreation areas. The choice to operate a small number of rooms is mainly dictated by the accommodation's need to provide personalized services, as well as to ensure forthwith communication between guests and employees.

Star Categories

The majority of BHs are 4* accommodations (45% of units and beds, respectively, see figure 3. Bed capacity is distributed more evenly between 3* and 5* boutique hotel accommodations, since 3* BHs are more numerous but, as mentioned above, much smaller in size (19 vs. 33 rooms).

Figure 3. Distribution of boutique hotels based on star classification

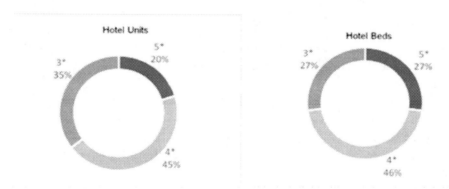

The evolution of BHs in Greece, as can be seen in Figure 4, is linked to the improvement of the quality aspects of the Greek hotel industry that occurred mainly during the last decade. In fact, based on BH opening data, accelerated growth rates have been recorded during the period 2010-2021 both for all BHs (7,5%) and for 5* and 4* accommodations (12% και 9% respectively). boutique hotel growth is linked to the increasing number of hotel units belonging to the three higher classification categories. This trend has prevailed during the last decade and is inversely proportional to the size of these accommodations. Please note, at this point, that hotels established during the period 1950-1999 although not originally boutique hospitality concept adepts, proceeded during the 21st century to an overhaul of their space, combined with capacity changes and/or star classification upgrades. Moreover, many of these establishments changed owner/operator.

Figure 4. The evolution of Boutique hotels over time, based on their opening period

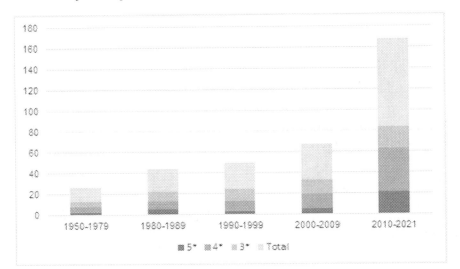

Boutique Hotels Typology

According to their location, BHs can be grouped into two main categories: Boutique Resorts Hotel (BrH) and Boutique City Hotels (BcH). In the case of Greece, there are more Boutique Resorts Hotels mainly due to the prevailing "sun and sea" tourism development concept. The characteristics of these hotel resorts are the following:

a. Boutique resort hotels (island): They represent the majority of certified accommodations and are deployed in the South Aegean Region (figure 5) and especially in the Cyclades (which account for 77.2% of their overall capacity, i.e. 60 units with a total of 3,116 beds). More specifically, boutique hotel spatial concentrations are to be found on the islands of Santorini and Mykonos, with mainly 5 and 4 star units, followed by the islands of Paros, Naxos and Folegandros, with mainly 4* and 3* units. Moreover, the presence of BrHs, mainly 4* units, is strong and expected to increase significantly in the coming years, on the island of Crete (with 31.7%), and in the Ionian Islands Region (with 12.1%).

b. Boutique resort hotels (inland): boutique hotels are also dynamically present in continental Greece and in particular in developing tourist areas, such as the area of Halkidiki in the Region of Central Macedonia, and, as often as not, in areas with strong traditional features, such as the region of Mount Olympus in the Regional Unit of Pieria, the municipality of Eastern Mani in the Peloponnese, in Metsovo and Zagorochoria (Papigo, Vitsa, Aristi), in Parga in the Region of Epirus and in Portaria in Thessaly.

The BrHs are, for the most part, seasonal units. They are mostly located in points of exceptional natural beauty, as well as in areas with strong cultural features. These units stand out thanks to a combination of traditional architecture with elements of modern aesthetics. Modern amenities in the room, especially those related to technology, are "masked" where necessary, so as not to disrupt the aesthetics of the room and the surrounding spaces. The majority of these hotels boast a restaurant, swimming pools (including private pools, in 4-star units and above), rejuvenation and wellness services, cultural event spaces, etc.

Figure 5. Regional distribution of BHs (hotel beds)

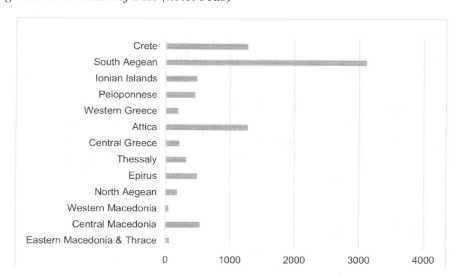

The Boutique city hotels (BcHs) are mainly continuous operation hotels located in:

- key commercial areas of the urban centres of Athens and Thessaloniki.
- suburbs of cities, in periurban areas, and especially in areas with a high per capita income (Kifisia, Glyfada, Vouliagmeni, etc.).
- urban centres visited by tourists (Ioannina, Kalamata, Nafplio, Heraklion, Rethymnon, Argostoli, Rhodes Town.).

The BcHs located in the centre or suburbs of big cities are mainly housed in neoclassical buildings but also in apartment buildings that are typical examples of Greek urban architecture of the inter-war and post-World War II period. The design of these hotels is usually characterised by an attempt to use suitable contemporary materials that match the listed building and local architecture, thus bringing out the value of both the building and the area. Hotel common areas are decorated with objects of high aesthetics, works of modern art, art deco and often pop art. These hotels typically boast a restaurant, lounge bar and a number of small multi-purpose rooms. Moreover, the high-tech amenities installed in the rooms often classify the latter as "smart rooms". BcHs located in smaller towns are usually housed in traditional and listed buildings, which are examples of the local architectural tradition, etc..

In mid-2021, during the phase of long-term recovery from the pandemic (May – August), there was growing demand for BH certification, mainly by newly established 4* category hotels, in the regions of South Aegean, Crete, and most especially in Athens. At the same time, however, there was growing interest in the establishment of BHs in developing destinations, such as Sifnos, Karpathos, Kalymnos, Kea and Katerini. This trend, during the phase of long-term recovery from the COVID-19 pandemic, is linked, both to the main goal of these accommodations, which is to provide personalized services and evoke emotions of "warm hospitality" in consumers, and to the key trend for authenticity and identity, given that, BrHs in particular, are frequently fully aligned with local architecture and design patterns, and their operation is directly linked to the socio-economic structure of the destinations in which they are located, as well as to existing attractions and outdoor tourism activities.

Upgraded Amenities and Services

The main focus of boutique hotels is experience based differentiation. Nowadays, the term "differentiated accommodation experience" does not simply suggest a full service package that will cover the customers' basic needs of sleep, food and hygiene. It mainly refers to the cultural experience customers expect to enjoy during their stay. Therefore, the main aim of a BHs is rather than to offer goods and services, to create experiences that evoke rare emotions capable of moving and seducing the tourist-consumer.

A detailed analysis of the type of amenities and services offered by BHs to their guests indicates that upgraded services, mainly at room/apartment level, are of four different types:

- The bed size is bigger than the minimum mandatory hotel bed size,
- There is a choice of bed pillows,
- BHs deliver dailies (digital) newspapers and magazines
- as well as new generation TV set in suites in almost all 5* and 4* accommodations, and more than 70% of 3* BHs.

Moreover, more than 70% of BHs of all three categories offer cable or satellite TV services, optional laptop services and magnifying bathroom mirror. 90% of 5* and 4* star accommodations, and over 50% of 3* BHs boast an espresso coffee machine. With regard to catering services, all BHs offer the option of breakfast room service, beyond the hours set for breakfast (for 3 hours), while more than 50% cater for special dietary needs (including gluten-free products, children's menus, healthy diet menus, request custom menus, etc.).

Moreover, all 5* hotels and the vast majority of 4* accommodations offer concierge service and turn down options. Also, more than 70% of all category BHs have a library and increased hospital staff to bed ratio (minimum of one/ 6 beds, for a hotel in full operation), let alone that the majority of these hotels provide their staff with a hotel operation manual. More than half of BH accommodations in all three star categories offer free transfer of their customers to and from the point of entry to/exit from the destination. It is also worth noting that over 50% of BHs in the 5* and 4* categories have a gym area of at least 20 sq.m., and a spa area (which includes at least two of the following: sauna steam bath, jacuzzi and two types of wellness treatments or massage). BHs are investing in the Food & Beverage segment as this segment has increased participation in their profits. For this reason, BHs focus on creating ambient dining spaces including an assortment of diversified breakfast and lunch menus (signatures dishes και cokctails) combined to "unforgettable experiences" such as the opportunity to meet the chef or food tasting sessions, etc..

FUTURE RESEARCH DIRECTIONS

Issues of global crisis management issues, which affecting tourism and hospitality. The spread of the Covid-19 is a paradigm of crisis management. In mid-2022, 2.5 years after the declaration of the pandemic, the discuss is focused on the shape of all tourism components for the transition of the sector to an improved situation of sustainable development. In this context, a future research effort can study the macroeconomic aspects and impacts of the strong trend, observed mainly in the last 10 years, in the Greek territory for the development of modern forms of tourism accommodation and products (such as boutique hotels, glamping, etc.), where their main objective is the management of personalized tourist experiences.

CONCLUSION

Nowadays, consumer choices are increasingly motivated by the "self-realization" of their tourist-related expectations. In fact, as Urierly N. (2005) points out, all shifts in tourism experience reflect the transition from a modern approach, in which tourism has been seen as "distinct" from everyday life, to a post-modern approach, where tourism is integrated in our daily experiences as an expression of life. In this context, the importance of a tourist travel and stay is determined and depends on the meaning that the travel and the arising experience have for each of us. Thus, the nature of the tourism product, and especially that of the hospitality industry, is redefined as the result of a negotiation, in which the services and products offered are constantly renewed and reshaped based on the desires, preferences and expectations of tourists, in the context of an ever-changing tourist consumption process. In this context, the Greek hospitality industry is constantly called upon to adapt and respond.

Boutique hotels in Greece are a successful example of the resilience of hospitality businesses during the periods of both the financial crisis and, subsequently, of the COVID-19 pandemic, given that the very nature of their services and products, enables them to immediately respond and adapt to new situations and cater for evolving consumer needs, ultimately striving for survival and for the return to a new reality of sustainable tourism development. The HCH, as the state's institutional advisor on issues of tourism policy and development, and as an organization that responsibly promotes hotel industry entrepreneurship, has designed innovative programs that encourage hoteliers to embrace modern and sustainable business practices. Nowadays, there is growing demand for BH certification, mainly by newly established 4* category hotels, in the regions of South Aegean, Crete and Athens. This trend is linked to the main goal of this hospitality product, which is to provide personalized services and evoke emotions of "warm hospitality" in consumers. The "Boutique hotel" seal is a distinct hotel industry product that aims to upgrade the competitiveness of Greek hotels by encouraging them to enhance and improve the quality of their services, so that they can provide their guests with new and differentiated experiences. The integrated business ecosystem of certification for small hotels with distinctive characteristics is, initially, a way to distinguish and recognise innovative design and services and, as a second step, a way to help accommodations that offer products of high added value to stand out. During the brief period of its existence, the programme has supported the establishment of a dynamic network of small accommodations in almost all of Greece and has become a seal of quality and recognition of hotels that offer unique hospitality experiences on a daily basis. At the same time, the programme has focused on designing a comprehensive customer driven communication strategy.

REFERENCES

Aggett, M. (2007). What has influenced growth in the UK's boutique hotel sector? *International Journal of Contemporary Hospitality Management, 19*(2), 169–177. doi:10.1108/09596110710729274

Ahmad, N. F., Hemdi, M. A., & Othman, D. N. (2017). Boutique hotel attributes and guest behavioral intentions. *Journal of Tourism. Hospitality & Culinary Arts, 9*(2), 257–266.

Akbulaev, N. (2021). Funding research certification programs in the sphere of tourism. In & M. Ozsahin (Ed.), New Strategic, Social and Economic Challenges in the Age of Society 5.0 Implications for Sustainability. European Proceedings of Social and Behavioural Sciences. European Publisher. doi:10.15405/epsbs.2021.12.04.27

Albazzaz, A., Birnbaum, B., Brachfeld, D., Danilov, D., Kets de Vries, O., & Moed, J. (2003). Lifestyles of the rich and almost famous: the boutique hotel phenomenon in the United States. High Tech Entrepreneurship and Strategy Group Project, Insead Business School, Fontainebleau.

Aliukeviciute, M. (2012). Boutique hotels' evolution. *International Journal of Contemporary Hospitality Management,* 1–3.

BLLA. (Boutique & Lifestyle Lodging Association). (2021). *Boutique and lifestyle hotels and properties—Definitions.* BLLA. http://www.blla.org

Callan, R. J., & Fearon, R. (1997). Town house hotels – an emerging sector. *International Journal of Contemporary Hospitality Management, 9*(4), 168–175. doi:10.1108/09596119710185855

Caterer Search. (2005). Market snapshot: Boutique hotels. In *Caterer and Hotelkeeper.* https://www.thecaterer.com/news/hotel/market-snapshot-boutique-hotels

Crouch, D., & Desforges, L. (2003). The sensuous in the tourist encounter: The power of the body in tourist studies. *Tourist Studies, 3*(1), 5–22. doi:10.1177/1468797603040528

Drewer, P. (2005). *Key note market report plus, 2005: Hotels* (20th ed.). Key Note.

Erkutlu, H. V., & Chafra, J. (2006). Relationship between leadership power bases and job stress of subordinates: Examples from boutique hotels. *Management Research News, 29*(5), 285–297. doi:10.1108/01409170610674419

Flick, U. (2006). *An introduction of qualitative research* (3rd ed.). Sage.

Freund de Klumbis, D., & Munsters, W. (2005). Developments in the hotel industry: design meets historic properties. In M. Sigala & D. Leslie (Eds.), *International Cultural Tourism.* Elsevier Butterworth Heinemann.

Georgiadou, M. E. (1981). *Hotel Economics.* Papazisi.

Haven-Tang, C., & Jones, E. (2006). Using local food and drink to differentiate tourism destinations through a sense of place. *Journal of Culinary Science & Technology, 4*(4), 69–86. doi:10.1300/J385v04n04_07

HCH. (Hellinic Chamber of Hotels 2019). *Boutique hotel Trademark: Regulation.* BLLC. http://www.boutique-hotel.gr

Herstein, R., Gilboa, S., Gamliel, E., Bergera, R., & Ali, A. (2018). The Role of Private Label Brands in Enhancing Service Satisfaction in the Hotel Industry: Comparing Luxury and Boutique Hotels. *Services Marketing Quarterly*, *39*(2), 140–155. doi:10.1080/15332969.2018.1437250

Horner, S., & Swarbrooke, J. (2005). *Leisure marketing: a global perspective*. Butterworth-Heinemann.

Hussein, A. S., Hapsari, R. D. V., & Yulianti, I. (2018). Experience quality and hotel boutique customer loyalty: Mediating role of hotel image and perceived value. *Journal of Quality Assurance in Hospitality & Tourism*, *19*(4), 442–459. doi:10.1080/1528008X.2018.1429981

Ioannides, D., & Debbage, K. (1997). Post-fordism and flexibility: The travel industry polyglot. *Tourism Management*, *18*(4), 229–241. doi:10.1016/S0261-5177(97)00019-8

Jana, A., & Chandra, B. (2016). Mediating role of customer satisfaction in the mid market hotels: An empirical analysis. *Indian Journal of Science and Technology*, *9*(1), 1–16. doi:10.17485/ijst/2016/v9i1/81973

Jones, L. D., Day, J., & Quadri-Felitti, D. (2013). Emerging definitions of boutique and lifestyle hotels: A delphi study. *Journal of Travel & Tourism Marketing*, *30*(7), 715–731. doi:10.1080/10548408.2013.827549

Judd, D. R. (2006). Commentary: Tracing the commodity chain of global tourism. *Tourism Geographies*, *8*(4), 323–336. doi:10.1080/14616680600921932

Kadir, S. A., Jamaludin, M., & Awang, A. R. (2019). Accessibility Adaptation in Heritage Boutique Hotels: A review on literature. *Environment-Behaviour Proceedings Journal*, *4*(10), 103–108. doi:10.21834/e-bpj.v4i10.1633

Khosravi, S., Malek, A., & Ekiz, E. (2014). Why Tourists are Attracted to Boutique Hotels: Case of Penang Island, Malaysia. *Journal of Hospitality and Tourism*, *12*(1), 26–41.

Kontis, A. P., & Gkoumas, A. (2017). "Greek Breakfast": A New Tourism Brand Name for an Age-Long Gastronomy Tradition. In A. Kavoura, P. Sakas, & P. Tomaras (Eds.), *Strategic Innovative Marketing: 5th IC-SIM, Athens, Greece 2016* (pp. 235–244). Springer. doi:10.1007/978-3-319-56288-9_32

Lim, W. M., & Endean, M. (2009). Elucidating the aesthetic and operational characteristics of UK boutique hotels. *International Journal of Contemporary Hospitality Management*, *21*(1), 38–51. doi:10.1108/09596110910930179

Loureiro, S. M. C., Rita, P., & Sarmento, E. M. (2020). What is the core essence of small city boutique hotels? *International Journal of Culture, Tourism and Hospitality Research*, *14*(1), 44–62. doi:10.1108/IJCTHR-01-2019-0007

MacNaghten, P., & Urry, J. (2000). Bodies of nature. *Body & Society*, *6*(3/4), 1–16. doi:10.1177/1357034X00006003001

Malcheva, M. (2018). Competitive advantages of boutique hotels in the context of a sharing economy. *ИзвестиянаСъюзанаучените- Варна. СерияИкономическинауки*, *7*(3), 71–83.

McNeill, D. (2009). The airport hotel as business space. *Geografiska Annaler. Series B, Human Geography*, *91*(3), 219–228. doi:10.1111/j.1468-0467.2009.00316.x

Middleton, V. T., & Hawkins, R. (1998). *Sustainable tourism: A marketing perspective*. Butterworth-Heinemann.

Pavlidis, P. (2000). *Hotel Marketing* (4th ed.). Interbooks.

Pippirs, C., & Steckenbauer, S. (2022). Case study – spa destination branding – a strategic realignment process of five Bavarian thermal spas. *International Journal of Spa and Wellness*, *30*(Aug), 1–12. doi: 10.1080/24721735.2022.2117009

Poon, A. (1989). Competitive strategies for New tourism. In C. P. Cooper (Ed.), *Progress in –Tourism Recreation and Hospitality Management* (pp. 91–102). Belhaven Press.

Prentice, R. C. (2001). Experiential Cultural Tourism: Museums and the Marketing of the New Romanticism of Evoked Authenticity. *Museum Management and Curatorship*, *19*(1), 5–26. doi:10.1080/09647770100201901

Rabontu, I. C., & Niculencu, G. (2009). Boutique hotels – New appearances in hotel industry in Romania. *Annals of the University of Petrosani. Economics*, *9*(2), 209–214.

Research Institute for Tourism. (2020). The Greek hotel in the years of crisis 2008-2018. Athens: Research Institute for Tourism

Sasidharan, V., Sirakaya, E., & Kerstetter, D. (2002). Developing countries and tourism ecolabels. *Tourism Management*, *23*, 161–174.

Rogerson, J. M. (2010), The boutique hotel industry in South Africa: definition, scope, and organization. *Urban Forum*, *21*, 425-439.

Shaw, G., & Williams, A. M. (2004). *Tourism and tourism spaces*. Sage Publications. doi:10.4135/9781446220528

Teo, C. C. J., Chia, G. H., & Khoo, H. P. M. (1998). *Size really does matter (when you're small): the critical success factors behind boutique hotels in Singapore*. [Research paper, Nanyang Business School, Singapore: Nanyang Technological University].

Teo, P., & Chang, T. C. (2009). Singapore's postcolonial landscape: boutique hotels as agents. In T. Winter, P. Teo, & T. C. Chang (Eds.), *Asia on tour: exploring the rise of Asian tourism* (pp. 81–96). Routledge.

Timothy, D., & Teye, V. (2009). *Tourism and the lodging sector*. Butterworth-Heinemann.

Todd, G., & Mather, S. (1995). *The International Hotel Industry. Corporate strategies and Global Opportunities*. The Economist Intelligence Unit.

Urry, J. (1994). *Consuming places*. Routledge.

Van Hartesvelt, M. (2006). Building a better boutique hotel. *Lodging Hospitality*, 32–44.

Victorino, L., Verma, R., Plaschka, G., & Dev, C. (2005). Service innovation and customer choices in the hospitality industry. *Managing Service Quality*, *15*(6), 555–576. doi:10.1108/09604520510634023

Vlami, A. (2021). The Developments and challenges of hospitality in greece for the financial sustainability of tourism: the case of boutique hotels. In D. L., Balsalobre, O. M., Driha, M., Shahbaz (eds.), *Strategies in Sustainable Tourism, Economic Growth and Clean Energy*. Spain: Springer.

Walterspiel, *G. (1969)*, *Einführung in die Betriebswirtschaftslehre des Hotels*, Wiesbaden.

WTTC. (World Travel & Tourism Council). (2020), *Coronavirus Brief*. WTTC. https://www.wttc.org/-/media/files/wttc-coronavirus-brief-external-3003.pdf?la=en

Compilation of References

Acs, Z. J., Arenius, P., Hay, M., & Minniti, M. (2005). *Global Entrepreneurship Monitor. 2004 Executive Report.* Babson & London Business School.

Agarwal, P. (2021). Shattered but smiling: Human resource management and the wellbeing of hotel employees during COVID-19. *International Journal of Hospitality Management, 93*, 102765. doi:10.1016/j.ijhm.2020.102765 PMID:36919177

Aggett, M. (2007). What has influenced growth in the UK's boutique hotel sector? *International Journal of Contemporary Hospitality Management, 19*(2), 169–177. doi:10.1108/09596110710729274

Ahmad, N. F., Hemdi, M. A., & Othman, D. N. (2017). Boutique hotel attributes and guest behavioral intentions. *Journal of Tourism. Hospitality & Culinary Arts, 9*(2), 257–266.

Ahmed, E., Kilika, J., & Gakenia, C. (2021). Progressive convergent definition and conceptualization of organizational resilience: A model development. *International Journal of Organizational Leadership, 10*(4), 385–400. doi:10.33844/ijol.2021.60599

Akbulaev, N. (2021). Funding research certification programs in the sphere of tourism. In & M. Ozsahin (Ed.), New Strategic, Social and Economic Challenges in the Age of Society 5.0 Implications for Sustainability. European Proceedings of Social and Behavioural Sciences. European Publisher. doi:10.15405/epsbs.2021.12.04.27

Al-Ababneh, M. M. (2021). The implementation of Total Quality Management (TQM) in the hotel industry. *International Journal of Tourism and Hospitality, 1*(1), 25–34. doi:10.51483/IJTH.1.1.2021.25-34

Albazzaz, A., Birnbaum, B., Brachfeld, D., Danilov, D., Kets de Vries, O., & Moed, J. (2003). Lifestyles of the rich and almost famous: the boutique hotel phenomenon in the United States. High Tech Entrepreneurship and Strategy Group Project, Insead Business School, Fontainebleau.

Albrecht, S. L., Bakker, A. B., Gruman, J. A., Macey, W. H., & Saks, A. M. (2015). Employee engagement, human resource management practices and competitive advantage: An integrated approach. *Journal of Organizational Effectiveness: People and Performance, 2*(1), 7–35. doi:10.1108/JOEPP-08-2014-0042

Aldrich, H. E. (2012). The emergence of entrepreneurship as an academic field: A personal essay on institutional entrepreneurship. *Research Policy, 41*(7), 1240–1248. doi:10.1016/j.respol.2012.03.013

Ali, S.R., Sweis, R.J., Saleh, F.M. and Sarea, A.M. (2018). Linking soft and hard Total Quality Management practices: Evidence from Jordan. *International Journal Business Excellence, 14*.

Aliukeviciute, M. (2012). Boutique hotels' evolution. *International Journal of Contemporary Hospitality Management, 1–3.*

Compilation of References

Aljarah, A., Emeagwali, L., Ibrahim, B., & Ababneh, B. (2018). Does corporate social responsibility really increase customer relationship quality? A meta-analytic review. *Social Responsibility Journal*, *16*(1), 28–49. doi:10.1108/SRJ-08-2018-0205

Alvord, S. H., Brown, L. D., & Letts, C. W. (2004). Social entrepreneurship and societal transformation, an exploratory study. *The Journal of Applied Behavioral Science*, *40*(3), 260–262. doi:10.1177/0021886304266847

Amelung, B. and Moreno, A. (2009). Impacts of climate change in tourism in Europe, PESETA-tourism study. *JRC Scientific and Technical Reports EUR, 24114*.

Amnesty. (2022). Η ιστορία της Οικουμενικής Διακήρυξης των Δικαιωμάτων του. *Ανθρώπου*.

Anderson, A. R. (2000). Paradox in the Periphery: An Entrepreneurial Reconstruction? *Entrepreneurship and Regional Development*, *12*(2), 91–109. doi:10.1080/089856200283027

Anderson, A. R., & McAuley, A. (1999). Marketing Landscapes: The Social Context. *Qualitative Market Research*, *2*(3), 176–188. doi:10.1108/13522759910291680

Ang, S., Van Dyne, L., Koh, D., Yee Ng, K., Templer, K., Tay, C., & Chandrasekar, A. (2007). Cultural intelligence: Its measurement and effects on cultural judgment and decision making, cultural adaptation and task performance. *Management and Organization Review*, *3*(3), 335–371. doi:10.1111/j.1740-8784.2007.00082.x

Anholt, S. (2010). *Places Identity, Image, and Reputation*. Palgrave Macmillan Hampshire.

Antunes, M. G., Texeira, Q., & Justino, M. R. (2017). The relationship between innovation and total quality management and the innovation effects on organizational performance. *International Journal of Quality & Reliability Management*, *34*(9), 1474–1492. doi:10.1108/IJQRM-02-2016-0025

Apetrei, A., Ribeiro, D., Roig, S., & Mas, A. (2013). El emprendedor social – una explicación socio-intercultural, CIRIEC-España. *C.I.R.I.E.C. España*, *78*, 37–52. www.ciriec-revistaeconomia.es

Arcaro, J. (1995). *Quality in Education: An Implementation Handbook*. St. Lucie Press.

Ardichvili, A.; Gasparishvili, A. (2003). Russian and Georgian Entrepreneurs and Non-Entrepreneurs: A Study of Value Differences. *Organization Studies*, *24*(1), 29-46.

Armstrong, M. (2008). *Strategic human resource management. A guide to action* (4th ed.). Kogan Page.

Artinger, S., Vulkan, N., & Shem-Tov, Y. (2015). Entrepreneurs negotiation behavior. *Small Business Economics*, *44*(4), 737–757. doi:10.100711187-014-9619-8

Ashton, D., & Green, F. (1996). *Education, training, and the global economy*. Edward Elgar.

Assarroudi, A., Heshmati Nabavi, F., Armat, M. R., Ebadi, A., & Vaismoradi, M. (2018). Directed qualitative content analysis: The description and elaboration of its underpinning methods and data analysis process. *Journal of Research in Nursing*, *23*(1), 42–55. doi:10.1177/1744987117741667 PMID:34394406

Au, C. H., Kevin, K. K. W., & Chiu, D. K. W. (2022). Managing users' behaviors on open content crowdsourcing platform. *Journal of Computer Information Systems*, *62*(2), 1125–1135. doi:10.1080/08874417.2021.1983487

Auernhammer, J., & Roth, B. (2021). The origin and evolution of Stanford University's design thinking: From product design to design thinking in innovation management. *Journal of Product Innovation Management*, *38*(6), 623–644. doi:10.1111/jpim.12594

Austin, J., Stevenson, H., & Wei-skillern, J. (2003). Social Entrepreneurship and Commercial Entrepreneurship: Same, Different, or Both? *Working Paper Series*, No. 04-029, Harvard Business School.

Avdikos, V. (2014). *The cultural and creative industries in Greece*. Epikentro Publications.

Azzone, G., & Noci, G. (1998). Seeing ecology and "green" innovations as a source of change. *Journal of Organizational Change Management*, *11*(2), 94–111. doi:10.1108/09534819810212106

Baker, R. J. (2015). *Pricing on Purpose: Creating and Capturing Value. Pricing on Purpose: Creating and Capturing Value*. Wiley Blackwell. doi:10.1002/9781119201366

Barney, J. B. (1995). Looking inside for competitive advantage. *The Academy of Management Executive*, *9*(4), 49–61. doi:10.5465/ame.1995.9512032192

Barney, J. B., & Wright, P. M. (1998). On becoming a strategic partner: The role of human resources in gaining competitive advantage. *Human Resource Management*, *37*(1), 31–46. doi:10.1002/(SICI)1099-050X(199821)37:1<31::AID-HRM4>3.0.CO;2-W

Baum, J. R., Frese, M., Baron, R. A., & Katz, J. A. (2007). Entrepreneurship as an area of psychology study: an introduction. *The Psychology of Entrepreneurship*, 1-18.

Baum, T. (2015). Human resources in tourism: Still waiting for change? A 2015 reprise. *Tourism Management*, *50*, 204–212. doi:10.1016/j.tourman.2015.02.001

Baum, T., & Hai, N. T. T. (2020). Hospitality, tourism, human rights and the impact of COVID-19. *International Journal of Contemporary Hospitality Management*, *32*(7), 2397–2407. doi:10.1108/IJCHM-03-2020-0242

BBC News. (2020). Trump's virus travel ban on Europe comes into force. *BBC News*. https://www.bbc.com/news/world-us-canada-51883728

BBC News. (2022). *'Syria Crusader castle Krak des Chevaliers has war scars', BBC News*. BBC.

BBC News. (2022). *'Ukraine war: On the front line of the battle for Kharkiv'. BBC News*. BBC.

Becker-Olsen, K. L., Cudmore, B. A., & Hill, R. P. (2006). The impact of perceived corporate social responsibility on consumer behavior. *Journal of Business Research*, *59*(1), 46–53. doi:10.1016/j.jbusres.2005.01.001

Bednar, P., & Grebenicek, P. (2012). Mapping Creative Industries in the Zlin Region. *Journal of Competitiveness*, *4*(1), 20–35. doi:10.7441/joc.2012.01.02

Begley, T.M.; Tan, W.L. (2001). The Socio-Cultural Environment for Entrepreneurship: A Comparison between East Asian and Anglo-Saxon Countries. *Journal of International Business Studies*, *32*(3), 537-553.

Belias, D. and Trihas, N. (2022). Investigating the Readiness for Organizational Change: A Case Study from a Hotel Industry Context/Greece. *Journal of Tourism & Management Research*.

Belias, D., & Trihas, N. (2022a). The relationship of the change context with the resilience of hotels: Proposal for a Research Framework on Hotels during the Covid-19 crisis. *ECRM, 21st European Conference on Research Methodology for Business and Management Studies*, Aveiro, Portugal.

Belias, D., & Trihas, N. (2022b). Human Resource Training of front office employees and change management in hospitality sector during crisis. *4th International Conference on Finance, Economics, Management and IT Business*. Scite Vents.

Compilation of References

Belias, D., & Trihas, N. (2022c). Human Resource Training of Front Office Employees and Change Management in Hospitality Sector during Crisis. In *Proceedings of the 4th International Conference on Finance, Economics, Management, and IT Business*. Research Gate.

Belias, D., & Trihas, N. (2022e). How can we measure the "Resistance to Change?" An exploratory Factor Analysis in a sample of employees in the Greek Hotel Industry. In *IACUDIT 2022 Conference Proceedings*. Research Gate.

Belias, D., & Trihas, N. (2022f). How can we measure the "Success of Change Management?" An exploratory Factor Analysis in a sample of employees in the Greek Hotel Industry. *In IACUDIT 2022 Conference Proceedings*. Research Gate.

Belias, D., Papademetriou, C., Rossidis, I. and Vasiliadis L. (2020a). Strategic Management in the Hotel Industry: Proposed Strategic Practices to Recover from COVID- 19 Global Crisis. *Academic Journal of Interdisciplinary Studies, 9*(6).

Belias, D., Papademetriou, C., Rossidis, I., & Vasiliadis L. (2020). Strategic Management in the Hotel Industry: Proposed Strategic Practices to Recover from COVID- 19 Global Crisis. *Academic Journal of Interdisciplinary Studies, 9*(6), 130 – 138. . doi:10.36941/ajis-2020-0117

Belias, D., Rosidis, I., & Velissariou, E. (2018). Shapting the consumers' behaviour who are using Airbnb- The case of airbnb's users in Greece. In Katsoni V. and Velander K., (Eds.) The Cultural and Sustainability Synergies. Springer. doi:10.1007/978-3-030-12453-3_10

Belias, D., Rossidis, I., & Valeri, M. (2022) Tourism in crisis: the impact of climate change on the tourism industry. Valeri M. (Eds.), Tourism risk. Crisis and Recovery Management? Emerald. doi:10.1108/978-1-80117-708-520221012

Belias, D., Rossidis, I., Lazarakis, P., Mantas, C. & Ntalakos, A. (2022d). *Analyzing organizational factors in Greek Tourism Services*. Corporate & Business Strategy Review.

Belias, D., Rossidis, I., Ntalakos, A., & Trihas, N. (2022b). Digital Marketing: The Case of Digital Marketing Strategies on Luxurious Hotels. *Conference Proceedings of Centeris – DTI4T22 – Workshop on Digital Transformation & Industry 4.0 technologies*, Lisboa, Portugal.

Belias, D., Rossidis, I., Papademetriou, C., & Valeri, M. (2022c). Destination Governance: The Role of Local Authorities in Greek Tourism Marketing. In Valeri M. (Ed.) New Governance and Management in Touristic Destinations, 1- 18. IGI Global.

Belias, D., Rossidis, I., Papademetriou, C., Mantas C. (2020c). Job Satisfaction as affected by Types of Leadership: A Case Study of Greek Tourism Sector. *Journal of Quality Assurance in Hospitality & Tourism, 10*(3), 39 – 45. doi:10.1 080/1528008X.2020.1867695

Belias, D., Rossidis, I., Vasiliadis, L., & Papademetriou, C. (2021). Utilizing strategic tools in hotel industry in the era of pandemic. *Proceedings of the 37th International Business Information Management Association (IBIMA)*, Cordoba, Spain.

Belias, D., Vasiliadis, L., & Mantas, C. (2020). The human resource training and development of employees working on luxurious hotels in Greece. *Cultural and Tourism Innovation in the Digital Era*, 639-648.

Belias, D., Velissariou, E., & Rossidis I. (2019). The contribution of HRM on the development of effective organizational culture in hotel units - The case of Greek hotels. *Smart Tourism as a Driver for Culture and Sustainability*, 603-618.

Belias, D., Velissariou, E., & Rossidis, I. (2018). The contribution of HRM on the development of effective organizational culture in hotel units - The case of Greek hotels. In Exploring smart tourism: The cultural and sustainability synergies. Springer.

Belias, D., Velissariou, E., & Rossidis, I. (2018). The contribution of HRM on the development of effective organizational culture in hotel units—The case of Greek hotels. In Exploring smart tourism: The cultural and sustainability synergies. Springer.

Belias, D. (2020). Research Methods on the Contribution of Robots in the Service Quality of Hotels. In *Strategic Innovative Marketing and Tourism* (pp. 939–946). Springer. doi:10.1007/978-3-030-36126-6_104

Belias, D., Mantas, C., & Tsiotas, D. (2019). The impact of corporate culture in the performance of the front desk employees - The case of five-star hotels in Greece. In *Smart tourism as a driver for culture and sustainability* (pp. 563–576). Springer. doi:10.1007/978-3-030-03910-3_38

Belias, D., Rossidis, I., Papademetriou, C., & Lamprinoudis, N. (2020b). The Greek Tourism Sector: An analysis of Job Satisfaction, Role Conflict and Autonomy of Greek Employees. *Journal of Human Resources in Hospitality & Tourism.*

Belias, D., Rossidis, I., Papademetriou, C., & Mantas, C. (2021). Job Satisfaction as Affected by Types of Leadership: A Case Study of Greek Tourism Sector. *Journal of Quality Assurance in Hospitality & Tourism.*

Belias, D., Rossidis, I., Sotiriou, A., & Malik, S.Case Study in Greek Seasonal Hotels. (2022). Workplace Conflict, Turnover, and Quality of Services. Case Study in Greek Seasonal Hotels. *Journal of Quality Assurance in Hospitality & Tourism*, 2022. doi:10.1080/1528008X.2022.2065655

Belias, D., & Trichas, N. (2022) Strategic HRM approaches as mediators to change management I the tourism industry: Potential and prospects for future research. *Proceedings of Academicsera International Conference*, Hamburg, Germany.

Belias, D., & Trichas, N. (2022c) Strategic HRM approaches as mediators to change management in the tourism industry: Potential and prospects for future research. *Proceedings of Academicsera International Conference*, Hamburg, Germany.

Belias, D., & Trihas, N. (2022a). The relationship of the change context with the resilience of hotels: Proposal for a Research Framework on Hotels during the Covid-19 crisis. *ECRM, 21st European Conference on Research Methodology for Business and Management Studies,* Aveiro, Portugal.

Belias, D., & Trihas, N. (2022d). Investigating the Readiness for Organizational Change: A Case Study from a Hotel Industry Context/Greece. *Journal of Tourism & Management Research*, 7(2), 1047–1062. doi:10.5281/zenodo.7090337

Belias, D., Trivellas, P., Koustelios, A., Serdaris, P., Varsanis, K., & Grigoriou, I. (2017). Human Resource Management, Strategic Leadership Development and the Greek Tourism Sector. In V. Katsoni, A. Upadhya, & A. Stratigea (Eds.), *Tourism, Culture and Heritage in a Smart Economy. Springer Proceedings in Business and Economics.* Springer. doi:10.1007/978-3-319-47732-9_14

Belias, D., Trivellas, P., Koustelios, A., Serdaris, P., Varsanis, K., & Grigoriou, I. (2017a). Human Resource Management, Strategic Leadership Development and the Greek Tourism Sector. Tourism, Culture and Heritage in a Smart Economy, 189-205. In V. Katsoni, A. Upadhya, & A. Stratigea (Eds.), *Tourism, Culture and Heritage in a Smart Economy. Springer Proceedings in Business and Economics.* Springer.

Belias, D., & Vasiliadis, L. (2021). A Conceptual Study of Proposing a Model to Use Robots in Hospitality Industry based on the Empirical Evidences. *Journal of Tourism and Management Research.*, 6(1), 830–841. doi:10.26465/ojtmr.2018339544

Belias, D., & Vasiliadis, L. (2022). Robots on the Tourist Industry—A Review for Future Research Directions. In V. Katsoni & A. C. Şerban (Eds.), *Transcending Borders in Tourism Through Innovation and Cultural Heritage. Springer Proceedings in Business and Economics.* Springer. doi:10.1007/978-3-030-92491-1_23

Compilation of References

Belias, D., Vasiliadis, L., & Mantas, C. (2020). *The Human Resource Training and Development of Employees Working on Luxurious Hotels in Greece*. Cultural and Tourism Innovation in the Digital Era. doi:10.1007/978-3-030-36342-0_49

Belias, D., Vasiliadis, L., & Rossidis, I. (2021b). The Intention and Expectations of Modern Robotic Technologies in the Hotel Industry. *Journal of Quality Assurance in Hospitality & Tourism*. doi:10.1080/1528008X.2021.1995566

Belias, D., Vasiliadis, L., & Velissariou, E. (2020b). Internal Marketing in Tourism: The Case of Human Resource Empowerment on Greek Hotels. In V. Katsoni & T. Spyriadis (Eds.), *Cultural and Tourism Innovation in the Digital Era. Springer Proceedings in Business and Economics*. Springer., doi:10.1007/978-3-030-36342-0_43

Belias, D., Velissariou, E., Koustelios, A., Varsanis, K., Kyriakou, D., & Sdrolias, L. (2017b). The Role of Organizational Culture in the Greek Higher Tourism Quality. In A. Kavoura, D. Sakas, & P. Tomaras (Eds.), *Strategic Innovative Marketing. Springer Proceedings in Business and Economics*. Springer. doi:10.1007/978-3-319-56288-9_10

Benavides-Velasco, C. A., Quintana-García, C., & Marchante-Lara, M.Velasco, B. (2014). Total quality management, corporate social responsibility and performance in the hotel industry. *International Journal of Hospitality Management*, *41*, 77–87. doi:10.1016/j.ijhm.2014.05.003

Benita, F. (2019). On the performance of creative industries: Evidence from Mexican metropolitan areas. *Papers in Regional Science*, *98*(2), 825–842. doi:10.1111/pirs.12403

Benzaquen, J., Carlos, M., Norero, G., Armas, H., & Pacheco, H. (2019). Quality in private health companies in Peru: The relation of QMS & ISO 9000 principles on TQM factor. *International Journal of Healthcare Management*, 1–9.

Bhattacharya, C. B., & Sen, S. (2003). Consumer–company identification: A framework for understanding consumers' relationships with companies. *Journal of Marketing*, *67*(2), 76–88. doi:10.1509/jmkg.67.2.76.18609

Bhattacharya, C. B., & Sen, S. (2004). Doing better at doing good: When, why, and how consumers respond to corporate social initiatives. *California Management Review*, *47*(1), 9–24. doi:10.2307/41166284

Bittán, M. (2017). El emprendimiento empresarial. *Disponible*. http://bit.ly/1R5erPv.

Blake, J. (2015). *International Cultural Heritage Law*. Oxford University Press. doi:10.1093/acprof:oso/9780198723516.001.0001

BLLA. (Boutique & Lifestyle Lodging Association). (2021). *Boutique and lifestyle hotels and properties—Definitions*. BLLA. http://www.blla.org

Blštáková, J., Joniaková, Z., Jankelová, N., Stachová, K., & Stacho, Z. (2020). Reflection of Digitalization on Business Values: The Results of Examining Values of People. *Management in a Digital Age Sustainability*, *2020*(12), 5202.

Boix, R., Capone, F., De Propris, L., Lazzeretti, L., & Sanchez, D. (2016). Comparing creative industries in Europe. *European Urban and Regional Studies*, *23*(4), 935–940. doi:10.1177/0969776414541135

Bonham, C., Edmonds, C., & Mak, J. (2006). The impact of 9/11 and other terrible global events on tourism in the United States and Hawaii. *Journal of Travel Research*, *45*(1), 99–110. doi:10.1177/0047287506288812

Boselie, P. (2014). *Strategic human resource management: A balanced approach* (2nd ed.). McGraw-Hill Education.

Bosworth, G., & Farrell, H. (2011). Tourism Entrepreneurs in Northumberland. *Annals of Tourism Research*, *38*(4), 1474–1494. doi:10.1016/j.annals.2011.03.015

Bowen, H. R. (2013). *Social responsibilities of the businessman*. University of Iowa Press. doi:10.2307/j.ctt20q1w8f

Bowma, M., Davies, P. G. G., Redgwell, C., & Lyster, S. (2010). *Lyster's International Wildlife Law*. Cambridge University Press. doi:10.1017/CBO9780511975301

Boxall, P., & Purcell, J. (2016). *Strategy and human resource management* (4th ed.). Palgrave. doi:10.1007/978-1-137-40765-8

Braun, V., & Clarke, V. (2006). Using thematic analysis in psychology. *Qualitative Research in Psychology, 3*(2), 77–101. doi:10.1191/1478088706qp063oa

Breiter, D., & Kline, S. F. (1995). Benchmarking quality management in hotels. *FIU Hospitality Review, 13*(2), 45–52.

Brinbaum, R. (2000). *Management Fads in Higher Education: Where They Come from, What They Do, Why They Fail*. Jossey-Bass Inc.

Brinbaum, R., & Deshotels, J. (1999). Has the Academy Adopted TQM? *Planning for Higher Education, 28*, 29–37.

Brockett, R. G., & Hiemstra, R. (1991). *Self Direction in Adult Learning Perspectives: on Theory, Research and Practice*. Routledge.

Brockhaus, R. H. (1980). Risk taking propensity of entrepreneurs. *Academy of Management Journal, 23*(3), 509–520. doi:10.2307/255515

Brookfield, S. D. (2009). Self-directed learning, in International Handbook of Education for the Changing World of Work. Springer Science and Business Media.

Budeanu, A. (2007). Sustainable tourist behaviour–a discussion of opportunities for change. *International Journal of Consumer Studies, 31*(5), 499–508. doi:10.1111/j.1470-6431.2007.00606.x

Byrd, R. (2021). Qualitative research methods.

Byrd, E. T. (2007). Stakeholders in sustainable tourism development and their roles: Applying stakeholder theory to sustainable tourism development. *Tourism Review, 62*(2), 6–13. doi:10.1108/16605370780000309

Cabrini, L., Simpson, M., & Scott, D. (2009). *From Davosto Copenhagenandbeyond:advancingtourism's response to climate change*. SDT. www.sdt.unwto.org

Calado, L., Rodrigues, A., Silveira, P., & Dentinho, T. (2011). Rural Tourism Associated with Agriculture as An Economic Alternative for the Farmers. *European Journal of Tourism, Hospitality and Recreation, 2*(1), 155–174.

Calderón, F., & Gamarra, E. (2004), Crisis, Inflexión y Reforma del Sistema de Partidos en Bolivia. Cuadernos de Futuro. La Paz, La Paz, Bolivia.

Callan, R. J., & Fearon, R. (1997). Town house hotels – an emerging sector. *International Journal of Contemporary Hospitality Management, 9*(4), 168–175. doi:10.1108/09596119710185855

Candy, P. C. (1991). *Self-Direction for Lifelong Learning: A Comprehensive Guide to Theory and Practice*. Jossey-Bass Publishers.

Canela, J., & Navarro, M. (2017). Profile of the consumer who values responsible and smart tourism in the hotel industry. *Management Decision, 50*(5), 972–988.

Cantarero, S., González-Loureiro, M., & Puig, F. (2017). Efectos de la crisis económica sobre el emprendimiento en empresas de economía social en España: un análisis espacial. *REVESCO. Revista de Estudios Cooperativos,* (125), 24-48. https://www.redalyc.org/articulo.oa?id=367/36754074002

Compilation of References

Carroll, A. B. (2015). Corporate social responsibility (CSR) is on a sustainable trajectory. *Journal of Defense Management, 5*(2), 1–2. doi:10.4172/2167-0374.1000132

Cascone, S. (2022). *Hiding Art in Basements, Returning Loans, Reopening as Bomb Shelters: How Ukraine's Museums Are Handling the Russian Invasion.*

Caterer Search. (2005). Market snapshot: Boutique hotels. In *Caterer and Hotelkeeper.* https://www.thecaterer.com/news/hotel/market-snapshot-boutique-hotels

CBC radio. (2022). *This museum director is staying in Kyiv as Ukrainian culture comes under fire.* CBD Radio.

Cerezo-Narváez, A., Córdoba-Roldán, A., Pastor-Fernández, A., Aguayo-González, F., Otero-Mateo, M., & Ballesteros-Pérez, P. (2019). Training competences in industrial risk prevention with lego® serious play®: A case study. *Safety (Basel, Switzerland), 5*(4), 81. doi:10.3390afety5040081

Chand, M. (2010). The impact of HRM practices on service quality, customer satisfaction and performance in the Indian hotel industry. *International Journal of Human Resource Management, 21*(4), 551–566. doi:10.1080/09585191003612059

Chan, M. M. W., & Chiu, D. K. W. (2022). Alert driven customer relationship management in online travel agencies: Event-condition-actions rules and key performance indicators. In A. Naim & S. Kautish (Eds.), *Building a brand image through electronic customer relationship management* (pp. 286–303). IGI Global. doi:10.4018/978-1-6684-5386-5.ch012

Channa, N. A., Shah, S. M. M., & Ghumro, N. H. (2019). Uncovering the link between strategic human resource management and crisis management: Mediating role of organizational resilience. *Annals of Contemporary Developments in Management & HR (ACDMHR),* 2632-7686.

Chan, T. T. W., Lam, A. H. C., & Chiu, D. K. W. (2020). From Facebook to Instagram: Exploring user engagement in an academic library. *Journal of Academic Librarianship, 46*(6), 102229. doi:10.1016/j.acalib.2020.102229 PMID:34173399

Chan, V. H. Y., & Chiu, D. K. W. (2023). Integrating the 6C's motivation into reading promotion curriculum for disadvantaged communities with technology tools: A case study of Reading Dreams Foundation in rural China. In A. Etim & J. Etim (Eds.), *Adoption and use of technology tools and services by economically disadvantaged communities: Implications for growth and sustainability.* IGI Global.

Chan, V. H. Y., Chiu, D. K. W., & Ho, K. K. W. (2022). Mediating effects on the relationship between perceived service quality and public library app loyalty during the COVID-19 era. *Journal of Retailing and Consumer Services, 67,* 102960. doi:10.1016/j.jretconser.2022.102960

Chatzopoulou, E., & Xanthopoulou, P. (2021). What drive customers to spread the word and be loyal? Factors influencing e-loyalty and eWOM to OTA's websites. *International Journal of Cultural and Digital Tourism.*

Chell, E., Nicolopoulou, K., & Karataş-Özkan, M. (2010). Social entrepreneurship and enterprise: International and innovation perspectives. *Entrepreneurship and Regional Development, 22*(6), 485–493. doi:10.1080/08985626.2010.488396

Chen, G. (1997). A review of the concept of Intercultural Sensitivity. Bienal Convention of the Pacific and Asian Communication Association, Honolulu, Hawaii.

Cheng, W., Tian, R., & Chiu, D.K.W. (2023) Travel vlogs influencing tourist decisions: Information preferences and gender differences. *Aslib Journal of Information Management.* doi:10.1108/AJIM-05-2022-0261

Cheng, S. C., & Kao, Y. H. (2022). The impact of the COVID-19 pandemic on job satisfaction: A mediated moderation model using job stress and organizational resilience in the hotel industry of Taiwan. *Heliyon, 8*(3), 09134. doi:10.1016/j.heliyon.2022.e09134 PMID:35342829

Cheng, W. W. H., Lam, E. T. H., & Chiu, D. K. W. (2020). Social media as a platform in academic library marketing: A comparative study. *Journal of Academic Librarianship*, *46*(5), 102188. doi:10.1016/j.acalib.2020.102188

Chen, R. (2015). The impact of tourism development on traditional village style. *Journal of Lanzhou Institute of Education*, *31*(9), 57–58.

Chen, Y., Chiu, D. K. W., & Ho, K. K. W. (2018). Facilitating the learning of the art of Chinese painting and calligraphy at Chao Shao-an Gallery. *Micronesian Educators*, *26*, 45–58.

Cheung, L. S. N., Chiu, D. K. W., & Ho, K. K. W. (2022). A quantitative study on utilizing electronic resources to engage children's reading and learning: Parents' perspectives through the 5E instructional model. *The Electronic Library*, *40*(6), 662–679. doi:10.1108/EL-09-2021-0179

Cheung, T. Y., Ye, Z., & Chiu, D. K. W. (2021). Value chain analysis of information services for the visually impaired: A case study of contemporary technological solutions. *Library Hi Tech*, *39*(2), 625–642. doi:10.1108/LHT-08-2020-0185

Cheung, V. S. Y., Lo, J. C. Y., Chiu, D. K. W., & Ho, K. K. W. (2023). Predicting Facebook's influence on travel products marketing based on the AIDA model. *Information Discovery and Delivery*, *51*(1), 66–73. doi:10.1108/IDD-10-2021-0117

Chin, G. Y. L., & Chiu, D. K. W. (2023). RFID-based robotic process automation for smart museums with an alert-driven approach. In R. Tailor (Ed.), *Application and adoption of robotic process automation for smart cities*. IGI. Global.

Chiu, D. K. W., & Ho, K. K. W. (2022a). Special selection on contemporary digital culture and reading. *Library Hi Tech*, *40*(5), 1204–1209. doi:10.1108/LHT-10-2022-516

Chiu, D. K. W., & Ho, K. K. W. (2022b). Editorial: 40th anniversary: Contemporary library research. *Library Hi Tech*, *40*(6), 1525–1531. doi:10.1108/LHT-12-2022-517

Chiu, D. K. W., Yueh, Y. T., Leung, H. F., & Hung, P. C. (2009). Towards ubiquitous tourist service coordination and process integration: A collaborative travel agent system with semantic web services. *Information Systems Frontiers*, *11*(3), 241–256. doi:10.100710796-008-9087-2

Cho, A., Lo, P., & Chiu, D. K. W. (2017). *Inside the world's major East Asian collections: One Belt, One Road, and beyond*. Chandos Publishing.

Christaller, W. (1963). Some considerations of tourism location in Europe: The peripheral regions – underdeveloped countries – recreation areas. *Regional Science Association Papers*, *12*, 95–105.

Chung, A. C. W., & Chiu, D. K. W. (2016). OPAC usability problems of archives: A case study of the Hong Kong Film Archive. [IJSSOE]. *International Journal of Systems and Service-Oriented Engineering*, *6*(1), 54–70. doi:10.4018/IJS-SOE.2016010104

Chung, C., Chiu, D. K. W., Ho, K. K. W., & Au, C. H. (2020). Applying social media to environmental education: Is it more impactful than traditional media? *Information Discovery and Delivery*, *48*(4), 255–266. doi:10.1108/IDD-04-2020-0047

Ciampa, D. (1992). *Total Quality: A User's Guide for Implementation*. Addison-Wesley.

Cloninger, C. R. (2004). *Feeling good: The science of well-being*. Oxford University Press.

Cloninger, C. R., Svrakic, D. M., & Przybeck, T. R. (1993). A psychobiological model of temperament and character. *Archives of General Psychiatry*, *50*(12), 975–990. doi:10.1001/archpsyc.1993.01820240059008 PMID:8250684

Collings, D. G., Wood, G. T., & Szamosi, L. T. (2019). *Human resource management. A critical approach* (2nd ed.). Routledge.

Compilation of References

Coltman, T. R., Devinney, T. M., Midgley, D. F., & Venaik, S. (2008). Formative versus reflective measurement models: Two applications of formative measurement. *Journal of Business Research, 61*(12), 1250–1262. doi:10.1016/j.jbusres.2008.01.013

Connell, J., & Gibson, C. (2004). World Music: Deterritorializing Place and Identity. *ERA, 2010*(3), 28. doi:10.1191/0309132504ph493oa

Connelly, M., Gilbert, J., Zaccaro, S., Threlfall, K., Marks, M., & Mumford, M. (2000). Exploring the relationship of leadership skills and knowledge to leader performance. *The Leadership Quarterly, 11*(1), 65–86. doi:10.1016/S1048-9843(99)00043-0

Consulting, B. (2010). Mapping the Creative Industries: A Toolkit. *Creative and Cultural Economy series, 2,* 1–33. https://www.britishcouncil.org/mapping_the_creative_industries_a_toolkit_2-2.pdf

COVID-19 Coronavirus Pandemic . (2020). WorldoMeters. https://www.worldometers.info/coronavirus/

Covid-19 in Iceland . (2020). Covid.com. https://www.covid.is/data

Cowling, M., & Taylor, M. (2001). Entreprenerurial Women and Men: Two Different Species? *Small Business Economics, 16*(3), 167–175. doi:10.1023/A:1011195516912

Craig, Clarke, F. L., & Amernic, J. H. (1999). Scholarship university business schools Cardinal Newman, Creeping corporatisation and farewell to the "disturber of the peace". *Accounting, Auditing & Accountability Journal, 12*(5), 510–524. doi:10.1108/09513579910298453

Crick, J. M. (2021). Qualitative research in marketing: What can academics do better? *Journal of Strategic Marketing, 29*(5), 390–429. doi:10.1080/0965254X.2020.1743738

Crnogaj, K., Rebernik, M., Hojnik, B. B., & Gomezelj, D. O. (2014). Building a model of researching the sustainable entrepreneurship in the tourism sector. *Kybernetes, 43*(3/4), 377–393. doi:10.1108/K-07-2013-0155

Croce, V. (2018). With growth comes accountability: could a leisure activity turn into a driver for sustainable growth? *Journal of Tourism Futures.*

Croce, V., & Maggi, R. (2007). From the ideal to the real destination: tourists' location choice for holiday experience. In T. Bieger & P. Keller (Eds.), *Productiveness in Tourism* (pp. 69–81). ESV.

Crouch, D., & Desforges, L. (2003). The sensuous in the tourist encounter: The power of the body in tourist studies. *Tourist Studies, 3*(1), 5–22. doi:10.1177/1468797603040528

Cunha, C., Kastenholz, E., & Carneiro, M. J. (2020). Entrepreneurs in rural tourism: Do lifestyle motivations contribute to management practices that enhance sustainable entrepreneurial ecosystems? *Journal of Hospitality and Tourism Management, 44,* 215–226. doi:10.1016/j.jhtm.2020.06.007

D W. (2022). *Ukraine calls Putin's passport plan 'criminal.* Deutsche Welle.

D'yakonova, I. I., Kravchuk, A. V., Sheliuk, A. A., & Haber, J.-E. (2020). Quantitative methods estimation of the competitiveness of insurance companies in the context of sustainable development. *Financial and Credit Activity Problems of Theory and Practice, 3*(34), 366–380. doi:10.18371/fcaptp.v3i34.215575

Dai, C., & Chiu, D. K. W. (2023). (in press). Impact of COVID-19 on reading behaviors and preferences: Investigating high school students and parents with the 5E instructional model. *Library Hi Tech.* doi:10.1108/LHT-10-2022-0472

Dale, B.G. (2003). Managing Quality.

209

Dana, L. P. (1999). The Social Cost of Tourism: A Case Study of Ios. *Cornell Hospitality Quarterly*, *40*(4), 60–63. doi:10.1177/001088049904000414

Dancin, M. T., Dancin, D. A., & Tracey, P. (2011). Social Entrepreneurship: A Critique and Future Directions. *Organization Science*, *22*(5), 1203–1213. doi:10.1287/orsc.1100.0620

Dathe, T., Dathe, R., Dathe, I., & Helmold, M. (2022). CSR as Part of the Corporate Strategy. In *Corporate Social Responsibility (CSR), Sustainability and Environmental Social Governance (ESG)* (pp. 1–22). Springer. doi:10.1007/978-3-030-92357-0_1

Davies, J., et al. (2001). Leadership in higher education. *Total Quality Management*, *12*(7 and 8), 1025-1030.

Davis, J. S., & Morais, D. B. (2004). Factions and enclaves: Small towns and socially unsustainable tourism development. *Journal of Travel Research*, *43*(1), 3–10. doi:10.1177/0047287504265501

Davis, K. (1973). The case for and against business assumption of social responsibilities. *Academy of Management Journal*, *16*(2), 312–322. doi:10.2307/255331

De la Garza Carranza, M. T., & Egri, C. (2010). Managerial cultural intelligence and small business in Canada. *Management Review*, *21*(3), 353–371. doi:10.1688/1861-9908_mrev_2010_03_dela-G

de Paulo, A. F., De Oliveira, S. V. W. B., & Porto, G. S. (2017). Mapping impacts of open innovation practices in a firm competitiveness. *Journal of Technology Management & Innovation*, *12*(3), 108–117. doi:10.4067/S0718-27242017000300011

Dees, J. G. (2001). *The meaning of social entrepreneurship, Comments and suggestions contributed from the*. Social Entrepreneurship Funders Working Group.

Dehter, M. (2002). Problema conocido, no es más problema. *Justo Ahora*. http://www.justoahora.com/nws/v15.htm#1

Del Solar, S. (2010). *Emprendedores en el aula. Guía para la formación en valores y habilidades sociales de docen-tes y jóvenes emprendedores*. Fondo Multilateral de Inversiones del Banco Interamericano de Desarrollo.

Deming, W.E. (1986). *Out of the Crisis*. Massachusetts Institute of Technology Centre for Advanced Engineering Study.

Deng, S., & Chiu, D. K. W. (2023). Analyzing Hong Kong Philharmonic Orchestra's Facebook community engagement with the Honeycomb Model. In M. Dennis & J. Halbert (Eds.), *Community engagement in the online space* (pp. 31–47). IGI. Global. doi:10.4018/978-1-6684-5190-8.ch003

Deng, W., Chin, G. Y.-l., Chiu, D. K. W., & Ho, K. K. W. (2022). (in press). Contribution of literature thematic exhibition to cultural education: A case study of Jin Yong's Gallery. *Micronesian Educators*, *32*.

Dewey, J. (1897). My Pedagogic Creed. *School Journal*, *54*(3), 77–80.

Diario Correo. (2014). Crece la demanda por gimnasios. *Diario Correo*. https://diariocorreo.pe

Diario Gestión. (2015). El emprendimiento en el Perú: De la necesidad a la oportunidad. *Diario Correo*.

Dill, D. (1995). Through Deming's Eyes A Cross-National Analysis of Quality Assurance Policies in Higher Education. *Quality in Higher Education*, *1*(2), 95–110. doi:10.1080/1353832950010202

Ding, S. J., Lam, E. T. H., Chiu, D. K. W., Lung, M. M., & Ho, K. K. W. (2021). Changes in reading behavior of periodicals on mobile devices: A comparative study. *Journal of Librarianship and Information Science*, *53*(2), 233–244. doi:10.1177/0961000620938119

Dodds, R., & Joppe, M. (2005). *CSR in the Tourism Industry?: The Status of and Potential for Certification, Codes of Conduct and Guidelines*. IFC.

Compilation of References

Dong, G., Chiu, D. K. W., Huang, P.-S., Lung, M. M., Ho, K. K. W., & Geng, Y. (2021). Relationships between research supervisors and students from coursework-based Master's degrees: Information usage under social media. *Information Discovery and Delivery*, *49*(4), 319–327. doi:10.1108/IDD-08-2020-0100

Downe-Wamboldt, B. (1992). Content analysis: Method, applications, and issues. *Health Care for Women International*, *13*(3), 313–321. doi:10.1080/07399339209516006 PMID:1399871

Drašković, B. and Džunić, M., (2020). *The Importance of Human Resources for Effective Implementation of Crisis Management Tools in Tourism and Hospitality Industry*. 5th International Thematic Monograph: Modern Management Tools and Economy of Tourism Sector in Present Era.

Drewer, P. (2005). *Key note market report plus, 2005: Hotels* (20th ed.). Key Note.

Duan, W., & Lei, N. (2014). Zhangjiatong Village, Tiantai, Zhejiang Province: Protection and renewal of traditional villages based on micro-intervention strategy. *Beijing Planning and Construction*, *2014*(5), 50–57.

Dunne, D. (2018). Implementing design thinking in organizations: An exploratory study. *Journal of Organization Design*, *7*(1), 16. doi:10.118641469-018-0040-7

Dym, C. L., Agogino, A. M., Eris, O., Frey, D. D., & Leifer, L. J. (2006). Engineering design thinking, teaching, and learning. *IEEE Engineering Management Review*, *34*(1), 65–90. doi:10.1109/EMR.2006.1679078

Dyrtr, Z. (2006). *Good business name* (1st ed.). Alfa Publishing.

Earley, P. C., & Peterson, R. S. (2004). The elusive cultural chameleon: Cultural intelligence as a new approach to intercultural training for the global manager. *Learning and Education*, *1*(1), 100–115. doi:10.5465/amle.2004.12436826

ECampusOntario, Virtual Learning Strategy (VLS), (2021) *Foresight Report: Lifelong Learning Empowering lifelong learners and creating opportunities for growth.* VLS Reports Outline.

Eduard, L. (1926). *The meaning of adult education.* New Republic.

Elsbach, K. D., & Stigliani, I. (2018). Design Thinking and Organizational Culture: A Review and Framework for Future Research. *Journal of Management*, *44*(6), 2274–2306. doi:10.1177/0149206317744252

Emmanuel, B., & Priscilla, O. A. (2022). A Review of Corporate Social Responsibility and Its Relationship with Customer Satisfaction and Corporate Image. *Open Journal of Business and Management*, *10*(2), 715–728. doi:10.4236/ojbm.2022.102040

Encarta. (2008). Lifelong learning. *Encarta.* http://encarta.msn.com/dictionary_561547417/lifelong_learning.html

Erkutlu, H. V., & Chafra, J. (2006). Relationship between leadership power bases and job stress of subordinates: Examples from boutique hotels. *Management Research News*, *29*(5), 285–297. doi:10.1108/01409170610674419

Escobar, A. L., López, R. R., Campos, A. M., & López-Felipe, T. (2020). Differences between women and men regarding the security measures required of the hotel sector to deal with COVID-19.

European Centre for Disease Prevention and Control (ECDC). (2020). *COVID-19 Situation update worldwide.* ECDC. https://www.ecdc.europa.eu/en/geographical-distribution-2019-ncov-cases [28/10/2020]

European University Association ASBL. (2021). *Meeting skills and employability demands: Thematic Peer Group Report. Learning & Teaching Paper #13. 12 Mar 2021. Report* (P. McSweeney & T. Zhang, Eds.).

Evans, C., & Lewis, J. (2018). *Analysing semi-structured interviews using thematic analysis: Exploring voluntary civic participation among adults.* SAGE Publications Limited.

Explainers, F. P. (2022). *Museums, memorials, and monuments under attack: The cultural catastrophe in Ukraine*. Firstpost.

Ezeamuzie, N.M., Rhim, A.H.R., Chiu, D.K.W., & Lung, M. M.-W. (2022). Exploring gender differences in foreign domestic helpers' mobile information usage. *Library Hi Tech*. doi:10.1108/LHT-07-2022-0350

Fatma, M., & Rahman, Z. (2015). Consumer perspective on CSR literature review and future research agenda. *Management Research Review*, *38*(2), 195–216. doi:10.1108/MRR-09-2013-0223

FCO (The Foreign & Commonwealth Office). (2020). *Foreign Secretary advises all British travelers to return to the UK now*. FCO. https://www.gov.uk/government/news/foreign-secretary-advises-all-british-travellers-to-return-to-the-uk-now [28/10/2020]

Feather, J. (2006). Managing the documentary heritage: issues from the present and future. *Preservation management for libraries, archives and museums*, 1-18.

Fennell, D. A. (2017). *Eco-Tourism* (4th ed.). Routledge.

Fletcher, R., Murray, I. M., Blázquez-Salom, M., & Asunción, B. R. (2020). Tourism, degrowth, and the COVID-19 Crisis. POLLEN *Ecology Network*. https://politicalecologynet-work.org/2020/03/24/tourism-degrowth-and-the-covid-19-crisis/ [18/10/2020]

Fletcher, R. (2014). Romancing the wild. In *Romancing the Wild*. Duke University Press.

Flick, U. (2006). *An introduction of qualitative research* (3rd ed.). Sage.

Flynn, B. B., Schroeber, R. C., & Sakakibaba, S. (1994). A framework for quality management research and an associated measurement instrument. *Journal of Operations Management*, *11*(4), 339–366. doi:10.1016/S0272-6963(97)90004-8

Font, X., & Lynes, J. (2018). Corporate social responsibility in tourism and hospitality. *Journal of Sustainable Tourism*, *26*(7), 1027–1042. doi:10.1080/09669582.2018.1488856

Foote, J., Gaffney, N., & Evans, J. R. (2010). Corporate social responsibility: Implications for performance excellence. *Total Quality Management*, *21*(8), 799–812. doi:10.1080/14783363.2010.487660

Formichella, M. M. (2004). *El concepto de emprendimiento y su relación con la educación, el empleo y el desarrollo local*. Tres Arroyos.

Fornet-Betancourt, R. (2005). Filosofía intercultural. In: Salas Astrain, Ricardo. (Coord.). (2005). Pensamiento crítico latinoamericano. Conceptos fundamentales. Ediciones Universidad católica Silva Henríquez (UCSH). (Chile).

Fornet-Betancourt, R. (2000). *Interculturalidad y globalización. Ejercicios de crítica filosófica intercultural en el contexto de la globalización*. DEI.

Fornet-Betancourt, R. (2009). *Tareas y propuestas de la filosofía intercultural*. Editorial Mainz.

Foster, J. J. (2003). Motywacja w miejscu pracy. In N. Chmiel (Ed.), *Psychologia Pracy I Organizacjii*. GWP.

Franchi, E. (2022). What is cultural. *Khan Academy. ICOMOS. (2002). International Cultural Tourism Charter. Principles And Guidelines for Managing Tourism at Places of Cultural and Heritage Significance*. ICOMOS International Cultural Tourism Committee. .

Franco, S., Caroli, M. G., Cappa, F., & Del Chiappa, G. (2020). Are you good enough? CSR, quality management and corporate financial performance in the hospitality industry. *International Journal of Hospitality Management*, *88*, 102395. doi:10.1016/j.ijhm.2019.102395

Freire, P. (1970). *Pedagogy of the oppressed*. Seabury Press.

Compilation of References

Freund de Klumbis, D., & Munsters, W. (2005). Developments in the hotel industry: design meets historic properties. In M. Sigala & D. Leslie (Eds.), *International Cultural Tourism*. Elsevier Butterworth Heinemann.

Frow, P., & Payne, A. (2011). A stakeholder perspective of the value proposition concept. *European Journal of Marketing, 45*(1), 223–240. doi:10.1108/03090561111095676

Fuguitt, G. V. (1965). The growth and decline of small towns as a probability process. *American Sociological Review, 30*(3), 403–411. doi:10.2307/2090721

Fyall, A., & Garrod, B. (1996). Sustainable heritage tourism: Achievable goal or elusive ideal? In M. Robinson, N. Evans, & P. Callaghan (Eds.), *Managing cultural resources for tourism* (pp. 50–76). British Education Publisher.

Gaddefors, J., & Cronsell, N. (2009). Returnees and Local Stakeholders Co-Producing the Entrepreneurial Region. *European Planning Studies, 17*(8), 1191–1203. doi:10.1080/09654310902981045

Gaither, N. (1996). *Production and Operations Management*. Duxbury Press.

Gander, J. (2018). Competing in the creative and cultural industries. In *Strategic Analysis* (pp. 9–28). Routledge. doi:10.4324/9781315644592-2

Gao, W., Lam, K. M., Chiu, D. K. W., & Ho, K. K. W. (2021). A big data analysis of the factors influencing Movie Box Office in China. In Z. Sun (Ed.), *Handbook of research on intelligent analytics with multi-industry applications* (pp. 232–249). IGI Global. doi:10.4018/978-1-7998-4963-6.ch011

Garay, L., & Font, X. (2012). Doing good to do well? Corporate social responsibility reasons, practices and impacts in small and medium accommodation enterprises. *International Journal of Hospitality Management, 31*(2), 329–337. doi:10.1016/j.ijhm.2011.04.013

García, A.M.; García, M.G. (2007). Diferencias culturales y comportamiento emprendedor... *Revista Europea de Dirección y Economía de la Empresa, 16*(4), 47-68.

Garrison, D. (1997). *Self-directed learning: toward a comprehensive model*. Academic Search Complete.

Garrison, D. R. (1997). Self directed learning: Toward a comprehensive model. *Adult Education Quarterly, 48*(1), 18–29. doi:10.1177/074171369704800103

Gartner, W. B. (1985). A conceptual framework for describing the phenomenon of new venture creation. *Academy of Management Review, 10*(4), 694–706. doi:10.2307/258039

Georgiadou, M. E. (1981). *Hotel Economics*. Papazisi.

Gerlach, A. (2003). Sustainable entrepreneurship and innovation, Centre for Sustainability Management, University of Lueneburg. In *Conference Proceedings of Conference Corporate Social Responsibility and Environmental Management* (pp. 1-10). Springer.

Getzner, M., Vik, M. L., Brendehaug, E., & Lane, B. (2014). Governance and management strategies in national parks: Implications for sustainable regional development. *International Journal of Sustainable Society, 6*(1-2), 82–101. doi:10.1504/IJSSOC.2014.057891

Ghaderi, M., Rigi, A., & Salimi, J. (2015). Investigation of present teaching performance assessment system problems and preposition of an appropriate model by technology: Sciences classrooms. *International Journal of Educational and Psychological Researches, 1*(2), 179–185. doi:10.4103/2395-2296.152257

Ghandour, A. (2019). Crafting a web-unique value proposition using the concept analysis technique. *Global Business and Economics Review, 21*(1), 14–25. doi:10.1504/GBER.2019.096853

Ghosh, R. N., & Siddique, M. A. B. (Eds.). (2017). *Tourism and economic development: Case studies from the Indian ocean region*. Routledge. doi:10.4324/9781315235981

Ghosh, S. (2020). Asymmetric impact of COVID-19 induced uncertainty on inbound Chinese tourists in Australia: Insights from nonlinear ARDL model. *Quantitative Finance and Economics*, *4*(2), 343–351. doi:10.3934/QFE.2020016

Giakoumis, I., & Pitas, I. (1998, May). Digital restoration of painting cracks. *Proceedings of the 1998 IEEE International Symposium on Circuits and Systems* (Cat. No. 98CH36187) (Vol. 4, pp. 269-272), IEEE.

Gil-Alana, L. A., & Huijbens, E. H. (2018). Tourism in Iceland: Persistence and seasonality. *Annals of Tourism Research*, *68*, 20–29. doi:10.1016/j.annals.2017.11.002

Gilliland, S. W., & Landis, R. S. (1992). Quality and quantity goals in a complex decision task: Strategies and outcomes. *The Journal of Applied Psychology*, *77*(5), 672–681. doi:10.1037/0021-9010.77.5.672

Glaesser, D. (2006). *Crisis management in the tourism industry*. Elsevier. doi:10.4324/9780080464596

Glaveli, N. (2020). Corporate social responsibility toward stakeholders and customer loyalty: Investigating the roles of trust and customer identification with the company. *Social Responsibility Journal*.

Goleman, D. (2005). *La Práctica de la Inteligencia Emocional*. 18va. Edición. Editorial

Gond, J. P., & Nyberg, D. (2017). Materializing power to recover corporate social responsibility. *Organization Studies*, *38*(8), 1127–1148. doi:10.1177/0170840616677630

Gong, J. Y., Schumann, F., Chiu, D. K. W., & Ho, K. K. W. (2017). Tourists' mobile information seeking behavior: An investigation on China's youth. [IJSSOE]. *International Journal of Systems and Service-Oriented Engineering*, *7*(1), 58–76. doi:10.4018/IJSSOE.2017010104

Goodman, L. A. (1961). Snowball sampling. *Annals of Mathematical Statistics*, *32*(1), 148–170. doi:10.1214/aoms/1177705148

Gössling, S., Ring, A., Dwyer, L., Andersson, A. C., & Hall, C. M. (2016). Optimizing or maximizing growth? A challenge for sustainable tourism. *Journal of Sustainable Tourism*, *24*(4), 527–548. doi:10.1080/09669582.2015.1085869

Gössling, S., Scott, D., & Hall, C. M. (2020). Pandemics, tourism and global change: A rapid assessment of COVID-19. *Journal of Sustainable Tourism*, *29*(10), 1–20.

Government of Iceland. (2020). Iceland implements Schengen and EU travel restrictions. Government of Iceland. https://www.government.is/diplomaticmissions/embassy-article/2020/03/20/Iceland- implements-Schengen-and-EU-travelrestrictions-/

Grapsas, N. (2003). Absurdities, acritics, radicals, historical elements. In D. Lekkas (ed.), Arts II Overview of Greek Music and Dance. Patras: E.A.P.

Gravetter, F. J., & Forzano, L. A. (2009). Research methods for the Behavioral Science. Wadsworth, Cengage Learning.

Grover, K. (2015). Online social networks and the self-directed learning experience during a health crisis. *International Journal of Self-Directed Learning*, *12*, 1–15.

Gursoy, D., Chi, C. G., & Dyer, P. (2010). Locals' attitudes toward mass and alternative tourism: The case of Sunshine Coast, Australia. *Journal of Travel Research*, *49*(3), 381–394. doi:10.1177/0047287509346853

Compilation of References

Guzzo, R. F., Abbott, J., & Lee, M. (2022). How CSR and well-being affect work-related outcomes: A hospitality industry perspective. *International Journal of Contemporary Hospitality Management, 34*(4), 1470–1490. doi:10.1108/IJCHM-06-2021-0754

Hagelborg, E. (2018). *CSR as a customer loyalty driver: Within the energy industry.* Semantic Scholar.

Hahn, T., Figge, F., Pinkse, J., & Preuss, L. (2018). A paradox perspective on corporate sustainability: Descriptive, instrumental, and normative aspects. *Journal of Business Ethics, 148*(2), 235–248. doi:10.100710551-017-3587-2

Hakim, L. (2020). COVID-19 and the Moment to Evaluate Tourism Euphoria, Indonesia. *Journal of Indonesian Tourism and Development Studies, 8*(2), 119–123. doi:10.21776/ub.jitode.2020.008.02.09

Hall, C. M. (2003). Politics and place: An analysis of power in tourism communities. In S. Singh, D. J. Timothy, & R. K. Dowling (Eds.), *Tourism in destination communities* (pp. 99–114). CABI. doi:10.1079/9780851996110.0099

Hall, C. M., Prayag, G., & Amore, A. (2018). *Tourism and resilience: Individual, organizational and destination perspectives.* Channelview.

Halpern, J. M., & Halpern, B. K. (1972). *A Serbian village in historical perspective.* Holt, Rinehart and Winston.

Hammer, M. R., Bennett, M. J., & Wiseman, R. L. (2003). *Measuring socio-intercultural sensitivity: The socio-intercultural development inventory.* International Inventory. *International Journal of Intercultural Relations, 27,* 421–443. doi:10.1016/S0147-1767(03)00032-4

Hanh, V. T. H. (2006). Canal-side highway in Ho Chi Minh City (HCMC), Vietnam – Issues of urban cultural conservation and tourism development. *GeoJournal, 66*(3), 165–186. doi:10.100710708-006-9024-1

Harmadyova, V. (1997). Occupational Mobility in the Transformation Process of Czech and Slovak Society, *Sociología, 29*(5), 505-536.

Harrington, H. J., & Trusko, B. (2017). *Maximizing Value Propositions to Increase Project Success Rates. Maximizing Value Propositions to Increase Project Success Rates.* Productivity Press. doi:10.1201/b16786

Harrison, J. S., & Wicks, A. C. (2013). Stakeholder theory, value, and firm performance. *Business Ethics Quarterly, 23*(1), 97–124. doi:10.5840/beq20132314

Harvey, L. (1995). Beyond TQM. *Quality in Higher Education, 1*(2), 123–146. doi:10.1080/1353832950010204

Hassan, A. (2012). The Value Proposition Concept in Marketing: How Customers Perceive the Value Delivered by Firms– A Study of Customer Perspectives on Supermarkets in Southampton in the United Kingdom. *International Journal of Marketing Studies, 4*(3). doi:10.5539/ijms.v4n3p68

Haven-Tang, C., & Jones, E. (2006). Using local food and drink to differentiate tourism destinations through a sense of place. *Journal of Culinary Science & Technology, 4*(4), 69–86. doi:10.1300/J385v04n04_07

Hayes, C., & Graham, Y. (2020). Understanding the building of professional identities with the LEGO® SERIOUS PLAY® method using situational mapping and analysis. Higher Education. *Skills and Work-Based Learning, 10*(1), 99–112. doi:10.1108/HESWBL-05-2019-0069

Hayton, J. C., George, G., & Zahra, S. A. (2002). National culture and entrepreneurship: A review of behavioral Research. *Entrepreneurship Theory and Practice, 26*(4), 33–52. doi:10.1177/104225870202600403

HCH. (Hellinic Chamber of Hotels 2019). *Boutique hotel Trademark: Regulation.* BLLC. http://www.boutique-hotel.gr

Heimstädt, M., & Friesike, S. (2021). The odd couple: Contrasting openness in innovation and science. Innovation. *Organization and Management, 23*(3), 425–438. doi:10.1080/14479338.2020.1837631

Hendl, J. (2016). *Kvalitativní výzkum* (1st ed.). Portál.

Herstein, R., Gilboa, S., Gamliel, E., Bergera, R., & Ali, A. (2018). The Role of Private Label Brands in Enhancing Service Satisfaction in the Hotel Industry: Comparing Luxury and Boutique Hotels. *Services Marketing Quarterly, 39*(2), 140–155. doi:10.1080/15332969.2018.1437250

Hesmondhalgh, David. (2008). *Cultural and Creative Industries*. Sage. . doi:10.4135/9781848608443.n26

He, Z., Chiu, D. K. W., & Ho, K. K. W. (2022). Weibo analysis on Chinese cultural knowledge for gaming. In Z. Sun (Ed.), *Handbook of research on foundations and applications of intelligent business analytics* (pp. 320–349). IGI Global. doi:10.4018/978-1-7998-9016-4.ch015

Higgins-Desbiolles, F. (2018). Sustainable tourism: Sustaining tourism or something more? *Tourism Management Perspectives, 25*, 157–160. doi:10.1016/j.tmp.2017.11.017

Higgins-Desbiolles, F. (2020). Socialising tourism for social and ecological justice after COVID-19. *Tourism Geographies, 22*(3), 610–623. doi:10.1080/14616688.2020.1757748

Higgs, P., Cunningham, S., & Bakhshi, H. (2008). Beyond the creative industries: Mapping the creative economy. *Nesta.* https://www.nesta.org.uk/publications/reports/assets/features/beyond_the_creative_industries

Hinterhuber, H. H. (2004). *Strategische Unternehmensführung: I. Strategisches Denken* (Vol. 7). Walter de Gruyter.

Hisrich, R., & Peters, M. (1992). *Entrepreneurship: starting, developing, and managing a new enterprise.* Irwin Publishing. doi:10.1002/jsc.4240040409

Hodgetts, R., & Kuratko, D. (2001). *Effective small business management.* Harcourt College Publishers.

Hoffman, A. J. (2018). The next phase of business sustainability. *Stanford Social Innovation Review, 16*(2), 34–39.

Hofstede, G. (2007) *Geert Hofstede Cultural Dimensions.* Hofstede. www.geert-hofstede.com

Hofstede, G. (2001). *Cultures and Organizations. Software of the Mind.* McGraw-Hill.

Holjevac, I. A. (1996). Total quality management for the hotel industry and tourism. *Tourism and Hospitality Management, 2*(1), 67–80. doi:10.20867/thm.2.1.8

Hollinshead, K. (1988). First-blush of the Longtime: The Market Development of Australia's Living Aboriginal Heritage. Tourism Research: Expanding Boundaries. In *Proceedings of the 19th annual conference of the Tourism Research Association*, Lake City: University of Utah.

Horner, S., & Swarbrooke, J. (2005). *Leisure marketing: a global perspective.* Butterworth-Heinemann.

Ho, S. K., & Wearn, K. (1995). A TQM Model for Higher education and training. *Training for Quality, 3*(2), 25–33. doi:10.1108/09684879510087503

House, R., Hanges, P., Javidan, M., & Dorfman, P. (2004). *Culture, Leadership and Organizations: the GLOBE Study of 62 Societies.* Sage Publications.

House, R., Javidan, M., Hanges, P., & Dorfman, P. (2002). Understanding cultures and implicit leadership theories across the globe: An introduction to project GLOBE. *Journal of World Business, 37*(1), 3–10. doi:10.1016/S1090-9516(01)00069-4

Compilation of References

Houston, D. (2008). Rethinking Quality and Improvement in Higher Education. *Quality Assurance in Education, 16*(1), 61–79. doi:10.1108/09684880810848413

Huang, A., De la Mora Velasco, E., Marsh, J., & Workman, H. (2021). COVID-19 and the future of work in the hospitality industry. *International Journal of Hospitality Management, 97*, 1–13. doi:10.1016/j.ijhm.2021.102986 PMID:34720330

Huang, P. S., Paulino, Y., So, S., Chiu, D. K. W., & Ho, K. K. W. (2021). Editorial - COVID-19 pandemic and health informatics (Part 1). *Library Hi Tech, 39*(3), 693–695. doi:10.1108/LHT-09-2021-324

Huang, P.-S., Paulino, Y. C., So, S., Chiu, D. K. W., & Ho, K. K. W. (2022). Guest editorial: COVID-19 pandemic and health informatics part 2. *Library Hi Tech, 40*(2), 281–285. doi:10.1108/LHT-04-2022-447

Huang, P.-S., Paulino, Y. C., So, S., Chiu, D. K. W., & Ho, K. K. W. (2023). Guest editorial: COVID-19 pandemic and health informatics part 3. *Library Hi Tech, 41*(1), 1–5.

Hu, B. (2012). Present situation and protection of traditional villages and their cultural relics in China. *Guangming Daily, 1*(15), 7.

Hudson, R. (2001). *Producing Places*. Guilford.

Hughes, M., Weaver, D., & Pforr, C. (2015). *The practice of sustainable tourism: resolving the paradox*. Routledge. doi:10.4324/9781315796154

Hussein, A. S., Hapsari, R. D. V., & Yulianti, I. (2018). Experience quality and hotel boutique customer loyalty: Mediating role of hotel image and perceived value. *Journal of Quality Assurance in Hospitality & Tourism, 19*(4), 442–459. doi:10.1080/1528008X.2018.1429981

Hutasuhut, I., Adruce, S., A., Z. and Jonathan, V. (2020). How a learning organization cultivates self-directed learning. *Journal of Workplace Learning, 33*(5), 334-347

Ibrahim, N., & Masud, A. (2016). Moderating role of entrepreneurial orientation on the relationship between *entrepreneurial skills, environmental factors and entrepreneurial intention: A pls approach. Management Science Letters, 6*(3), 225–236. doi:10.5267/j.msl.2016.1.005

ICOM. (2022). *ICOM Call for Donations to Support Museums and Museum Professionals in Ukraine*. ICOM.

INEI. (2017). *Censos 2017*. Instituto Nacional de Estadística e Informática. www.censos2017.inei.gob.pe/red atam/

Innocenti, N., & Lazzeretti, L. (2019). Do the creative industries support growth and innovation in the wider economy? Industry relatedness and employment growth in Italy. *Industry and Innovation, 26*(10), 1152–1173. doi:10.1080/1366 2716.2018.1561360

International Council of Museums. (n.d.) *Κώδικας Δεοντολογίας του ICOM για τα Μουσεία. ΔΙΕΘΝΕΣ ΣΥΜΒΟΥΛΙΟ ΜΟΥΣΕΙΩΝ ΕΛΛΗΝΙΚΟ ΤΜΗΜΑ*. ICM. http://icom-greece.mini.icom.museum/wp- content/uploads/sites/38/2018/12/code-of-ethics_GR_01.pdf

Ioannides, D., & Debbage, K. (1997). Post-fordism and flexibility: The travel industry polyglot. *Tourism Management, 18*(4), 229–241. doi:10.1016/S0261-5177(97)00019-8

Ioannides, D., & Gyimóthy, S. (2020). The COVID-19 crisis as an opportunity for escaping the unsustainable global tourism path. *Tourism Geographies, 22*(3), 624–632. doi:10.1080/14616688.2020.1763445

Islam, T., Islam, R., Pitafi, A. H., Xiaobei, L., Rehmani, M., Irfan, M., & Mubarak, M. S. (2021). The impact of corporate social responsibility on customer loyalty: The mediating role of corporate reputation, customer satisfaction, and trust. *Sustainable Production and Consumption, 25*, 123–135. doi:10.1016/j.spc.2020.07.019

217

Jackson, M. N., Meade, M. A., & Ellenbogen, P. B. K. (2006). Perspectives on networking, cultural values, and skills among African American men with spinal cord injuries: A reconsideration of social capital theory. *Journal of Vocational Rehabilitation, 25*, 21–33.

Jaén, I., & Fernandez-Serrano, J. & Liñan Francisco. (2013). Valores culturales, nivel de ingresos y actividad emprendedora. *Revista de Economía Mundial, 35*, 35–52.

Jamal, T., & Getz, D. (1999). Community roundtables for tourism-related conflicts: The dialetics of consensus and process structures. *Journal of Sustainable Tourism, 7*(3&4), 290–313. doi:10.1080/09669589908667341

Jana, A., & Chandra, B. (2016). Mediating role of customer satisfaction in the mid market hotels: An empirical analysis. *Indian Journal of Science and Technology, 9*(1), 1–16. doi:10.17485/ijst/2016/v9i1/81973

Jeffrey, B., & Troman, G. (2011). The construction of performative identities. *European Educational Research Journal, 10*(4), 484–501. doi:10.2304/eerj.2011.10.4.484

Jiang, L. (2012). *Study on the gains and losses of the early eco-museum and its continuation in China* [Master's thesis]. Chongqing Normal University.

Jiang, T., Lo, P., Cheuk, M. K., Chiu, D. K. W., Chu, M. Y., Zhang, X., Zhou, Q., Liu, Q., Tang, J., Zhang, X., Sun, X., Ye, Z., Yang, M., & Lam, S. K. (2019). 文化新語:兩岸四地傑出圖書館、檔案館及博物館傑出工作者訪談 (New Cultural Dialog: Interviews with Outstanding Librarians, Archivists, and Curators in Greater China). Hong Kong: Systech publications.

Jiang, X., Chiu, D. K. W., & Chan, C. T. (2023). Application of the AIDA model in social media promotion and community engagement for small cultural organizations: A case study of the Choi Chang Sau Qin Society. In M. Dennis & J. Halbert (Eds.), *Community engagement in the online space* (pp. 48–70). IGI Global. doi:10.4018/978-1-6684-5190-8.ch004

Jiricka-Pürrer, A., Brandenburg, C., & Pröbstl-Haider, U. (2020). City tourism pre-and post-covid-19 pandemic–Messages to take home for climate change adaptation and mitigation? *Journal of Outdoor Recreation and Tourism, 31*(1), 1–6. doi:10.1016/j.jort.2020.100329

Jóhanesson, G. T., & Huijbens, E. H. (2010). Tourism in times of crisis: Exploring the discourse of tourism development in Iceland. *Current Issues in Tourism, 13*(5), 419–434. doi:10.1080/13683500.2010.491897

Johannot-Gradis, C. (2015). Protecting the past for the future: How does law protect tangible and intangible cultural heritage in armed conflict? *International Review of the Red Cross, 97*(900), 1253–1275. doi:10.1017/S1816383115000879

Johnson Tew, P., Lu, Z., Tolomiczenko, G., & Gellatly, J. (2008). SARS: Lessons in strategic planning for hoteliers and destination marketers. *International Journal of Contemporary Hospitality Management, 20*(3), 332–346. doi:10.1108/09596110810866145

Johnstone, H., & Lionais, D. (2004). Depleted Communities and Community Business Entrepreneurship: Revaluing Space Through Place. *Entrepreneurship and Regional Development, 16*(3), 217–233. doi:10.1080/0898562042000197117

Jones, K. B. (2012). The transformation of the digital museum. In P. F. Marty & K. Jones (Eds.), *Museum informatics* (pp. 25–42). Routledge.

Jones, L. D., Day, J., & Quadri-Felitti, D. (2013). Emerging definitions of boutique and lifestyle hotels: A delphi study. *Journal of Travel & Tourism Marketing, 30*(7), 715–731. doi:10.1080/10548408.2013.827549

Judd, D. R. (2006). Commentary: Tracing the commodity chain of global tourism. *Tourism Geographies, 8*(4), 323–336. doi:10.1080/14616680600921932

Compilation of References

Jugănaru, I. D. (2020). Mass Tourism during the Coexistence with the New Coronavirus. The Predictable Evolution of the Seaside Tourism in Romania. Ovidius University Annals. *Series Economic Sciences*, *20*(1), 171–179.

Juran, J. M., & Gryna, F. M. (1993). *Quality Planning and Analysis: From Product Development through Use*. McGraw-Hill.

Kadir, S. A., Jamaludin, M., & Awang, A. R. (2019). Accessibility Adaptation in Heritage Boutique Hotels: A review on literature. *Environment-Behaviour Proceedings Journal*, *4*(10), 103–108. doi:10.21834/e-bpj.v4i10.1633

Kallimopoulou, E. (2009). *Paradosiaka Music, Meaning and Indetity in Modern Greece*. Ashgate Publishing.

Kaplan, R. (2015). Who has been regulating whom, business or society? The mid-20th-century institutionalization of 'corporate responsibility' in the USA. *Socio-economic Review*, *13*(1), 125–155. doi:10.1093er/mwu031

Karia, N., & Asaari, M. H. A. H. (2006). The effects of total quality management practices on empoyees' work-related attitudes. *The TQM Magazine*, *18*(1), 30–43. doi:10.1108/09544780610637677

Kasworm, C. E. (1983). An examination of self-directed contract learning as an instructional strategy. *Innovative Higher Education*, *8*(1), 45–54. doi:10.1007/BF00889559

Kavoura, A., & Sahinidis, A. G. (2015). Communicating corporate social responsibility activities in Greece in a period of a prolonged economic crisis. *Procedia: Social and Behavioral Sciences*, *175*, 496–502. doi:10.1016/j.sbspro.2015.01.1228

Khan, M. A., Yasir, M., & Khan, M. A. (2021). Factors Affecting Customer Loyalty in the Services Sector. *Journal of Tourism and Services*, *12*(22), 184–197. doi:10.29036/jots.v12i22.257

Khan, Y. K., & Arshad, A. S. M. (2019). Innovation Ecosystem in the Small and Medium Enterprises. *Journal of Management Info*, *6*(1), 51–54. doi:10.31580/jmi.v6i1.461

Khosravi, S., Malek, A., & Ekiz, E. (2014). Why Tourists are Attracted to Boutique Hotels: Case of Penang Island, Malaysia. *Journal of Hospitality and Tourism*, *12*(1), 26–41.

Kim, M., Yin, X., & Lee, G. (2020). The effect of CSR on corporate image, customer citizenship behaviors, and customers' long-term relationship orientation. *International Journal of Hospitality Management*, *88*, 102520. doi:10.1016/j.ijhm.2020.102520

King, T. F., Hickman, P. P., & Berg, G. (1977). *Anthropology in historic preservation: Caring for culture's clutter*. Academic Press.

Knowles, M. S. (1968). Andragogy, not pedagogy. *Adult Leadership, 16*(10), 350–352, 386.

Knowles, M. (1980). *The modern practice of adult education: Andragogy versus pedagogy*. Cambridge Adult Education.

Knowles, M. S. (1975). *Self-Directed Learning: A Guide for Learners and Teachers*. Cambridge Books.

Knowles, M. S. (1984). *Andragogy in action: Applying modern principles of adult learning*. Jossey-Bass Publishers.

Knowles, M. S. (1984). *The adult learner: A neglected species*. Gulf Publishing.

Knowles, M. S. (1989). *The making of an adult educator*. Jossey-Bass.

Knowles, M. S., Elwood, R., Holton, R. III, & Swanson, A. (1998). *The Adult Learner: The Definitive Classic in Adult Education and Human Resource Development* (5th ed.). Heinemann.

Kokkosis, C. & Tsartas, P. (2001), Sustainable tourism development and environment. *Athens: Review*

Kolb, D. A., & Fry, R. (1975). Toward an applied theory of experiential learning. In C. Cooper (Ed.), *Studies of group process* (pp. 33–57). Wiley.

Komarova, I. P., & Ustyuzhanin, V. L. (2017). Problems of companies' sustainable competitiveness. *Espacios, 38*(62).

Konstantinides, D. (2021). *Comparative approach to the evaluation of secondary school teachers with elements and influences from the private sector.* Neapolis University Pafos.

Konstantinides, D. D., & Reppa, A. (2021). Adopting an approach of entrepreneurial excellence to teacher evaluation in Greece and Cyprus during the first twenty years of the 21st century. *Educational Cycle, 9*(2), 49–65.

Konstantinides-Vladimirou, K. (2013). *Mid-career teacher motivation and implications for leadership practices in secondary schools in Cyprus.* University of Nottingham: School of Education.

Konstantinides-Vladimirou, K. (2015). Cypriot secondary school teachers' professional life phases: A research-informed view of career-long motivation. *International Journal of Multidisciplinary Comparative Studies, 2*(1-3), 33–55.

Kontis, A. P., & Gkoumas, A. (2017). "Greek Breakfast": A New Tourism Brand Name for an Age-Long Gastronomy Tradition. In A. Kavoura, P. Sakas, & P. Tomaras (Eds.), *Strategic Innovative Marketing: 5th IC-SIM, Athens, Greece 2016* (pp. 235–244). Springer. doi:10.1007/978-3-319-56288-9_32

Kou, H., & Zhang, S. (2015). Changes in the protection of traditional villages under the background of new rural construction. *Chinese Cultural Heritage, 2015*(001), 12–17.

Koutiva, M., Belias, D., Flabouras, I., & Koustelios, A. (2019). The Effects of Workplace Well-being on Individual"s Knowledge Creation Outcomes. A Study Research among Hotel Employees. *International Conference on Strategic Innovative Marketing and Tourism.* Springer.

Koutiva, M., Belias, D., Flabouras, I., & Koustelios, A. (2019). The Effects of Workplace Well-being on Individuals Knowledge Creation Outcomes. A Study Research among Hotel Employees. *International Conference on Strategic Innovative Marketing and Tourism.* Springer.

Koutiva, M., Belias, D., Nietos, I. F., & Koustelios, A. (2020). The Effects of Workplace Well-Being on Individual's Knowledge Creation Outcomes: A Study Research Among Hotel Employees. In A. Kavoura, E. Kefallonitis, & P. Theodoridis (Eds.), *Strategic Innovative Marketing and Tourism. Springer Proceedings in Business and Economics.* Springer. doi:10.1007/978-3-030-36126-6_118

Kranawetleitner, T., Krebs, H., Kuhn, N., & Menner, M. (2020). Needs Analyses with LEGO® SERIOUS PLAY®. In Lecture Notes in Computer Science (including subseries Lecture Notes in Artificial Intelligence and Lecture Notes in Bioinformatics) (pp. 99–104). Springer Science and Business Media Deutschland GmbH. doi:10.1007/978-3-030-61814-8_8

Kulenović, M., Folta, M., & Veselinović, L. (2021). The Analysis of Total Quality Management Critical Success Factors. *Quality Innovation Prosperity, 25*(1), 88–102. doi:10.12776/qip.v25i1.1514

Kumar, D. (2020). Corona Virus: A Review of COVID-19. *Eurasian Journal of Medicine and Oncology, 4*(6), 15–23.

Kumar, R., & Mishra, R. (2020). Linking TQM Critical Success Factors to strategic goal: Impact on Organizational Performance. *Journal of Mechanical and Civil Engineering, 17*(3), 1–13.

Kusluvan, S. (2003). *Managing employee attitudes and behaviors in the tourism and hospitality industry.* Nova Science Publishers, Inc.

Kuzminsky, S. C., & Gardiner, M. S. (2012). Three-dimensional laser scanning: Potential uses for museum conservation and scientific research. *Journal of Archaeological Science, 39*(8), 2744–2751. doi:10.1016/j.jas.2012.04.020

Compilation of References

Lachman, R. (1980). Toward measurement of entrepreneurial tendencies. *Management International Review*, 108–116.

Lai, Y. L., & Cai, W. (2022). Enhancing post-COVID-19 work resilience in hospitality: A micro-level crisis management framework. Sage. https://journals.sagepub.com/doi/pdf/10.1177/14673584221075182

Lam, A. H. C., Ho, K. K. W., & Chiu, D. K. W. (2023). Instagram for student learning and library promotions? A quantitative study using the 5E Instructional Model. *Aslib Journal of Information Management*, 75(1), 112–130. doi:10.1108/AJIM-12-2021-0389

Lane, B. (2005). Sustainable rural tourism strategies: A tool for development and conservation. *Revista Interamericana de Ambiente y Turismo-RIAT*, 1(1), 12–18.

Lashua, B., Spracklen, K., & Long, P. (2014). Introduction to the special issue: Music and Tourism. *Tourist Studies*, 14(1), 3–9. doi:10.1177/1468797613511682

Latif, K. F., Pérez, A., & Sahibzada, U. F. (2020). Corporate social responsibility (CSR) and customer loyalty in the hotel industry: A cross-country study. *International Journal of Hospitality Management*, 89, 102565. doi:10.1016/j.ijhm.2020.102565

Lau, K. P., Chiu, D. K., Ho, K. K., Lo, P., & See-To, E. W. (2017). Educational usage of mobile devices: Differences between postgraduate and undergraduate students. *Journal of Academic Librarianship*, 43(3), 201–208. doi:10.1016/j.acalib.2017.03.004

Lau, K. S. N., Lo, P., Chiu, D. K. W., Ho, K. K. W., Jiang, T., Zhou, Q., Percy, P., & Allard, B. (2020). Library, learning, and recreational experiences turned mobile: A comparative study between LIS and non-LIS students. *Journal of Academic Librarianship*, 46(2), 102103. doi:10.1016/j.acalib.2019.102103

Lau, R. S. M., & Anderson, C. A. (1998). A three-dimensional perspective of total quality management. *International Journal of Quality & Reliability Management*, 15(1), 85–98. doi:10.1108/02656719810199277

Lawrence, S., & Sharma, U. (2002). Commodification of education and academic labour: Using the balanced scorecard in a university setting. *Critical Perspectives on Accounting*, 13(5-6), 661–677. doi:10.1006/cpac.2002.0562

Laws, E. (1995). *Tourist destination management: Issues, analysis and policies*. Routledge.

Laws, E., Prideaux, B., & Chon, K. S. (2007). *Crisis management in tourism*. Cabi., doi:10.1079/9781845930479.0000

Lazzeretti, L., Boix, R., & Capone, F. (2008). Do creative industries cluster? Mapping creative local production systems in Italy and Spain. *Industry and Innovation*, 15(5), 549–567. doi:10.1080/13662710802374161

Le, D., & Phi, G. (2021). Strategic responses of the hotel sector to COVID-19: Toward a refined pandemic crisis management framework. *International Journal of Hospitality Management*, 94, 102808. doi:10.1016/j.ijhm.2020.102808 PMID:34785839

Lee D Y and Tsang E W K. (2001). The Effect of Entrepreneur Personality, Background and Network Activities on Venture Growth, *Journal of Management Studies, 38*(4), pp 583-602.

Lee, G. O. M., & Warner, M. (2005). Epidemics, labour markets and unemployment: The impact of SARS on human resource management in the Hong Kong service sector. *International Journal of Human Resource Management*, 16(5), 752–771. doi:10.1080/09585190500083202

Legge, K. (1995). *Human resource management: Rhetorics and realities*. Macmillan Press LTD. doi:10.1007/978-1-349-24156-9

Lekkas, D. (2003). Theories of Greek traditional music. In D. Lekkas (Ed.), *Arts II Overview of Greek Music and Dance* (Vol. III, pp. 151–346). EAP.

Lema, J. (2009). Continuous learning: A competitive advantage for the tourism industry. *International Journal of Tourism and Travel, 2*(2), 16-30.

Leung, K., Ang, S., & Tan, L. (2014). Intercultural competence. *Annual Review of Organizational Psychology and Organizational Behavior, 1*(1), 489–519. doi:10.1146/annurev-orgpsych-031413-091229

Levenson, H. (1974). Activism and powerful others: Distinctions within the concept of internal-external control. Journal of Personality Assessment, 38 (4), Light, P.C. (2009). Social entrepreneurship revisited. *Stanford Social Innovation Review, 7*(3), 21–22.

Lew, A. (2020). How to create a better post-COVID-19 World. *Medium.* https://medium.com/new-earth-consciousness/creating-a-better-post-covid-19-world-36b2b3e8a7ae

Liang, T. C., & Wong, E. S. F. (2020). Sustainable development: An adaptive re-use solution for the hospitality industry. *Worldwide Hospitality and Tourism Themes, 12*(5), 623–637. doi:10.1108/WHATT-06-2020-0047

Lifestyle Desk. (2022). *Who is Maria Prymachenko, the Ukrainian artist whose artworks were nearly destroyed at a museum.* The Indian Express.

Lim, W. M., & Endean, M. (2009). Elucidating the aesthetic and operational characteristics of UK boutique hotels. *International Journal of Contemporary Hospitality Management, 21*(1), 38–51. doi:10.1108/09596110910930179

Lin, T., & De Guzman, F. D. (2007). *Tourism for pro-poor and sustainable growth: Economic analysis of tourism projects.* Asian Development Bank.

Linca, A. C., Stanciulescu, G. C. J., & Bulin, D. (2013). The importance of niche tourism in sustainable development. *Calitatea, 14*(2), 385.

Li, S., Chiu, D. K. W., & Ho, K. K. W. (2023). Social media analytics for non-governmental organizations: A case study of Hong Kong Next Generation Arts. In Z. Sun (Ed.), *Driving socioeconomic development with big data: Theories, technologies, and applications* (pp. 277–295). IGI Global.

Lisi, D. & Malo, M. A. (2017). The impact of temporary employment on productivity. The importance of sectors' skill intensity. *Journal for Labour Market Research, 50,* 258–271.

Liu, M. T., Liu, Y., Mo, Z., Zhao, Z., & Zhu, Z. (2019). How CSR influences customer behavioural loyalty in the Chinese hotel industry. *Asia Pacific Journal of Marketing and Logistics, 32*(1), 1–22. doi:10.1108/APJML-04-2018-0160

Liu, Y., Chiu, D. K. W., & Ho, K. K. W. (2023). Short-form videos for public library marketing: Performance Analytics of Douyin in China. *Applied Sciences (Basel, Switzerland), 13*(6), 3386. Advance online publication. doi:10.3390/app13063386

Liu, Z. (2003). Sustainable tourism development: A critique. *Journal of Sustainable Tourism, 11*(6), 459–475. doi:10.1080/09669580308667216

Li, Y., Pinto, M. C. B., & Diabat, A. (2020). Analyzing the critical success factor of CSR for the Chinese textile industry. *Journal of Cleaner Production, 260,* 120878. doi:10.1016/j.jclepro.2020.120878

Locke, E. A., & Latham, G. P. (1990). *A theory of goal setting and task performance.* Prentice-Hall, Inc.

Locke, E. A., & Latham, G. P. (2006). *New Directions in Goal setting. Current directions in psychological science.* SAGE Publications.

Compilation of References

Loots, E., Neiva, M., Carvalho, L., & Lavanga, M. (2021). The entrepreneurial ecosystem of cultural and creative industries in Porto: A sub-ecosystem approach. In *Growth and Change* (Vol. 52, pp. 641–662). John Wiley and Sons Inc., doi:10.1111/grow.12434

Lo, P., Chan, H. H. Y., Tang, A. W. M., Chiu, D. K. W., Cho, A., Ho, K. K. W., See-To, E., He, J., Kenderdine, S., & Shaw, J. (2019). Visualising and revitalising traditional Chinese martial arts – Visitors' engagement and learning experience at the 300 years of Hakka KungFu. *Library Hi Tech*, *37*(2), 273–292. doi:10.1108/LHT-05-2018-0071

Lo, P., Hsu, W.-E., Wu, S. H. S., Travis, J., & Chiu, D. K. W. (2021). *Creating a global cultural city via public participation in the Arts: Conversations with Hong Kong's leading arts and cultural administrators*. Nova Science Publishers.

Loureiro, S. M. C., Rita, P., & Sarmento, E. M. (2020). What is the core essence of small city boutique hotels? *International Journal of Culture, Tourism and Hospitality Research*, *14*(1), 44–62. doi:10.1108/IJCTHR-01-2019-0007

Ludvigsen, J. A. L., & Hayton, J. W. (2020). Toward COVID-19 secure events: Considerations for organizing the safe resumption of major sporting events. *Managing Sport and Leisure*, *25*(6), 1–11.

Luo, X., & Bhattacharya, C. B. (2006). Corporate social responsibility, customer satisfaction, and market value. *Journal of Marketing*, *70*(4), 1–18. doi:10.1509/jmkg.70.4.001

Lynch, K. (2014). New managerialism: The impact on education. *Concept*, *5*(3), 1–11.

MacNaghten, P., & Urry, J. (2000). Bodies of nature. *Body & Society*, *6*(3/4), 1–16. doi:10.1177/1357034X00006003001

Madanat, H., & Khasawneh, G. (2017). Impact of total quality management implementation on effectiveness of human resource management in the jordanian banking sector from employee's perspective. *Academic Strategy Management Journal*, *16*, 114–148.

Mäe, R. (2016). The Creative Industries: A discourse-theoretical approach. *International Review of Social Research*, *5*(2), 78–87. doi:10.1515/irsr-2015-0007

Mahdad, M., De Marco, C. E., Piccaluga, A., & Di Minin, A. (2020). Harnessing adaptive capacity to close the pandora's box of open innovation. *Industry and Innovation*, *27*(3), 264–284. doi:10.1080/13662716.2019.1633910

Mahjabeen, Z., Shresha, K. K., & Dee, J. A. (2009). Rethinking community participation in urban planning: The role of disadvantaged groups in Sydney metropolitan strategy. *Australasian Journal of Regional Studies*, *15*(1), 45–63.

Mair, J., & Martí, I. (2006). Social entrepreneurship research: A source of explanations, prediction, and delight. *Journal of World Business*, *41*(1), 36–44. doi:10.1016/j.jwb.2005.09.002

Mak, M. Y. C., Poon, A. Y. M., & Chiu, D. K. W. (2022). Using social media as learning aids and preservation: Chinese martial arts in Hong Kong. In S. Papadakis & A. Kapaniaris (Eds.), *The digital folklore of cyberculture and digital humanities* (pp. 171–185). IGI Global. doi:10.4018/978-1-6684-4461-0.ch010

Malcheva, M. (2018). Competitive advantages of boutique hotels in the context of a sharing economy. *ИзвестиянаСъюзанаучените- Варна. СерияИкономическинауки*, *7*(3), 71–83.

Maldonado, K. (2007). La socio-interculturalidad de los negocios internacionales Universidad del Rosario. *Empresa, Bogotá (Colombia)*, *6*(12), 261–291.

Mallapaty, S. (2020). What the cruise-ship outbreaks reveal about COVID-19. *Nature*, *580*(7801), 18–28. doi:10.1038/d41586-020-00885-w PMID:32218546

Mann, R. S. (1992). *The development of a framework to assist in the implementation of TQM*. [PhD Thesis, University of Liverpool, UK].

Mann, R. H., Clift, B. C., Boykoff, J., & Bekker, S. (2020). Athletes as community; athletes in community: Covid-19, sporting mega-events and athlete health protection. *British Journal of Sports Medicine, 54*(18), 1071–1072. doi:10.1136/bjsports-2020-102433 PMID:32303522

Marchington, M., & Wilkinson, A. (2005). *Human resource management at work. People management and development* (3rd ed.). Chartered Institute of Personnel and Development.

Maroudas, L., Kyriakidou, O. & Vacharis, A. (2008). *Employees' motivation in the luxury hotel industry: the perceived effectiveness of human-resource practices.* Taylor and Francis.

Marshal, R., & Tucker, M. (1992). *Thinking for a living.* Basic Books.

Martínez, P., & Del Bosque, I. R. (2013). CSR and customer loyalty: The roles of trust, customer identification with the company and satisfaction. *International Journal of Hospitality Management, 35,* 89–99. doi:10.1016/j.ijhm.2013.05.009

Martin, J. N., & Nakayama, T. K. (2010). *Intercultural Communication in Contexts* (5th ed.). McGraw-Hill.

Martin, R. L., & Osberg, S. (2007). Social entrepreneurship: The case for definition. *Stanford Social Innovation Review, 5*(2), 27–39.

Marty, P. F. (2010). Museum informatics. In Encyclopedia of library and information sciences (3rd ed., pp. 3717-3725).

Masouras, A., Komodromos, I., & Papademetriou, C. (2019). Cyprus's wine market: Influencing factors of consumer behaviour as part of destination marketing. In Strategic Innovative Marketing and Tourism: 7th ICSIMAT, (pp. 637-644). Springer International Publishing.

Masouras, A. (2019). *Entrepreneurship in Small and Medium-Sized Enterprises.* Nova Science Publishers.

Matiza, V. M. (2020). The Role of Creative Industries in Economic Development: The Human Factor Development Approach. *African Journal of Inter/Multidisciplinary Studies, 2*(1), 50–61. doi:10.51415/ajims.v2i1.833

Mayer, H., Habersetzer, A., & Meili, R. (2016). Rural–urban linkages and sustainable regional development: The role of entrepreneurs in linking peripheries and centers. *Sustainability, 8*(8), 745. doi:10.3390u8080745

McClelland, D. (1971). *The achievement Motive in Economic Growth Entrepreneurship and economic development.* P. Kilby.

McCool, S. (2009). Constructing partnerships for protected area tourism planning in an era of change and messiness. *Journal of Sustainable Tourism, 17*(2), 133–148. doi:10.1080/09669580802495733

McCusker, S. (2020). Everybody's monkey is important: LEGO® Serious Play® as a methodology for enabling equality of voice within diverse groups. *International Journal of Research & Method in Education, 43*(2), 146–162. doi:10.108 0/1743727X.2019.1621831

McDonald, L. M., & Rundle-Thiele, S. (2008). Corporate social responsibility and bank customer satisfaction: A research agenda. *International Journal of Bank Marketing, 26*(3), 170–182. doi:10.1108/02652320810864643

McGlone, P. (2022). A lab in rural Virginia is racing to preserve Ukraine's cultural heritage. *Washington Post.*

Mcgrath, V. (2009). Reviewing the Evidence on How Adult Students Learn: An Examination of Knowles' Model of Andragogy. *Adult Learner: The Irish Journal of Adult and Community Education,* p 99-110.

McNeill, D. (2009). The airport hotel as business space. *Geografiska Annaler. Series B, Human Geography, 91*(3), 219–228. doi:10.1111/j.1468-0467.2009.00316.x

Compilation of References

Meho, L. I. (2006). E-mail interviewing in qualitative research: A methodological discussion. *Journal of the American Society for Information Science and Technology, 57*(10), 1284–1295. doi:10.1002/asi.20416

Mergen, E., & Stevenson, W. (2002). Sowing the seeds of quality: Quality at the source. *Total Quality Management, 13*(7), 1015–1020. doi:10.1080/0954412022000017085

Merriam, S. B., & Bierema, L. L. (2013). *Adult Learning: Linking Theory and Practice.* Jossey-Bass, John Wiley and Sons.

Merriam, S. B., Caffarella, R., & Baumgartner, L. (2007). *Learning in Adulthood: A Comprehensive Guide.* Jossey-Bass Publishers.

Metaxas, T., & Tsavdaridou, M. (2010). Corporate social responsibility in europe: Denmark, Hungary and Greece. *Journal of Contemporary European Studies, 18*(1), 25–46. doi:10.1080/14782801003638679

Meuser, T., Gugliucci, M., & Weaver, S. (2020). *Intergenerational Learning in Higher Education.* The Evolllution. https:// evolllution.com/attracting-students/todays_learner/intergenerational-learning-in-higher-education/

Mezirow, J. (1978). Perspective Transformation. *Adult Education Quarterly, 28*(2), 100–110. doi:10.1177/074171367802800202

Middleton, A., Gunn, J., Bassilios, B., & Pirkis, J. (2014). Systematic review of research into frequent callers to crisis helplines. *Journal of Telemedicine and Telecare, 20*(2), 89–98. doi:10.1177/1357633X14524156 PMID:24518928

Middleton, V. T., Fyall, A., Morgan, M., & Ranchhod, A. (2009). *Marketing in travel and tourism.* Routledge.

Middleton, V. T., & Hawkins, R. (1998). *Sustainable tourism: A marketing perspective.* Butterworth-Heinemann.

Milakovich, M. E. (1995). *Improving Service Quality.* Lucie Press.

Mirzapour, M., Toutian, S. S., Mehrara, A., & Khorrampour, S. (2019). The strategic role of human resource management in crisis management considering the mediating role of organizational culture. *International Journal of Human Capital in Urban Management, 4*(1), 43–50.

Mitchell, R. K., Busenitz, L. W., Bird, B., Marie Gaglio, C., Mcmullen, J. S., Morse, E. A., & Smith, J. B. (2007). The central question in entrepreneurial cognition research 2007. *Entrepreneurship Theory and Practice, 31*(1), 1–27. doi:10.1111/j.1540-6520.2007.00161.x

Mitchell, R. K., Smith, B., Seawright, K. W., & Morse, E. A. (2000). Cross-cultural cognitions and the venture creation decision. *Academy of Management Journal, 43*(5), 974–993. doi:10.2307/1556422

MOEC - Ministry of Education, Culture, Sport, and Youth (2019). *New system of teacher evaluation.* MOEC.

Mohammed, A., & Rashid, B. (2018). A conceptual model of corporate social responsibility dimensions, brand image, and customer satisfaction in Malaysian hotel industry. *Kasetsart Journal of Social Sciences, 39*(2), 358–364. doi:10.1016/j.kjss.2018.04.001

Mohanty, R. P., & Behera, A. K. (1996). TQM in the service sector. *Work Study, 45*, 13–17.

Mondal, M., & Haque, S. (2017). SWOT analysis and strategies to develop sustainable tourism in Bangladesh. *UTMS Journal of Economics (Skopje), 8*(2), 159–167.

Moriano, J. A., Trejo, E., & Palací, J. (2001). El perfil psicosocial del emprendedor: un estudio desde la perspectiva de los valores. Revista de psicología Social 2001, p. 230.

Müller, S., & Korsgaard, S. (2018). Resources and bridging: The role of spatial context in rural entrepreneurship. *Entrepreneurship and Regional Development, 30*(1-2), 224–255. doi:10.1080/08985626.2017.1402092

Murad, A., & Rajesh, K. S. (2010). Implementation of Total Quality Management in Higher Education. *Asian Journal of Business Management*, 2, 9–16.

Mysteskyi Arsenal. (2002). *Exhibitions*. Mysteskkyi Arsenal.

Navarro Jurado, E., Ortega Palomo, G., & Torres Bernier, E. (2020). *Propuestas de reflexio_n desde el turismo frente al COVID-19. Incertidumbre, impacto y recuperacio_n.* Universidad de Malaga. https://www.i3t.uma.es/wp-content/uploads/2020/03/Propuestas-Reflexiones-Turismo-ImpactoCOVID_i3tUMA.pdf [28/10/2020]

Neumann, T. W. (2022). Heritage legilsation, the introduction of: disciplining through law. In Encyclopaedia of Global Archaeology. Springer.

Ng, A. W., & Tavitiyaman, P. (2020). Corporate social responsibility and sustainability initiatives of multinational hotel corporations. In *International business, trade and institutional sustainability* (pp. 3–15). Springer. doi:10.1007/978-3-030-26759-9_1

Ngoc Su, D., Luc Tra, D., Thi Huynh, H. M., Nguyen, H. H. T., & O'Mahony, B. (2021). Enhancing resilience in the Covid-19 crisis: Lessons from human resource management practices in Vietnam. *Current Issues in Tourism*, 24(22), 3189–3205. doi:10.1080/13683500.2020.1863930

Ngozwana, N. (2020). The Application of Adult Learning Theory (andragogy) by Adult Educators and Adult Learners in the Context of Eswatini. UJOE, 3(1).

Nickson, D. (2007). *Human resource management for the hospitality and tourism industries*. Elsevier. doi:10.4324/9780080469461

Ni, J., Chiu, D. K. W., & Ho, K. K. W. (2022). Exploring Information search behavior among self-drive tourists. *Information Discovery and Delivery*, 50(3), 285–296. doi:10.1108/IDD-05-2020-0054

Ntalakos, A., Belias, D., & Koustelios, A. (2022c). The relationship between Leadership Styles & Communication – Effect on Team Efficiency: The case of Greek Hotel Businesses' employees. In *IACUDIT 2022 Conference Proceedings*. Springer.

Ntalakos, A., Belias, D., & Koustelios, A. (2022e). *The relationship between Leadership Styles & Communication – Effect on Team Efficiency: The case of Greek Hotel Businesses' employees.* In IACUDIT 2022, Semantic Scholar.

Ntalakos, A., Belias, D., & Tsigilis, N. (2022d). Leadership Styles and Group Dynamics in the tourism industry. In *IACUDIT 2022 Conference Proceedings*. Research Gate.

Ntalakos, A., Belias, D., Koustelios, A., & Tsigilis, A. (2022a). Effect of Covid-19 on the Tourism Industry: Opportunities and Threats in Covid-19 Era. *4th International Conference on Finance, Economics, Management and IT Business*. Scitepress. 10.5220/0011065200003206

Ntalakos, A., Belias, D., Koustelios, A., & Tsigilis, A. (2022b). *Organizational Culture and Group Dynamics in the tourism industry.* 5th International Conference on Tourism Research 2022 (ICTR22) Porto, Vila do Conde, Portugal (ESHT). 10.34190/ictr.15.1.150

Ntalakos, A., Belias, D., Koustelios, A., & Tsigilis, N. (2022). Effect of Covid-19 on the Tourism Industry: Opportunities and Threats in Covid-19 Era. In *Proceedings of the 4th International Conference on Finance, Economics, Management and IT Business*, (pp. 107-114). Research Gate.

Ntalakos, A., Belias, D., Koustelios, A., & Tsigilis, N. (2022). Effect of Covid-19 on the Tourism Industry: Opportunities and Threats in Covid-19 Era. In *Proceedings of the 4th International Conference on Finance, Economics, Management and IT Business*. SciTePress.

Compilation of References

Ntalakos, A., Belias, D., Koustelios, A., & Tsigilis, N. (2022c). Organizational Culture and Group Dynamics in the Tourism Industry. *Proceedings of the 5th International Conference on Tourism Research 2022*, (pp. 286-293). Research Gate.

Ntalakos, A., Belias, D., Trihas, N. (2022b). The Impact of Covid -19 on Hospitality and Tourism Industry in Greece. *International Journal of Science and Research Methodology, 21*(1), 190–200

Ntalakos, A., Belias, D., & Trihas, N. (2022b). (in press). The Impact of Covid – 19 on Hospitality and Tourism Industry in Greece. International Journal of Science and Research Methodology. *Human Journals*.

Ntalakos, A., Rossidis, I., & Belias, D. (2022d). Trait Emotional Intelligence & Leadership: A study of managers and employees. *21st European Conference on Research Methodology for Business and Management Studies,* Aveiro, Portugal.

O'Keefe, R. (2006). *The Protection of Cultural Property in Armed Conflict*. Cambridge University Press. doi:10.1017/CBO9780511494260

O'Keefe, R., Péron, C., Tofig, M., & Ferrari, G. (2016). *Protection of Cultural Property, Military Manual*. Manual.

Oakland, J. S. (1993). *Total Quality Management: The Route to Improving Performance*. Butterworth-Heinemann.

Ollila, S., & Elmquist, M. (2011). Managing open innovation: Exploring challenges at the interfaces of an open innovation arena. *Creativity and Innovation Management, 20*(4), 273–283. doi:10.1111/j.1467-8691.2011.00616.x

Osterwalder, A., & Pigneur, Y. (2010). *Business Model Generation - A handbook for visionaries, Game Changers and challengers striving to defy outmoded business models and design tomorrow's enterprises. The Medieval Ous: Imitation.* Rewriting, and Transmission in the French Tradition. http://0-search.ebscohost.com.library.uark.edu/login.aspx?direct=true&db=mzh&AN=1996055971&site=ehost-live

Ostrovska, O. (2022). *The Invasion of Ukraine Is a War Against All Democratic States. As We Fight for Our Liberty, Here Are 5 Ways the Art World Can Help.* Artnet.

Pablo López, I., Begoña Santos, U., & Bueno Hernández, Y. (2004). *Las dimensiones del perfil emprendedor contraste empírico con emprendedores de éxito.* Universidad Autónoma de Madrid. https://www.uv.es/motiva/libromotiva/51PabloSantosBueno.pdf

Pachoulidis, K. (2007). *The national identity of Greek Cypriots: a socio-psychological genetic approach.* [Unpublished doctoral dissertation, Panteion University of Social and Political Sciences].

Paiva, T., Ribeiro, M., & Coutinho, P. (2020). R&D collaboration, competitiveness development, and open innovation in R&D. *Journal of Open Innovation, 6*(4), 1–18. doi:10.3390/joitmc6040116

Pande, M., & Bharathi, S. V. (2020). Theoretical foundations of design thinking – A constructivism learning approach to design thinking. *Thinking Skills and Creativity, 36*, 100637. doi:10.1016/j.tsc.2020.100637

Papadimitriou, D. B., Rodousakis, N., & Zezza, G. (2022). *Is Greece on the Road to Economic Recovery (No. sa_3_22).* Levy Economics Institute.

Pappas, M., & Pitas, I. (2000). Digital color restoration of old paintings. *IEEE Transactions on Image Processing, 9*(2), 291–294. doi:10.1109/83.821745 PMID:18255399

Park, E., Kim, W. H., & Kim, S. B. (2022). How does COVID-19 differ from previous crises? A comparative study of health-related crisis research in the tourism and hospitality context. *International Journal of Hospitality Management, 103*, 103199. doi:10.1016/j.ijhm.2022.103199 PMID:36540129

Parmar, B. L., Freeman, R. E., Harrison, J. S., Wicks, A. C., Purnell, L., & De Colle, S. (2010). Stakeholder theory: The state of the art. *The Academy of Management Annals, 4*(1), 403–445. doi:10.5465/19416520.2010.495581

Paschalidis, G. (2002) Introduction to Culture, Volume A. Patra: EAP Publications

Pavlidis, P. (2000). *Hotel Marketing* (4th ed.). Interbooks.

Pawar, D. V. (2014). Internal and External Customers. International Journal for Research in Management and Pharmacy, 3(5).

Peabody, M. A., & Turesky, E. F. (2018). Shared Leadership Lessons: Adapting LEGO® SERIOUS PLAY® In Higher Education. *International Journal of Management and Applied Research*, 5(4), 210–223. doi:10.18646/2056.54.18-015

Pearce, P. L., Filep, S., & Ross, G. F. (2010). *Tourists, Tourism and the Good Life*. Routledge. doi:10.4324/9780203845868

Peredo, A. M., & Mclean, M. (2006). Social entrepreneurship: A critical review of the concept. *Journal of World Business*, 41(1), 56–65. doi:10.1016/j.jwb.2005.10.007

Pérez, A., & Del Bosque, I. R. (2015). Corporate social responsibility and customer loyalty: Exploring the role of identification, satisfaction and type of company. *Journal of Services Marketing*, 29(1), 15–25. doi:10.1108/JSM-10-2013-0272

Pérez-Aranda, J. A., & Boronat-Navarro, M. (2022). Which corporate social responsibility issues do consumers perceive as relevant to be evaluated in the hotel sector? *European Journal of International Management*, 17(1), 60–85. doi:10.1504/EJIM.2022.119746

Pforr, C., & Hosie, P. J. (2008). Crisis management in tourism. Preparing for recovery. *Journal of Travel & Tourism Marketing*, 23(2-4), 249–264. doi:10.1300/J073v23n02_19

Pike, J., & Barnes, R. (1996). *TQM in Action: A practical approach to continuous performance improvement*. Chapman and Hall.

Pippirs, C., & Steckenbauer, S. (2022). Case study – spa destination branding – a strategic realignment process of five Bavarian thermal spas. *International Journal of Spa and Wellness*, 30(Aug), 1–12. doi:10.1080/24721735.2022.2117009

Pizzorno, A. (1985). *Sobre la racionalidad de la opción democrática, en CLACSO, Los límites de la democracia* (Vol. 2). CLACSO.

Polyzos, S., Samitas, A., & Spyridou, A. E. (2020). Tourism demand and the COVID-19 pandemic: An LSTM approach. [23/10/2020]. *Tourism Recreation Research*, 1–13. https://www.tandfonline.com/doi/full/10.1080/02508281.2020.1777053

Poon, A. (1989). Competitive strategies for New tourism. In C. P. Cooper (Ed.), *Progress in –Tourism Recreation and Hospitality Management* (pp. 91–102). Belhaven Press.

Porfírio, J. A., Carrilho, T., & Mónico, L. S. (2016). Entrepreneurship in different contexts in cultural and creative industries. *Journal of Business Research*, 69(11), 5117–5123. doi:10.1016/j.jbusres.2016.04.090

Poria, Y., Butler, R., & Airey, D. (2001). Clarifying Heritage Tourism. *Annals of Tourism Research*, 28(4), 1047–1049. doi:10.1016/S0160-7383(00)00069-4

Porras, J., Oliveras, G., & Vigier, H. (2013). Probabilidades de éxito para la creación de empresas: Implicancias sobre la educación emprendedora. *Revista FIR*, 2(4), 42–48. doi:10.15558/fir.v2i4.45

Post, J. E., Preston, L. E., & Sauter-Sachs, S. (2002). *Redefining the corporation: Stakeholder management and organizational wealth*. Stanford University Press. doi:10.1515/9781503619692

Prajogo, D. I. (2005). The comparative analysis of TQM practices and quality performance between manufacturing and service firms. *International Journal of Service Industry Management*, 16(3), 217–228. doi:10.1108/09564230510601378

Compilation of References

Prajogo, D. I., & Sohal, A. S. (2006). The integration of TQM and technology/R & D management in determining quality and innovation performance. *Omega: The International Journal of Management Science, 34*(3), 296–312. doi:10.1016/j.omega.2004.11.004

Prakash, K. B., & Reddy, M. P. S. (2020). Eco-tourism-the enabler and enhancer of sustainable growth. *Innov. Econ. Policy Res., 1*(1), 16–23.

Prentice, R. C. (2001). Experiential Cultural Tourism: Museums and the Marketing of the New Romanticism of Evoked Authenticity. *Museum Management and Curatorship, 19*(1), 5–26. doi:10.1080/09647770100201901

Prentice, R., & Andersen, V. (2013). Festival as creative destination. *Annals of Tourism Research, 30*(1), 7–30. doi:10.1016/S0160-7383(02)00034-8

Prud'homme van Reine, P. (2017). The culture of design thinking for innovation. *Journal of Innovation Management, 5*(2), 56–80. doi:10.24840/2183-0606_005.002_0006

Ρόκου, Τ. (2022). Δράσεις υπέρ προστασίας του ουκρανικού πολιτισμού ζήτησε στην ΕΕ η Λ. Μενδώνη. *Travel Daily News.*

Quintana-García, C., Marchante-Lara, M., & Benavides-Chicón, C. G. (2018). Social responsibility and total quality in the hospitality industry: Does gender matter? *Journal of Sustainable Tourism, 26*(5), 722–739. doi:10.1080/09669582.2017.1401631

Raaij, B. V. (2016). *Jihadist krijgt 9 jaar cel voor vernieling cultureel erfgoed.* De Volkstrant.

Rabontu, I. C., & Niculencu, G. (2009). Boutique hotels – New appearances in hotel industry in Romania. *Annals of the University of Petrosani. Economics, 9*(2), 209–214.

Radziszewska Czestochowa, A. (2014). Socio-intercultural dimensions of entrepreneurship. *Journal of Socio-intercultural Management, 6*(2), 35–47. doi:10.2478/joim-2014-0010

Rahmafitria, F., Pearce, P. L., Oktadiana, H., & Putro, H. P. (2020). Tourism planning and planning theory: Historical roots and contemporary alignment. *Tourism Management Perspectives, 35*, 1–9. doi:10.1016/j.tmp.2020.100703

Rahman, M. R. A., Nor, M. Y. M., & Wahab, J. L. A. (2020). Does Total Quality Management Influence Teacher Quality? An empirical analysis. *International Journal of Academic Research in Business & Social Sciences, 11*(1), 250–260.

Ramlawati, & Putra, A.H.P.K. (2018). Total Quality Management as the Key of the Company to Gain the Competitiveness, Performance Achievement and Consumer Satisfaction. *International Review of Management and Marketing, 8*(5), 60-69.

Rasoolimanesh, S. M., Ramakrishna, S., Hall, C. M., Esfandiar, K., & Seyfi, S. (2020). A systematic scoping review of sustainable tourism indicators in relation to the sustainable development goals. *Journal of Sustainable Tourism*, 1–21. doi:10.1080/09669582.2020.1775621

Rauch, A., & Frese, M. (2007). Born to be an entrepreneur? Revisiting the personality approach to entrepreneurship. *The Psychology of Entrepreneurship*, 41-65.

Raya, A. B., Andiani, R., Siregar, A. P., Prasada, I. Y., Indana, F., Simbolon, T. G. Y., Kinasih, A. T., & Nugroho, A. D. (2021). Challenges, open innovation, and engagement theory at craft smes: Evidence from Indonesian batik. *Journal of Open Innovation, 7*(2), 121. doi:10.3390/joitmc7020121

Razzouk, R., & Shute, V. (2012). What Is Design Thinking and Why Is It Important? *Review of Educational Research, 82*(3), 330–348. doi:10.3102/0034654312457429

Research Institute for Tourism. (2020). The Greek hotel in the years of crisis 2008-2018. Athens: Research Institute for Tourism

Revans Reg, W. (1982). *The Origin and Growth of Action Learning*. Chartwell-Bratt.

Revista Andina (2017). Tacna: el futuro se escribe en el Sur. *Andina*. www.andina.pe

RFE/RL. (2022). *Live Briefing: Russia Invades Ukraine. Radio Free Europe*. .

Richards, G. (2003). What is Cultural Tourism? A. van Maaren, A. (Ed.), Erfgoed voor Toerisme. Weesp: Nationaal Contact Monumenten.

Richins, H., & Pearce, P. (2000). Influences on tourism development decision making: Coastal local government areas in eastern Australia. *Journal of Sustainable Tourism*, *8*(3), 207–225. doi:10.1080/09669580008667359

Risteskia, M., Kocevskia, J., & Arnaudov, K. (2012). Spatial planning and sustainable tourism as basis for developing competitive tourist destinations. *Procedia: Social and Behavioral Sciences*, *44*, 375–386. doi:10.1016/j.sbspro.2012.05.042

Rita, P., Oliveira, T., & Farisa, A. (2019). The impact of e-service quality and customer satisfaction on customer behavior in online shopping. *Heliyon*, *5*(10), e02690. doi:10.1016/j.heliyon.2019.e02690 PMID:31720459

Roccas, S., Sagiv, L., Schwartz, S. H., & Knafo, A. (2002). The Big Five Personality Factors and Personal Values. *Personality and Social Psychology Bulletin*, *28*(6), 789–801. doi:10.1177/0146167202289008

Roche, W. K., & Teague, P. (2012). Business partners and working the pumps: Human resource managers in the recession. *Human Relations*, *65*(10), 1333–1358. doi:10.1177/0018726712451282

Rogers, R.E. (2013). *Implementation of Total Quality Management A Comprehensive Training Program*. The Haworth Press, Inc.

Rogerson, C. (2006). Creative Industries and Urban Tourism: South African Perspectives. *Urban Forum*, (17), 149-166.

Rogerson, J. M. (2010), The boutique hotel industry in South Africa: definition, scope, and organization. *Urban Forum*, *21*, 425-439.

Rokou, T. (2022). Δράσεις υπέρ προστασίας του ουκρανικού πολιτισμού ζήτησε στην ΕΕ η Λ. Μενδώνη. *Travel Daily News*.

Romagosa, F. (2020). The COVID-19 crisis: Opportunities for sustainable and proximity tourism. *Tourism Geographies*, *22*(3), 1–5. https://www.uab.cat/doc/article_turisme_postcovid_francesc_romagosa.pdf. doi:10.1080/14616688.2020.1 763447

Rossidis, I., Belias, D., & Vasiliadis, L. (2021b). Strategic Human Resource Management in the International Hospitality Industry. An Extensive Literature Review. *Culture and Tourism in a Smart, Globalized, and Sustainable World*, 337-346.

Rossidis, I., & Belias, D. (2020). Combining Strategic Management with Knowledge Management: Trends and International Perspectives. *International Review of Management and Marketing*, *10*(3), 39–45. doi:10.32479/irmm.9621

Rossidis, I., Belias, D., & Aspridis, G. (2020). *Change Management and Leadership (Διαχείριση Αλλαγών και Ηγεσία)*. Tziolas. (in Greek)

Rossidis, I., Belias, D., Papailias, S., Tsiotas, D., Niavis, S., & Vasiliadis, L. (2019). The Use of Customer Relations Management's Digital Technologies from Greek Hotels. In A. Kavoura, E. Kefallonitis, & A. Giovanis (Eds.), *Strategic Innovative Marketing and Tourism. Springer Proceedings in Business and Economics*. Springer. doi:10.1007/978-3-030-12453-3_9

Compilation of References

Rossidis, I., Belias, D., Varsanis, K., Papailias, S., Tsiotas, D., Vasiliadis, L., & Sdrolias, L. (2019b). Tourism and Destination Branding: The Case of Greek Islands. In A. Kavoura, E. Kefallonitis, & A. Giovanis (Eds.), *Strategic Innovative Marketing and Tourism. Springer Proceedings in Business and Economics*. Springer. doi:10.1007/978-3-030-12453-3_11

Rossidis, I., Belias, D., & Vasiliadis, L. (2021). Strategic Hotel Management in the "Hostile" International Environment. In V. Katsoni & C. van Zyl (Eds.), *Culture and Tourism in a Smart, Globalized, and Sustainable World. Springer Proceedings in Business and Economics*. Springer. doi:10.1007/978-3-030-72469-6_21

Rossidis, I., Belias, D., & Vasiliadis, L. (2021). Strategic Human Resource Management in the International Hospitality Industry. An Extensive Literature Review. In V. Katsoni & C. van Zyl (Eds.), *Culture and Tourism in a Smart, Globalized, and Sustainable World. Springer Proceedings in Business and Economics*. Springer. doi:10.1007/978-3-030-72469-6_22

Rossman, G. B., & Rallis, S. F. (2011). *Learning in the field: An introduction to qualitative research*. Sage.

Rothmann, S., & Coetzer, E. P. (2003). T*he Big Five Personality Dimensions and Job Performance. SA Journal of Industrial Psychology, 29*(1), 68–74. doi:10.4102ajip.v29i1.88

Rowley, T. J. (1997). Moving beyond dyadic ties: A network theory of stakeholder influences. *Academy of Management Review, 22*(4), 887–910. doi:10.2307/259248

Rudd, M. A., & Davis, J. A. (1998). Industrial Heritage Tourism at the Bingham Canyon Copper Mine. *Journal of Travel Research, 36*(3), 85–89. doi:10.1177/004728759803600310

Rusque, A. M. (2004). *Reflexiones en torno a un programa emprendedor para universidades Latinoamericanas.* I Congreso Emprendedurismo y V Reunión Anual Red Motiva: El emprendedor innovador y las empresas de I+D+I. Universitat de Valencia.

Saad, S. (2013). Contemporary challenges of human resource planning in tourism and hospitality organizations: A conceptual model. *Journal of Human Resources in Hospitality & Tourism, 12*(4), 333–354. doi:10.1080/15332845.2013.790246

Sachs, S., & Rühli, E. (2011). *Stakeholders matter: A new paradigm for strategy in society*. Cambridge University Press. doi:10.1017/CBO9781139026963

Sadler-Smith, E., Hampson, Y., Chaston, I., & Badger, B. (2003). Managerial behavior, entreprenurial style and small firms performance. *Journal of Small Business Management, 41*(1), 47–67. doi:10.1111/1540-627X.00066

Sahinidis, A. G., & Kavoura, A. (2014). Exploring corporate social responsibility practices of Greek companies. *Zeszyty Naukowe Małopolskiej Wyższej Szkoły Ekonomicznej w Tarnowie,* (2 (25)), 185–193.

Sakthivel, P. B., Rajendran, G., & Raju, R. (2005). TQM implementation and students' satisfaction of academic performance. *The TQM Magazine, 17*(6), 573–589. doi:10.1108/09544780510627660

Sallis, E. (1993). *TQM in Education*. Kogan Page.

Santana-Quintero, M., & Addison, A. C. (2007, September). Digital tools for heritage information management and protection: The need of training. In T. G. Wyeld, S. Kenderdine, & M. Docherty (Eds.), Lecture notes in computer science: Vol. 4820. *Virtual Systems and Multimedia* (pp. 35–46). Springer. doi:10.1007/978-3-540-78566-8_4

Santos-Roldán, L., Castillo Canalejo, A. M., Berbel-Pineda, J. M., & Palacios-Florencio, B. (2020). Sustainable Tourism as a Source of Healthy Tourism. *International Journal of Environmental Research and Public Health, 17*(15), 53–59. doi:10.3390/ijerph17155353 PMID:32722271

Sarasvathy, S. D. (2001). Causation and effectuation: Toward a theoretical shift from economic inevitability to entrepreneurial contingency. *Academy of Management Review, 26*(2), 243–263. doi:10.2307/259121

Sarasvathy, S. D. (2004). The questions we ask and the questions we care about: Reformulating some problems in entrepreneurship research. *Journal of Business Venturing*, *19*(5), 707–717. doi:10.1016/j.jbusvent.2003.09.006

Sasidharan, V., Sirakaya, E., & Kerstetter, D. (2002). Developing countries and tourism ecolabels. *Tourism Management*, *23*, 161–174.

Saxena, M. M. (2021). Obstacles in accomplishing Total Quality Management in Higher Education. *International Research Journal of Education and Technology*, *2*(2), 33–41.

Sbonias, K. (2002). Cultural approaches and interpretations of the Past. In K. Sponias (ed.), The concept of culture, aspects of Greek culture. Patras: E.A.P.

Schaper, M. (Ed.). (2016). *Making ecopreneurs: Developing sustainable entrepreneurship*. CRC Press. doi:10.4324/9781315593302

Schengen Visa Info. (2020). *EU decides to close all Schengen borders for 30 days*. Schengen Visa Info. https://www.schengenvisainfo.com/news/breaking-eu- decides-toclose-all-schengen-borders-for-30-days/

Scheyvens, R., Carr, A., Movono, A., Hughes, E., Higgins-Desbiolles, F., & Mika, J. P. (2021). Indigenous tourism and the sustainable development goals. *Annals of Tourism Research*, *90*, 103260. doi:10.1016/j.annals.2021.103260

Schreck, P. (2011). Reviewing the business case for corporate social responsibility: New evidence and analysis. *Journal of Business Ethics*, *103*(2), 167–188. doi:10.100710551-011-0867-0

Schulz, S. A., & Masters, R. J. (1997). Total quality management: The Deming food processing connection. *Journal of Food Products Marketing*, *4*(1), 61–70. doi:10.1300/J038v04n01_06

Shackleton, V., & Wale, P. (2002). Przywództwo I zarządzanie. In N. Chmiel (Ed.), *Psychologia Pracy I Organizacji*. Gdańskie Wydawnictwo Psychologiczne.

Shahmohammadi, N. (2017). The Evaluation of Teachers' Job Performance Based on Total Quality Management (TQM). *International Education Studies*, *10*(4), 58–64. doi:10.5539/ies.v10n4p58

Shahril, M. (2005). Amalan pengajaran guru yang bekresan: Kajian di beberapa sekolah menengah di Malaysia. *Jurnal Fakulti Pendidikan Universiti Malaya*, 1-14.

Shane, S., & Venkataraman, S. (2000). The promise of entrepreneurship as a field of research. *Academy of Management Review*, *25*(1), 217–226. doi:10.5465/amr.2000.2791611

Shapero, A. (1975). The Displaced, Uncomfortable Entrepreneur. *Psychology Today*, *9*(6), 83–88.

Shaver, K. G., & Scott, L. R. (1991). Person, process, choice: The psychology of new venture creation. *Entrepreneurship Theory and Practice*, *16*(2), 23–45. doi:10.1177/104225879201600204

Shaw, G., & Williams, A. M. (2004). *Tourism and tourism spaces*. Sage Publications. doi:10.4135/9781446220528

Siakalli, M., & Masouras, A. (2020). Factors that influence tourist satisfaction: An empirical study in Pafos. In Strategic Innovative Marketing and Tourism: 8th ICSIMAT, (pp. 459-466). Springer International Publishing.

Siakalli, M., Masouras, A., & Papademetriou, C. (2017). e-Marketing in the hotel industry: marketing mix strategies. In Strategic Innovative Marketing: 4th IC-SIM, (pp. 123-129). Springer International Publishing.

Siakwah, P., Musavengane, R., & Leonard, L. (2020). Tourism governance and attainment of the sustainable development goals in Africa. *Tourism Planning & Development*, *17*(4), 355–383. doi:10.1080/21568316.2019.1600160

Compilation of References

Sila, S., & Ebrahimpour, M. (2003). Examination and comparison of the critical factors of total quality management (TQM) across countries. *International Journal of Production Research*, *41*(2), 235–268. doi:10.1080/0020754021000022212

Sirdeshmukh, D., Singh, J., & Sabol, B. (2002). Consumer trust, value, and loyalty in relational exchanges. *Journal of Marketing*, *66*(1), 15–37. doi:10.1509/jmkg.66.1.15.18449

Skagias, K., Belias, D., Vasiliadis, L., & Christos, P. (2022). Digital Tourist Marketing: The Latest Developments and Recommendations on How Mykonos Can Take Advantage of Digital and Influencer Marketing. In V. Katsoni & A. C. Şerban (Eds.), *Transcending Borders in Tourism Through Innovation and Cultural Heritage. Springer Proceedings in Business and Economics*. Springer. doi:10.1007/978-3-030-92491-1_60

Skagias, K., Vasiliadis, L., Belias, D., & Papademetriou, C. (2021). From mass tourism and mass culture to sustainable tourism in the post-covid19 era: The case of Mykonos. In V. Katsoni & C. van Zyl (Eds.), *Culture and Tourism in a Smart, Globalized, and Sustainable World. Springer Proceedings in Business and Economics*. Springer. doi:10.1007/978-3-030-72469-6_23

Slocum, J. (2004), *Comportamiento Organizacional*. Cengage Learning Editores.

Smith, A. D. (2000). National identity. (trans. E. Peppa). Athens: Odysseus.

Smith, B. R., & Stevens, C. E. (2010). Different types of social entrepreneurship: The role of geography and embeddedness on the measurement and scaling of social value. *Entrepreneurship & Regional Development: An International Journal*, *22*(6), 575–598. doi:10.1080/08985626.2010.488405

Sophocleous, H. P., Masouras, A., & Papademetriou, C. (2019). Brand as a strategic asset for cultural organisations: A proposal for the forthcoming cultural institution of Pafos. In Strategic Innovative Marketing and Tourism: 7th ICSIMAT, (pp. 735-743). Springer International Publishing. doi:10.1007/978-3-030-12453-3_85

Spencer, B., & Lange, E. (2014). *The Purposes of Adult Education: An Introduction* (3rd ed.). Thompson Educational Publishing.

Stanco, F., Battiato, S., & Gallo, G. (Eds.). (2011). *Digital imaging for cultural heritage preservation: Analysis, restoration, and reconstruction of ancient artworks*. CRC Press.

Stevenson, H., & Wei-Skillern, J. (2003). Social Entrepreneurship and Commercial Entrepreneurship: Same, Different, or Both? *Working Paper Series, No. 04-029*. Harvard Business School.

Stevenson, D. (2007). *Cities and Urban Cultures* (I. Pentazou, Trans.). Critical Scientific Library Publications.

Stoll, L., & Seashore Louis, K. (2007). *Professional learning communities: divergence, depth and dilemma*. Open University Press.

Suen, R. L. T., Tang, J., & Chiu, D. K. W. (2020). Virtual reality services in academic libraries: Deployment experience in Hong Kong. *The Electronic Library*, *38*(4), 843–858. doi:10.1108/EL-05-2020-0116

Sugianto, S., & Soediantono, D. (2022). Literature Review of ISO 26000 Corporate Social Responsibility (CSR) and Implementation Recommendations to the Defense Industries. *Journal of Industrial Engineering & Management Research*, *3*(2), 73–87.

Su, L., Swanson, S. R., Hsu, M., & Chen, X. (2017). How does perceived corporate social responsibility contribute to green consumer behavior of Chinese tourists: A hotel context. *International Journal of Contemporary Hospitality Management*, *29*(12), 3157–3176. doi:10.1108/IJCHM-10-2015-0580

Sullivan Mort, G., Weerawardena, J., & Carnegie, K. (2003). Social entrepreneurship: Towards conceptualization. *International Journal of Nonprofit and Voluntary Sector Marketing*, *8*(1), 76–88. doi:10.1002/nvsm.202

Sung, Y. Y. C., & Chiu, D. K. W. (2022). E-book or print book: Parents' current view in Hong Kong. *Library Hi Tech*, *40*(5), 1289–1304. doi:10.1108/LHT-09-2020-0230

Sun, X., Chiu, D. K. W., & Chan, C. T. (2022). Recent digitalization development of buddhist libraries: A comparative case study. In S. Papadakis & A. Kapaniaris (Eds.), *The digital folklore of cyberculture and digital humanities* (pp. 251–266). IGI Global. doi:10.4018/978-1-6684-4461-0.ch014

Svendsen, A. C., & Laberge, M. (2005). Convening stakeholder networks: A new way of thinking, being and engaging. *Journal of Corporate Citizenship*, *2005*(19), 91–104. doi:10.9774/GLEAF.4700.2005.au.00013

Talib, F., & Rahman, Z. (2010). Critical success factors of TQM in service organizations: A proposed model. *Services Marketing Quarterly*, *31*(3), 363–380. doi:10.1080/15332969.2010.486700

Tari, J. J., Claver-Cortes, E., Pereira-Moliner, J., & Molina-Azorin, J. F. (2010). Levels of quality and environmental management in the hotel industry: Their joint influence on firm performance. *International Journal of Hospitality Management*, *29*(3), 500–510. doi:10.1016/j.ijhm.2009.10.029

Tauringana, V., & Chithambo, L. (2015). The effect of DEFRA guidance on greenhouse gas disclosure. *The British Accounting Review*, *47*(4), 425-444.

Taylor, B. (1995). *Self-directed learning: revisiting an idea most appropriate for middle school students*. Paper presented at the Combined Meeting of the Great Lakes and Southeast International Reading Association, Nashville, TN.

Teo, C. C. J., Chia, G. H., & Khoo, H. P. M. (1998). *Size really does matter (when you're small): the critical success factors behind boutique hotels in Singapore*. [Research paper, Nanyang Business School, Singapore: Nanyang Technological University].

Teo, P., & Chang, T. C. (2009). Singapore's postcolonial landscape: boutique hotels as agents. In T. Winter, P. Teo, & T. C. Chang (Eds.), *Asia on tour: exploring the rise of Asian tourism* (pp. 81–96). Routledge.

Tepelus, C. (2010). 6 Corporate Social Responsibility. *Understanding the sustainable development of tourism*, 110.

Theologou, K. (2007). The Value of Memory for a Society. *Intellectum3*, 1-17. https://www.intellectum.org/articles/issues/intellectum3/ITL03P053069_H_aksia_tis_mnimis.pd

Thiagaragan, T., Zairi, M., & Dale, B. G. (2001). A proposed model of TQM implementation based on an empirical study of Malaysian industry. *International Journal of Quality & Reliability Management*, *18*(3), 289–306. doi:10.1108/02656710110383539

Thorpe, V. (2022). Crimes against history: mapping the destruction of Ukraine's culture. *The Guardian*.

Thurley, S. (2005). Into the future. Our strategy for 2005-2010. In *Conservation Bulletin* [English Heritage] (pp. 49). https://content.historicen gland.org.uk/i mages-books/publications/conservation-bulletin- 49/cb4926-27.pdf/

Tien, C., Lo, H. C., & Lin, H. W. (2011). The economic benefits of mega events: A myth or a reality? A longitudinal study on the Olympic Games. *Journal of Sport Management*, *25*(1), 11–23. doi:10.1123/jsm.25.1.11

Timothy, D., & Teye, V. (2009). *Tourism and the lodging sector*. Butterworth-Heinemann.

Todd, G., & Mather, S. (1995). *The International Hotel Industry. Corporate strategies and Global Opportunities*. The Economist Intelligence Unit.

Compilation of References

Tomalin, B. (2009). Applying the principles: Instruments for intercultural business training. In A. Feng, M. Byram, & M. Fleming (Eds.), *Becoming interculturally competent through education and training* (pp. 115–131). Multilingual Matters. doi:10.21832/9781847691644-010

Tracey, P., Phillips, N., & Jarvis, O. (2011). Bridging institutiona lentrepreneurship and the creation of new organizational forms: A multilevel model. *Organization Science*, *22*(1), 60–80. doi:10.1287/orsc.1090.0522

Tran, D. (2021). *OECD Skills Outlook 2021: why lifelong learning is essential for modern society. Digital skills and Jobs Platform*. European Union. https://digital-skills-jobs.europa.eu/en/latest/news/oecd-skills-outlook-2021-why-lifelong-learning-essential-modern-society

Tribus, M. (1993). Why Not Education: Quality Management in Education. *Journal for Quality and Participation*, *16*, 12–21.

Tsaur, S. H., & Lin, Y. C. (2004). Promoting service quality in tourist hotels: The role of HRM practices and service behavior. *Tourism Management*, *25*(4), 471–481. doi:10.1016/S0261-5177(03)00117-1

Tse, H. L., Chiu, D. K. W., & Lam, A. H. C. (2022). From reading promotion to digital literacy: An analysis of digitalizing mobile library services with the 5E Instructional Model. In A. Almeida & S. Esteves (Eds.), *Modern reading practices and collaboration between schools, family, and community* (pp. 239–256). IGI Global. doi:10.4018/978-1-7998-9750-7.ch011

Tsiotas, D., Niavis, S., Belias, D., & Sdrolias, L. (2020). What Can the TripAdvisor Tell Us About the Complaints Management Strategies? The Case of the Greek Hotels. In A. Kavoura, E. Kefallonitis, & P. Theodoridis (Eds.), *Strategic Innovative Marketing and Tourism. Springer Proceedings in Business and Economics*. Springer. doi:10.1007/978-3-030-36126-6_111

Turner, L., & Ash, J. (1975). *The Golden Hordes: International Tourism and the Pleasure Periphery*. Constable.

Tyson, S., & Witcher, M. (1994). Getting in gear: Post recession HR management. *Personnel Management*, *26*(8), 19–23.

Τμήμα, Δ. (2009). Κώδικας Δεοντολογίας του ICOM για τα Μουσεία. New York Times (2022). Russia attacks Ukraine. *The New York Times.* .

U. a. (2022). What Happened on Day 94 of the War in Ukraine. *The New York Times.* .

UNESCO. (1995). *The 1954 Hague Convention for the Protection of Cultural Property in the Event of Armed Conflict and its two (1954 and 1999) Protocols*. UNESCO.

UNESCO. (2022). *UNESCO's statement on the recent developments in Ukraine*. UNESCO.

Urbano, D., Toledano, N., & Soriano, D. R. (2010). Analyzing social entrepreneurship from an institutional perspective: Evidence from Spain. *Journal of Social Entrepreneurship*, *1*(1), 54–69. doi:10.1080/19420670903442061

Urry, J. (1994). *Consuming places*. Routledge.

Valdivia, M. (2018). Cultural and creative industries in Mexico: The role of export-oriented manufacturing metro areas. In *Creative Industries and Entrepreneurship: Paradigms in Transition from a Global Perspective* (pp. 262–282). Edward Elgar Publishing Ltd. doi:10.4337/9781786435927.00021

van de Vrande, V., de Jong, J. P. J., Vanhaverbeke, W., & de Rochemont, M. (2009). Open innovation in SMEs: Trends, motives and management challenges. *Technovation*, *29*(6–7), 423–437. doi:10.1016/j.technovation.2008.10.001

Van der Auwera, S. (2013). International Law and the Protection of Cultural Property in the Event of Armed Conflict: Actual Problems and Challenges. *The Journal of Arts Management, Law, and Society*, *43*(4), 175–190. doi:10.1080/1 0632921.2013.841114

Van Hartesvelt, M. (2006). Building a better boutique hotel. *Lodging Hospitality*, 32–44.

Vardalier, P. (2016). Strategic approach to human resources management during crisis. In Procedia - Social and Behavioral Sciences, *12th International Strategic Management Conference,* Antalya, Turkey.

Varela, B., & Pacheco, G. (2018). Comprehensive evaluation of the internal and external quality control to redefine analytical quality goals. *Biochemia Medica, 28*(2), 1–11. doi:10.11613/BM.2018.020710 PMID:30022885

Varsanis, K., Belias, D., Kakkos, N., Chondrogiannis, M., Rossidis, I., & Mantas, C. (2019). The Relationship Between Service Quality and Customer Satisfaction on Luxurious Hotels So to Produce Error-Free Service. In A. Kavoura, E. Kefallonitis, & A. Giovanis (Eds.), *Strategic Innovative Marketing and Tourism. Springer Proceedings in Business and Economics.* Springer. doi:10.1007/978-3-030-12453-3_8

Verheul, I., Van Stel, A., & Thurik, R. (2006). Ex-plaining Female and Male Entrepreneurship at the Country Level. *Entrepreneurship and Regional Development, 18*(2), 151–183. doi:10.1080/08985620500532053

Vernon, J., Essex, S., Pinder, D., & Curry, K. (2005). Collaborative policymaking: Local sustainable projects. *Annals of Tourism Research, 32*(2), 325–345. doi:10.1016/j.annals.2004.06.005

Vickers, I., & Lyon, F. (2014). Beyond green niches? Growth strategies of environmentally-motivated social enterprises. *International Small Business Journal, 32*(4), 449–470. doi:10.1177/0266242612457700

Victorino, L., Verma, R., Plaschka, G., & Dev, C. (2005). Service innovation and customer choices in the hospitality industry. *Managing Service Quality, 15*(6), 555–576. doi:10.1108/09604520510634023

Viera, A., Pérez, A., & Paredes, M. (2008). La pedagogía crítica y las competencias de emprendedurismo en estudiantes universitarios. *Pensamiento y Gestión*, (24), 43–62.

Vilá, R. (2006). La dimensión afectiva de la competencia comunicativa intercultural en la Educación Secundaria Obligatoria: Escala de Sensibilidad Intercultural. Revista de Investigación Educativa, 2, 353–372.

Virvidakis, S. (2003). Problems of defining the concept of folk creation. In D. Lekkas (ed.), Arts II overview of Greek music and dance. Patras: E.A.P, 59-66

Viterouli, M., & Belias, D. (2021). *True Organizational Learning Culture as a key to unlocking Operational Performance: A Critical Review.* International Business Information Management Association, 37th IBIMA Conference, Cordoba, Spain.

Viterouli, M., & Belias, D. (2021). True Organizational Learning Culture as a key to unlocking Operational Performance: A Critical Review. *Proceedings of the 37th International Business Information Management Association (IBIMA),* Cordoba, Spain.

Viterouli, M., Belias, D., & Koustelios, A. (2021). *Organizational Performance Enhancement via Adult Education Driven Principles in HR Management.* Leadership and Governance (ECMLG 2021), 17th European Conference on Management, Valletta, Malta.

Viterouli, M., Belias, D., Koustelios, A., & Tsigilis, N. (2022). Refining Employees' Engagement by incorporating Self-Directedness in Training and Work Environments. *Proceedings of the 18th European Conference on Management Leadership and Governance.* ACI.

Vlami, A. (2021). The Developments and challenges of hospitality in greece for the financial sustainability of tourism: the case of boutique hotels. In D. L., Balsalobre, O. M., Driha, M., Shahbaz (eds.), Strategies in Sustainable Tourism, Economic Growth and Clean Energy. Spain: Springer.

Compilation of References

Vo-Thanh, T., Vu, T. V., Nguyen, N. P., Nguyen, D. V., Zaman, M., & Chi, H. (2021). COVID-19, frontline hotel employees' perceived job insecurity and emotional exhaustion: Does trade union support matter? *Journal of Sustainable Tourism*, 1–18.

Waitt, G. (2000). Consuming heritage: Perceived historical authenticity. *Annals of Tourism Research*, *27*(4), 835–862. doi:10.1016/S0160-7383(99)00115-2

Walker, D. M. (2003). *Doing business internationally*. McGraw-Hill.

Walterspiel, *G. (1969)*, *Einführung in die Betriebswirtschaftslehre des Hotels*, Wiesbaden.

Wan, L. C., Chan, E. K., & Luo, X. (2020). Robots Come to Rescue: How to reduce perceived risk of infectious disease in Covid19-stricken consumers? *Annals of Tourism Research*. https://www.ncbi.nlm.nih.gov/pmc/articles/PMC7550303/pdf/main.pdf [28/10/2020]

Wang, C. K.; Wong, P.K. (2004). Entrepreneurial Interest of University Students in Singapore, *Tech-novation*, *24*(2), 163-172.

Wang, J., Deng, S., Chiu, D. K. W., & Chan, C. T. (2022). Social network customer relationship management for orchestras: A case study on Hong Kong Philharmonic Orchestra. In N. B. Ammari (Ed.), *Social customer relationship management (Social-CRM) in the era of Web 4.0* (pp. 250–268). IGI Global. doi:10.4018/978-1-7998-9553-4.ch012

Wang, Y., & Lo, H. (2003). Customer-focused performance and the dynamic model for competence building and leveraging: A resource based-view. *Journal of Management Development*, *22*(6), 483–526. doi:10.1108/02621710310478486

Weaver, D. B. (2014). Asymmetrical dialectics of sustainable tourism: Toward enlightened mass tourism. *Journal of Travel Research*, *53*(2), 131–140. doi:10.1177/0047287513491335

Weerawardena, J., & Mort, G. S. (2006). Investigating social entrepreneurship: A multidimensional model. *Journal of World Business*, *41*(1), 21–35. doi:10.1016/j.jwb.2005.09.001

Wengel, Y. (2020). LEGO® Serious Play® in multi-method tourism research. *International Journal of Contemporary Hospitality Management*, *32*(4), 1605–1623. doi:10.1108/IJCHM-04-2019-0358

Wengel, Y., McIntosh, A., & Cockburn-Wootten, C. (2020). A critical consideration of LEGO® SERIOUS PLAY® methodology for tourism studies. *Tourism Geographies*, *23*(1–2), 162–184. doi:10.1080/14616688.2019.1611910

Wennekers, S., Thurik, R., Van Stel, A. & Noorderhaven, N. (2010). *Uncertainty avoidance and the rate of business ownership across 21 OECD countries 1976-2004*. Springer Berlin Heidelberg.

Wheeler, S., Passmore, J., & Gold, R. (2020). All to play for: LEGO® SERIOUS PLAY® and its impact on team cohesion, collaboration and psychological safety in organisational settings using a coaching approach. *Journal of Work-Applied Management*, *12*(2), 141–157. doi:10.1108/JWAM-03-2020-0011

Wilkins, C. (2011). Professionalism and the post-performative teacher: New teachers reflect on autonomy and accountability in the English school system. *Professional Development in Education*, *37*(3), 389–409. doi:10.1080/19415257.2010.514204

Winkler, M., & Dosoudil, V. (2011). On Formalization of the Concept of Value Proposition. *Service Science*, *3*(3), 194–205. doi:10.1287erv.3.3.194

Wong, A. K.-k., & Chiu, D. K. W. (2023). Digital Transformation of museum conservation practices: A value chain analysis of public museums in Hong Kong. In R. Pettinger, B. B. Gupta, A. Roja, & D. Cozmiuc (Eds.), *Handbook of research on the digital transformation digitalization solutions for social and economic needs* (pp. 226–242). IGI. Global. doi:10.4018/978-1-6684-4102-2.ch010

World Health Organization. (2020a). *Q&A on coronavirus (COVID-19).* WHO. https://www.who.int/emergencies/diseases/novel- coronavirus2019/question-and-answers-hub/q-a-detail/q-a-coronaviruses

World Health Organization. (2020b). WHO timeline – COVID-19. WHO. https://www.who.int/news-room/detail/27-04-2020-who-timeline---covid-

World Tourism Organization (2022). *World Tourism Barometer, 20*(1). WTO.

World Tourism Organization. (2020). *AL ULA Framework for Inclusive Community Development through Tourism Executive Summary* IE University, Spain.

World Travel & Tourism Council. (2019). Travel & tourism economic impact 2019. World Travel & Tourism Council. https://wttc.org/Research/Economic-Impact

World Travel and Tourism Council. (2021). Staff Shortages. World Travel and Tourism Council.

WTTC. (World Travel & Tourism Council). (2020), *Coronavirus Brief.* WTTC. https://www.wttc.org/-/media/files/wttc-coronavirus-brief-external-3003.pdf?la=en

Xanthopoulou, P., & Kefis, V. (2016). Redefining CSR as an innovative tool in crisis times: The Greek approach. *International Journal of Social Research Methodology, 4*(4), 1–18.

Xu, C., Lam, A. H. C., & Chiu, D. K. W. (2023). Antique bookstores marketing strategies as urban cultural landmark: A case analysis for Suzhou Antique Bookstore. In M. Rodrigues & M. A. M. Carvalho (Eds.), *Exploring niche tourism business models, marketing, and consumer experience.* IGI Global.

Xu, H., Wan, X., & Fan, X. (2014). Rethinking authenticity in the implementation of China's heritage conservation: The case of Hongcun Village. *Tourism Geographies, 16*(5), 799–811. doi:10.1080/14616688.2014.963662

Xu, Y. (2015). Discussion on the protection and renewal of public space in traditional villages - Taking Cangtai Village, Jianshui County, Honghe Prefecture as an example. *Value Engineering, 34*(14), 203–205.

Yao, L., Lei, J., Chiu, D. K. W., & Xie, Z. (2023). Adult learners' perception of online language English learning platforms in China. In A. Garcés-Manzanera & M. E. C. García (Eds.), *New approaches to the investigation of language teaching and literature.* IGI Global.

Yi, Y., & Chiu, D.K.W. (2023). Public information needs during the COVID-19 outbreak: A qualitative study in mainland China. *Library Hi Tech.* doi:10.1108/LHT-08-2022-0398

Yip, K. H. T., Chiu, D. K. W., Ho, K. K. W., & Lo, P. (2021). Adoption of mobile library apps as learning tools in higher education: A tale between Hong Kong and Japan. *Online Information Review, 45*(2), 389–405. doi:10.1108/OIR-07-2020-0287

Yoon, J., Sung, S., & Ryu, D. (2020). The role of networks in improving international performance and competitiveness: Perspective view of open innovation. *Sustainability (Switzerland), 12*(3), 1269. Advance online publication. doi:10.3390u12031269

Yoshino, N., Taghizadeh-Hesary, F., & Otsuka, M. (2021). Covid-19 and Optimal Portfolio Selection for Investment in Sustainable Development Goals. *Finance Research Letters*, *38*, 101695. Advance online publication. doi:10.1016/j.frl.2020.101695 PMID:32837379

Yu, P. Y., Lam, E. T. H., & Chiu, D. K. W. (2022b). *Operation management of academic libraries in Hong Kong under COVID-19*. Library Hi Tech. doi:10.1108/LHT-10-2021-0342

Yu, C. P., Chancellor, H. C., & Cole, S. T. (2011). Measuring residents' attitudes toward sustainable tourism: A reexamination of the sustainable tourism attitude scale. *Journal of Travel Research*, *50*(1), 57–63. doi:10.1177/0047287509353189

Yuen, K. F., Thai, V. V., & Wong, Y. D. (2016). Are customers willing to pay for corporate social responsibility? A study of individual-specific mediators. *Total Quality Management & Business Excellence*, *27*(7-8), 912–926. doi:10.1080/14783363.2016.1187992

Yu, H. Y., Tsoi, Y. Y., Rhim, A. H. R., Chiu, D. K. W., & Lung, M. M. W. (2022a). Changes in habits of electronic news usage on mobile devices in university students: A comparative survey. *Library Hi Tech*, *40*(5), 1322–1336. doi:10.1108/LHT-03-2021-0085

Yusuf, S. M., & Aspinwall, E. (2000). TQM Implementation Issue: Review and Case Study. *International Journal of Operations & Production Management*, *20*(6), 634–655. doi:10.1108/01443570010321595

Zaccaro, S., Mumford, M., Connelly, M., Marks, M., & Gilbert, J. (2000). Assesment of leader problem solving capabilities. *The Leadership Quarterly*, *11*(1), 37–64. doi:10.1016/S1048-9843(99)00042-9

Zairi, M. (1995). Total Quality Education for superior performance. *Training for Quality*, *3*(1), 29–35. doi:10.1108/09684879510082238

Zelensky, V. (2022). *Twit* [Status update]. Twitter.

Zeng, B., & Gerritsen, R. (2014). What do we know about social media in tourism? A review. *Tourism Management Perspectives*, *10*, 27–36. doi:10.1016/j.tmp.2014.01.001

Zenk, L., Primus, D. J., & Sonnenburg, S. (2021). Alone but together: Flow experience and its impact on creative output in LEGO® SERIOUS PLAY®. *European Journal of Innovation Management*, *25*(6), 340–364. doi:10.1108/EJIM-09-2020-0362

Zeppal, H., & Hall, C. (1991). Selling Art and History: Cultural Heritage and Tourism. *Tourist Studies*, *2*, 47–55.

Zhang, H., Luo, Y., Liu, H., Wang, Y., Chen, Q., & Tan, X. (2017). Research status and prospect of digital protection technology for traditional villages in China. *Resource development and market*, *33*(08), 912-915.

Zhang, S. (2013). Protection and inheritance of intangible cultural heritage as a cultural ecology: Theoretical thinking and problem analysis of China's conservation practice. *Journal of Tongji University: Social Science Edition*, *2013*(5), 58–66.

Zhang, T., Chen, J., & Hu, B. (2019). Authenticity, quality, and loyalty: Local food and sustainable tourism experience. *Sustainability*, *11*(12), 34–37. doi:10.3390u11123437

Zhang, X., Lo, P., So, S., Chiu, D. K. W., Leung, T. N., Ho, K. K. W., & Stark, A. (2021). Medical students' attitudes and perceptions towards the effectiveness of mobile learning: A comparative information-need perspective. *Journal of Librarianship and Information Science*, *53*(1), 116–129. doi:10.1177/0961000620925547

Zhang, Z., Waszink, A., & Wijngaard, J. (2000). An instrument for measuring TQM implementation for Chinese manufacturing companies. *International Journal of Quality & Reliability Management*, *17*(7), 730–755. doi:10.1108/02656710010315247

Zhou, M., Geng, G., & Wu, Z. (2012). *Digital Preservation Technology for Cultural Heritage*. Springer. doi:10.1007/978-3-642-28099-3

Zhuang, Y., Zhu, F., Chiu, D. K. W., Ju, C., & Jiang, B. (2014). A personalized travel system based on crowdsourcing model. In X. Luo, J. X. Yu, & Z. Li (Eds.), Lecture notes in computer science: Vol. 8933. *Advanced Data Mining and Applications* (pp. 163–174). Springer. doi:10.1007/978-3-319-14717-8_13

Zientara, P., & Zamojska, A. (2018). Green organizational climates and employee pro-environmental behaviour in the hotel industry. *Journal of Sustainable Tourism*, *26*(7), 1142–1159. doi:10.1080/09669582.2016.1206554

Πανταζόπουλος, Τ. (2022). *Γιατί ηχούν «τύμπανα πολέμου» στα σύνορα Ουκρανίας - Ρωσίας*. Lifo.

About the Contributors

Andreas Masouras teaches at the University of Neapolis in Pafos. He is expertise in Marketing Management and Qualitative Social Research. Dr. Masouras is a graduate of the Doctor Management program from Monarch Business School and PhD candidate in Institutional Economics at the University of Peloponnese. Dr. Masouras also holds an MPhil in Media from the University of Brighton, a BA degree in Communication and Mass Media from the National Kapodistrian University of Athens, LLB from Neapolis University and a M.Sc. in Globalization, Media and Culture from the University of Glamorgan in Wales (South Wales University) as well as a Postgraduate Diploma in Management Studies (with specialization in media) from the National Awarding Body of the United Kingdom. Opposite of media studies, Dr. Masouras holds a postgraduate certificate in university education from the University of Brighton.He is a founding member and Head of the Research Institute of Applied Communication in Cyprus. Andreas has been a Visiting Research Fellow at Antwerp University in Belgium, at the Central European University in Hungary and at Fordham University, NY.

Christos Papademetriou teaches at the University of Neapolis in Pafos since 2010. He is an Assistant Professor in Management – Human Resources Management at the School of Economics, Administration and Computer Science. He is a Coordinator of the Distance Master in Business Administration (DMBA). He was teaching in the Department of Business Administration at the Open University of Cyprus (2017-2020). He obtained a BA (Hons) in Accounting and Business (2001) and MA in International Management (2002) from the University of Sunderland. He was awarded also a BSc (Hons) in Computing and the Postgraduate Certificate in Information Systems from the University of Portsmouth. He holds a doctorate (PhD) in Social Science from the University of Leicester, UK. The title of his thesis is "Investigating the Impact of Sequential Cross-Cultural Training on the Level of Sociocultural and Psychological Adjustment of Expatriate Mangers".

Dimitrios Belias is a Human Resource Management scientist. Holder of BSc, MSc, MEd, PhD, PostDoc, University of Thessaly. He has published more than 230 papers in internationals and Greek refereed journals and conference presentations in the areas of Organization Behavior, Human Resource Management, TQM, Educational Management and Tourism Management. He has also been a regular reviewer for 15 scientific journals and is currently a member in many scientific and professional bodies.

Sofia Anastasiadou is a Professor of Statistics and Research Methodology at the University of Western Macedonia (UOWM). Her teaching focuses in the field of cognitive Research Methodology (Quantitative and Qualitative), Educational Research and Statistical Data Analysis, Big Data. She has written three books on Statistics and Research Methodology and has published over 280 articles in International and Greek Journals as well as in International and Greek Conferences. She has participated in scientific dialogues/round tables in more than 200 lectures at International and Greek Conferences. She has organized and co-organized Greek and International Scientific Conferences. She is also a Member of a number of Scientific Committees of International Conferences and is an Associate Editor in a number of International Journals.

***

Dickson K.W. Chiu received the B.Sc. (Hons.) degree in Computer Studies from the University of Hong Kong in 1987. He received the M.Sc. (1994) and the Ph.D. (2000) degrees in Computer Science from the Hong Kong University of Science and Technology (HKUST). He started his own computer consultant company while studying part-time. He has also taught at several universities in Hong Kong. His teaching and research interest is in Library & Information Management, Service Computing, and E-learning with a cross-disciplinary approach, involving library and information management, e-learning, e-business, service sciences, and databases. The results have been widely published in around 300 international publications (most of them have been indexed by SCI/-E, SSCI, and EI, such as top journals MIS Quarterly, Computer & Education, Government Information Quarterly, Decision Support Systems, Information Sciences, Knowledge-Based Systems, Expert Systems with Application, Information Systems Frontiers, IEEE Transactions, including many taught master and undergraduate project results and around 20 edited books. He received a best paper award in the 37th Hawaii International Conference on System Sciences in 2004. He is an Editor (-in-chief) of Library Hi Tech, a prestigious journal indexed by SSCI (impact factor 2.357). He is the Editor-in-chief Emeritus of the International Journal on Systems and Service-Oriented Engineering (founding) and International Journal of Organizational and Collective Intelligence, and serves in the editorial boards of several international journals. He co-founded several international workshops and co-edited several journal special issues. He also served as a program committee member for around 300 international conferences and workshops. Dr. Chiu is a Senior Member of both the ACM and the IEEE, and a life member of the Hong Kong Computer Society. According to Google Scholar, he has over 5,300 citations, h-index 39, i-10 index 109, ranked worldwide 1st in "LIS," "m-learning," and "e-services."

Stalo Georgiou is a member of the Special Teaching Staff in Psychology Department, School of Health Science at Neapolis University Pafos. She holds an Undergraduate Degree (BMus Music) Musicology at Hull University in United Kingdom, first Postgraduate Degree in Music Composition (MSc) from Hertfordshire University in UK, second master's degree (MSc) in Public Administration, Educational Management and Administration and a PhD in Music Composition for Films and Media in Hertfordshire University. Moreover, she is a PhD candidate for her 2nd PhD (in final process for viva), at Neapolis University Pafos, at Department of Economics and Business. The title of her 2nd PhD is: Effective verbal and non-verbal communication Techniques in the Educational process and the psychological components that effect. She holds a Diploma in Journalism and Media. Dr. Georgiou has composed Music for several films (not narrative films, short films and animated films) and theatre performances and musicals, in Cyprus and UK.nAt the same time, she has received several awards from international competitions, and has been an organizer and Judge in Music Talent shows and competitions in the United Kingdom.

About the Contributors

Athanasios Koustelios is a Professor in the Department of Business Administration at the University of Thessaly, Greece. He has published more than 120 papers in International and Greek refereed journals and has more than 180 conference presentations. His research expertise is in the area of human resource management and organizational behaviour.

Apple Hiu Ching Lam obtained her degree of Bachelor of Business Administration (Honours) in International Business from City University of Hong Kong (2016) and degree of Master of Science in Library and Information Management with distinction from the University of Hong Kong (2020). She is a doctoral student in Education at the University of Hong Kong. Her current research interests are social media in library, user education, and the 5E Instructional Model.

Josue Aaron Lopez-Leyva is a professor of subjects related to innovation and interdisciplinary capstone projects at CETYS University.

Angelos Ntalakos is a PhD Candidate in Business Administration, University of Thessaly, Larisa, Geopolis, 41500, Greece.

Plimakis - Contributing Author| **Sifis Plimakis** is Assistant Professor of Public Policy at the Department of Political Science and International Relations, University of Peloponnese. He studied political science at the University of Crete, public management at postgraduate level at the University of Liverpool and awarded his PhD in public – private partnerships from the University of Athens. He conducted a two-year post-doctoral research on strategic planning and performance measurement in public sector, at Rutgers University, National Center for Public Performance. He has taught public policy and public management lessons at the National School of Public Administration, Aristotle University of Thessaloniki and ASPAITE. His research interests are focused on strategic planning and organizational change implementation in public sector, public policy design and evaluation and the alternative models for public services provision. He has extensive experience in the design and implementation of administrative reform programs in Greece and abroad and has worked as an expert for the EU and other international organizations in the field of public sector reorganization.

Miguel Angel Ponce-Camacho is a full-time professor in the school of engineering at CETYS Universidad.

Ioannis Rossidis holds a bachelor degree in Business Administration from University of Piraeus, a MBA from University of the Aegean, a Msc in Health Management from the National School of Public Health and a Phd in Administrative Science from Panteion University, Public Administration Department (national scholarship). Dr. Rossidis has been teaching over the last decade in undergraduate and post graduate programs in various Greek and Cypriot Universities. Dr. Rossidis has also worked as Financial Director in the Hellenic Quality Assurance& Accreditation Agency, as Ministry of Finance, Piraeus Bank and ATE Bank executive and as manager in Leivatho Hotel (4star). Dr. Rossidis, has contributed to various conferences while he has authored numerous published papers (80 in total). His research interests are administrative science, change management, public management, knowledge management

About the Contributors

Eliza Sharma is an assistant Professor at Symbiosis International University, Bengaluru. She has more than 13 years of working experience and has published 50-plus research papers. Her area of research is sustainability, CSR, SDGs, and tourism.

Megha Tamang is Dean of Christ (Deemed University), Bangalore Yeshwanthpur Campus and Associate Professor.

Nikolaos Trihas holds a PhD in e-Tourism, a Master Degree (M.Sc.) in "Tourism Planning, Administration and Policy", and a B.Sc. in Business Administration from the University of the Aegean, Greece. Currently, he is an Assistant Professor in the Department of Business Administration and Tourism at the Hellenic Mediterranean University in Greece, and a tutor at the Hellenic Open University, where he lectures courses on marketing, management and tourism.

Nikolaos Tsigilis is an Associate Professor in the Department of Journalism and Mass Media Communication, Aristotle University of Thessaloniki, Greece. He has published more than 120 papers in International and Greek refereed journals and has a variety of conference presentations. His research expertise is in the area of methodology and psychometrics of Social Sciences.

Omar Vargas-González is a professor at Tecnologico Nacional de Mexico Campus Ciudad Guzman. Fields of research: Entrepreneurship Economics, Statistics, Mathematical, Information and Computing Sciences.

José G. Vargas-Hernández is a research professor, and has an M.B.A.; Ph.D. Member of the National System of Researchers of Mexico and a research professor at Tecnológico Mario Molina Unidad Zapopan formerly at University Center for Economic and Managerial Sciences, University of Guadalajara. Professor Vargas-Hernández has a Ph. D. in Public Administration and a Ph.D. in Organizational Economics. He has undertaken studies in Organisational Behaviour and has a Master of Business Administration, published four books and more than 200 papers in international journals and reviews (some translated to English, French, German, Portuguese, Farsi, Chinese, etc.) and more than 300 essays in national journals and reviews. He has obtained several international Awards and recognition.

Mary Viterouli has had teaching experience of over twenty years and is now also working as a Deputy Director at the Vocational Institute of DYPA in Chalkida. Her scientific interests revolve around Strategic Management, Human Resources Management, Adult Education, Sociology and English Literature. She holds two Bachelor's Degrees, two Master's Degrees and is now a PhD Candidate at the University of Thessaly, Greece.

Vlami Aimilia is an Assistant Professor in Tourism Economics and Tourism Development, at Agricultural University of Athens (AUA). She received her M.S. in Tourism Planning, Management and Policy, from University of Aegean and her Ph.D in Tourism Economics & Development, from University of Patras. Dr. Vlami was a Scientific Advisor at Hellenic Chamber of Hotels, over 10years. Her main research interests are tourism economics, planning and development, hospitality and regional development.

244

About the Contributors

Panagiota Xanthopoulou is a Postdoctoral Researcher and Academic Fellow of the Department of Business Administration at the University of West Attica. She studied at the Panteion University of Social and Political Sciences where she completed her postgraduate and doctoral studies. Her teaching and research interests include Public Administration, Entrepreneurship & Innovation and Distance Education. Her research has been published in international and Greek scientific journals and has also been presented at international scientific conferences. She also works as a collaborating teaching staff in Universities of Greece and Cyprus.

Yixin Zuo received the Bachelor's degree in Public Affairs Management from Nanjing Agriculture University and the Master's degree in Library and Information Management from the University of Hong Kong. She once participated in the Student Research Training and organized a project about the protection of traditional villages. As a result, she published two articles about culture management as the first author in Southern Agriculture Journal. She joined two short-term internships at Jiangsu Folk Museum and Sanqin Daily in 2016 and 2017, respectively. Her undergraduate thesis focuses on government management of traditional culture and won the second prize in her school and an outstanding graduate award, while this chapter is based on her master's capstone project. Her research interests are in information management and E-learning.

Index

A

Alternative tourism 77, 79, 84-86, 89
Andragogy 21, 30, 33-34, 36, 39-40
Artifacts 148, 154

C

Capability Building 42-43, 50, 59
Consumer Behavior 14, 18
Corporate Responsibility 1, 6, 16, 18
Covid-19 20-26, 29, 40, 60-61, 65, 67, 69-78, 80-81, 84-85, 88-91, 106, 141-144, 147, 181-182, 193, 195
Covid-19 Pandemic 20-22, 29, 61, 65, 73, 77, 80, 85, 91, 141, 144, 181, 193, 195
Creative Industries 93-94, 102-106, 127-128
crisis management 25-26, 28, 38, 60, 64-68, 73-75, 195
Cultural Diplomacy 119, 152
Cultural Heritage 76, 88, 111, 114, 120-121, 128-136, 139-141, 144, 146-161, 186
Cultural Identity 119-120, 122
Cultural Objects 152, 156
Culture Heritage Preservation 134
Customer Loyalty 1, 13, 15-17, 19, 197
Customer Trust 1-2, 19, 66

D

Design Thinking 93, 95, 97-106
Digital management of cultural heritage 147
Digital restoration 132, 143, 147, 150-151
Digital technologies 91, 130, 132-133, 138, 141, 147-150, 185
Digitization of cultural heritage 132, 148
Domestic Prosperity 20

E

Entrepreneurial profile 43, 46, 59

Entrepreneurship 40, 42-59, 79, 81-82, 89, 100-101, 106, 108-109, 114-117, 195-196

F

Famous Artists 152

H

Heritage preservation 129, 132-135, 139, 146, 148
Heritage tourism 127-130, 132-133, 136-138, 140-141, 148
hospitality sector 20, 22, 28-29, 36-37, 60-62, 66, 69-72, 88, 184, 187
Hotel Industry 1-4, 7, 12-14, 16-19, 27, 37, 41, 72-74, 87-88, 165, 176, 178, 181-186, 188, 191, 195-198
Hotel Management 19, 41, 75, 91, 163

I

Innovative Experience 93
Intangible cultural heritage 120-121, 130, 134-135, 139, 147-149, 151, 153, 159, 161
Interculturality 59

L

Legal Protection 152, 157
Lego® Serious Play® 93, 95-106

M

Music Tradition 119, 124, 126

P

Personalised Experience 181
Post-pandemic era 77, 83-87
Professional Learning Community 163

Index

R

Regional Development 20, 58, 93-95, 98, 101-102, 107, 109-110, 114-117

S

Self-Initiation 20, 35-36
Socio-intercultural 42-43, 45-54, 56-57, 59
Strategic Human Resource Management 41, 60, 62, 68, 71, 73, 75, 91
Student Learning 145, 164, 166, 176
Student-Centeredness 163, 171
Sustainable heritage tourism development 130, 140, 148
Sustainable tourism 4-5, 15, 17-18, 76-78, 80-81, 83-86, 89-92, 108-110, 112-114, 116-118, 121, 127, 145, 181, 187, 195, 198-199

T

Tangible cultural heritage 133, 148-149, 152

Tourism Developments 181
Tourism Policy 5, 19, 187, 195
Tourist Identity 119
TQM 27-28, 37, 163-169, 174-180
Traditional Music 119-120, 123, 125-127
Traditional village 129-131, 133, 142, 148
Traditional Villages 129-133, 136, 141, 143-144, 146-147, 149

U

UNESCO 121, 153, 155, 157-158, 162
Unique Design Concept 181, 186, 188
Upgraded Services 181-182, 185, 187, 189, 194

V

Value Proposition Concept 93, 95, 98, 104

Recommended Reference Books

IGI Global's reference books are available in three unique pricing formats:
Print Only, E-Book Only, or Print + E-Book.

Order direct through IGI Global's Online Bookstore at
www.igi-global.com or through your preferred provider.

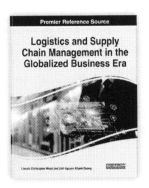

ISBN: 9781799887096
EISBN: 9781799887119
© 2022; 413 pp.
List Price: US$ 250

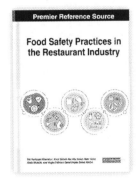

ISBN: 9781799874157
EISBN: 9781799874164
© 2022; 334 pp.
List Price: US$ 240

ISBN: 9781668440230
EISBN: 9781668440254
© 2022; 320 pp.
List Price: US$ 215

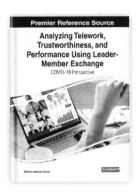

ISBN: 9781799889502
EISBN: 9781799889526
© 2022; 263 pp.
List Price: US$ 240

ISBN: 9781799885283
EISBN: 9781799885306
© 2022; 587 pp.
List Price: US$ 360

ISBN: 9781668455906
EISBN: 9781668455913
© 2022; 2,235 pp.
List Price: US$ 1,865

Do you want to stay current on the latest research trends, product announcements, news, and special offers?
Join IGI Global's mailing list to receive customized recommendations, exclusive discounts, and more.
Sign up at: **www.igi-global.com/newsletters.**

Publisher of Timely, Peer-Reviewed Inclusive Research Since 1988

www.igi-global.com   Sign up at www.igi-global.com/newsletters   facebook.com/igiglobal   twitter.com/igiglobal   linkedin.com/igiglobal

Ensure Quality Research is Introduced to the Academic Community

Become an Evaluator for IGI Global Authored Book Projects

   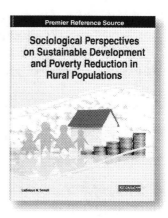

The overall success of an authored book project is dependent on quality and timely manuscript evaluations.

Applications and Inquiries may be sent to:
development@igi-global.com

Applicants must have a doctorate (or equivalent degree) as well as publishing, research, and reviewing experience. Authored Book Evaluators are appointed for one-year terms and are expected to complete at least three evaluations per term. Upon successful completion of this term, evaluators can be considered for an additional term.

If you have a colleague that may be interested in this opportunity, we encourage you to share this information with them.

Easily Identify, Acquire, and Utilize Published Peer-Reviewed Findings in Support of Your Current Research

IGI Global OnDemand

Purchase Individual IGI Global OnDemand Book Chapters and Journal Articles

For More Information:
www.igi-global.com/e-resources/ondemand/

Browse through 150,000+ Articles and Chapters!

Find specific research related to your current studies and projects that have been contributed by international researchers from prestigious institutions, including:

- Accurate and Advanced Search
- Affordably Acquire Research
- Instantly Access Your Content
- Benefit from the InfoSci Platform Features

"It really provides an excellent entry into the research literature of the field. It presents a manageable number of highly relevant sources on topics of interest to a wide range of researchers. The sources are scholarly, but also accessible to 'practitioners'."

– Ms. Lisa Stimatz, MLS, University of North Carolina at Chapel Hill, USA

Interested in Additional Savings?

Subscribe to

Learn More

Acquire content from over 128,000+ research-focused book chapters and 33,000+ scholarly journal articles for as low as US$ 5 per article/chapter (original retail price for an article/chapter: US$ 37.50).

7,300+ E-BOOKS.
ADVANCED RESEARCH.
INCLUSIVE & AFFORDABLE.

IGI Global e-Book Collection

- **Flexible Purchasing Options** (Perpetual, Subscription, EBA, etc.)
- Multi-Year Agreements with **No Price Increases** Guaranteed
- **No Additional Charge** for Multi-User Licensing
- No Maintenance, Hosting, or Archiving Fees
- Continually Enhanced & Innovated **Accessibility Compliance Features** (WCAG)

Handbook of Research on Digital Transformation, Industry Use Cases, and the Impact of Disruptive Technologies
ISBN: 9781799877127
EISBN: 9781799877141

Handbook of Research on New Investigations in Artificial Life, AI, and Machine Learning
ISBN: 9781799886860
EISBN: 9781799886877

Handbook of Research on Future of Work and Education
ISBN: 9781799882756
EISBN: 9781799882770

Research Anthology on Physical and Intellectual Disabilities in an Inclusive Society (4 Vols.)
ISBN: 9781668435427
EISBN: 9781668435434

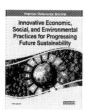

Innovative Economic, Social, and Environmental Practices for Progressing Future Sustainability
ISBN: 9781799895909
EISBN: 9781799895923

Applied Guide for Event Study Research in Supply Chain Management
ISBN: 9781799889694
EISBN: 9781799889717

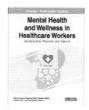

Mental Health and Wellness in Healthcare Workers
ISBN: 9781799888130
EISBN: 9781799888147

Clean Technologies and Sustainable Development in Civil Engineering
ISBN: 9781799898108
EISBN: 9781799898122

Request More Information, or Recommend the IGI Global e-Book Collection to Your Institution's Librarian

For More Information or to Request a Free Trial, Contact IGI Global's e-Collections Team: eresources@igi-global.com | 1-866-342-6657 ext. 100 | 717-533-8845 ext. 100